beat MERCHANTS

Also by Alan Clayson

CALL UP THE GROUPS:
The Golden Age of British Beat, 1962–67

BACK IN THE HIGH LIFE:
A Biography of Steve Winwood

ONLY THE LONELY:
The Life and Artistic Legacy of Roy Orbison

THE QUIET ONE:
A Life of George Harrison

RINGO STARR:
Straight Man or Joker?

DEATH DISCS:
Ashes To Smashes
– An Account of Fatality in the Popular Song

BACKBEAT –
Stuart Sutcliffe: The Lost Beatle
(with Pauline Sutcliffe)

ASPECTS OF ELVIS
(ed. with Spencer Leigh)

beat MERCHANTS

The Origins, History, Impact and Rock Legacy of the 1960's British Pop Groups

Alan Clayson

BLANDFORD

A BLANDFORD BOOK

First published in paperback in the UK 1996 by Blandford
A Cassell Imprint
Cassell plc
Wellington House
125 The Strand, London WC2R 0BB

Previously published in hardback 1995

Distributed in the United States by Sterling Publishing Co., Inc. 387 Park Avenue South, New York, NY 10016-8810

Distributed in Australia by Capricorn Link (Australia) Pty Ltd, 2/13 Carrington Road, Castle Hill, NSW 2154

A Cataloguing-in-Publication Data entry for this title is available from the British Library

ISBN 0-7137-2462-5

Typeset by Litho Link Ltd, Welshpool, Powys, Wales
Printed in Great Britain by Hartnolls Limited, Bodmin, Cornwall

CONTENTS

TO **JOHN TOBLER** ⸻

ACKNOWLEDGEMENTS

I am grateful for the co-operation, trust and privileged information I have received over the years from many musicians, famous and obscure, including Hans Alehag, Frank Allen, Wally Allen, Ian 'Tich' Amey, Don Andrew, Rob Arnold, Mick Avory, Maurice Bacon, Roger Barnes, Cliff Bennett, Andre Barreau, Christina Balfour, Alan Barwise, Dave Berry, John Bloomfield, Barry Booth, Robert Boughton, Bruce Brand, Chris Britton, Bob Brunning, Les Calvert, Ian Campbell, Louis Cennamo, Jeff Christopherson, Dave Clark, Allan Clarke, Terry Clarke, Liz Coley, Sharon Collins, Frank Connor, Eric E. Cooke, Mike Cooper, Pete Cox, Don Craine, Tony Crane, Michael d'Abo, Tony Dangerfield, Danny D'Arcy, Spencer Davis, Helen Deeble, Dave Dee, Denis D'Ell, Rod Demick, Jackie Doe, Chris Dreja, Colin Drummond, Richie Earles, Mike Evans, Wayne Fontana, Freddie Garrity, Steve Gibbons, Gary Gold, Chris Gore, Eric Goulden, Keith Grant, Norman Haines, Dave Harding, John Harries, Mike Hart, Gail Hendricks, David Hentschel, Penny Hicks, Tony Hicks, Tim Hill, Graham Hobbs, Stuart Hobday, Alan Hope (Kerry Rapid), Nick Horne, Malcolm and Lee Hornsby, Mark 'Swordfish' Hunt, Marsha Hunt, Rick Huxley, Neil Innes, Tony Jackson, Roy Jarvis, Garry Jones, Paul Jones, Chris 'Ace' Kefford, Billy Kinsley, Chris Kirtley, Billy J. Kramer, Graham Knight, Denny Laine, Graham Larkbey, Gary Le Port, Andy Lockwood, John Duff Lowe, Kenny Lynch, Dave Maggs, Sir Charles Marling, Phil May, Ruth McCartney, Jim McCarty, Tom McGuinness, Dennis Mills, Zoot Money, Adrian Moulton, Russell Munch, Sandy Newman, Gary Noble, John Ozoroff, Jessica Palin, Dave Parkington, Andy Pegg, Mike Pender, Eddie Phillips, Ray Phillips, Ray Pinfold, Brian Poole, Keith Powell, Reg Presley, Mike Read, Mike Robinson, Rob Rose, Paul Samwell-Smith, Jim Simpson, Mike Smith, Norman Smith, Henry Smithson, Louis Spyrou, the late Vivian Stanshall, Lord David Sutch, Mike Sweeney, Jeff Taggart, Andy Taylor, Dick Taylor, Gary Thomas, John Townsend, Paul Tucker, Mark Turauskis, Twinkle, Chris Warman, Roger Watson, Ron Watts, Clifford White, Frank White, Mark Wilkins, Val Wiseman, Fran Wood and Pete York.

Very special thanks are in order for my commissioning editor Stuart Booth for his faith in me and the intrinsic merit of this project; his battles on its behalf; his encouragement as I worked at it, and for seeing it through to publication.

Particular debts of gratitude are also owed to Colin Baylis, Aimee Blythe, Carol Boyer, Rob Bradford, Faith Brooker, Ron Cooper (of *Zabadak!*), Trevor Dann, Andy Davis, Kevin Delaney, Peter Doggett (of *Record Collector*), Ian Drummond, John Elphick (of Hickies Ltd.), Ian Forsyth, Pete Frame, Ann Freer, Helen Gummer, Cecilia Gyampoh, Herman Hamerpagt, Bill Harry, Michael Heatley, Martin Hockley (of *Carousel*), Dave Humphreys, Lennart Wrigholm, Allan Jones (of *Melody Maker*), Sam Leach, Brian Leafe, Spencer Leigh, Richard MacKay, Steve Maggs, Mark Paytress, Colin Miles (of *See For Miles*), Steve Morris (of *Brum Beat*), Russell Newmark, Mike Ober, Chris Phipps, April Relf, John Repsch, Simon Robinson, Johnny Rogan, Peter Rowe, Jacqueline Ryan (of *Trogg Times*), Charles and Deborah Salt, Miranda Stonor, Pauline Sutcliffe, John Tobler, Andrea Marie Tursso, Marthy Van Lopik and especially Rochelle Levy. I would also like a big round of applause for Christine Bones and Mike Neal of *The Beat Goes On* (1, Marasca End, Colchester, Essex, CO2 0DL).

It may be obvious to the reader that I have received help from sources that prefer not to be mentioned. Nevertheless, I wish to express my appreciation of what they did.

Thanks are also due in varying degrees to Andy Anderton, Jane and Eddie Armstrong, B&T Typewriters, Robert Bartel, Pete Barton, John Battersby, Alf Bicknell, Jane Blackstock, Kathryn Booth, Maryann Borgon, Andrew Boyd, Kevin Brew, Jackie Brind, Eva Maria Brunner, Roy Bull, Paul Cassin, Clive Chandler, Dawn Chaplin, Chris Charlesworth, Ray Coleman, Jackie Craine, Brian and Hilary Cresswell, Margaret Cutts, Doreen Davies, Marilyn Demick, PJ Dempsey, John Dingle, Roger Dopson, J. Drabble, Helen Drummond, Paul Du Noyer, Finola Dwyer, Geoffrey Ellis, Ron Ellis, Mark and Clare Ellen, Tim and Sarah Fagan, Bob Fisher, Katy Foster-Moore, Kathi and Rick Fowler, Simon Frith, Mark Georgeson, Jill Gore, Philippa Goulden, Oliver Gray, Louise Harrison, Caroline Hartley, Dawn and Wilf Harvey, David Hawley, Bill Heckle, Paul Hearne, Giulia Hetherington, Terri Hemmert, Susan Hill, Angie Hobbs, Mark Hodgkinson, David Horn, Barney Hoskyns, Kevin Howlett, Susie Hudson, Howard Hugues, Caroline Humphreys, Graham Humphreys, Mark Hutchinson, John Irvin, Dave Jones, Ron Jones, Andrew Kilderry, Neil Kinnock, Yvonne Lambourne, Mark and Carol Lapidos, Jon Lewin, Mark Lewisohn, Jane Lindsay, Jack Lyons, Stephen Macdonald, Helen Maggs, Kevin Manning, Fraser Massey, Angie McCartney, Judy McGaugh, Tom McKee, Phil McMullen (of *Ptolemaic Terrascope*), Bill Mielenz, Bruce Miller, Chris and Julia Morris, Lynda Morrison, Bert Muirhead, Stefan Mlynek, Julia New, Martin Nicholls, Malcolm Noble, James Norrish, Darryl Paddick, Carolyn Pinfold, John Platt, Wally Podrazik, Pam Poole, Nik Powell, Laine and Jule Rawlinson, Evan and

Lynne Reynolds, Paul Richards, Richard Riding, Cindy and Mary Rock, George and Penny Rowden, Liam Ryan, Nick Saloman, David Sanderson, Caroline Scott, Liz and Malcolm Shakespeare, Harry Shapiro, Greg Shaw, Maggie Simpson, Reg Singleton, Phil Smee, Iain Softley, Mark St. John, Keith Strong, Peter Sullivan, Stephen Taylor, Tony Theobald, Rowland Thomas, Trish Thomas, Michael Towers, Dr Geoff Trodd, John Wagstaff, Alison Walster, Mike Watkinson, Chris Welch, Derek Whiteley, Richard Widmore, Pamela Wiggin and Ted Woodings – plus Inese, Jack and Harry for coping with my absence in spirit when closeted away for months in a room which looked as if someone had chucked a hand-grenade into it.

Alan Clayson

PROLOGUE: *CALL UP THE GROUPS!*

In 1985, Alan Clayson and the Argonauts celebrated their tenth unsuccessful year in showbusiness. A significant engagement the previous year had been at a charity function in an asylum. After deducting overheads for a fortnight's tour of Ireland in 1977, I had been uncertain whether to spend my cut of what remained on a box of matches or a pair of shoelaces. At any given booking around that time, I was always worried that we were going to be lynched.

Whilst recognizing faults, I remain convinced that my artistic purpose has been misunderstood and that it is merely a matter of time before I Make It. As Robert Louis Stevenson wrote: 'Our business in life is not to succeed but to continue to fail in good spirits.' Forgetting the 'in good spirits' bit, I've been this way since 19. . .63.

I was twelve then, and about to grow to manhood during the British beat boom and its aftermath. While some teacher or other prattled on, I'd be stealing illicit squints beneath desk-top level at *Melody Maker*, as others would at *War Picture Library*, *The Hotspur* or selected passages from *Lady Chatterley's Lover*. The reason why the *Western Morning News* would one day describe me as the 'A.J.P. Taylor of the pop world' was that the so-called trivialities of pop were more meaningful to me than anything that Farnborough Grammar School could impart. As homework was neglected in the evenings, sometimes the records said it for me – a Pretty Things B-side, 'I Can Never Say', was one particularly articulate speech of the heart as I traced a guitar in the vapour on my bedroom window and wondered why my mother didn't understand.

Transfixed by the Rolling Stones on ITV's *Arthur Haynes Show*, I was disturbed by my father's remarks about how low-brow it all was, but could anyone old enough to have fought Hitler have guessed that beat groups would be more than a 'passing phase' – as evangelist Billy Graham put it when the Beatles conquered North America? Even fourteen-year-old Steve Winwood, then about to join a semi-professional pop group, 'had the mistaken impression that rock 'n' roll was a juvenile thing'.

Moving the clock forward twenty-odd years – 'odd' being a key word – Winwood was high in the US Hot 100, and I was functioning on keyboards with Dave Berry and the Cruisers, having progressed in six weeks from sight-reading at a funereal pace to banging out the entire set by heart as the street where I lived shuddered. Later, I was one of Screaming Lord Sutch's Savages, and then Twinkle's bass player and self-appointed musical director of her 1993 comeback.

Around that time, I collaborated with former Yardbird Jim McCarty on 'Moonlight Skater', a number which, when recorded by Dave Berry, had every requirement of a Christmas Number One, but none that have yet interested major record companies. Jim's fiftieth birthday party at London's 100 Club in July 1993 brought together representatives from every trackway of his professional life. Among those queueing for the buffet were former members of the Yardbirds, Renaissance, the McCarty Blues Band and the British Invasion All-Stars plus Richard MacKay, editor of *Yardbirds World*, the magazine for those with an insatiable appetite for all things Yardbird.

And then there was me, hoping I wouldn't let slip some inane remark if Jeff Beck spoke to me. He passed me a plate of sandwiches and I said, 'Thank you', an exchange I have since made out to be less fleeting. Some listeners were excited enough to demand, word for word, my exaggeration of both this encounter with Jeff and further details of the star-studded event where it occurred.

Beck, McCarty, Dave Berry and other *dramatis personae* from 1960s beat groups aroused the emotions from the start. Like provincial football teams, local musicians would acquire a tremendous grassroots following of those who'd recall bitterly how, with a Top 50 entry or two, this singer or that group later betrayed them by defecting to London. Most of the prodigals, however, returned, after going off the boil soon after the first flush of success. Those that didn't usually jumped on the next bandwagon before the rest, even impregnating it with a certain originality.

It might have provided a shadowy link to 'higher' artistic expression for some, but the strongest motive for even the most ill-favoured youth to be in a pop group was sex. After the Pill (and before AIDS), there was licence to make eye-contact with short-skirted 'birds' with urchin faces and pale lipstick, who ringed the stage front, ogling with unmaidenly eagerness the enigma of untouchable lads-next-door. Now and then, the attire, bone structure and slow-and-easy movements of a dancing Ace Face would be noticed, but otherwise a kind of *droit de seigneur* prevailed for those on the bandstand.

Beat groups, you see, were almost always male – which was why the publicity machine of both the Applejacks and the Honeycombs was geared towards the respective gimmicks of bass guitarist Megan Davies and drummer Honey Langtree. Further exceptions included the Lindys, the McKinleys, the Liverbirds, Tiffany's Dimensions, the Tracks, the Orchids, the

She Trinity, Evesham's all-girl Rayvons and the Beat-Chics whose 1964 revival of a Bill Haley number begins '*his* Skinny Minnie is a crazy chick . . .' Every other girl knew her place as either a member of a dance exhibition troupe like Sheffield's Dolly Rockers or Liverpool's Shimmy-Shimmy Queens, an occasional supplier of onstage glamour who simply sat on a stool in the midst of a group or, less passively, a 'featured vocalist', regarded as either an abberation or a breath or fresh air in a sphere dominated by male bonding.

Behind the public intimacies of off-mike comments and momentary eye contacts, there was often territory forbidden and inexplicable to outsiders: jokes side-splitting to nobody else; the open state of masochistic warfare between two guitarists who both want to play lead; a singer who is everybody's best pal onstage and full of venomous character assassinations in the van; a bearded drummer twinkling with pride when the schoolboy saxophonist takes a solo, and a tacit implication in a seemingly innocuous announcement that sparks off a hastily unplugged amplifier and a slammed backstage fire door.

Though we can learn much from verbatim accounts, the more salacious amongst us would like the impossible: videos of, for example, a Rolling Stones recording session around 1967 when three members were in danger of going to prison; to be a fly on the wall in a dressing room shared by the Top 10 combo that in 1964 contained two homosexuals; or to sample with their own sensory organs Dave Davies' feelings about his elder brother and fellow Kink.

You might not actually want to know what kind of people members of a favourite outfit are in private life. If they turned out to be Right Bastards, the records would never sound the same, too many illusions shattered. Emulation of heroes is a vital part of growing up, affecting the clothes you can't afford, the hairstyle you're forbidden to have, and the manner in which you mouth into a hairbrush-as-microphone in front of the bedroom mirror. Much of my teenage self-image was formed with several successive groups and individuals lurking in the shadows in much the same way as the giants of 1950s classic rock might have in turn influenced them.

This account is unquestionably affected by my own preferences and considerations about who or what might be prototypical of any particular musical style of the age – as well as the experience and knowledge gained since 1985 when my first book, *Call Up The Groups!: The Golden Age Of British Beat, 1962–67*, was published. Care had, nevertheless, been taken to define as widely as possible the myriad social, cultural, economic, environmental and other factors that polarize and prejudice what is generally known about the beat boom already. Much new and rediscovered evidence was brought to light as I waded through oceans of archive material and screwed myself up to talk to complete strangers about events that took place up to forty years ago. Crucially, though it concerns a historical period potentially as dry and academic as any other, *Beat Merchants* is meant to be as entertaining as the music that inspired it.

"*Winds of the world, give answer!*
They are whimpering to and fro –
And what should they know of England
Who only England know?"

The English Flag, *Rudyard Kipling*

1 VOICES IN THE WILDERNESS

As the Vietnam War can be traced back to some early medieval trade agreement, so the origins of British beat might lie in those 'musical evenings' that preceded television – 'especially amongst working class people', reckoned Chris 'Ace' Kefford, later bass guitarist with the Move. 'My mum and grandad both played the piano with "boxing glove" left hands.' Front parlours might not have tinkled as frequently with the strains of Handel, Debussy or Sir Arthur Sullivan, but even as late as the 1940s many were still set a-tremble to sonorous renderings of 'Greensleeves', 'Danny Boy', 'The Road to Mandalay' or an eye-rolling 'Spaniard That Blighted My Life', Al Jolson's 1913 million-seller. Before being packed off to bed, a child might be led forth, glistening with embarrassment, to the centre of the room to pipe out 'Donkey Riding', 'Billy Boy' or maybe a hymn.

Such ditties might have been absorbed during primary school music lessons, sitting cross-legged round an upright piano in the main hall and – quite a new idea – in *Singing Together* and other BBC Home Service radio broadcasts to schools. Amid the dashing white sergeants, drunken sailors, Li'l Liza Janes and John Barleycorns – seldom heard formally outside ceilidhs, eisteddfods, barn dances and similar events – musical theory was taught as a kind of mathematics in which a dotted crochet was expressed diagrammatically by 'three of the little milk bottles you have at school' as refreshment at morning playtime.

From a school recorder group, children could graduate to brass or woodwind – but piano and guitar were often easier because the learning process was easier to understand than those of, say, saxophone or French horn on which, no matter how many holes your fingers covered, you'd sometimes emit exactly the same note (if you got any note at all). Some were put off by unpredictable harmonics that set the teeth on edge – though it was often the unevenness of those very molars that precipitated such squeaks.

Such mouths were better employed in festival chorales and Boy Scout gang shows – not to mention church choirs where in ruffs, surplices and cassocks, children faced each other across the chancel up to three times every Sunday, cantillating the holy sounds, novel and unintelligible at seven, over-familiar and rote-learnt at thirteen.

The discovery that, execrable though you may be, a grown-up audience is actually listening to you singing or playing an instrument can create false impressions of personal talent in the immature mind – and so, from a musical genesis both ecclesiastical and domestic, would begin many a tranfiguration to pop stardom.

Much depended on where you lived. London was then as now the storm centre of the British music business. Other cities might have been years rather than miles away then. Swollen pivots of commerce though they had become, these provincial outposts forged opportunities for musical development beyond trumping a euphonium in a Remembrance Day procession. A specific example is that of Mendelssohn conducting the world premier of *Elijah* in Birmingham, which resounds still with a reputable symphony orchestra, youth choir (containing in the late 1950s both Muff and Steve Winwood and Moody Blue-in-waiting Ray Thomas) and international jazz festival.

Founded in 1947, the Second City's Hot Club had metamorphosed into the Jazz Record Society. Aided by crackling 78 rpm records, its members would convene to discuss such esoterica as 'small band Ellingtonia'. Not so cerebral was Aston's Jazz Studio One, the brainchild of a Gordon Andrews, and a platform on which parochial jazzers could blow. Further north, Blackpool hosted the Mineworkers' National Brass Band Contest every November. There you might come across a trumpeter from Huddersfield, far less conscious of being 'arty' than a Londoner, even claiming not to be particularly musical, but automatically buying a ticket for a Town Hall jazz concert.

In middle-class living rooms, regardless of who was present, a parent would often switch off a radio set if it was broadcasting what was taken to be jazz. With geometrically-patterned linoleum the only hint of frivolity in many such homes, the drab post-war era was epitomized by a father who would relax over an after-dinner crossword in slippers, baggy trousers and 'quiet' cardigan. Shackled to homework, his adolescent – not 'teenage' – son would glower and wonder if this was all there was. Perish the thought but you might be better off as the yob offspring of some Tyneside navvy who wouldn't threaten disinheritance if you dared to come downstairs in an American tie.

The United States seemed the very wellspring of everything glamorous from Coca-Cola to the Ink Spots whose humming polyphony enraptured the kingdom's theatres during a 1947 tour. Priscilla White, a Merseyside docker's daughter, was typical of many an English lass who 'lived in a world where the model of all that was good in life was in a Doris Day movie'.[1]

Concern was expressed in a 1957 feature in *Everybody's Weekly*, a now defunct something-for-everyone journal. 'Are We Turning Our Children Into Little Americans?'[2] it asked – for, as well as crew-cuts bristling on young scalps and Barkis remarking that Mrs Peggotty 'sure knows her cooking' in a

US cartoon-strip edition of *David Copperfield*, almost as incredible were the Wild West films that British youth had come to consume. No one ever talked thataway. Neither would a pub landlady fail to bat an eyelid if some hombre was plugged full of daylight in the lounge bar. A god had descended on London once when Roy Rogers rode *a* Trigger from his hotel to Leicester Square Odeon. To many youngsters – including future Rolling Stones Mick Jagger and Keith Richards – Rogers, Gene Autry, Hopalong Cassidy and other singing cowboys with guitars were significant early influences.

Others were impressed by presentations that marked the passing of the music hall. The young could forget about spelling tests and chanted multiplication tables as a magician sawed his buxom assistant in half, and Max Miller told the one about his wife and the nudist who came to use the telephone. It was called 'music hall' because each artiste made use of the pit orchestra if only for a rumble of timpani as a rabbit was produced from a top hat. Usually the bill would contain an entirely musical act; a singer more often than not. In the 1950s, however, you'd be less likely to be serenaded with 'Danny Boy' or 'The Road to Mandalay' than 'How Much Is That Doggie In The Window?', 'Mambo Italiano' or something else from the newly-established *New Musical Express* record and sheet music sales charts.

These and, later in the evening, more sombre music formed the soundtrack to adolescent parties in living rooms transformed into dens of iniquity – especially when the host's parents were away – by dimming table lamps with headscarves and pushing back armchairs to create an arena for smooching as a prelude to snogging and attacks of 'desert sickness', a pre-1970 euphemism for fondling (desert sickness: wandering palms).

Coming from a record player in a corner were the sounds of the plastic 45 rpm records that started to supercede brittle 78s after 1955 – a streamlining that was an apt herald of the 'teenager', a word newly coined to denote those who, 'twixt twelve and twenty', were now specific targets for advertising, thanks to the post-war economic boom. Yet a girl still wore socks well into her teens, and a sure sign of growing up was when she pulled on nylon stockings held up by a suspender belt. Boys were still supposed to dress like little men – men like their teachers in dark business suits with elephant folds obliterating any inkling of body shape round the seat.

This 'quiet' style was reflected in school uniforms of black 'bomber' shoes, grey flannels, blazer, tie and white or grey shirt as local authorities meekly fell into line with state education policy and its compounding of mediocrity – and an often demoralising regime epitomized by academic streaming. Passing the Eleven-Plus examination and so going to a grammar school rather than a secondary modern – where all the 'failures' went – was a desirable social coup for ambitious parents. When the ITV soap opera *Coronation Street* was young, Ken Barlow – then a teacher – was once depicted refusing a bribe to rig results so that a town councillor's son could attend Market Wetherby Grammar.

All but the most liberal educational establishments discouraged anything to do with popular music, bar that which wasn't far removed from the most trifling 'classical' music. In this, they were supported some of the way by the British Broadcasting Corporation, a universal aunt with a stranglehold over the nation's electric media. Some supposed that the sounds they picked up on the Light Programme were 'square' because they were listening on a cheap wireless but, from new Braun transistor to cumbersome mahogany radio-gram, it was the same on all of them: huge helpings of string-laden musak oozing from the orchestras of Geraldo, Mantovani or Ted Heath, and pruned-down arrangements of *Tales of Hoffman* and Handel's 'Largo'. On television, the 'William Tell Oveture' was used as theme to the imported *Lone Ranger* series.

Likewise, as far as more overt 'pop' was concerned, the BBC gave the public only that decent music it ought to like – hence *The Black and White Minstrel Show*, *The Perry Como Show*, strict tempo supremo Victor Sylvester's *Come Dancing*, *Spot the Tune* with Marion Ryan, and Cy Grant's calypsos on Cliff Michelmore's topical *Tonight*.

Also directed at the over-thirties were programmes monopolized by singers such as The Beverley Sisters and Donald Peers ('The Cavalier of Song'), and musical interludes in shows centred on acts like ventriloquist's dummy Archie Andrews – with intriguing harmonica incidental music – 'Mr Pastry', and Lancastrian schoolboy Jimmy Clitheroe. Otherwise, there was *Children's Favourites*: 'Where Will the Baby's Dimple Be', 'The Runaway Train', 'The Ballad of Davy Crockett' and other record requests aired by 'Uncle Mac'. Older siblings – and mighty square ones at that – made do with *Quite Contrary*, built round Ronnie Hilton, a former apprentice engineer from Leeds, who for want of anyone better was cited by the *NME* as 1955's most popular British vocalist. His rival as BBC radio's most omnipresent singer was Lee Lawrence, an ex-ENSA trouper with a similar neo-operatic tenor.

The search for anything teenage was as fruitless on Independent Television (ITV) which began in 1956 with weekly spectaculars starring Patti Page ('The Singing Rage') and our own Dickie Valentine, straight from some palais bandstand. While *Round About Ten* was a bit racy in its embrace of Humphrey Lyttelton's Jazz Band, the inclusion of the Teenagers, a winsome boy-girl ensemble in 'Forces Sweetheart' Vera Lynn's *Melody Cruise*, was something of a false dawn. In between 'How Much Is That Doggie In The Window?' and Lee Lawrence's 'cover' of the quasi-religious 'Crying in the

Chapel', there was no middle ground. As in the 1940s, you jumped from nursery rhymes to Perry Como as if the connecting years were spent in a coma.

'With-it' vicars, off-duty teachers and like do-gooders in cardigans tried harder with youth clubs that embraced wholesome pursuits like ping-pong, slide-shows and a 'Brains Trust' on current affairs. Bored silly, formerly tractable young men would get themselves expelled from such places by blatantly brandishing a cigarette or letting slip a 'bloody'. If not reinstated after scandalized parents forced an apology, they'd take to the streets, smoking and saying 'bloody' – and even 'bugger' – unreproached whilst denouncing the youth club as 'kids' stuff'. If there was no other action going, the boldest might return *en bloc* to wreck the place, snarling with laughter as the grown-up in charge pleaded ineffectually – though clerics were sometimes able to limit the damage because of their dog-collars and the juvenile invaders' superstitious terror of eternal punishment for sin.

The notion of smashing up the youth club might have come from Marlon Brando – as leather-clad 'Johnny' – and his motorcycle thugs' raid on a small US town in the then UK-banned film *The Wild One*. Another role model was James Dean who left this vale of misery in a spectacular car crash on 30 September 1955. In that same year's *Rebel Without A Cause*, he'd demonstrated that, unlike delinquent Brando, you didn't have to come from the wrong side of the tracks to qualify as a sullenly introspective ne'er-do-well. Even the most nicely-spoken lad could now mooch down to the corner shop with hunched shoulders, hands rammed in pockets, and chewing gum in a James Dean half-sneer.

Nevertheless, particularly on desolate housing estates and within industrial and dockland hinterlands, pedestrians would cross over to avoid a swaggering phallanx of Teddy Boys, out for more than boyish mischief. If the attitude was derived largely from Brando and Dean, the appearance of the most menacing teenage cult of the 1950s was almost entirely British. Attired like Edwardian rakes with a touch of the Mississippi riverboat card-sharp, they were usually undersized, homely and of depressed circumstances, but some actually succeeded in growing fearsome, scimitar-like sideburns. They prowled the streets in gangs with brass rings adorning their fists like knuckledusters, and belts studded with washers stolen from work.

Along with the sports coat and 'sensible' shoes, mothballed forever were the cavalry twills. Round the legs now were drainpipes that were what one of my older relations would call 'crude' round the thighs and crotch. A short-back-and-sides was only a memory, and longer tresses were teased into a lavishly whorled glacier of Brylcreem.

They'd barrack in cinemas – except during the sexy bits when they'd go all quiet – and barge without paying into dancehalls, especially ones where Teds and 'coloureds' were barred. Once inside, they'd be studied (not always surreptitiously) by 'birds' with ruby-red lips, tight sweaters, wide belts and pony-tails who, in their imaginations at least, were as elfin as Audrey Hepburn in 1953's *Roman Holiday.*

Sticking with films, the dance hall scene of 1957's *The Hell Drivers* is a boorish but not untypical instance of adult male social behaviour in the 1950s. If pursuit of romance was either unsuccessful or not the principal mass objective of the expedition, Teds would seek more brutal sensual recreation. If you so much as glanced at them, the fun could be *you*. A meek reproof by the victim sparked off the first Teddy Boy murder on a London heath in 1954. Afterwards came hellfire sermons, questions in Parliament, plays like Bruce Walker's *Cosh Boy* (that suggested flogging was the only answer) and movies such as *These Dangerous Years* – featuring a teenage troublemaker reformed by a spell in the army – and *Violent Playground* (with local boy Freddie Fowell as a gangleader). Both films were made in 1957, set on Merseyside and supposedly reflected the corruptness of the 'new' cult.

However, as it had been with *The Wild One*, such moral crusades backfired, and even more fine young people went to the bad after metaphorically tasting the forbidden fruit on celluloid. Those who weren't in a position to buy Teddy Boy 'brothel creepers', the three-quarter length drape jacket with velvet collar and all the other finery, could still radiate the required anti-everything stance. 'When I was at Yardley Wood Secondary Modern – a dump, very rough,' recalled Ace Kefford, 'my school uniform was cheap black jeans sewn up as tight as I could get 'em, black shirt, red waistcoat off my grandad, greased-back hair. We had a gang at school, real dead-end kids who broke into shops and pinched cigarettes, but I think that's how a lot of groups formed – as an extension of that.'

Yet careers advisors would urge that, unless you'd been born into showbusiness, it was unwise to see popular music as a viable career. See, nearly all of these record folk were into their thirties before achieving worthwhile recognition after servitude in an established band. It was a facile life anyway. Few lasted very long. Those that did often operated from the wings. After overseeing the Stargazers' 1953 'hit parade' topper, 'Broken Wings', Dick Rowe, for example, 'arrived' as chief producer and talent spotter for the Decca record company, working similar magic for Lita Roza and Dickie Valentine. Even more prolific a hitmaker was Norrie Paramor, a mild, bespectacled gentleman who'd spent years in metropolitan dance outfits. He was quite middle-aged when appointed Artists and Repertoire manager of Columbia, an EMI subsidiary.

Stars that benefited from the know-how of such men were usually solo performers who took their cue from North America – where the wildest act on the circuit was Johnnie Ray, the 'Prince of Wails'. Against the heavily masculine images of Frankie Laine, Tennessee Ernie Ford and even Dickie Valentine, frail Ray was an unlikely star with his hearing-aid visible from the gallery as, on cue, he collapsed in tears during 'Cry', and turned on the thwarted eroticism of 'Such a Night'.

Women had hysterics and circle stalls buckled wherever he went. Yet Johnnie became dismayingly human to a certain Richard Starkey – later, Ringo Starr – of Liverpool who was among the rapt crowd watching him sip coffee in a window of the city's Adelphi Hotel but 'he was eating in fancy restaurants and waving at people from big hotels, and I thought, "That's the life for me!"'[3]

Though Ray anticipated the exhibitionism that would pervade rock 'n' roll, the intrinsic content of his repertoire was pretty much the same as that emitted from lustier throats during merry evenings in the local boozer when drinkers would be drawn into 'Bye Bye Blackbird', 'Alexander's Ragtime Band', 'Somebody Stole My Gal', 'Hi Lili Hi Lo' and other cosy singalongs. Furthermore, when Ray, Cab Calloway, Jo Stafford, Guy Mitchell, the Platters and other exotic Americans included Britain on their world tour itineraries, you'd be compelled to fidget through endless centuries of jugglers, trick cyclists and like variety turns. Sometimes, US headliners scarcely bothered with a backwater like Britain with its cold and rain, only two television channels, lard-and-chips in fly-blown wayside cafes with no diners' toilets, and no ice in your drink. A night at the London Palladium would often be the sole concession to Limey customers.

No Yank of any importance would travel far into the provinces for less than a king's ransom. Therefore, you had to fall back on cheaper local entertainment. Even Teds were among five million adult Britons who went ballroom dancing every Saturday to, say, Cambridge's John Goddard Orchestra or, long resident at Croydon's Orchid Ballroom, The Johnny Howard Big Band, cranking out the evening's veletas and square tangos in customary stiff formal garb.

Yet these contained fragments of portent. The fathers of such as Dave Berry, Paul McCartney, The Who's Pete Townshend and other 1960s pop stars were veterans of such outfits. Moreover, Dave Clark would 'remember seeing the Eric Delaney Band when I was young. This guy got up in front and had timpani with the pedals on them, and he did his thing. It was very jazzy, but I said, "God, he looks good!" And it was very simple. That's the one bit of inspiration that I always recall.'[4] Finally, as well as requests for 'The Anniversary Waltz', 'Charmaine' and 'Que Sera Sera', there was always some young smart alec who wanted 'Rock Around the Clock'.

Ted Heath didn't think rock 'n' roll would come to Britain. 'You see, it is primarily for the coloured population.'[5] But penetrating the BBC and its rival's snug realms of red-nosed reindeers and Christmas alphabets as 1955 mutated into 1956 was a 'cover' of black rhythm-and-blues unit Sonny Dae and the Knights' 'Rock Around the Clock' by Bill Haley and the Comets, a paunchy dance combo from Detroit. It was a hit with all but the most serious-minded teenagers after parental blood ran cold at its metronomic clamour. Incited by the newspapers, girls jived in gingham and flat ballet shoes while secretive penknives slit cinema seats when Haley's B-movie of the same name – 'the old backstage plot spiced with the new music' quoth *Picturegoer*[6] – reached these isles.

Haley himself came over to beg pardon of the press for his Comets' knockabout stage routines but, what with this 'rock' nonsense going so well, it would have been daft not to have played up to it, wouldn't it? Even with four concurrent entries in the UK 'charts', Bill and his 'rock 'n' roll' turned out more harmless than Johnnie Ray had proved to be. After Kay Starr's 'Rock and Roll Waltz' smash in 1956, the Creep, hula-hoops, the Cha-Cha-Cha, the UK-only Double-Decker, the Hand Jive – rather limited in physical satisfaction – and, its steps lost in the mists of time, the Slippin' Skin had been proffered as the next fad. However, rock 'n' roll put forward a more suitable and enduring champion than Haley or Starr in a Mr E. A. Presley, a Tennesseean who dressed as a hybrid of amusement arcade hoodlum and nancy-boy.

With 'common' good looks, Elvis Presley wasn't married and tubby like Haley but, as the first photograph[7] of him published in Britain testified, a delinquent type like Brando with Brooding Intensity *à la* Dean. His brilliantined but girly cockade was offset by sideburns down to his earlobes. Rearing up in seedy-flash 'cat' clothes – pink socks, circulation-impeding slacks, check shirt and box jacket – this 'unspeakably untalented and vulgar young entertainer', as a TV guide had him, made adult flesh creep.

Unlike Bill Haley, Presley had no qualms about onstage frolics that involved hip-swivelling, doing the splits and rolling about as if he had a wasp in his pants. With an electric guitarist shifting from simple frills to full-blooded clangorous solo, Presley's first single had been a jumped-up treatment of a negro blues. From then on, his shout-singing and sulky balladeering had become both adored and detested throughout the free world.

Of the new sensation's debut UK release, 'Heartbreak Hotel', the *NME* wrote, 'If you appreciate good singing, I don't suppose you'll manage to hear this disc all through.'[8] Reports of Presley's unhinged go-man-go sorcery in concert caused Methodist preacher and jazz buff Dr Donald Soper (later Lord Soper) to wonder 'how intelligent people can derive satisfaction from something which is emotionally embarrassing and intellectually ridiculous.'[9]

What more did Elvis need to be the rage of teenage Britain?

To the disgust of Dr Soper, Johnny Dankworth – 1949's 'Musician of The Year' in *Melody Maker* – and other purists, certain jazz and swing band musicians, set up contingent rock 'n' roll combos, their drummers twirling sticks gratuitously during numbers in which subtle bebop cross-rhythms had no part. Lionel Hampton's raucous nod to rock 'n' roll during a 1956 concert at the Royal Festival Hall prompted Dankworth to voice his displeasure from the audience. Newly-lapsed British jazz percussionists like Tony Crombie, Rory Blackwell, even Eric Delaney, were now socking a crude but powerful off-beat less like that of Haley – whose 'Rock Around the Clock' rim-shots were actually quite tricky – than those of Louis Jordan, Fats Domino, Bill Doggett, Big Joe Turner and other US 'jump-blues' exponents of the late 1940s, thereby battling against charges of gold-digging because, agreed Brian Bird, clergyman founder of the Boxford Jazz Club, 'blues is the main content of jazz'.[10]

Needing no such justification, the John Barry Seven were formed in 1957 with guitarist Vic Flick, pianist Les Reed and other 'real musicians' as a multi-functional ingredient of package tours and pop TV, sounding mock-tijuana by choice. Group Six, however, merely titled the two genteel vibraphone-led jazz instrumentals that constituted a 1957 single, 'Rockin' the Blues' and 'Rock-A-Boogie'. Clinging more firmly to the new craze's coat-tails, Gordon Andrews of Jazz Studio One had become – as he'd tell you himself – 'Birmingham's *only* rock 'n' roll singer'[11] as he cut up rough at the Casino Ballroom to the accompaniment of the Unsquare Men.

The first single by Ronnie Scott's former vocalist Art Baxter, with the Rockin' Sinners, was 'Shortnin' Bread Rock'. As Chuck Berry, a genuine North American rocker, was seen derisively duck-walking with his red guitar in *Jazz On a Summer's Day*, a US film documentary, Britain's response was to engage the Kirchins, whose record debut was 'Rockin' And Rollin' at the Darktown Strutters' Ball', for a jazz extravaganza at a Clacton holiday camp.

Well, you have to move with the times, as did Lee Lawrence with 1956's spoof 'Rock 'n' Opera' that namechecked Elvis, Gene Vincent, Tommy Steele and other newcomers who were lessening his chances of ever returning to the hit parade. Then there was Victor Sylvester's sanitized rock 'n' roll sequence on *Come Dancing*, and Clinton Ford's rocked-up 'Nellie Dean'. An EP from the Rock 'n' Rollers on Embassy, the cheap Woolworth's label, was also unconsciously and mildly amusing, but more attractive was 'Sweet Old-Fashioned Boy' by Terry Thomas Esq. and his Rock 'n' Roll Rotters, notable for the distinguished character actor's haw-haw interjections of 'dig those crazy sounds, Daddio' and 'See you later, alma mater' *ad nauseum*.

Norrie Paramor provisioned Columbia with a token 'rock 'n' roll' act in

Tony Crombie's Rockets. Though too critically blinkered to see rock 'n' roll being more than 'an American phenomenon – and they do it best', Paramor realized that no one in London had much idea. Singers were too plummy, arrangements too polite – and session musicians too bland. Among those thus earning their tea break were the Ted Taylor Four with their hearts in jazz, the Cliff Adams Singers, who would one day mark the end of the BBC radio weekend with the depressing *Sing Something Simple*, and guitarist Bert Weedon who'd landed on his feet as featured soloist with Mantovani, Ted Heath and, by the early fifties, Cyril Stapleton's BBC show Band – heard thrice weekly on the Light Programme. By 1956, Bert was leading his own quartet, but if records like 'Guitar Boogie Shuffle' made the Top 10, his bread-and-butter was record dates for domestic artistes from Dickie Valentine and Alma Cogan to the new breed of Presley-esque teen idols headed by Tommy Steele.

Though the accolade belonged morally to Bert, his middle-aged hireling, Tommy began winning music press popularity polls as Best Guitarist after a 1956 Number One with 'Singing the Blues' – arguably more creditable than Guy Mitchell's original – and it seemed that British rock 'n' roll was here to stay for a while yet, no matter how abhorrent its noise and gibberish to those no longer young.

Pragmatism ruled, however, and soon the hunt was up for more money-making morons in the Presley mould. Needless to say, these sprouted thickest in the States where dull-witted talent scouts saw Louisiana fireball Jerry Lee Lewis as just an Elvis who substituted piano for guitar, and hollered arrogance for hot-potato-in-the-mouth mumbling. While Capitol was lumbered with a pig-in-a-poke in crippled, unco-operative Gene Vincent – 'The Screaming End' – Acuff-Rose would snare two-for-the-price-of-one in the Everly Brothers, whose delinquent-angel faces and double-edged bluegrass harmonies had propelled them into charts far beyond their native Kentucky.

Repeated listening to 'Bye Bye Love', *risqué* 'Wake Up Little Susie' and subsequent smashes brought home to aspiring British imitators how rock 'n' roll could be simultaneously forceful and romantic. British double-acts like the Dene Boys, the Dowlands and the Allisons were direct imitations of Don and Phil Everly – though Bill and Brett Landis, an EMI duo, at least wrote their own songs – while fans attempting to describe the early Beatles' vocal interplay found it simplest to say that it sounded like the Brothers too.

Black Presleys like Chuck Berry, Bo Diddley and Little Richard had appeared; then female ones like Wanda Jackson and Janis Martin; mute ones in guitarists Duane Eddy and – a Red Indian too – Link Wray who achieved the extra-tonal shading on his global smash, 'Rumble', through preparatory jabbing of pencils into amplifier speakers. The resulting buzzings and rattlings were comparable to the battered vocal nuances of Ray Charles – a Presley black *and* blind – on the call-and-response 'What'd I Say', which had him trading 'heys' and 'yeahs' with his female trio, the Raelettes, like a gospel exhorter with his congregation. Emasculations by inhibited home-reared rockers of 'What'd I Say', 'Sticks and Stones' and further Charles set-works were common on British stages long into the 1960s, as were tries at 'Honey Don't', 'Lend Me Your Comb' and other songs from the portfolio of Carl Perkins, an unsexy Elvis – but not as unsexy as bespectacled Buddy Holly, a Texan singing guitarist who dominated his group, the Crickets.

Making up for a manifest deficit of teen appeal, gangling Buddy possessed other creative talents – not least of which was an ability to write, with various Crickets, simple but atmospheric songs tailored to his elastic adenoids. In the ascendant too was another composer, Eddie Cochran, a multi-talented Oklahoman Elvis, whose 'Summertime Blues' and other singles outlined the trials of adolescence.

Off-the-cuff examples of would-be Elvii further afield were Mickie Most from South Africa and Australia's Johnny O'Keefe. More awkward were Ricky Fulton and the kilted Andy Stewart, each pushed briefly as a Scottish Elvis. Tommy Steele remained Presley's English 'answer' – 'just as talented or just as revolting according to the way you feel' said *Everybody's Weekly*[2] – before entering showbiz proper as an all-round entertainer. In his wake emerged the diverse likes of Terry Dene and actor Anthony Newley who both paralleled Elvis mainly in that they endured National Service – Terry in unhappy, career-destroying fact; Anthony in silver screen fiction as 'Jeep Jackson' in *Idol On Parade*.

After the soundtrack EP made the Top 20, Newley followed up with a crack at Lloyd Price's 'Personality'. Such syndication was anticipated, even welcomed, by US pop stars as it brought their music, if not their records, to another territory of teenagers with money to waste. Rather than pre-empting Elvis, Newley and other Britons gave themselves a more sporting chance by mechanically reproducing discs by lesser known Americans like Price. On the radio, these could sound virtually identical to the originals – though among exceptions were Bernard Bresslaw's gormless 'Charlie Brown' as opposed to the Coasters' streetwise hustler, and comedian Charlie Drake's amazing go at Bobby Darin's 'Splish Splash' that justified *NME* reviewer Derek Johnson's critique that Drake's was 'as down-to-earth a piece of rock 'n' roll as anyone could wish to hear on disc.'[12]

There were no takers for the medley of nursery rhymes by canine vocal group the Singing Dogs, but a veritable pack of Britons fought over Marty Robbins' jogalong 'The Story of My Life'. The war was won by Michael

Holliday who, with Robbins on the other side of the Atlantic, was better able to promote his version in concert and on TV. Tommy Steele had a more unfair advantage with 'Come On Let's Go', originally by Ritchie Valens, killed in the same 1959 aeroplane disaster as Buddy Holly.

After a controversial tour by Jerry Lee Lewis that same year, Sir Frank Medlicotte, MP, pointed out in Parliament that 'we have enough rock 'n' rollers of our own without importing them'. Why bring Elvis over when plenty of British lads could do the job just as well? In quantity, we had more than enough duplicates of almost every US pop sensation during these Dark Ages of British beat. Outside the hit parade, the first homogenous local rock 'n' roll groups were already banning themselves from adult functions on which they might have otherwise depended for virtually all their bookings had they played 'decent' music.

Salisbury's Johnny Nicholls and the Dimes were led by a genuine American, and from Sheffield had emanated a mild media stir when the twenty-one-year-old Earl of Wharncliffe joined the Musicians Union in 1956 in order to drum with a rock 'n' roll combo led by Ted Pell, a chap who then vanishes from the pages of history, as would another Steel City unit, the Four Imps, with their rehearsed patter and close harmonies – though they contained future TV funnyman Dougie Brown, and would sometimes back Lyn Sheppard, later comedienne Marti Caine.

Other regions also cradled perpetrators of interminable teenage racket whether the Bobby Bell Rockers from Seaforth – in existence since Bell (né Crawford) had seen Freddie Bell and the Bellboys in Haley's *Rock Around the Clock* movie in 1956 – Glasgow's Kansas City Counts, Jerry Storm and the Falcons of Burnley or Johnny Vincent and his Alley Cats on the Isle of Wight. Generally, the 'Somebody and the Somebodies' dictate regarding the group's name held good, differentiating between the 'star' and backing outfit from which might be drawn 'featured vocalists' whenever he needed a rest. Johnny Nicholls, for example, frequently waved in to the central microphone his high-spirited schoolboy guitarist, Dave Harman.

Despite the existence of these grassroots alternatives to national hit parade contenders, it was when the continental commercial station Radio Luxembourg began broadcasting pop showcases in English that the BBC light entertainment division, despite finding rock 'n' roll noxious, felt more obliged to cater for its fans. Worse, ITV broke a tacit 'toddlers' truce' by filling what was previously a blank screen between six and seven p.m. with the like of *Dance Roof Party*, a Scottish regional effort with teenagers dancing to bands playing current favourites.

The Corporation countered with *Six-Five Special*, designed to keep teenagers quiet while mum and dad put the little ones to bed. It was co-produced by Jack Good, true originator of British pop TV. Once president of Oxford University Drama Society, he'd been a stand-up comic before enrolling on a BBC training course. His final test film had been about Freddie Mills, the champion boxer, who was to resurface on *Six-Five Special* because, though Dr Soper might have watched it 'as a penance',[9] it sought to preserve a little decency by employing such upstanding interlocutors as Mills and disc-jockey Pete Murray – who abhorred Elvis.

'Rock and roll' was to be by the likes of singing trombonist Don Lang and his 'Frantic Five', and Wee Willie Harris who'd been bruited as London's – and, by implication, the entire country's – very own Jerry Lee Lewis, though he was less a teen idol than a clown in outsized polkadot bow-tie, silly grin and hair dyed shocking pink. Neither was he above banal publicity stunts like a 'feud' with blue-rinsed Larry Page 'the Teenage Rage'. Though Harris himself composed 'Rockin' at the 2i's' as a debut 45, he – like Page – relied mostly on US covers on the understanding that most home consumers were unlikely to have heard the originals before he rehashed them on *Six-Five Special*.

The show's pop regulars also embraced entertainers such as Everton's Russ Hamilton with his gentle lisp, and the King Brothers who were of the same stamp as the Four Imps for, despite producing a xerox of 'Wake Up Little Susie', they were born to do show tunes. Dickie Valentine wasn't yet too square to appear either, nor was Joe 'Mr Piano' Henderson.

Though he'd become evangelical about rock 'n' roll, Good's old-maidish superiors obliged him to balance it and the other pop with comedy, string quartets and self-improving features on sport and hobbies. This brief also allowed traditional jazz, ethnic blues by visiting black Americans such as Big Bill Broonzy (with his novel twelve-string guitar) and, a by-product of both forms, skiffle – which was to be dominated throughout its prime in 1957 by another *Six-Five Special* guest, Tony 'Lonnie' Donegan.

2 THE DONEGAN EFFECT

Though skiffle was derived from the rent parties, speakeasies and Dust Bowl jug bands of the US Depression, 'rockabilly', its closest relation in primeval rowdiness, gripped the imagination of young America infinitely harder. Rockabilly employed conventional rather than home-made instruments – and, while retaining a washboard for percussion, even those skiffle outfits who made the UK hit parade tended to abandon the makeshift too, thereby adulterating the form for purists, still divided over the policy of The Chris Barber Jazz Band who, as an intermission from the interweaving of the front line horns, had introduced in 1951 The Washboard Wonders: Beryl Bryden on washboard and Barber himself on orthodox double bass (rather than one made with broom-handle and tea-chest) accompanying guitarist and banjoist Lonnie Donegan's brace of blues-tinged North American folk songs.

This became the highlight of the act. From the Barber outfit's *New Orleans Joys* in 1954, Donegan's 'Rock Island Line' – from the catalogue of walking musical archive Huddie 'Leadbelly' Ledbetter – was issued eventually as a single which, after months in the domestic charts, was a US hit too. However, none of Lonnie's many subsequent UK smashes caught on with the American teenager as they did with his Limey cousin who, on teaching himself a few guitar chords, could (and generally did) form an amateur combo in the Donegan image – but with a repertoire that tended to incorporate rock 'n' roll and its attendant physical jerks, until some nit-picker insisted that they stay seated rent-party style, and stick soley to the folksy likes of 'Lil' Liza Jane', 'This Little Light of Mine' and 'Railroad Bill'.

In 1958, the Vipers – once Tommy Steele's backing combo, and then second only to Lonnie in the skiffle hierarchy – released a cover of Eddie Cochran's 'Summertime Blues'. However, ex-serviceman Donegan, steeped in traditional jazz, reviled rock 'n' roll as 'a gimmick'. Like all gimmicks, it is sure to die the death. Nothing makes me madder than to be bracketed with those rock 'n' roll boys'.[6] Yet, despite himself, Donegan – with his stage name lifted from blues singer, Lonnie Johnson – was a more homogeneously British equivalent of Elvis than Tommy Steele, through his vivacious processing of black music for a white audience, singing in an energetic whine far removed from the gentle polish of other UK pop stars.

If he looked like a used car salesman offstage, the 'King of Skiffle' could be mesmeric in concert, creating true hand-biting excitement as he piled into numbers his group didn't know; took on and resolved risky extemporizations, and generated a sweaty, exhilarating intensity never before experienced in British pop. In retrospect, it is not silly to put him on a par with Jimi Hendrix.

Donegan's impact rippled across decades of British pop. If his 'Railroad Bill' – rooted in a slave work 'holler' – hadn't much to do with sixpence (2½p) for a British Railways sandwich, at least it had been sufficiently anglicized (with 'new words and music') not to be sneered at – as was, say, singing comedy actor Jim Dale's unspeakable cover of 'All Shook Up'.

As exemplified by later chart strikes such as 'Grand Coolie Dam' and 'Battle of New Orleans', Lonnie delved deeply into white Americana too, encompassing Woody Guthrie, bluegrass, spirituals, Cajun and even Appalachian music – which, in its minimal melodic variation was the formal opposite of jazz. Perhaps the best-known item from this source was 'Go Tell Aunt Nancy', another from Leadbelly who, like Big Bill Broonzy and one-man-band Jesse Fuller, had absorbed white folk music as well as blues, during an eventful life.

The scholarly natures of other skifflers also dictated digging beneath the music's chewing-gum flavoured veneer. So began their haunting of Dobell's in Charing Cross Road, Strickland's in Soho, Carey's Swing Shop in Streatham and rare provincial stores like Plymouth's Hot Record Shop and Leicester's Moore and Stanworth's that also specialized in imported merchandise from skiffle's blues and hillbilly sources whether uproarious jug bands like Gus Cannon's Jug Stompers from Texas or the grippingly personal styles of pre-war bluesmen such as Robert Johnson.

Skiffle thus brought all manner of vigorous alien idioms to an impoverished and derivative UK pop scene. Moreover, like punk after it, anyone who'd mastered basic techniques could have a go at skiffle – and the more do-it-yourself the sound, the better. No one howled with derision at tea-chest bass, a washboard tapped with thimbles, rasping comb-and-paper, dustbin-lid cymbals, biscuit tin snare drum and other instruments fashioned from household implements. Among more elaborate options were banking on a given venue's piano – veteran of other parish activities – being playable, and investing in a 'Viceroy Skiffle Board', a 'tapbox' advertised in the *NME* with miniature drum, washboard, cowbell and hooter that, for 39s 11d (£1.99½p), was 'ideal for parties and playing along with radio and gramophone' – thereby placating mothers irked by drumsticks smiting the furniture instead. You could then save up for a Broadway 'Kat' snare-and-cymbal set costing £10 4s.

Percussion and slashed acoustic rhythm guitar were at the core of the contagious backbeat. In an *NME* advice column, Bob Cort, one of skiffle's lesser icons, dwelt too on 'visual effect', emphasizing that 'some sort of uniform is a great help – though ordinary casual clothes are perhaps best as long as you all wear exactly the same.'[13]

Musically, however, the highest ideal was to forge an individual style even with set-works like 'Midnight Special', 'Black Girl', 'Careless Love' and 'The House of the Rising Sun', a soaring whorehouse ballad recorded by both Big Bill Broonzy and Josh White. 'That's where half the enjoyment lies,' pontificated Bob Cort, 'in experimenting with ideas.'[13] Dickie Bishop and his Sidekicks' 'Cumberland Gap', for example, deviated from that of Donegan in its swapping of guitar *obligato* for a jigging fiddle.

Once the guitar had been associated mainly with Latinate heel-clattering but now it was what Elvis and Lonnie played. In April 1957, the *Daily Mirror* quipped 'Springtime Is Stringtime!'[14] as 'Cumberland Gap' became Donegan's first Number One, and a London musical instrument firm with two thousand unfulfilled orders from guitars indented a West German manufacturer for a further six thousand. Though some might attend the flamenco guitar lessons laid on by some senior schools, young men's motives for taking up the instrument were regarded as somewhat suspect by leading guitar tutor Ivor Mairants. 'Some lads,' he believed, 'are buying them just to hang on their shoulders.'[14]

A group frequently had an embarrassment of superfluous guitarists within a nebulous line-up. Most grappled with chords, but this rudimentary impetus could be overlaid by a 'lead guitarist' plucking runs and solos. He was usually the one who'd taken the trouble to learn properly. Positioning yet uncalloused fingers on the taut strings, he pored over 'When the Saints Go Marching In', 'Simple Blues For Guitar' and other exercises prescribed in *Play in a Day*, a tutor book devised by Bert Weedon, before progressing on to *Play Every Day*, a more advanced manual with pieces by Charlie Christian and Django Reinhardt.

Daily practice drew to light an appreciation of the more gifted electric guitarists of classic rock. Coalescing the hep-cat couplets of rockabilly, Carl Perkins' harsh picking was as cutting as the vocal on his best-remembered hit, 'Blue Suede Shoes'. Much admired too were Jerry Lee Lewis's guitarist Roland Janes, Cliff Gallup of Gene Vincent's Blue Caps, and Scotty Moore, creator of the heart-stopping second guitar break in Presley's 'Hound Dog'. When Elvis defected to RCA, he was co-produced by Chet 'Mr Guitar' Atkins, master of the 'Nashville Sound', with first refusal of all daily record sessions in the aptly-named 'Music City USA'. Less jaunty but as highly regarded, Duane Eddy had blueprinted a 'twangy' approach which involved booming melodies on the three lower strings.

So inspired, the most dedicated skiffle guitarists would work at it until fingertips hardened, and the purchase of a more worthy instrument – an electric model maybe – could be considered. From a kit advertised in *Melody Maker*, it was feasible to solder together an amplifier 'with a ten-watt punch' which was transportable in a school satchel. Neither was it laughable for a group warily magnifying its volume to simply shove a microphone through the hole in an acoustic and wire it into the workings of a record-player.

Many adolescents were taking skiffle seriously enough to labour over a guitar fretboard late into the evening to the detriment of even that modicom of homework necessary to avert the cane or a detention. Yet the outlook in some schools had become open-minded enough for skiffle not to be seen as an evil but a more effective means of arousing interest in music than could be achieved through the tedium of diminished fifths and Brahms' *German Requiem*.

While some teachers were active in extra-mural skiffle clubs, musical parents too were glad enough to give a few pointers when their offspring took up skiffle – which was harmless as long as it didn't interefere with schoolwork. Most children agreed, and, if their skiffle group fell apart – as most did – within a year, weren't that dismayed because it was seen as a vocational blind alley, a folly to be cast aside on departure to the world of work, the marriage bed, or National Service. Indeed, mainstay Ray Stuart's call-up papers meant the end of the Mainliners, South Yorkshire's leading skiffle unit.

Willing to perform for as little as a round of fizzy drinks, most groups existed for the benefit of performers rather than audience anyway, but there were hundreds of them in every shire, each led generally by an aspirant Donegan whose innate bossiness had him at stage-centre, singing through his nose, and thrashing that E-chord on a digit-lacerating six-string for all he was worth.

Appearances were confined mainly to wedding receptions, youth clubs, church fetes and street parties – though Joe Brown's Spacemen were fixtures in the saloon of his parents' Plaistow pub. At moments of high drama, Joe would turn round abruptly and play his guitar on the back of his head. In nearby Essex, the County Ramblers moved from knees-ups at Widdington Village Hall to RAF Debden's Sergeants' Mess.

If somebody gave your group actual money for playing, you might be sufficiently overwhelmed to tumble through your parents' front door afterwards, recounting details of the engagement at the top of your voice and flourishing the ten-shilling (50p) note you'd been given from petty cash. The first time was the only time in many cases, and the greatest night anyone could ever remember was not marred by a repeat performance.

Not everyone, however, was doing it simply for a hobby. Day jobs weren't exactly showbusiness but they'd do while skiffle still served as a path to a living as a professional entertainer. You'd appoint someone with access to a telephone as 'manager' to get your bookings, and, if none were forthcoming, you'd open your own venue in some back room or starkly-lit basement, boldly stretching out a limited set over an entire evening; the bass player's fingers bleeding by the finish. The Five Nutters – from which would spring Johnny Kidd and the Pirates – were one such outfit, omnipresent at their own KKK club in Willesden.

Like nascent punk groups would decades later, it was not unknown for an audacious skiffle ensemble to gatecrash another act's show. The scenario was timeless: immediately on entering a youth club, a group leader's presence is requested in the office. The organiser can't recall booking them. Perhaps it had been negotiated via one of the more credulous members of the committee. He permits them twenty minutes as support to the billed attraction, the Brian Gammidge Combo.

Not letting personal dislike deter them either, cinema proprietors began offering 'Teenage Shows' every Saturday morning, thus giving local skifflers another forum, and enabling the madder local youths to make-believe they were Elvis Presleys, now and then evoking more audience enthusiasm than many nationally famous pop singers.

Free of charge too, ambitious groups would try to get on the bill of any other talent showcase whether it was in village hall or some Victorian monstrosity in the middle of the city. Virtually the only avenue from insignificance to stardom was taking a brief turn under a local theatre's proscenium in itinerant contests like *Search For Stars*, overseen by ITV's Carroll Levis. This forefather of Hughie Green's *Opportunity Knocks* countered the rival channel's *Bid For Fame*. Up against such disparate acts as blindfolded knife-throwers and comedy impressionists, you were judged by volume of applause in the finale.

Other such tournaments included those instigated by *The People* newspaper with holiday camp potentate Billy Butlin, and the more explicit 1957 All-England Skiffle championship – in which the John Henry Group, led by the man who would become Chris Farlowe, triumphed – and *Singing in Harmony* whose heat at Sheffield's Locarno was won in 1958 by Malcolm Green and David Grundy with an Everly Brothers number.

Of similar persuasion, two Salford boys, Allan Clarke and Graham Nash, singing together as 'Ricky and Dane', did well in 1959's *Search for Stars* final at the Manchester Hippodrome, but if they could not seize the ultimate prize of exposure on *The Carroll Levis Show*, at least they came out of it with a more promising date sheet for a while. A list that had once signified a month's work became a week's, but 'after that you were on your own', elucidated Cilla White, 'Agents never saw themselves as more than bookers.'[1]

Newcastle guitarists Brian Rankin and Bruce Welch had chosen to go directly to source. After his Crescent City Skiffle Group won a South Shields Jazz Club talent competition, Rankin went professional on joining Welch in the Railroaders. Moving to London, Brian – assuming the *nom de théâtre* 'Hank B. Marvin' – and Bruce operated briefly as the Geordie Boys before enlistment in what would evolve into the Shadows.

Their stamping ground was Soho clubs like Chas McDevitt's Skiffle Cellar, where Tommy Steele and Terry Dene used to play. It was still prestigious in 1958, and even skifflers in the sticks deemed worthwhile a booking either there – or, in the same square mile, at the 2i's (run by Doctor Death, a former wrestler), the Gyre and Gimble and Trafalgar Square's Safari Club, in case foremost pop impresario Larry Parnes or a svengali like him noticed them. In these hang-outs – notably the 2i's – Harry Webb, Reg Smith and Terry Nelhams were then awaiting respective destinies as Cliff Richard, Marty Wilde and Adam Faith.

One evening in 1958 at the Safari Club, Dame Fortune smiled wanly on an Alan Caldwell of Liverpool – ostensibly down south to take part in an athletics championship. After an impromptu solo performance, he secured his Texan Skiffle Group a one-song slot on Radio Luxembourg's *Skiffle Club*, recorded in Manchester. Historically, they were the first such Scouse act to so broadcast – a fact not much appreciated at the time.

Just as eager to succeed, the Saints, a handful of Norwich schoolboys, ran away from home to audition there. Two of them, guitarists Kenny Packwood and Tony Sheridan, stayed on to back Marty Wilde, a more successful testee. Hitmakers from later eras of British pop – among them Spencer Davis, Gary Glitter and, all the way from Glasgow, Alex Harvey – tried out at the Safari and its rival clubs too. The Davis group, named the Saints too, also busked for pennies while looking out for policemen at various West End tube stations. With their earnings, they recorded a privately-pressed single, hedging their bets with a coupling of 'Midnight Special' and Buddy Holly's 'Oh Boy!'.

There was also a fellow called David Edward Sutch who, one night in 1959, had mounted a metropolitan pub stage to entertain his mates with a parody of a pop star. With amused cheers still ringing in his ears, David decided to become the antithesis of the Presley and Donegan copyists competing for Doctor Death's attention at the 2i's, after convincing a Sudbury outfit that, although he had intended initially to manage them, he could better serve as front man. Screaming Lord Sutch and his Horde of Savages' first paid booking at a Harrow working men's club brought instant parochial notoriety.

Beyond Greater London, skiffle still prevailed in vaguely differing regional shades. Birmingham, for example, leaned towards jazz, while in the West Country, groups like the Avon Cities Skiffle – who issued 'This Little Light of Mine' on their own Tempo Records – and the Satellites, led by ex-Dime Dave Harman (who'd adopted the stage surname 'Dee'), betrayed roots in Morris Dance sides in their employment of mandolin and piano accordion. The north-western ports up to Glasgow were inclined to have more of a country-and-western bias. There were over forty cowboy outfits operational in what had been christened 'the Nashville of the North'. Playin' the kinda music folk like a-tappin' their boot leather to, they covered all waterfronts from Slim Whitman' falsetto 'sweetcorn' to the 'hard' country of Hank Williams with its unusual preoccupation with rhythm.

As TV series such as *Rawhide*, *Wagon Train*, *Cheyenne* and *Gunsmoke* were popular, the Wild West affected the names of groups and individuals like Clay Ellis and the Raiders, the James Boys (after pistol-packin' Jesse), Johnny Ringo and the Colts, the Texans, and Clint Reno who reverted to his given name of Tony Jackson on throwing in his lot with the Searchers (after a 1956 John Wayne movie). Many accrued accessories like cowboy boots, stetsons and, if they could grow them, stringy desperado beards.

Merseyside skiffle groups also plundered sea shanties like 'Maggie May' and 'Liverpool Lou'. Folk traditions in other areas left their marks too. Surviving skiffle, the Ian Campbell Folk Group, stalwarts of the Midlands folk scene, contained future Fairport Convention violinist Dave Swarbrick, who was usually introduced as 'the Black Country Cowboy'. Among many outlets for Swarbrick and other local folk artistes was the Boggery Club, which convened in a Solihull rugby club pavilion. Learning his comedian's craft there, a Robert Davis would gain later renown as Jasper Carrot and a chaperoned Steve Winwood was, from his earliest teens, playing floor spots as a change from bookings with his big brother's Muff Woody Jazz Band – who had started in skiffle.

The skiffle antecedent of the trad jazz craze of the early 1960s was less significant than its longer-term effect on the beat boom. The Beatles rose from the ashes of the Quarry Men and the Texan Skiffle Group – for whom both George Harrison and Manchester's Graham Bonnet (cousin of the three brothers who would constitute the Bee Gees) auditioned after the fame of the lads who'd been on *Skiffle Club* had spread. George was turned down because of his youth, even though, on transferring from washboard to guitar, he'd been leader of the Rebels – a name duplicated by many other skiffle groups throughout the country, including one in South Wales containing future political leader Neil Kinnock, and another that recorded for Parlophone, a subsidiary of EMI, one of London's four major record labels.

3 WORKERS' PLAYTIME

Ray Charles at London's Hammersmith Odeon in 1961 'was one of the greatest things I've ever seen'[15] to sixteen-year-old Gary Brooker who, on returning to his native Southend, began the formation of the Paramounts. Initially, Charles numbers filled around half their set. Yet, of all the elements that coalesced to produce the beat boom, perhaps the single most influential event had been when fated Buddy Holly and the Crickets – two guitars, double bass and drums – undertook British dates in March 1958.

'How these boys manage to make such a big, big sound with such limited instrumentation baffles me'[16] gasped a reviewer after the quartet closed the show at a Kilburn cinema with a half-hour mixture of their own and rivals' hits. Among schoolboys who found the Crickets' stage act and compact sound instructive were Mick Jagger, Dave Clark and Brian Poole who, from Kent, North London and Essex respectively, caught the Crickets in the capital too. At the Manchester stop were Ricky and Dane, and a spindly youth named Garrity, lately parted from a girlfriend who'd disapproved of him singing in a new group called Freddie and the Dreamers in which he wore black horn-rimmed spectacles – as would Hank Marvin and Brian Poole after he'd approached boys at his Barking secondary school about forming his own Crickets with himself as Buddy Holly.

One metropolitan Teddy Boy has merited the nickname 'Sunglasses Ron' as he has never removed the said shades since reading of Buddy's death not quite a year later. Wiltshire guitarist Trevor 'Dozy' Davies 'cried all the way home. Yes, he was a big hero.'[17] That day too, British newspapers had bristled with Holly who was written off as a has-been in his own land. Yet his US flops had often been huge sellers in Britain, and many UK artists were to pay vinyl respects down the years: the Quarry Men's 'That'll Be The Day' on a 1960 demo; 'Listen To Me' from the Searchers; The Rolling Stones' maiden Top 10 entry with 'Not Fade Away'; Dave Berry's 'Maybe Baby'; Peter and Gordon's – and, in 1983, Cliff Richard's – 'True Love Ways'; 'Well All Right' (with a lyrical update) by Blind Faith; Humble Pie's 'Heartbeat'; Steeleye Span's *a capella* 'Rave On'; Mud's 1975 chart-topper with 'Oh Boy' in the same style, Wreckless Eric's 'Crying Waiting Hoping', and an entire 1980 album of Holly by, well, the Hollies.

After Buddy's British tour, it was no coincidence that sales of electric guitars boomed, especially those of either genuine or copied sunburst Fenders the same as his – though, at Wilson Peck, then Sheffield's only musical equipment shop, a Frank White became the first UK owner of a twin-necked Gibson, a gleaming white object like one Elvis was to pretend to play in one of his movies. However, Plymouth's Music Centre was more typically supplying plenty of Holly-esque Fenders to just-formed groups like the Hepcats, Dave Lee and the Staggerlees, the Zodiacs and the Black Shadows.

The Crickets had demonstrated how rock 'n' roll could progress without getting too complex. Most of their originals were inspired doctorings of R & B style cliches as shown by 'I'm Looking For Someone to Love' with a stock blues sequence, and 'Not Fade Away', built round Bo Diddley's patented *shave-and-a-haircut-six-pence* rhythm. On seeing Buddy's boys at the Liverpool Philharmonic, Paul McCartney suggested to school chum George Harrison that they too write their own songs. A study of chord charts on sheet music revealed that three basic structures recurred: the 'three chord trick', the twelve-bar blues (a variation) and the I-VI minor-IV-V ballad cliché. Sometimes, these were infused with a 'middle-eight' or bridge passage. These findings were the foundation of the first efforts at composition by McCartney and John Lennon, leader of the Quarry Men, and a keener collaborator than George.

It was understood that, should the Quarry Men – or whatever they decided to call it – fold, John and Paul would make a go of it purely as writers. Two other boys, Roger Cook and Roger Greenaway of The Kestrels, an outfit from Bristol, were hoping to do the same. After all, jobbing tunesmiths were staples of the record business. In New York's Brill Building, there was even a songwriting 'factory' where such combines as Goffin and King, Tepper and Bennett, and Mann and Weill churned out assembly-line pop for the masses. Why too couldn't two northern teenagers called McCartney and Lennon, and a pair of West Country lads like Cook and Greenaway?

Though musically untrained, a London printer named Lionel Bart and actor Mike Pratt had together penned hits for Tommy Steele and Marty Wilde; Jerry Lordan, an ex-comedian, wrote for Anthony Newley, and a Johnny Worth from Cheam would soon be doing the same – under an alias – for Adam Faith who, with further help from the John Barry Seven augmented with strings ('Stringbeat') would be a Top 30 fixture until a trough in 1963. Worth foisted Faith rejects onto smaller luminaries like David Macbeth, Jimmy Justice and Mark Wynter as Bart had tossed 'Why the Chicken', title song from his West End show, to Dave Sampson and the Hunters, relegating a Tepper-Bennett item to the B-side.

Johnny Worth was lead vocalist with the Raindrops. Other singers such as

Marty Wilde, Billy Fury, Johnny Gentle, Johnny Kidd and Frank Ifield would all show promise as songwriters, and be allowed to place their efforts mostly on royalty-earning B-sides. For most UK rock 'n' roll musicians, however, composing was incidental to their artistic self-image. Nothing British was up to US standards anyway. Moreover, where did it get you? As everyone knew, if anything unfamiliar was attempted on stage, dancers tended to sit it out. Group originals just weren't done, and it was usually presumed that, when an artiste boasted that he was recording his own material, his handlers had hired Worth, Bart, Mitch Murray, Geoff Stephens or some other professional based in Denmark Street — London's Tin Pan Alley — to come up with numbers solely for him.

This had become the case with Hertfordshire's Cliff Richard after a 1958 demonstration tape by him and his backing unit, the Drifters, arrived on Norrie Paramor's desk. With no rock 'n' roller to speak of currently on Columbia's roster, Paramor contracted Richard, intending to play it safe with a US cover with the Ken Jones Orchestra, until persuaded to risk the Drifters (soon renamed the Shadows) on the session and push one of their originals, 'Move It', as the A-side. After this came within an ace of topping the charts, a policy was instigated by Paramor whereby nearly all future Richard singles would be of items untried by US acts — among them his first three Number Ones: Lionel Bart's 'Living Doll', 'Travellin' Light' commissioned from Tepper and Bennett, and 1960's 'Please Don't Tease' by old Norrie himself.

That spring, Eddie Cochran co-starred with Gene Vincent on their first 'scream circuit' trek round Britain: 'A Fast Moving Anglo-American Beat Show'. Supporting players like Joe Brown were flattered but not quite at ease when Eddie and Gene chose to travel in the charabanc rather than be chauffeured like the stars they were — for, almost as stimulating to precursors of the beat boom as Buddy Holly, Cochran inspired local guitarists to follow the tour as far as pocket money or a working man's wage would allow to learn from a distance what they could about his terse, resonant technique. Joe Brown was later able to pass on Eddie's hint about using an unwound extra-light third string — the secret of his agile bending of middle register 'blue' notes.

Among Britons in artistic debt to Vincent were Vince Taylor, Johnny Kidd, Mansfield's Shane Fenton — and a Cal Danger who was under the aegis of Hampshire promoter Bob Potter. A show in Aldershot impressed Jeff Beck who, afterwards, asked Potter point-blank if he could join the musicians backing Danger, Kerry Rapid and the other singers in the troupe. After a successful audition, Jeff — ostensibly still studying at Wimbledon Art College — left home to play lead guitar in something as near as dammit to Gene and the Blue Caps.

At the behest of producer Jack Good, Vincent had arrayed himself in biker

leathers before setting foot on the inspired Jack's ITV pop showcase, *Oh Boy!*
With a more electric atmosphere that its pious predecessor, *Six-Five Special*,
Oh Boy! was a parade of acts following each other so quickly that the
screaming studio audience, urged on by Good, scarcely had pause to draw
breath – though screams became cheers for the resident Vernons Girls,
choreographed singers recruited from among employees of the Liverpool
Football Pools company.

Over on BBC, the children's series, *Crackerjack*, generally featured one
pop act per week, but it was disregarded by most teenage viewers of more – if
less exciting – televised pop from the *Oh Boy!* stencil. *Drumbeat* had
launched Adam Faith among its mix of rock 'n' rollers like Vince Eager and
Roy Young (a Jerry Lee Lewis from Oxford), crooner Dennis Lotis, the John
Barry Seven (held over from *Oh Boy!*), vocal groups the Raindrops and the
Kingpins, and Bob Miller and the Millermen, an all-purpose combo that
would pop up like rocks in the stream on later sub-*Oh Boy!* programmes like
Cool For Cats, *Wham!*, the short-lived *Dig This!*, *For Teenagers Only* and
Boy Meets Girls.

Implicit in the last title was the emphasis on male stars. Quite a few were
studs from the stable of the celebrated manager Larry Parnes who groomed
them, and liked to give them names that juxtaposed the run-of-the-mill with
the technicolor. Marty Wilde was one of his boys – as was Vince Eager, Duffy
Power, Billy Fury, Nelson Keene, Julian X, Dickie Pride, Johnny Gentle,
Georgie Fame and so on.

Bar Fury and, until he married, Wilde, none of them were potential
usurpers of Cliff Richard's throne as England's Elvis. Though designated 'The
Sheik of Shake' for his trademark onstage convulsions, diminutive Dickie
Pride found that his face was not his fortune. He and nearly all the rest
specialized in American covers – though there were chancy exceptions like
Duffy Power's arrangement of ragtime stand-by 'Ain't She Sweet', which
planted feet in both the trad jazz and rock 'n' roll camps.

Most put up a reasonable show on the scream circuit and, if lucky, on TV.
However, those few that had hits were finished by the mid-1960s – except for
late developer Georgie Fame who, as Clive Powell, a Fats Domino soundalike
from Greater Manchester, had been identified by Rory Blackwell as the X-
factor in the Dominoes, an outfit working a Welsh holiday camp season. On
joining Blackwell's Blackjacks for a stint in an Islington ballroom, Powell was
spotted and rechristened by Larry Parnes who visualized him at first as one
who could be moulded as a variety entertainer of the Tommy Steele kidney.
However, when Clive-Georgie's humble spot on his new handler's *Big Beat*
series of shows was not instantly impressive, a contingency plan was
formulated. Why not create a band round Georgie to back Billy Fury?

The official story of Fury's genesis goes that, goaded by his pal, self-styled 'rock 'n' roll comedian' Jimmy Tarbuck, Ronnie Wycherley had insinuated his way into Marty Wilde's dressing room at Birkenhead's Essoldo Theatre. There and then, he played songs he'd written to Wilde and Larry Parnes. Enthralled by Ronnie's high cheekbones and restless eyes, Parnes squeezed him into the show. Wycherley's knees knocked and his voice was tremulous with terror, but the girls all thought it was part of the act. An 'overnight sensation', he joined the troupe as 'Billy Fury'. Next, Larry dressed him in gold lamé, and his metamorphosis from unemployed tugboat hand to teen idol was set in motion. Billy-Ronnie rarely spoke to fans. It was said that he was self-conscious about a Scouse accent that sounded ambiguously alien and 'common' to anyone south of Birmingham.

Yet Willesden-bred Johnny Kidd's elocution was a problem for his manager, Don Toy, who, in common with most other 1960s starmakers, had torn chapters from Larry Parnes' book. Eve Taylor had changed Terry Nelhams to Adam Faith, and, as well as Cal Danger, subtle Bob Potter had an Eddie Sex on his books. Conversely, others were to reverse the Parnes dictum via the punchy symmetry of unusual first name and ordinary surname as in Shane Fenton, Shel Naylor and Shadows bass guitarist Jet Harris – a fancy extended further into the 1960s with Thunderclap Newman and Hurricane Smith.

Back at the turn of the decade, the accepted way in which a manager got a client noticed was to put him on a package tour with the endless backstage anecdotes about how Gene Vincent answered a heckler at the Glasgow Empire, and bitter squabbles over who'd do 'Whole Lotta Shakin'' or 'What I'd Say' wherein a vocalist could, over ten minutes, take it down easy, talk to the audience, build the tension to raving panic before sweeping into the wings, leaving 'em wanting more.

Time limitations truncated such exhibitions on TV and new pop offerings on the Light Programme such as *Music with a Beat*, *Saturday Club* and Sunday morning's *Easybeat*. Rock 'n' roll was also infiltrating *Workers' Playtime* in which the lack of individuality at the microphone of the resident singers, Danny Street and Russ Sainty, was ideal, as they duplicated the hits of others.

As a portion of its two-hour length was allotted to acts that weren't of national renown, the most innovative of these shows was *Saturday Club*, hosted by Brian Matthew who, though he announced Billy Fury as he would *Sportsview*, at least forewent inane yap and got on with the job.

It was recorded in Birmingham which, in 1959, was where the motorway from London terminated.

This was also the geographical limit of the pool from which the entertainment industry was usually prepared to fish for its talent. Though Manchester had a plethora of radio and television stations, the likes of Ronnie Hilton, Russ Hamilton, Michael Holliday and the Vernons Girls had had to head to the capital to Make It. 'In the noise and heat of a tailor's shop,' cooed *Everybody's Weekly*, 'a nineteen-year-old negress from Liverpool thinks of crooning in a West End night club.'[18] The same impossible visions appeared before Alan Caldwell, Dave Grundy and Malcolm Green, Freddie Garrity, the Quarry Men, Ricky and Dane, Dave Lee, Frank White and Dozy Davies as Adam Faith's image flickered from *Drumbeat*.

For all of them, skiffle had long lost its flavour on the bedpost overnight – because groups who still used instruments made from kitchen utensils had become *passé* and restricted – not least because washboard and tea-chest bass players had trouble joining the Musicians' Union and were thus prohibited from defiling the stages at some venues where tin-pot skifflers were now lucky to be booked at all.

Skiffle had also become insufferably square after Dickie Valentine's big-band cover of 'Putting on the Style', Lonnie Donegan's second Number One. Hacking the word 'skiffle' from the name of his Group, Lonnie was broadening his appeal with comedy routines, cracks at showbiz evergreens like 'Over the Rainbow', and by fusing skiffle with pub singalong and British folk music, *viz* 'Knees Up Mother Brown', 'Have a Drink On Me' and other gems from the golden days of empire. His final chart-topper was an overhaul of a Liverpool ditty, 'My Old Man's a Fireman on the Elder-Dempster Line'.

'My Old Man's a Dustman' was, nonetheless, more palatable than 'experiments with skiffle' at London University, and a company director with a trimmed beard hollering behind his banjo about dem ole cotton fields back home – for among sharper nails in skiffle's coffin was growing approval from adults. 'Never before have so many young people made their own music,'[19] one aged television pundit had chortled back in *Six-Five Special* prehistory. A hastily-assembled skiffle group at Scott Base had gone to town on 'My Bonnie Lies Over the Ocean' to greet Dr Vivian Fuchs after his trans-Antarctic expedition in 1958.

This *Boy's Own Paper* incident had spurred church youth club supervisors to seize upon skiffle as a means of nurturing youthful Christianity – as demonstrated on *Pops with a Purpose*, an EP – extended play – disc of 'with-it' bible-bashing by the Rev. Canon E.C. Blake whose posh warbling only just stayed in key to accompaniment by his Twentieth Century Church Light Music Group. 'He feels strongly', ran the sleeve notes', 'that the Gospel must be taught and proclaimed through a medium with which its hearers are familiar.'[20]

With abominations like this and a Camberwell vicar's *Skiffle Mass* making a cheerful noise unto the God of Jacob, it was small wonder that teenagers came to prefer either loafing about in streets or recreation grounds of an evening, or frequenting expresso coffee bars that, though thickest in city centres, had penetrated the furthest-flung suburbs where transport cafes, and even the cellars of private houses, were converted over the space of a half-term holiday into light-catering archetypes of the early 1960s, complete with juke boxes loaded with the coin-operated sounds of Elvis, Gene, Cliff, Billy *et al.*

The more sophisticated coffee bars installed a video juke box called a Scorpitone. Whatever happened to it? Maybe too few record companies bothered with publicity film shorts to make it viable. Its contents ranged from Susan Maughan anticipating a date as 'Bobby's Girl' to 1963's 'Jack the Ripper' which brought Screaming Lord Sutch his closest to the UK hit parade. I was present in Macari's in Aldershot when two bus conductors, their faces alight with vacant ecstasy, spent an entire lunch hour and half a satchel of silver repeatedly watching David Sutch in full regalia and long-bladed dagger stalking Victorian tearsheets – 'nauseating trash' sneered *Melody Maker*.

Whether Macari's, Birmingham's Sombrero or the Waikiki in Cheltenham, nearly every bar-cum-club modelled itself on London shrines of British rock where it had all started for such as Sutch. 'As certain sections of the adult population go to the public house for relaxation,' sniffed one grammar school magazine editorial, 'so the younger generation goes to a coffee bar to contemplate the weird and wonderful vegetation.'[21] These new havens also made it possible to sit all evening, conversing with other teenagers, for the price of a transparent cup of frothy liquid. John Albon, now an Assistant Chief Constable, spent his adolescence in Brighton where 'they [adults] were concerned that we were going to coffee bars instead of doing homework and that these bars were corrupting the youth of Brighton. They wanted to introduce a borough regulation of Parliament to control them.'[22] Expected Sunday press condemnation of such houses of ill-repute, where boys smoked and girls were deflowered, may have been justified in certain provincial cases where neighbouring gardens were receptacles for cigarette butts and used rubber 'johnnies'.

As a change from the jukebox, many bars would book a group – but what kind of group now that skiffle was all but over? Twickenham's Dedicated Men were persisting with it as late as 1965, but the more 'sophisticated' skifflers that hadn't fallen by the wayside switched to jazz – scornfully donating their Donegan and Vipers records to jumble sales. At student union dances, they'd show off how grown-up they were by donning boaters or top hats and a variety of hacked-about formal wear, drinking heavily of cider, and launching into vigorous steps that blended a type of skip-jiving with the

Charleston in a curious bounding motion to the plinking and puffing of a trad band like the Pagan Jazzmen, a Newcastle college outfit in which an Eric Burdon slid trombone, or one in Cheltenham which digressed from ordained New Orleans precedent by roping in alto saxophonist Brian Jones.

'Appreciation' of other forms of jazz was a 'sign of maturity' too – particularly being 'sent' by Theolonius Monk, Dave Brubeck and Lewis, Meade Lux rather than Lewis, Jerry Lee. Buddy Rich was every clever dick's received idea of percussive splendour. Living in the Shadow of the Bomb, roll-necked beatniks and would-be college radicals exuded 'cool' by strewing modern jazz albums about their 'pads': the orchestral euphoria of Duke Ellington; the white swing of Woody Herman, Buddy Rich and rockin' Lionel Hampton; vocal dare-devilry from Anita O'Day, Peggy Lee and Mel Torme, and the soft fretting of Charlie Christian and Wes Montgomery. More rousing was blaring bebop from Charlie Mingus, the Jazz Messengers, Charlie Parker and Miles Davis, and the differing textural complexities of Ornette Coleman and Roland Kirk.

If better suited for cabaret than a mob impatient for Marty Wilde, 'Moanin'' by singing 'jazz sage' Jon Hendricks would be popular in the post-soundcheck jam sessions behind stage curtains on package tours, and after it was recorded in 1962 by ex-Vernons Girl Lyn Cordell. Similarly, Mose Allison's 'Parchman Farm' would be revived later by both John Mayall and Georgie Fame. Steve Winwood was another who felt more comfortable with 'the bluesier side of modern jazz, although I always preferred the jazz people who had an element of pop in their music.'[23]

Far from Blackpool Tower and wheezy Magnificats, the fluid electric organ beneath the hands of 'Brother' Jack McDuff and, later, Jimmy Smith and Richard 'Groove' Holmes bordered on the jazzy pop that was acceptable in hip circles where some had also been introduced to the early 1960s equivalent of glue-sniffing, i.e. buying a Vick inhaler from the chemist's and isolating that part of it that contained an excitant called benzedrine. This, you then ate.

It was a tacky way of getting 'high' but that was the nearest you could get to sharing something with doomed musical icons whose credibility was enhanced by having some sort of addiction. The originator of Peggy Lee's 'Fever', Little Willie John, was an alcoholic who died in jail – and there were junkies galore, direct from the ghetto. It was enough, nevertheless, if you were merely black: the Twisted Voice of the Underdog. This was where Ray Charles – black, blind and mainlining on heroin – came into his own. He was pop – even rock 'n' roll, if you like – but as a jazz pianist, he was excellent, and his long catalogue of vocal records was punctuated by occasional all-instrumental albums. He'd also worked with Count Basie and, on 1959's

Soul Brothers LP, with Milt Jackson of the Modern Jazz Quartet. Charles was so worshipped that a British female fan offered him her eyes.

The same equation as that linking Charles to Marty Wilde existed between British and American jazzers, i.e. you'd never beat the Yanks but you could have fun and even make a little money displaying your inferiority complex. Some were more interested in the 'money' aspect than others. Denis Payton, saxophonist with Tottenham's Dave Clark Five, had once been in the Mike Jones Combo, a jazz quartet that Clark was, supposedly, managing. Burnley's Bobby Elliott could tell a similar tale. With cymbals carefully positioned horizontally like Buddy Rich's, he'd splattered patterns and accents across bar-lines in a club trio that supported visitors like Harold McNair and Don Rendell. Though 'modern jazz was all I ever listened to, and all I ever watched,'[24] Bobby was to capitulate to the pop and higher engagement fees of Jerry Storm and the Falcons. Pete Morgan likewise left Oxford's Climax Jazz Band for what became the Fourbeats 'after much heart-searching arithmetic'. Better-known lapsed jazz drummers include Charlie Watts, Mick Avory and Pete York who were also to yield to temptation from what York used to refer to disdainfully as 'these bloody pop groups'.

It is intriguing to tally how many 'bloody pop groups' from every phase of the mid-1960s beat boom had roots in the college beatnik jazz scene. Random examples are the Rolling Stones, the Animals, the Yardbirds, the Kinks, the Pretty Things, the Bonzo Dog Doo-Dah Band, the Move and Pink Floyd. Many a tight-trousered lead singer or clenched-teeth guitarist may have once been an 'existentialist' with a baggy sweater and bumfluff beard like the barefoot characters who 'put on a jumper that's three feet long' and were caricatured in a spin-off 45 from *Eggheads*, a transient BBC TV series of 1961 starring Bryan Blackburn and Peter Reeves – a sort of Newman and Baddiel of their day – on a constant quest for female favours on the premise that 'if she thinks you're kinda brainy, she flips'.

Outside college portals, girls were less responsive to the dropping of buzz-words like 'Monk' and 'Brubeck' into seductive whisperings. The music more likely to impress them was from former skifflers who had backslid, via wary amplification, to rock 'n' roll and an increasingly more American Top 20. To reflect this new leaning, groups re-emerged with new handles – the James Boys, for instance, were now Kingsize Taylor and the Dominoes – and brushing invisible specks of dust from uniform stage costumes bespoken by a local tailor. At opposite extremes were Nero and the Gladiators in togas and laurel wreaths, and the Beatles who, if slovenly and leather-clad, had nevertheless assumed a corporate identity as precise as that of Nero's mob.

The change was also marked by an increase in both levels of musicianship and volume – even if groups tended to enrol new members for what they owned rather than how they played, and equipment could still be walked or bussed to local venues. Investment in proper[25] drumkits facilitated hand-and-foot co-ordination, accurate time-keeping and the beginnings of a naive style by trial and error as novice drummers irritated entire rows of terraces in the years before phrases like 'noise pollution' and 'environmental health'.

Guitarists in those days were nowhere as annoying. Before he discovered Cliff Gallup, Jeff Beck had copied Chet Atkins and the more countrified Merle Travis through 'a shortwave band on our radio, and I used to fiddle with it for hours on end. That was my first amplifier too. It was barely audible, but that was enough for me to feel, "Hey! I'm on the radio."' Chris Britton of Andover Grammar School needed no ego-massage on winning the Wiltshire challenge cup for a guitar instrumental and 'song with guitar'. The onset of puberty, however, had found him, like Jeff, looking for an opening in a pop group.

In nearby Salisbury, Roy Jarvis of Johnny Nicholls and the Dimes had acquired from New York an electric bass guitar, huge and played in an upright position like a double bass. Though Rory Blackwell and his Blackjacks also imported one of these new-fangled instruments via a 'Cunard Yank' as early as 1956, it was only after Freddie Bell's Bellboys appeared at the Liverpool Empire with one that Kingsize Taylor stampeded his bass player into buying a model. Soon, all groups not wishing to be anachronisms had to have an electric bass. Not only were they more portable, but they radiated inestimably greater depth of sound than a broomstick and tea-chest.

The post-skiffle group's work was often unsatisfying in substance once they had made the more significant financial commitment required now that pop was at its most harmless and ephemeral. Most of the fiercest practitioners of 1950s classic rock were by then dead (Buddy Holly, Eddie Cochran), gaoled (Chuck Berry), disgraced (Jerry Lee Lewis), in holy orders (Little Richard) or otherwise obsolete. The Everly Brothers were a year away from enlisting as marines when Elvis was demobbed both as sergeant and a tamed monster who was cranking out Italianesque ballads and infrequent, self-mocking rockers whilst he smirked in the direction of the Sinatra 'Rat Pack' who'd guested on his homecoming TV spectacular from Miami. It was probably the way Elvis had always wanted it, and so had the grubbing music industry who, isolating his more palatable all-American aspects, loaded the hit parades of North America – and, by extension, everywhere else – with insipidly handsome boys-next-door, all doe-eyes, hair spray and bashful half-smiles.

Their forenames – mainly Bobby – and piddle-de-pat records matched. If they faltered after a couple of Hot 100 entries, queueing round the block would be any number of substitute Bobbies raring to sing any piffle put in front of them – though former rockabilly rebel Roy Orbison Made It at last by transforming 1960's 'Only the Lonely', a trite Bobby exercise, into an unprecedented epic that combined hillbilly diction with operatic pitch.

Few Britons could equal Orbison's *bel canto* eloquence but Chuck Berry's celebrations in song of the pleasures available to US teenage consumers would remain prominent in the repertoire of nearly all young vocal-instrumental groups; his incarceration and lack of major British hits only boosting his cult celebrity. More erudite outfits were wondering whether to have a go too at 'Money' by Barrett Strong, the Marvelettes' 'Beechwood 45786' and other discs on Tamla-Motown whose first fistful of signings had been manoeuvred into the US Hot 100, though it would be years before anything from this promising Detroit label dented the British charts.

The only home-reared acts that London record moguls fussed over after the demise of skiffle were those whose records were glutinous with orchestration and their producers' ideas, or who aped Americans, even those Americans aping other Americans as in Ral Donner's Presley counterfeit, 'You Don't Know What You've Got', copied in 1961 by the Big Jim Sullivan Combo. Rare signs of resistance to US domination were still manifested in more successful domestic covers such as Gene McDaniels' 'Tower of Strength' by Frankie Vaughan and a certain Paul Raven.

The only pop phenomenon peculiar to Britain then was a traditional jazz revival around 1961. A line in the *Eggheads* single mentions 'Freud, Proust – and Acker Bilk' and, to the man in the street, trad was epitomized by this Somerset clarinettist, and the chart-topping Temperance Seven's stiff-upper-lip recreations of a 1920s dance band. From Bristol where Bilk was king, the pestilence had spread beyond the intellectual fringe and 'Ban the Bomb' marches to a proletariat where ACKER was studded on the backs of leather jackets where ELVIS or GENE once were.

Yet British rock 'n' roll hadn't been banned and bombed – merely suppressed. Cliff's 'Move It', 'Crazy Man Crazy' by Don Charles, Vince Taylor's 'Jet Black Machine', Don Lang's 'See You Friday' and climactic 'Shakin' All Over' from Johnny Kidd had all been earmarked initially as B-sides (and some remained so). You wonder how some artists might have turned out had they not acquiesced to additional executive advice to follow the Tommy Steele route with numbers like the chirpy 'Little White Bull' (from 1959's *Tommy the Toreador* film) and 'Must Be Santa'. On the other side of the same coin was 'Mrs Brown You've Got a Lovely Daughter', actor Tom Courtenay's song from ITV's *The Lads*.

After a fine start with *Serious Charge* and *Expresso Bongo*, Cliff Richard's movies had become semi-musicals of cheery unreality, almost as awful as those into which Elvis too was sinking. Vince Eager was 'Simple Simon' in

Southport Floral Hall's *Mother Goose* pantomine in 1960. Dickie Pride was still stunning 'em with his twitching when he recorded an album of Tin Pan Alley chestnuts in 1960 with Ted Heath's orchestra. Fans could be forgiven for assuming that he was trying to make it as a 'quality' entertainer like Frank Sinatra or Tony Bennett, whose flop singles were excused as being 'too good for the charts'. *Pride Without Prejudice*, however, was no *Songs For Swinging Lovers*.

Like Dickie, Marty Wilde had declared his wish to 'do the real class stuff like Sinatra'. Shortly before, he'd caused a sensation at the Bradford Gaumont when he took the stage not with 'corny and square' session musicians foisted on him by his record company, but four lads who'd backed him when he was still Reg Smith. 'It takes youngsters,' he'd explained, 'to play and feel the rock beat.'

If there were hardly any UK rock 'n' rollers regarded with awe now, they were a worthier strain than before. Indeed, Hounslow one-hit-wonder Vince Taylor had everything it took – except the voice – to be not only a second Gene Vincent but a contender for Presley's crown. Though their period of optimum impact was also around 1960, Johnny Kidd and the Pirates belonged to the years beyond the 1962 watershed too. Kidd, like Taylor after he'd emigrated to France, would always have plenty of work assured with or without chart entries, thanks in part to a melodramatic stage act enhanced with *Treasure Island* garb, galleon backdrop and blood-and-thunder taped overture. With a sparse crew of bass, drums and *one* guitar, Kidd was as fervent and devoted a stage performer as Lonnie Donegan, and one of few home-grown rockers who didn't go Bobby-smooth.

Screaming Lord Sutch couldn't even if he'd wanted to after Sunday newspapers and a BBC docmentary team homed in, remarking mostly on his pre-Rolling Stones long hair – briefly dyed green – before touching on the leopard skin loin cloth, the woad, a bath (for 'Splish Splash'), bull horns, monster feet, a collapsible cage, a caveman's club, the inevitable coffin and whatever else he'd laid his hands on in a persistent campaign for career-sustaining publicity. Sutch's horror spoofs verged on slapstick in an 'operation' that entailed the wrenching out of heart and liver (bought from the butcher's that afternoon), and, during 'Jack the Ripper', the simulated murder and mutilation of a 'prostitute', i.e. a Savage in wig and padded bra.

The music, of course, came second. In 1960, he'd been discovered by independent producer Joe Meek. The title of the debut 45, 'Big Black Coffin' had to be altered to a mollifying 'Till the Following Night' to give it the best possible chance, but, more so than Johnny Kidd, all Sutch's disc releases were secondary to criss-crossing Britain and then Europe in draughty, overloaded vans. Membership of his Savages served as an incubation shed for many future stars, among them Paul Nicholas – mid-1960s leader of Paul Dean and the Thoughts and then 1970s pop star and actor – who admitted that 'with David Sutch being more theatrical, I was learning another aspect of the business'. Jimmy Page, Ritchie Blackmore and pianist Nicky Hopkins were Savages too. All three also served as Crusaders under Neil Christian, a London vocalist, who, like Sutch, was to be cited as 'a pivotal figure in the development of British music'[27] for those other talents he'd once employed.

No recordings by Christian, Kidd, Sutch or Taylor were to allude to the Twist, as much the latest rave world-wide as trad was in Britain alone. Its Mecca was New York's Peppermint Lounge where, to the sound of Joey Dee and the Starliters, middle-aged trendsetters mingled with beatniks to do this 'most vulgar dance ever invented'.[28] Its Acker Bilk was Chubby Checker – vigorously aped in British TV demonstrations by a Rolly Daniels – but, from Sinatra and Elvis downwards, all manner of unlikely artists were issuing Twist 45s. Worse, it wouldn't go away because you were too spoilt for choice with alternatives like the Fly, the Shimmy-Shimmy, the Locomotion, the Slop, the ungainly Turkey Trot, the Mashed Potato, the Gorilla Walk, the Mickey's Monkey, the Hully Gully, the Hitch Hiker, the back-breaking Limbo, the Madison and, in Europe only, La Yenka and the Letkiss. Via a 1961 hit by the Temperance Seven, there was even a revival of the Charleston, and, a few months later, the Can-Can by Peter Jay and the Jaywalkers.

Nothing dates a 1960s movie more than the obligatory Twist sequence, and, to this day, the elderly will slip into it unconsciously whenever the music hots up at a dinner dance. By 1962, it had become squarer than skiffle but 'just to make sure we stayed up to date,' smiled *Crackerjack*'s Eamonn Andrews, 'we rounded off Edition One Hundred with . . . the Twist.'[29] Dance crazes generally indicate stagnation in pop, and Britain in 1961 had certainly been heaving with that. On the Light Programme were 'Mama's Doin' the Twist', by the Viscounts, the Kaye Sisters' 'Paper Roses', Tommy Bruce with a rocked-up 'Lavender Blue', Dave Carey's homage to 'Bingo' and 'Just Couldn't Resist Her With Her Pocket Transistor' from Alma Cogan – plus wall-to-wall slop-ballads that your grandmother liked by UK Bobbies such as Ronnie Carroll and Craig Douglas. Finally, the Mudlarks, spiritual descendants of *Melody Cruise*'s Teenagers, were voted the kingdom's Best Vocal Group in the *NME*.

Dire though it was, the Twist was all that was available if trad was too mellow. New clubs like Birmingham's Moat Twistacular and Ilford's Twist at the Top (after *Room at the Top*) were very much in business. Ilford even had its own Joey Dee and the Starliters in Wailin' Howie Casey and the Seniors who called their only album after the place – and Twist exhibition teams utilized time where an intermission skiffle group once did.

4 BIG NOISE FROM WINCHESTER

More jazzers than ever before were unashamedly jumping on the rock bandwagon. US drummer Cozy Cole's 'Topsy Part Two' had stood on the sidelines of the UK Top 30 in 1958. Based on a 1930s standard, it focused on a virtuoso solo. This was not the case with the younger Sandy Nelson, a Californian who was the percussion counterpart to Duane Eddy in that his best-remembered records, 'Teenbeat' and 'Let There Be Drums', were pared down to monotonous beat against a menacing guitar ostinato. He even had the nerve to thus refashion 'Big Noise From Winnekta' by Gene Krupa – then such a jazz legend that he was to the subject of a 1960 bio-pic.

Britain's closest equivalent to Sandy Nelson was, I suppose, Tony Meehan from the Shadows – in LP tracks like 'See You In My Drums' – but to both restore order and let the singer take a breather, dance hall sticksmen everywhere would be bullied into, say 'Big Noise From Winnekta' or 'Topsy Party Two', commanding the stage virtually alone under their own voodoo spell for minutes on end.

Unaccompanied paradiddles were less of a feature of other instrumentals – 'Rumble', Duane Eddy's, 'Peter Gunn' and, of course, 'Apache'. In 1960, this Jerry Lordan opus had been the first of many chart-toppers by the Shadows who, while backing and, later, composing songs for Cliff Richard, were allowed to record independently and, acknowledged generally as Britain's top instrumental act, would become nearly as famous as Cliff himself.

It might have been otherwise had Norrie Paramor had his way, and 'Apache' issued as B-side to a guitar rendering of 'The Quartermaster's Stores', the traditional forces favourite. Through Norrie, a butter-fingered phrase on the 'Apache' follow-up, 'Man of Mystery', went unchanged to EMI's pressing plant. Nevertheless, Hank B. Marvin remains the most omnipotent of British lead guitarists given those now-renowned musicians who began by copying him – and Bruce Welch: for much as John Lennon professed to despise the Shadows' showbiz polish, as a guitarist he'd 'vamp like Bruce does'.[30] Sniffing the wind, the Beatles were rehearsing (and writing) instrumentals in 1960, and George Harrison would pluck Bert Weedon's 'Guitar Boogie Shuffle' at the drop of a hat.

Weedon may be seen as King Marvin's *eminence grise* as even Hank had been among the many tyro guitarists who had furrowed their brows over *Play in a Day* – and Bert's records still lingered round the middle of the Top 40. The most notable was a rival attempt at 'Apache'. Though the Shadows were dismissive of it, they paid what they owed Bert by penning the self-referential 'Mr Guitar', his singles chart farewell.

It may have sparkled under Bert's digits, but the Fender Stratocaster will be forever associated with Hank Marvin whose reverberating, metallic picking and copious use of tremelo arm – its note-warping metal protrusion – was the inspirational source of the later fretboard fireworks of Pete Townshend, Alvin Lee, Dave Mason, Tony Iommi (despite losing the tops of two fingers in a factory accident), Ritchie Blackmore and others whose professional careers began in outfits that imitated the Shadows.

A sinister tremelo sound-curve would round off 'Before the Beginning', a latter-day release by Peter Jay and the Jaywalkers who, to the end, closed their act by playing and demonstrating the Can-Can, a display that reached back to the Shadows who iced their instrumentals with more intricately synchronized footwork.

Other groups took up the Shadows' slack; their leaders enticing bass players to peroxide their hair like Jet Harris, and the man on lead to sport lens-less Marvin horn-rims. Regardless of whether such individuals went that far, it was common in an out-of-the-way village dance around 1961 to witness a quartet happily presenting a set consisting almost entirely of deadpan Shadows copies.

A random sample of groups in this vein is the Packabeats, the ultra-cool Indifferents, the Crescents – with whom Jeff Beck made a debut at Tunbridge Wells – Blackpool's Executioners, the Remo Four in Liverpool and Winchester's Arapahos whose drummer had acquired a pair of timpani. Despite this gimmick, the Arapahos hadn't a hope in hell of gaining a recording contract, living where they were.

With a far stronger geographic advantage, North London's Raiders were fronted by sixteen-year-old Rod Stewart in 1960 when they were auditioned in a local church hall by Joe Meek who was seeking an instrumental act to record an item entitled 'Night of the Vampire'. Succumbing to the console boffin's masterplan, the unit thrust Stewart aside and, as the Moontrekkers, were rewarded with a solitary week in the Top 50 and a ban by a BBC worried about the single's creepy sound effects – wailing wind, creaking coffin lid *et al* – that Meek had also used on Lord Sutch's 'Til The Following Night' a few weeks earlier.

The Staccatos and Mandrake put up less of a chart fight with a couple of more orthodox Shadows-style 45s each. However, Bristol's Cougars, also on Parlophone, would spend nearly two months in the charts in 1963 with 'Saturday Nite at the Duck Pond', as robust a treatment of Tchaikovsky's

Swan Lake theme as Nero and the Gladiators' overhaul of Grieg's 'Hall of the Mountain King' had been two years earlier.

The Cougars and any number of parochially-esteemed instrumental groups were on a par technically with the Shadows. Derek Fell of the Executioners had once filled in for an indisposed Tony Meehan most proficiently, and the Krew Cats provided a more permanent replacement in the person of Brian Bennett after Meehan left in 1961.

When all four of his Shadows couldn't make a bill-topping slot on ITV's long-running *Sunday Night at the London Palladium* variety showcase, Cliff hired the Hunters, a group he'd known at his Cheshunt secondary modern. Though this show was their professional zenith, the Hunters also served Frank Kelly and Dave Sampson in the studio. Disbanding after drummer Norman Stacey's fatal car accident, ex-members were absorbed into Buster Meakle and the Daybreakers and then the more prestigious Adam Faith and the Roulettes.

Lower down the scale, the Cliftons (with bass player Bill Wyman) backed Dickie Pride for about as many dates as the Beatles did for Johnny Gentle on an eight-day slog round Scotland. The luckier Mustangs were used by every solo star – including Gene Vincent – that came to Pinhoe Youth Hall. This four-piece would add organ and saxophone 'to give the public more than exhibitions of twanging', explained leader Dave Vincent (no relation). 'People don't want to see you play the same things over and over again; you have to give them something different. That's why the group is learning several stage acts.'[31]

The Mustangs' exit from the Shadows' orbit was emulated less commendably by other groups like the Volcanos and the Telstars who preferred not to venture too far into the unknown. Instead, despite the huge capital outlay for a Vox Contintental organ, they latched onto the Tornados, the only true challengers to Hank, Jet *et al*'s suzerainty. Perhaps the greatest UK instrumental unit of the 1960s, the Tornados had succeeded Georgie Fame and the Blue Flames as Billy Fury's accompanists. They also alternated with the Outlaws and the Blue Men as house band in Joe Meek's London studio on records by solo vocalists like Ian Gregory, Pamela Blue and John Leyton – though it was the Outlaws, under Meek's direction, who were accountable in 1960 for the cantering propulsion of Leyton's 'Johnny Remember Me' smash.

The view I expressed in *Call Up The Groups!* in 1985 is unmodified. I still 'rate Joe Meek, as a record producer, far higher than Phil Spector for inventiveness and originality in his striking juxtaposition of funfair vulgarity and outer space aetheria.'[32] There are many who agree. Yet part of Meek's reputation hinges on music that was unavailable to Joe Average for thirty years. Excerpts from *I Hear A New World* had been circulated on two 1960 EPs only to audio dealers demonstrating these new-fangled 'stereo' gramophones – but the quantum jump of *I Hear A New World* is much the same as Marty McFly's futuristic rampage through 'Johnny B. Goode' at a 1954 high school hop in *Back to the Future*. With Heath Robinson machinery on which tape speed was controlled by finger pressure on a revolving spool, Meek transformed the dinky melodies, the Blue Men's workmanlike playing, and the clatter and ping of everyday sounds into something extraterrestrial.

Two years on, the Great Man still hadn't bothered to update his equipment, but on it he made the Tornados' 'Telstar'. Unbelievably, this quintessential British instrumental topped the US Hot 100 where no Limey group – not even the Shadows – had made much headway. Friction between Meek and Larry Parnes led to the cancellation of a lucrative Tornados tour of the States where there'd be no further advances. However, 'Telstar' played Eric the Red to the UK's pop invasion of the North American continent in 1964.

Younger pop journalists nowadays have been brought up to think that Meek was a poor man's Phil Spector – and it must be said that this weedy young New Yorker was certainly hot property around 1961 for his spatial 'wall of sound' technique whereby he'd multi-track an apocalyptic melange behind beehive-and-net-petticoat vocal groups such as the Crystals and the Ronettes.

A little of this rubbed off on Norrie Paramor who would offend Shadows purists by augmenting the four on disc with horn sections and his characteristic massed strings. Though the Shadows were to rule 1962's spring charts with 'Wonderful Land', their reliance on lavish violins to so do buttressed record company moguls' theories that groups with electric guitars were behind the times, and that what the kids wanted now were solo heart-throbs and smart-suited ensembles of the King Brothers-Mudlarks bent such as the Viscounts, the Kestrels and – 'Britain's *ace* vocal group' – The Brook Brothers whose so-so record sales were adjuncts to earnings on the road and as session singers.

Outfits in the same boat nailed their stylistic flag to commercial folk, as did Unit Four, a sort of Cheshunt 'supergroup' in its inclusion of Buster Meakle, Tommy Moeller – once a rival local attraction to Cliff Richard – and, briefly, ex-Hunter Brian Parker. They mingled folky items like 'Cotton Fields' and 'La Bamba' with 'Climb Every Moutain' from *The Sound of Music* and Nat 'King' Cole's sentimental 'When I Fall In Love', all draped in lush four-part harmony and soft, semi-acoustic backing.

If Unit Four resembled with-it Sunday school teachers in their slacks and Pete Murray cardigans, the Countrymen tried the Romany look with embroidered shirts and waistcoats as they roamed the lower reaches of the Top 50 in spring 1962 with 'I Know Where I'm Going'. Many rungs above them were the Springfields whose panda-eyed Dusty achieved spectacular solo success when the three split up the following year. In the same bag over the Atlantic, Peter, Paul and Mary were a product of New York's Greenwich Village where the civil rights movement had fused with folk song to be labelled 'protest'. This trio's first intrusion into the UK Top 30 was with 'Blowing in the Wind' by Village protest singer Bob Dylan, whose plaintive debut LP was acclaimed in the *NME* as 'most promising'[33] – though there were then few British converts to his downhome intonation and eccentric breath control.

Rather than Bob, however, North America was still taking to its heart the more saccharine sounds of Bobby, but Californian surf music was beginning to clog the ether too. Ruling this genre would be the Beach Boys, who celebrated surfing and its companion sport, hot-rod racing, with a rock 'n' roll chug overlaid with a breathtaking chorale.

No one in Britain had either the wherewithal to sing like the Beach Boys or the audacity to sing like Dylan – and, not as much of a truism as it seems, instrumental groups hardly sang at all. Neither the Shadows nor the Tornados issued any vocal singles until their respective ends were nigh. In any event, it had been assumed that as they'd cornered the market there were few openings for copycats beyond toeing a conventional line with pieces slick to the point of sterility and accompanying either some local Adonis in hair lacquer and Italian suit or a glamour puss such as Annabel Leventon, honey-blonde guest *chanteuse* with the Fourbeats.

Mike Berry *and* the Outlaws, Billy Fury *and* the Tornados, Tommy Bruce *and* the Bruisers, Russ Sainty *and* the Nu-Notes, Billy J. Kramer *with* the Dakotas, Mel Turner *and* the Mohicans: that was how you Made It: skulking in grey mediocrity behind someone who wasn't regarded as an integral part of the group. One way out was when the member with most visual appeal was singled out by manager or producer as token 'leader' (with all the attendant resentment that created) and even solo stardom as was the case with the Tornados' Viking-featured bass guitarist Heinz Burt.

Thanks, however, to the Shadows, if a group raised a few screams by association with a hit vocalist, it might be permitted pot-shots at the charts in its own right – as the Hunters were after the Cliff Richard episode with 'The Storm', a minor classic co-written by Brian Parker. Among other outfits momentarily going it alone were the Bruisers with 'Blue Girl', a vocal item no less; the Outlaws on an album, *Dream of the West*, and the Dakotas who infiltrated the Top 20 in 1963 with 'The Cruel Sea'.

All these (and most other groups) duplicated the Shadows' instrumental set-up – and, thereafter, the 1960s pop group stereotype: lead, rhythm and bass guitars plus drums. Yet the concept of single-note runs being cemented by rudimentary chord-strumming wasn't always adhered to as the roles of both guitarists often merged in the interlocking poignancy of *Play in a Day* virtuosity and good-bad rawness,

As well as the immovable tonality of keyboards, the trills, tootles and rasps of brass and woodwinds were also used sometimes as a foil to the dissonance and *legato* of guitars. Names in this genre that spring to mind are the Flee-Rekkers, Sounds Incorporated, the Mike Cotton Sound – a reformed trad band from St Albans – and Peter Jay (a non-singing drummer) and the Jaywalkers. Rather than the Tornados or Shadows, this minority of outfits had been stimulated instead by the John Barry Seven and fellow *Oh Boy!* residents Lord Rockingham's XI, as well as US combos like Johnny and the Hurricanes and the Piltdown Men, units that were also dominated by blowing instruments. UK 'answers' to the Piltdown bunch included the Flintstones and the Stonehenge Men, while 'Mad Goose', a medley of nursery rhymes by the Beachcombers, was not unlike Johnny and the Hurricanes' biggest UK strike, 'Rocking Goose'.

As well as being larger in number, these keyboards-and-horns ensembles were more flexible than two guitars-bass-drums acts, and, therefore, most often employed on scream circuit packages to kick off the first and second halves, and back a cache of vocalists. Sometimes they'd be used exclusively by a particular performer – as Sounds Incorporated would be by the ubiquitous Gene Vincent, The Beachcombers by a Pat Wayne and, of course, the Shadows by Cliff.

Shadows-sized stardom might have been off-limits for the common-or-garden guitarist practising in front of a wardrobe mirror, but glancing at short-sighted Hank and stunted Jet, you didn't need to be a hunk to join a group. After acned years as a Teddy Boy, many a group musician still believed you wouldn't guess that he was no Charles Atlas or Errol Flynn if his apparel was sufficiently gaudy. Under the abili of a stage act, a homely boy could make himself otherworldly with gold lamé, pink nylon, rings, medallions, shirts frilled like whipped cream, sequins, shifty sunglasses, skintight trousers, hair-dye, even make-up.

Attractive too was the implied camaraderie and workmanlike blokeism exemplified sometimes by taciturn brusqueness that translated to the uninitiated as 'being professional'. 'Some of those Shadows things,' said Jimmy Page, 'sounded like they were eating fish-and-chips while they were playing.'[32] Marital fetters counted for less than membership of some groups and being in on the restricted code, superstitions and folk-lore peculiar to them. In 1987's BBC TV drama, *Tutti Frutti* – about the fictional Majestics,

Glasgow's self-styled 'Kings of Rock' – a road manager disclosed that 'there's three outfits where blood ties don't count for that much: the Magic Circle, the Mafia and the Majestics.'[35]

When a couple of the fellows were called up, those left in Saffron Walden skiffle group, the Diamonds, loyally suspended activities until their confreres were free again, regrouping as 'Rod Clark and the Diamonds – the Band with Rhythm, Rock and Beat'. This air of all-lads-together was itself reminiscent of the barracks fraternizations of the soon-to-be-abolished National Service. 'We were the first generation that wasn't drafted,' theorized Dave Clark, then a film stunt man. 'You were told what to do, where to go, who to be. Then you got out of the service, got married, and worked a job in a factory. That was it. Had not the government stopped the draft, there would have been no Dave Clark Five, no Beatles, no Stones.'[34] Mind you, we'd have still had Rod Clark and the Diamonds.

Rod's namesake drummed with 'The Dave Clark Five Featuring Stan Saxon' until Saxon didn't show at an air base booking in Hertfordshire. Dave did not replace him, favouring the simpler expedient of asking pianist Mike Smith to sing. By so doing, the Five, in common with many other units, instigated a stylistic shift based on the concept that the Group could be a plausible means of both vocal *and* instrumental expression. It sprang too from the use of 'featured vocalists' who specialized in areas thought unsuitable for the usual singer. Swooping elegantly from bass grumble to falsetto shriek within a few bars, Lou Walters, bass player with Rory Storm and the Hurricanes (formerly the Texans) handled show-stopping ballads like 'Fever', the Everly Brothers' 'Let It Be Me' or Gershwin's 'Summertime'.

Newer outfits formed with no non-instrumentalist like Rory fronting them, and most members taking turns on lead vocals. A novel aspect of many of these emergent groups was an uncool enthusiasm and absence of Shadows-type fancy footsteps – or Shadows-type anything.

5 THE DAY WE WENT TO A RECORDING STUDIO

Most regions had spawned at least one hit parade entrant apiece during the 1950s. Nevertheless, if talent scouts from London found themselves in, say, Manchester, 'Entertainment Capital of the North', they rarely had the time to hear what was going on locally or negotiate the forty-odd miles west or east to do likewise in Liverpool or Sheffield, let alone towns inbetween where the last fish-and-chip shop closed at 10.30 p.m.

A lot of provincial groups weren't that concerned with national fame anyway. It boiled down to motivation. The Fourbeats came together to help maintain an Oxford theatre company, and myth has it that the Dave Clark Five were formed initially to raise the cash required for Dave's Tottenham rugby team to play an away match in Holland. In December 1960, 'The Jaguars and Their Electronic Organist' existed simply to vend 'rock and calypso music' at a Saturday youth club – 'Coffee Mornings with a Difference!' – and soundtrack a 'Modern Morality Play' at the Sunday school where bass guitarist Megan Davies and her drumming fiancé, Gerry Freeman, were teachers.

In 1960 too, Bern Elliott and the Fenmen evolved from boys fresh out of school who'd started drinking at the Jolly Fenman pub near Eltham, where London dissolves into Kent. They considered themselves fortunate to scrape up an interval spot amid the strict-tempo at Dartford's Scala Ballroom where their future manager, Ronnie Vaughan, was featured crooner. By 1961, a trivial round of parochial bookings had won them a reputation as the area's own Cliff and the Shadows – though, unlike Hank Marvin *et al*, The Fenman's forté was not instrumentals but severe four-part harmonies behind Bern's hip-shakin' lead vocal.

Also-rans on the North Kent scene were Danny Rogers and his Realms, all yet to leave Dartford Grammar. Guitarist Alan Dow, now a structural engineer, remembered 'Mick Jagger coming up to me during an interval in a sixth form concert. He asked, "Can I do a few numbers with you?" I said, "No, Mick. I think we are all right." He was playing all these weird records that no one else wanted to listen to.'[36]

Up in St Albans' fee-paying Abbey School, few pupils shared Rod Argent's classical preferences either – but then few had studied clarinet, violin and, crucially, keyboards to scholarship level like he had. Rod, however, was broadminded enough to have a go at pop with fellow sixth-formers of like mind. They didn't progress beyond rehearsals because of the difficulties Rod had in pressing keys and taking lead vocals simultaneously, despite recruiting a younger lad, Paul Arnold, to pluck a home-made bass. If Paul's enthusiasm for the nascent group – the Zombies – was lukewarm, to his eternal credit it was he who mentioned that he knew a chap called Colin Blunstone at the Boys' Grammar who could sing a bit.

With the addition of Blunstone's marvellous voice, the Zombies hawked their musical wares within a catchment area roughly outlined from Aylesbury to Hertford, Dunstable to the edge of London. Their primal set included the first group original, Argent's 'It's All Right with Me' and the show-stopping 'Summertime' from *Porgy and Bess* in which Colin exuded all the breathy sentience of a man who has been sprinting – and his athlete's physique was sufficient to draw cow-eyed attempts to grab his attention from front-row females.

Blunstone had an exceptionally clear voice. However, another lead vocalist might have been appreciated just as much for slurred diction and gravelly ranting *à la* Ray Charles, frequently straining a disjointed range past its limits through a muffled public address system. In context, the dominance of spontaneity over expertise was not unattractive, even gruffly charming – because, however inaudible without electronic assistance, such tortuous endowment still conveyed such exquisite brush-strokes of enunciation and inflection that a fractional widening of *vibrato* during a sustained note could be as loaded as the most anguished wail. This was the ace up the sleeves of Tommy Bruce, Chris Farlowe and Jimmy Powell, respective leaders of the Bruisers, the Thunderbirds and the Five Dimensions – and Joe Cocker who'd sung and blown mouth-organ whilst pounding a drum kit with the Cavaliers during their 1959 debut at a Methodist youth club in Sheffield.

Such an outfit's transition to semi-professionalism was usually assisted by the growth of a substantial fan following via regular performances in youth clubs, YMCA centres and Saturday morning cinema intervals. Then they might slip into a routine of maybe two or three bookings a week in an array of working men's clubs, Co-op halls, welfare institutes, sports pavilions, ice rinks, public houses and boarded-over swimming pools turned into ballrooms for the night. If there was no place to play, as in the skiffle days, you created one. The *Herald of Wales'* pop column related that Llanelli's Corncrackers 'are running their own L-Club – a teenage dancing centre above a local pub.'[37]

Certain groups would become synonymous with specific venues. With a backing group that included guitarist Roy Phillips (later of the Peddlers) and Chris Warman, drummer from another local outfit, the Lonely Ones, the

Dowlands were as much a fixture in the auditorium on Southampton's Royal Pier as Ricky Ford and the Cyclones were on 'Teenbeat Night' at Weston-super-Mare's Winter Gardens. Further inland, the Four Aces ruled Hereford's Hillside Ballroom as the Javelins did Cranford's St Dunstan's Youth Club. In 1961, the Hereford Lounge in Yardley had opened the Twitch club, later immortalized in a B-side by its former resident group, the Rockin' Berries. In the military borough of Aldershot, the Central resounded to Kerry Rapid and the Blue Stars – as Liverpool's Green Dolphin did to the Delacardos, and the Plaza in Belfast to the Golden Crusaders (with Van Morrison on saxophone) and Tony and the Telstars.

The Cossacks and the Jaguars tussled over Thursday nights at Worcester's plush 'Ot Spot – which boasted a disc library, bar and lounge area. Such power struggles were universal. In Salisbury, Durrington Youth Hall was the jackpot for the Chequers, the Coasters, Eddie Lane and the Strollers, the Beatniks, the Boppers, the Satellites and, with a big 'B' sewn on the top pockets of their jackets, Ronnie Blonde and the Bostons.

There were enemies within too. You can read what you like into this, but Ronnie Blonde and the Bostons played their last engagement together at Durrington in January 1962. A few months later, the Bostons returned, fronted by ex-Satellite Dave Dee – and Blonde was sighted vamping keyboards in the Coasters who already had a lead singer, albeit one with an incurable Buddy Holly fixation. Similar comings and goings took place in Torquay during a war over dates at the 400 Ballroom, down in the harbour, between the Telstars, the Barracudas and the Midnights.

Another Midnights was operational in Bristol, but such duplication of names only became confusing if groups advanced beyond defined territories. As well as two sets of Jaguars, the West Midlands contained three units called the Fortunes – and the Renegades of Birmingham would put nearby Worcester's Renegades' noses out of joint by chalking up a Finnish Number One in 1965. As well as the Viscounts in the charts, three instrumental outfits – two featuring saxophones – were to also bear the title until one changed to the Remo Four.

Dominoes was quite a standardized name too, what with three in Rotherham for some reason; another led by Kingsize Taylor, and a Reading edition whose versions of 'Bye Bye Johnny' and 'Yakety Yak' were issued on a 1960 charity flexi-disc. Liverpool's Karl Terry and the Cruisers were nothing to do with Dave Berry and the Cruisers over in Sheffield. In retrospect, there are also familiar-sounding rings to Tony Dunning and the Tremelos – who recorded a 1961 single, 'Pretend' – Dave Dee and the Deemen, the Nazz, the Cult, the Cimarrons – all from the Midlands – and a Sheffield quintet called the Who.

On going fully professional, the Rockin' Jaymen became the Beachcombers (from Birmingham!) in deference to the more established Peter Jay and the Jaywalkers, and the Jaybirds who replicated Top 20 entries for the cheap Embassy label. Later, they discovered that there was a Beachcombers in Wembley. On a higher plane, a Gary Kane and the Tornadoes in the West Country refused to budge, even after 'Telstar'. The Platters of Belfast maintained that they'd thought of it first too. The possibility of litigation from other internationally-renowned US acts caused Cliff Richard's Drifters to become the Shadows, and Salisbury's Coasters to become the Fabulous Roller Coasters, so you wouldn't wonder why they didn't do 'Charlie Brown'.

A flow-chart of recurring names for parochial groups unfolds like a word-association game. Native tribes of the Americas gave rise to Britain's various Cherokees, Apaches, Comanches, Commancheros, Dakotas, Aztecs and Incas. Pastoral farming and law enforcement north of Mexico brought forth Marshalls, Deputies, Lawmen, Vigilantes, Federals, Ramrods, Mustangs, Colts and Mavericks. The howling of Coyotes greeted an incorporeal small-hours cast of Vampires, Spectres, Phantoms, Demons, Hell's Angels and Hellions. Mystery also adhered to numerous Strangers, Nomads, Echoes, Zombies, Druids and Pyramids and inevitable genuflections towards the Shadows in Silhouettes and Shades.

After Screaming Lord Sutch and the Savages came Frankenstein and the Monsters, the Mersey Monsters, Ray Satan and the Devils, Count Lindsay III and the Skeletons, Torquay's Mel Fear and his Fantastic Phantoms (*sic*) and Paignton's Baron Grave and the Vampires. Prior to his formation of the Five Nutters, the mortal who was to be Johnny Kidd was leader of Bats Heath and the Vampires.

Other group names were inspired by precious stones (Sapphires, Emeralds, Jets, Diamonds), playing cards (Aces, Deuces), games (Blackjacks, Roulettes, Checkmates, Chessmen, Dominoes), inclement weather (Cyclones, Tornadoes, Tempests, Tempest Tornadoes, Hurricanes, Whirlwinds, Typhoons), times of day (Midnights, Midnighters, Daybreakers), makes of cars (Cortinas, Corvettes, Cadillacs, Zephyrs, Zodiacs, Pontiacs), the fiercer members of the cat family (Wildcats, Panthers, Cheetahs, Tigers), bird of prey – some mythical – (Falcons, Eagles, Thunderbirds), outer space (Meteors, Astronauts, Asteroids, Spacemen, Telstars, Rockets, Dimensions), social undesirables and aggressors (Outcasts, Outlaws, Stowaways, Invaders, Villains, Conquerors, Vikings, Saxons, Vagabonds, Banshees) – and even musical terms (Crescendos, Clefs, Chords, Downbeats, Off-Beats, Semitones).

Some worked hard on the words 'tone' or 'beat'. Unsurprisingly, the most common of this species was Beatniks, but there were Fourbeats, Fourtones,

Beatles, Greenbeats (Irish), Beat Boys (Larry Parnes' touring combo) and Bluetones too. Blue was also the most widespread colour (Blue Aces, Bluegenes, Blue Jeans, Blue Flames, Blue Notes, Blue Stars, Blue Men, Blue Chips, Blue Diamonds).

Vantennas, Shondells, Shantelles and Delmonts were among nomenclatures that didn't necessarily mean anything, but rolled easily off the tongue. There were also myriad Impalas, Detours, Chevrons, Valiants, Cascades and Dolphins.

The surname 'Storm' was a pervasive *nom de guerre* for lead singers – especially after Marty Wilde played 'Jett Storm' in his 1961 silver screen debut, *The Hellions*. As well as Jerry Storm and the Falcons and Rory Storm and the Hurricanes, there was Robb Storm and the Whispers, Ricky Storm and his Storm Cats from Mansfield, Southampton's Danny Storm and his Strollers, and variations like Billy Gray and the Stormers, Tony Gale and the Stormers and Johnny Tempest and the Cadillacs – the latter two both from Sheffield.

The Steel City's *Top Star Special* was the daddy of regional pop gazettes that covered local music. It was closely followed in 1961 by Bill Harry's celebrated *Merseybeat* on which Dennis Detheridge's *Midland Beat* and, to a lesser extent, the Torquay-based *South-West Scene* would be modelled. For the publicity they gave deserving acts, these journals sufficed as a stepping stone between rehearsing in front rooms and The Day We Went to a Recording Studio for all sorts of amateurs, bending over backwards in their hyperbole and bulk-buying issues with the voting coupon for polls to find out their area's most popular group.

That first editions frequently had to be reprinted after selling out within a morning demonstrated the strength of demand for venue information, news coverage, and articles about local pop personalities. *Merseybeat*'s aim was also to foster local musicians' self-expression beyond just hammering out 'Bony Moronie' down the Green Dolphin. As well as John Lennon's early prose, its pages also embraced travel notes from abroad and cartoons. Further extra-curricular activities encouraged by Bill Harry included a mini-pantomime that the Roadrunners put on one Christmas.

A more informal sense of solidarity was evidenced when, while the rest of the county slept, working rock 'n' rollers congregated in fixed places after hours. United by artistic purpose and mutual respect, parochial semi-professional outfits were civil enough to each other when unwinding after an evening's engagement in a coffee bar or late night watering hole like Sheffield's Stone House, or queueing at, say, Morgan's fish-and-chip shop in Birkenhead or Alex's Pie Stand in central Birmingham.

As they ambled past the rows of Bedfords, Commers and the occasional new Transit, rivalry would dissolve into ribald mateyness as musicians boasted, spread rumours, small-talked, borrowed equipment, betrayed confidences, schemed and had a laugh – or a cry if the booking had gone badly.'There was a great atmosphere – sort of all pals together, pursuing the same dreams,' recalled drummer Bev Ralston of Carl Wayne and the Vikings. 'I think a lot of bands formed, changed line-ups and broke up at Alex's Pie Stand.'[38]

They also provided false information of impending success for local pop journalists. Who would admit, for example, that they'd taken the stage that evening before the hall caretaker and his barking dog plus two Teddy Boys who left after the first song, setting off a fire extinguisher on the way out? All bookings were, so it was made out, triumphs in retrospect. *South-West Scene, Midland Beat, et al* missed a lot of great moments, apparently.

The most chronicled instance of British beat's *esprit de corps* was a merger of the Beatles with Gerry and the Pacemakers – as 'The Beatmakers' – one evening at Litherland Town Hall, but it wasn't unusual for, perhaps, Freddie Garrity to bound onstage for a couple of numbers with Wayne Fontana and the Jets at Manchester's Belle Vue, or guitarist Russ Ballard of Buster Meakle's Daybreakers to deputize for Brian Parker at a Hunters bash in Stevenage. All hatchets were buried temporarily when Salisbury's top groups all appeared for nothing at Durrington Youth Hall on 9 December 1960 for a fundraising *Youngsters 'Rock' and Help Refugees* concert before each individual outfit went back to more typical engagements in venues within easy reach. In those days, most groups only had instruments, puny amplifiers – thirty watts at most – and drums to transport. Some kind of PA system usually appeared by magic.

To an amused cheer, a lead vocalist – still given prominence on billings – seemed to imply with a wink that he might not be that brilliant technically, but that didn't matter because he had an indefinable something else. Should you wave at him from the audience or in the street, he might grin and wave back, making you think that, just for that moment, you were the only person that was important to him.

Group leaders, you see, were often indefatigable self-publicists. If the Shadows or Gene Vincent were on nearby, the local heroes might be noticeably present, nattering familiarly with the stars, if not actually performing. Carl Wayne made sure that when he and the Vikings opened for Jerry Lee Lewis at Birmingham Town Hall, they'd be pictured in *Midland Beat*[39] sharing a backstage joke with 'The Killer' – as if to infer that, but for a hit record or two, they were his equal.

Local pop celebrities would ensure, too, that their birthdays were public events on the understanding that everything that happened to them was worth communicating to the whole district – or the whole nation if possible. As early as 1960, the country at large first saw Dave Berry – formerly David Grundy of *Singing in Harmony* renown – via a non-story (and attendant photograph) about his big feet in the *Daily Mirror*.[40] A man of more extreme strategy, Phil Ball, the Boppers' guitarist, made the Wiltshire newspapers as early as 1959 for getting his hair cut Mohican-style for a bet.

To illustrate Carl Perkins 'Lend Me Your Comb', Rory Storm would sweep an outsize one through a precarious pompadour that kept falling over his eyes, but this was nothing to what he did when he and the Hurricanes played in the foyer of a local swimming baths. Mid-song, Rory pushed through the crowd, stepped up to the top board, stripped to scarlet trunks and dived in. When he later pushed even harder to see how far he could go, Storm plummeted from the glass dome of New Brighton's capacious Tower Ballroom and fractured his leg. He was, however, only concussed on an equally rash climb to a pillared balcony stage left at Birkenhead's Majestic.

Dangerous exhibitionism, peacock antics and publicity stunts became as commonplace as whist drives, but certain performers' dedication was such that they'd cry real tears during agonized *lieder* with the aid of an onion-smeared handkerchief. They might also resin their hair with paraffin wax which served the dual purpose of lending extra sheen and, as it ran down to soak shirts, making it look like they'd worked up one hell of a sexy sweat.

An extrovert like this sometimes became truly obnoxious with his 'penetrating' stares, primadonna tantrums, affectations of speech and gait, Brooding Intensity, and chopping untidy endings in the air when trying to pull a front-row girl. Private anxieties and dark nights of the ego turned easy affability into sly competitiveness against both other groups and any of his own backing musicians who might threaten direct onstage rivalry as, taking a break, he noted with trepidation the screams the drummer's crooning of 'Red Sails in the Sunset' evoked.

The unpleasantnesses that make pop groups what they are were often subtly and literally illustrated in publicity photographs in which the singer, with hands on hips, sneers gently in pride of place. One of the group who just then may be out of favour makes a wan attempt to lean further into lens range but is thwarted by an obstructing elbow.

Unsolicited, a rank-and-file member might make suggestions that undermined the stylistic determination and the various creative monopolies. If such a revolutionary didn't swiftly resign himself to just fretting guitar, an underhanded dismissal would be planned and put into action as soon as someone meeker came to light. Such machinations would punctuate a group history of discord, intrigues, *ménages à trois*, sulking, bitter jealousies, horrid conspiracies, punch-ups, unresolvable rows, walk-outs, homoerotic horseplay, snide remarks and a sax player who'd refuse to go on stage with a twit like that new guitarist.

A local group – let's call them 'Teddy and the Confessors' – begins as a passive vehicle for its leader's self-projection. Because Teddy imagines himself a firm enforcer of his own discipline, the Confessors have always had a rapid turnover of personnel: so rapid that transient members are often recruited on the day of a show. Even as the audience files into the hall, Teddy will be backstage hammering home the essentials of the entire set to such a stand-in, distracted by the old hands' tedious twelve-bar jamming, squabbles, tuning-up and psyching-up. When they hit the stage, the new boy might be clutching a scribbled chord sheet, knowing only the keys and non-existent arrangements. He'll look as if he wants the floor to swallow him up.

If he stays on as a full-time Confessor, he might be one of these fusspots who insists on a formal rehearsal. Though taken more seriously than actual performances, these degenerate into social occasions, owing largely to interruptions as late arrivals set up their gear. There'll also be premature departures motivated either by thirst or Teddy's ruthlessness in sticking to the job in hand. Over-sensitive souls will stride out, insulted, to licensed premises where his character and musicianship will be dissected with bitter intensity: 'He was busy with some tart during "Big Noise From Winnekta" last Saturday. We had to fill in with another instrumental until he panted on, zipping himself up. He can't sing either. Whether it's "Roll Over Beethoven" or "Only The Lonely", he just growls like a bear.'

With one eye on the clock and another on the waning patience of those still present, Teddy runs through numbers speedily and incompletely, frequently stopping after only two verses. 'Yeah! OK. That'll do. It goes on like that for another chorus, then there's a standard middle eight. After that, I'll point at whoever ought to solo. Get the picture? Right, let's have a go at . . .' There is little scope for much more instruction past the occasional, 'No, not dum-dum-de-diddly-*dum*. Try dum-dum-de-diddly-*dah*.' You never got any of this *rallentando* or counterpoint nonsense.

Not believing it's happening, a player turns up for his first engagement with Teddy and the Confessors. Backstage, he'll not be heartened at seeing Brooksie, the bass player, with his hand in bandages after a mishap at the saw mill. Brooksie's mixture of day job and alcohol has been causing concern. Giggling drunk or on another planet, on more than one night it'll seem, as if he'll never totter onstage. Although he always makes it, sometimes it may have been better if he hadn't.

Of the glut of electric guitarists, one is still waiting for a bigger incentive than being a Confessor to shell out on a workable amplifier. He was shocked when he found out one was necessary. With no amplifier or speaker in sight when groups mimed their singles on television, he could be forgiven for thinking that you had to plug 'electric' guitars directly into the mains.

Another Confessor elects to wash his hair in the hand-basin ten minutes before showtime, causing a half-hour delay and rendering a previously docile audience hostile. That afternoon, the drummer had phoned to say that he wasn't bloody coming. A substitute has been dragged from a TV meal with his slippers on, and is marinating the air with curses as he shambles onstage.

After the anticipated catcalls and desultory clapping from the horde before them, the group, driven by panic, lurches into the first number at twice the speed at which it was rehearsed, capsizing Teddy's vocal. Unco-ordinated, relentless drumming clatters behind seemingly random notes and chords chasing up and down fretboards. At the abrupt and unaccountable silence of his amp, Brooksie in pain gamely delivers inaudible goods. In his fancy dress before a unit teetering on disintegration, Teddy brazens it out, forgetting the words but daring the riff-raff to boo. Paraxodically, he's barely suppressing an urge to laugh out loud during the emotionally-charged spoken passage in 'Are You Lonesome Tonight' before it dies its death to a floor-tom rumble and Griz the pianist vamping inanely for a few unaccompanied extra bars.

A slumming 'real' musician, Griz perches, lazily smoking, on an amplifier rim. He interrupts a tempo announcement with a languid 'What key's this in, man?' – thus demonstrating to all the world his condescending superiority: he hadn't needed to rehearse this simplistic drivel, had he? 'Like, Z minus, man,' Teddy snaps testily. His tormentor, capitalizing on the situation, pretends to be deeply offended – 'That's it! I've had my fill of this crap anyway!' – but strides off into the wings effervescent with malicious glee. This was the thrill divine; his jazz cronies are at the back, witnessing this public repudiation of barbarian rock 'n' roll.

Afterwards, Griz guffaws as Teddy is harassed with enough minor problems to start World War 3. 'I want those PA speakers back by eleven on the dot or I'll never lend them again.' 'Lyn says I'm to be home by 10.30. Can you sort out a lift?' 'Oi, Elvis! If you don't get this electrical junk out of here in ten minutes, I'm locking up.' They love making Teddy twitch in this antithesis of pop and fame. 'Clive's decided not to lend Paul his amp (pause). What are you going to do about getting Paul an amp then, Teddy? You'd better tell Mr Arch about those keys that snapped off the hall piano during the Jerry Lee Lewis bit. If you don't, I will. We're not starting again until we've all had a pint – and I'm walking off if those lights get in my eyes. We're not . . .'

In self-defence, Teddy bites back. 'That flurry of bum notes you played in "White Lightning": they *were* bum notes, weren't they?' 'I'm perfectly aware that your function in the group is purely to blow sax and nothing else, but would you mind asking your next-door neighbour about borrowing the van? No? All right, I'll do it instead of eating lunch tomorrow.' 'No, I don't mind you missing the Sunday matinée because you've got to take your budgerigar for a walk.' 'Don't say "we" when you mean "I".'

Post-mortems on Teddy and the Confessors' few bookings include why they were ordered offstage at the Kiln Hall and sabotaged at a talent contest in Northley. When the bass amp cut out again at the All Hallows Young People's Club, 'Shakin' All Over' had shuddered to a halt to a spatter of sardonic applause, Teddy murmured something with 'bloody' in it on mike, and the curate felt entitled not to pay the group the agreed Coca-Colas and beans-on-toast and threw them out.

On the plus side, TV personality Geoffrey Adams ('PC Lauderdale' in *Dixon of Dock Green*) had declared them runners-up in a Battle of the Bands tournament in Southtown. There'd been another triumph too: the ramshackle grandeur of an uproarious Christmas dance at Eastford Abattoirs Social Club – even if it started awkwardly after Griz had had the bright idea of entering in pitch darkness to the *Quatermass and the Pit* music, taped off the TV. They'd groped onto the boards, colliding with microphone stands and other hardware, tripping over wires, bumping into people and even falling into the audience. When the tape petered out, the stark white lights came on to a scene not wholly welcoming. Instead of the galvanizing rundown into the opening item, there'd been thuds, amplified mutterings, electronic crackles, weird crashes and savage oaths feebly censored by feedback as the guitarists searched for their own or somebody else's inputs. Two guitars and Teddy's microphone were all – via two shared jacks – plugged lethally into one AC 30amp.

In a blizzard of distortion and unbalanced sound, Teddy counted in a malevolent 'Jet Black Machine'. Musically, it was worse than ever. Most numbers were still too fast; transitions from choruses to bridges were cluttered, and any arrangements shot to pieces despite bawled off-mike directives. Yet by the time they finally resolved into the playout of 'Hound Dog', Teddy and the Confessors had long been home and dry. All right, it was the season of goodwill, and both audience and group had had a few, but from initial disaster had come forth a hysterical gaiety.

During the up-tempo rockers, cavorting onlookers had assumed the role of rhythm section, stamping, clapping and squealing feathered party whoopers. A bunch of Brooksie's mates from the pub had even dared to clamber onstage to commandeer a mike, their extemporized backing vocals only slightly worse than those of the group. In the thick of flying streamers, the drummer had enjoyed a stylized mobbing during his 'Red Sails in the Sunset' while Teddy, to scattered screams, had pulled out every ham trick in the book in 'Hound

Dog', guarding his stardom with the passionate venom of a six-year-old with a new bike.

Of course, it couldn't last, wasn't meant to. In the wilds of Midshire, no big shot was ever likely to check out Teddy and the Confessors, even if Teddy had managed to get everyone in one place at one time. Structurally, they were never much of a group anyway. Too much depended on too many variables. As with the Jaguars and their Electronic Organist, no one except Teddy thought in terms of Making It, having hit records or 'Teddymania'. By 1962, all the principal *dramatis personnae* had dispersed to colleges, proper jobs or fatherhood. Teddy, however, kept the faith, and was spied miles away in Gonesville as the 'Dickie' in 'Dickie and the Lionhearts' until, stepping forward to make an opening announcement one night, he touched his microphone and, because persons unknown had been up to no good with the wiring of the PA system, promptly absorbed more than enough high voltage to kill him.

Teddy sacrificed his life for rock 'n' roll. If not as committed, some accompanists to lads like him were, nevertheless, solidly at the music's heart, ministering to overall effect. Often, at least as crucial as his playing was such an individual's neo-managerial strategems as he laid the group on with a hyperbolic trowel to this quizzical landlord or that disinterested social secretary.

Silver-tongued guile was brought into play in other ways too. Celebrity, if only parochial, can be a powerful aphrodisiac – and a perk of a musician's job was supposed to be readier access to coltish female charms than blokes who'd paid half-a-crown to shuffle about in the gloom past the burning footlights. Even if not conventionally handsome, he could still be the darling of the ladies who, in suede, fishnet and leather, clustered, tits bouncing, round the lip of the stage, chattering excitedly until the group was introduced. It was not unknown for fans to level none-too-friendly stares and even physical threats at a local star's 'bird', varnished nails sometimes raking her face to screeched curses.

Another side of such frightening adoration was the bellicose resolves of possessive boyfriends if a musician caught the wrong girl's attention – especially in palais frequented by what would be known later as 'Rockers': *Wild One*-esque motorcyclists in jeans, T-shirts and real or imitation black leather windcheaters, their greasy ducktails in direct descent from the Teds. There was bother too from members of Her Majesty's Armed Forces, compelled to wear their hair shaved halfway up the skull – which added to a built-in sense of defeat when on the look-out for sex.

At the Agincourt in Camberley one night, some soldiers in civvies, slit-eyed with beer and frustration, hurled chairs towards the narcissistic endeavours of one of Larry Parnes' charges who, maddened by incessant barracking, retaliated verbally. Leaving the stage without an encore, he quit the building and the town within ten minutes, leaving the group backing him to face the music. If there was going to be any kind of vendetta against them, they were uncertain of aid from the venue's promoter. To him, as long as the teenagers handed over the admission money and behaved themselves inside, he wasn't concerned about their deeds of destruction afterwards.

The squaddies came mob-handed: ugly people who wanted to make everything else ugly too. They watched like lynxes as the gear was transferred hurriedly via a fire door to the van. A minute dragged by with as yet no reason to start anything. Then the drummer replied 'Good evening' to an ''Ullo'. For being such a toffee-nosed git, he was thumped in the stomach. He collapsed onto the asphalt, gasping for breath. That, however, wasn't good enough. Beneath the sole back-porch light, bestial faces got an eyeful of unofficial spectator sport as the victim writhed about in a forest of kicking winkle-pickers, yelling in panic as blood cascaded from his face. Someone summoned a man who, hugging a biscuit tin half-full of coins, watched for a few seconds before scurrying away with a look of distaste. Take care of the pennies and the lads can take care of themselves.

This was not a rare occurrence. Saying much about Teignmouth's Landsdowne Ballroom – albeit situated next to the police station – and Liverpool's famous Cavern club was the infrequency of the violence that marred or supplemented pop evenings elsewhere. Wielding hatchets, hooligans with a grievance against an entertainer named Derry Wilkie converged on another Liverpool club, the Iron Door (formerly the Storyville), when his group were onstage.

Once, when the same venue was deserted, Rory Storm and the Hurricanes put forty ragged minutes of their stage set onto tape. Other outfits that could afford one of these weighty and expensive 'tape recorders' would rig one up likewise in a hall's most acoustically sympathetic corner to capture an audible gauge whereby performances could be measured against those of any opposition. The sound felt tremendous when the local Cliff Richard was cavorting onstage with his backing group bucking and lunging about him – but, as sonic vibrations *per se*, you should hear it on reel-to-reel afterwards! They were often more capable of musical effect than music, and who could manage more than an approximation if hall regulations required them to conclude an evening with the National Anthem?

Repertory choice was frequently governed by four-four time, rote-learnt chord patterns and immoderate fondness for particular musical keys; guitarists usually favouring E, A and G major. In the retractable sphere of recording, contrived atmospherics with reverberation units and echo chambers might improve matters – though facilities for overdubbing (superimpositions) were crude then – but, if you owned a tape recorder or even a studio, however primitive, you could keep playing your best songs until you got them right. The Cresters, from Bramley in Yorkshire, had such a place in the attic of the house belonging to the parents of group members, Richard (bass guitar) and John Harding (lead). Most of the equipment came courtesy of father's electrical goods business. With his family's blessing too, Birmingham teenager Jeff Lynne turned his front room into an Aladdin's cave of linked-up tape recorders, editing blocks and jack-to-jack leads.

Young experts like the Harding brothers and Jeff did not need to be told that after a song or 'information' has been taped, you have to listen to the 'playback', of what is referred to as a 'take'. If any parts of the performance are not accurate enough, you and your group can re-record just those sections and the recording engineer then cuts out the bad 'information' and patches in the new. Yet this simplistic litany was alien to the majority of British groups – mainly because there were few *bona fide* studios outside London other than customized garages, sheds and living rooms.

One of the more sophisticated was Newcastle's Mortonsound where Whitley Bay's Wild Cats – with future Animals guitarist Hilton Valentine – recorded an acetate LP. At Wolverhampton's Domino Studio, among those who coughed up £10 for an afternoon there were the Vendors, a quartet containing subsequent members of Slade. With a pound sign over every fretful quaver, Kingsize Taylor and the Dominoes recorded ten items in Crosby's Lambda Studio.

With the drummer they shared with the Cossacks, Worcester's Jaguars taped two instrumentals – 'Opus To Spring' and 'The Beat' – amidst sound-proofing mattresses at Henwick Road YMCA. These were issued on Impression, the city's own shoestring record label, and, allegedly, exhausted their unrepeated run of five hundred copies as a testament to the Jaguars' local popularity.

In a similar circumstance in Sheffield were Jimmy Crawford, a former swimming champion, and the Ravens – through whose ranks passed twin-necked Frank White, fast emerging as a staggering lead guitarist. However, Sol Byron and the Impacts were just as much stars in Glasgow, as Terry Lee and the Checkers were in Orpington, as Tommy Scott and the Senators in Pontypridd, as Brian Poole and the Tremeloes in Barking, as Deanie Sands and the Javelins in Belfast, as Peter Jay and his Jaywalkers in Great Yarmouth, as Wayne Fontana and the Jets in Oldham, as Dave Curtiss and the Tremors in Clacton, as Johnny and his Copycats in Buckie, as Gene Coburn and the Chimes in Brighton, as Cliff Richard and the Shadows in the hit parade.

There was, too, a growing preponderance of deserving outfits without a demarcated 'leader', such as the Echolettes from Walton-on-Thames, Liverpool's Beatles, the Executives in Blackpool, the Thunderbeats in Preston, Newent's Whirlwinds with their female vocalist and, winners of a national Boys' Club talent competition, the Eagles, pride of Bristol.

A vocalist called Valerie Mountain 'sat in' and would record with the Eagles – and, since finding herself microphone in hand one frolicsome evening at London's Esmeralda's Barn, Twinkle, another personable young lady, was granted a weekly two-song spot with the resident Trekkers. Other singers invited onstage by a group to be Cliff, Adam or Billy – or new schoolgirl star Helen Shapiro – for a while (and often feeling no end of a fool afterwards) might be one of a handful of freelance locals who performed with several different outfits.

Dave Berry moonlighted with the big band at Chesterfield's Victoria Ballroom. He raised his head higher above the parapet when, after much dogged negotiation, he and his regular backing combo, the Cruisers, along with the Twin Cities Rhythm Group and two coachloads of fans, brought Sheffield pop to London via a bold but troubled concert at the Shepherd's Bush Gaumont in 1960.

Such endeavours or driving for hours on the off-chance of Doctor Death letting them do a turn at the 2i's stoked up little substantial interest. Yet fully mobilized provincial acts continued to sharpen their profiles through the establishment of fan clubs, recurring local engagements and occasional side-trips further afield. The Beatles played to a mere handful of patrons on a wintry Saturday in 1961 in Aldershot's Queen's Road Palais, a booking arranged by Sam Leach, that most adventurous of Merseyside promoters. He'd hoped that their funny dialect and endearing lack of arranged routines would prove alluring to those nearer the heart of the UK music business than remote Liverpool. By word of mouth, Rory Storm and the Hurricanes drew over two hundred at the same faraway venue the following week. Though Sam then turned his back on Aldershot, Storm and his group continued a sporadic southern offensive on their own, venturing as far east as Norwich.

The lesson of Rory Storm's Aldershot statistic was that there was a potential market for his outfit outside Merseyside. Groups in other areas thought the same applied to them. As it was during the Carroll Levis era, so parochial was provincial pop that there seemed to be few realistic halfway points between obscurity and the Big Time, but if you weren't to be a Cliff Richard and the Shadows in the wider world, you could limit yourself to remaining cherished as one locally, even giving yourself regional identification like Jimmy Cullen and his *Avon*airs, The *Hull*aballoos, The *Mersey*beats and Pete *Devon* and the Drifters. After obtaining permission from the local council, Dartmouth's Sapphires wore the town's coat of arms on their uniform blazers.

As it had been when the Beatles pounced – however ineffectually – on Aldershot, aliens from beyond could still invade, some more electrifying than even the top local group. Certain areas, therefore, began manning barricades. There was, for example, a closed shop of venues from Redruth's Flamingo to Honiton's Marchioness Hall where only the likes of Torquay's Barry Safari and his Hunters ('Big Beat is their game'), Bristol's Johnny Carr and the Cadillacs and Redruth's own Dave Lee and the Staggerlees[41] tended to work.

Territorial defence was epitomized by an agency founded 'with the sole intention of stopping Brum groups playing at Worcester venues'[11]. Such embargos were relaxed for visitors of qualified national eminence as long as local acts supported – as the Boppers did to Gene Vincent at Basingstoke's Haymarket theatre. 'We used to meet at Jack Woodroffe's, where agents came in to see which groups were available for gigs that night,' recounted Ray Thomas of Birmingham's El Riot and the Rebels, 'like going all the way to somewhere like Ellesmere Port for ten quid. We would always end up supporting Screaming Lord Sutch or someone.'[38]

This was as far as most of them went, for as *Top Stars Special* pointed out, 'Coming from out-of-the-way Sheffield, our groups are shackled before they start.'[42] Provincial fetters were sometimes shaken off, as when Liverpool's Two Jays landed a season in a club on the Isle of Man, and the Eagles, after a slot in a cinema B-feature, snared a weekly showcase on Radio Luxembourg.

If even more inconveniently placed to strike at the heart of the land's pop industry, Shane Fenton and the Fentones sent a recording of one of their recitals to the Light Programme. Unhappily, before receiving a summons to report for a Corporation try-out, Fenton (alias John Theakston) died of rheumatic fever. The Fentones then convinced their road manager and general dogsbody, Bernard Jewry, to front them as the second Shane Fenton, and thus leapt from glum Mansfield to a residency on *Saturday Club*. Likewise, after the show's producer, Jimmy Grant, sounded them out in a Southend ballroom, Brian Poole and the Tremeloes' turn came in 1962.

The Country Gentlemen – Hampton Grammar sixth-formers – had seen the Promised Land rather more fleetingly in 1960 after 'With Love', composed by guitarist Paul Samwell-Smith and his brother, caused EMI recording manager John Schroeder to invite them to the firm's Abbey Road studio complex to tape it for a purpose that was then non-specific. 'It didn't work,' sighed self-effacing drummer Jim McCarty, 'because of me. Schroeder reckoned that Tony Meehan would have made a better job of it.'

Though EMI held an ace in Cliff Richard and the Shadows, it fought the same battle as the other labels, the battle for chart placings, the battle for money. There were internal conflicts too. George Martin, head of Parlophone, sought to provision it with some sort of equivalent to whatever sensations other EMI labels had thrown up. Among those tried so far were Dean Webb – a dishwasher from the 2i's who resembled Marty Wilde – and Shane Fenton and the Fentones, but none of his finds could match Johnny Kidd and the Pirates on HMV or Columbia's precious Cliff and the Shadows. Though a Parlophone artist, Adam Faith was someone else's production baby, and even he was waning when into George Martin's life in 1962 came a chap called Brian Epstein.

A major northern record retailer, Epstein could pull strings on behalf of the groups he managed. He'd already got Decca to send one of Dick Rowe's underlings to the Cavern to judge the Beatles – the first occasion that any London A & R man had ever visited Liverpool professionally. Few other provincials had the clout to enchant Rowe, Martin, Jimmy Grant, Joe Meek *et al* north of Birmingham or west of Swindon. Groups kept on mailing tapes over the edge of the world, but few requests to audition ever came from anyone important; they had quite enough guitar groups, thank you.

6 RAUS! RAUS! SCHNELL! SCHNELL!

In 1960, trad bands had been everywhere and the venues that counted, i.e. ones that paid more than a glass of Pepsi per man, remained stubbornly biased towards them, designating what should and shouldn't be played within their walls. Deductions from fees would ensue for any digressions, thus curtailing any deceitful opportunism from lowbrow rock 'n' rollers in disguise. Not knowing what to think, Larry Parnes sent on tour a group called the New Orleans Rockers that walked an uncomfortable line between the two.

The field was, therefore, narrowed for British groups dispensing a rock 'n' roll elixir that could only be swallowed neat. Small wonder that they responded to demands from abroad for cheap musical labour by impressarios affronted by clumsy native attempts to copy US pop. The principal areas of work were US military bases in France and Germany, ports like Amsterdam, Hamburg, Stockholm and Copenhagen, and Parisian clubs such as Le Golf Drouot that functioned despite government efforts to ban subversive *yé-yé* rock 'n' roll.

UK groups also began residencies in Marbella where the Spanish would soon be debasing their culture further by sanctioning the construction of pubs, fish-and-chip shops and further home comforts for British holiday-makers. Basking beneath a more watery sun, Ken Levy and the Phantoms left Cambridge for a lengthy spell in Scandinavian clubland in 1961, shortly before the city's Deejays – with singer Clive Sands, brother of one of that year's UK chart-toppers, Eden Kane – arrived in Sweden in an exchange approved by the Musicians' Union for the Spotniks, the country's Shadows soundalikes.

Two years earlier, Acker Bilk had been well-primed to capitalize on the trad boom through a six-week spot in a Dusseldorf hostelry where 'you just blew and blew and blew,' exhaled Acker, 'and had twenty minutes off for a drink, and then you were back blowing again'.[26] Just blowing, blowing blowing . . . Within months, however, trad was old hat and, from Kiel's Star Palaast to Cologne's Storyville, bastions of Teutonic jazz had converted to rock 'n' roll. The new policy was most rampant in Hamburg, Germany's largest port. 'The Germans were just coming to the end of their jazz era,' remembered Dave Dee, 'and the American rock 'n' roll thing had really taken off. For the Germans to bring in all these stars from America would have cost a fortune, and there they had, just across the Channel, these English blokes that were copying the Americans and doing it very well. So it was easy to bring them in for twenty quid a week and work them to death.'[48]

The first – and most significant – of these English blokes was Tony Sheridan, much changed from the absconding schoolboy in McDevitt's Skiffle Cellar. After serving Marty Wilde and then Vince Taylor, Tony had struck out on his own, leading a trio with Brian Bennett and (also fore-ordained to join the Shadows) Brian Locking on bass. Nevertheless, though Tony – a guitarist-singer of unusual flair – was stirring enough before *Oh Boy!* cameras in 1959, an invitation to be likewise on *Boy Meets Girls* was cancelled when, in his own publicist's word, Sheridan 'went haywire (failing to be on time, arriving without his guitar etc)'.[43]

Television was, therefore, closed to him, and only on sufferance did Larry Parnes allow Tony just ten minutes on the all-British supporting bill on the legendary Vincent-Cochran trek of 1960 – on which he displayed both an impetuous exuberance as a performer, and a wanton dedication to pleasing himself rather than the customers.

Three months later, Tony and a motley shower of other unemployed London-based rock 'n' rollers were in Hamburg, seizing songs by the scruff of the neck and wringing the life out of them. They'd been an instant and howling success with a clientele for whom the personality of the house band had been secondary to boozing, brawling and sex.

Later visitors to Hamburg picked up useful tips about stagecraft from Sheridan – nicknamed 'the Teacher' – who, after his Jets' farewell in December 1960, would favour using not a fixed backing band, but whatever group happened to be playing in the same club. Most felt honoured to be on the same stage, learning further tricks of the trade from him – though David Sutch likened Tony more to 'a sergeant-major. He was really snappy towards them.'

Doug Fowlkes and the Airdales, of the same late 1950s vintage, performed a similar miracle at Le Golf Drouot – as did Carl Wayne and the Vikings at the Storyville in Cologne. For £30 a week, 'you had to do seven hours a night, ten at weekends,' groaned their Ace Kefford, 'with just fifteen minutes off every hour.' Swansea's Jets would be likewise 'having a ball in Germany, playing from 7 p.m. to 1 p.m. during the week and 6 p.m. to 1 a.m. at weekends.'[44] They had been plucked from a residency at Oystermouth's Big T ballroom for a club tour commencing in Munich, just as their local rivals, the Blackjacks, started a similar three-month stint in France.

An expedition like this was sometimes the first occasion that a provincial musician ever breathed foreign air. When the group, giddy and stiff, finally reached its destination, they might find themselves unloading outside an auditorium plusher than the most salubrious hall they'd ever worked in Britain. The accommodation provided, however, may have sickened pigs: cramped, dingy rooms still full of the previous tenants' litter and sock-smelling frowziness; naked light bulbs coated with dust; improvized ash-trays and piss-pots; lumps of brittle plaster falling from walls so mildewed that it was as if they were covered with black-green wallpaper; not enough old camp beds to go round; waking up shivering to open-mouthed snores and the drummer breaking wind before rising to shampoo his hair in a sink in the club lavatory. 'I didn't know what to expect,' said Ace Kefford, 'but it was like a squat. It had no roof!'

Living conditions described politely as frugal on top of punishing work schedules either transformed a clumsy act into a hard one to follow or destroyed it completely. The legacy of Joe Cocker's Big Blues outfit almost starving during weeks of hard graft round US air bases in France was disbandment, and Joe being obliged to take a job in a Sheffield warehouse.

Sex and violence was in its infancy in Sheffield compared to cities abroad that had recognized red-light districts since the days of three-mast clippers. Amsterdam and Hamburg were especially noted for gartered erotica, *bierkeller* violence and a midnight *demi-monde* of gangsters and brothel madames. It wasn't uncommon for up to a dozen knuckle-dustered waiter-bouncers to lay into a single *schlager* – a man actively looking for a fight – amidst shattered tankards and upturned furniture. *Pour encourager les autres*, the blood-splattered victim would then be raised aloft weight-lifter style and pitched into the street. Such a person once stumbled from one Amsterdam niterie with a marlinspike embedded in his neck. A Hamburg store named the Armoury once displayed a sub-machine gun as well as flick-knives, coshes, pistols and other more conventional aids to keeping the peace.

All this was a trifle unsettling to most British youths – for, guest workers or not, a group's well-being depended on its standing with the local Mister Bigs and the wealthier madames from whom fear spread like cigar smoke. Partiality for certain UK outfits was manifested in crates of liquor and even plates of food being sent to sustain them whilst on stage and as prepayment for requests. The musicians all knew better than to show less than the fullest appreciation of these gifts. In between reprising some parochial Capone's favourite song over and over again, they might each be swigging liberally from a bottle of vintage champagne. Another advantage of being so terrifyingly honoured was extra-legal protection if ever they ran into grief within such a fan's sphere of protection. Falling on a clip-joint that had fleeced the Casuals, a hit squad in *Polizei* uniforms smashed every bottle, tumbler and mirror in the place before boarding it up.

Minors could also be unofficially exempted from curfew regulations that forbade them from frequenting night clubs after midnight; an immunity that could just as easily be withdrawn to secure deportation. 'When I was first in Germany,' elucidated drummer Paul Francis of the Vibrations, 'I had to alter the date of birth on my passport as I was officially under age. Every time I was asked to produce the passport, I was sure someone would twig.'[45] Someone did in the case of Beatle George Harrison who, months short of his eighteenth birthday, was expelled from West Germany forthwith.

The group had been a fortnight away from finishing a season at Hamburg's Kaiserkeller. It and most of the other Hamburg clubs that catered for teenagers were located in Der Grosse Freiheit, a tributary of the Reeperbahn – Rope Street. This dry translation belied its reputation as the neon starting point of innumerable evenings of perfumed temptation and living tableaux of flesh. I am prohibited by inbred prudishness from entering into distressing detail – bar stating that an hour on the Reeperbahn could be an eye-opener for anyone who assumed humans could only be sexually gratified without mechanical appliances and only with other humans.

Striptease palaces and whorehouses were to the Reeperbahm as steel to Sheffield. 'Everybody around the district,' George Harrison would remember fondly, 'were transvestites, pimps and hookers, and I was in the middle of that when I was seventeen.'[46] Amused by the memory, Ian 'Tich' Amey of Dave Dee and the Bostons recalled their first Hamburg jaunt when 'we spent nearly two months trying in vain to chat up two gorgeous ladies who used to stroll along the Reeperbahn. Just before we returned to England, we found out that they weren't girls at all but two fellows. Thank God none of us succeeded with the chat-up lines.'[45]

Back home, he might have fled if accosted by a prostitute in a dark doorway but, in a country where bartering in sex was less sheepish, a young British musician might suddenly lose his virginity in the robust caress of a bawd who'd openly exhibited her seamy attractions in a bordello window. 'They usually arrive knowing it all', moaned one of Tony Sheridan's Jets, 'and, sure enough, would go back to the UK with crabs, pox, "Hamburg throat". You name it, they had it.'[47]

When the sixties truly started swinging, many pop stars were showered with paternity suits. Many of them emanated from the Freiheit where, giving in to nature's baser urges, free-spirited frauleins would simply lock eyes with a selected male onstage with a jerking crotch-level Stratocaster, point at him whilst flexing a phallic forearm, and hope he got the message that tonight was to be his night.

The Freiheit was a narcotic ghetto as well as a sexual one. More knowingly inflicted than social disease were the headaches, rashes and other side-effects of chemicals swallowed initially to combat exhaustion and ensure that a performance in the grey of morning was as energetic as one at 7 p.m. 'The only problem with that,' warned Dave Dee, 'was that when we finished work, we couldn't sleep and went through the next day waiting for the pills to wear off. Of course, we were knackered again at four o' clock – so were asked for more pills.'[46] John Lennon might have capped this with 'What with playing, drinking and birds, how could you find time to sleep?'[49]

He and other British musicians' only previous experience of artificial euphoria might have been benzadrine from Vick inhalers. New to all were Preludin and Captigun tablets – amphetamine-based appetite suppressants – outlawed in Britain and only available on prescription in Germany. Yet they could be obtained illicitly with ease, and it was no hanging matter if you were caught with them. Therefore, for purposes other than fighting the flab, supplies were stocked for employees' use in most of Hamburg's all-night establishments by 1961 – though elsewhere the stimulant of choice was usually booze. 'To keep going, I popped a couple of pills,' admitted Ace Kefford, 'but we were more into getting legless on German beer.'

Some were introduced to amphetamines by students – for, as well as racketeers, sailors and tearaways, German clubs came to cater too for tourists, *Mittelstand* teenagers and intellectuals for whom exposure to the uproarious abandon of the UK groups and their trashy rock 'n' roll in the red-light mire provoked a horrified urge to reject jazz coolness altogether. Let's have some fun for a change. In reciprocation, immigrant rock 'n' rollers took sartorial, trichological and other cues from their new admirers – of which the most far-reaching was the Beatles' adoption of the *pilzen kopf* ('mushroom head') haircut as worn by Klaus Voorman, Astrid Kirchherr and other bohemians in Hamburg – though both the Kaye Sisters and Adam Faith in Britain had pre-empted the Beatles with similar brushed-forward styles.

The earnest attentions of the blue stocking set gave groups a new confidence, even if they were still technically immature. 'Germany boosted our morale', said West Drayton singer Cliff Bennett. 'For the first time, we seemed to be making a solid impression on our audiences.' This had been born also from night after night onstage. 'They go in for movement,' said Spencer Davis, 'Musical ability doesn't matter so much.'[50] Nevertheless, in the days before onstage monitors when vocal balance was achieved by simply moving back and forth on the mikes, breathtaking harmonies and instrumental prowess were hard-won but perfected in preparation for what lay ahead.

Putting on the agony for so long, you got better at capitalizing on, rather than shrinking from, an inability to pitch past a hoarse vocal compass without cracking. Rather than try to hit the high notes and fail, you extemporized huskily like a blues or gospel singer, as though the sentiment of a song was too intense for satisfactory verbal or expected melodic articulation. Outfits stopped duplicating recorded arrangements, choosing rather to pile up the pressure during infinitely-extended extrapolations of 'Whole Lotta Shakin'', 'Keep a-Knockin'', 'What'd I Say', even 'When the Saints Go Marching In' and other pieces with simple structures that required little instruction.

Groups became unpredictable on the boards. Infused with the fizz of amphetamines, a group might leap into an onslaught of endlessly inventive caperings, skylarks, amateur acrobatics and improvised comedy sketches. Some items might stop after a muddled verse or two, but one such as 'Whole Lotta Shakin'' could last a full hour during which all but the drummer might abandon instruments to appeal to dancers to clap along to what they recognized as the *mach schau* – later, corrupted to 'let's go' – beat: pounding hi-hat, snare and bass drum in the same lone four-in-a-bar rhythm for chorus after chorus amid yells of encouragement until the levelling guitars surged back in again and the snare reverted to its usual offbeat, and the hi-hat to eight quavers a bar while the bass drum continued to clump fours rather than its standard rock 'n' roll on-beat. Hitting solidly and defiantly a fraction slow, drummers invested material with stronger definition and increased tension. Whether originated by Sheridan's drummer or Pete Best of the Beatles, it would not be presumptuous to say that the subtleties of these rhythmic developments in Hamburg were to alter drumming procedures forever.

The most celebrated exponents of *mach schau* – a backbeat that a half-wit couldn't lose – were Dave Dee and the Bostons. Years later, it would underpin 'Hold Tight!', 'Hideaway', 'Touch Me Touch Me' and other hits they notched up as Dave Dee, Dozy, Beaky, Mick and Tich – and it was in the hothouse emergency of their Reeperbahn residencies where, *mach schau*-ing for hours on end, the group evolved from Wiltshire clodhoppers into, perhaps, Hamburg's most popular attraction. As it was with the Barron Knights and Freddie and the Dreamers too, informal clowning became stylized quasi-vaudevillian routines – and it quickly became apparent how much English-speaking seamen appreciated Dave's rich fund of dirty jokes.

Dee would notice too that, 'When you come home, you aren't half tight, musically tight. You don't know it's happening because you get tired.'[48] Encounters with the Fatherland wrought other more workmanlike groups whose loose ends had been firmly tied by the time they returned with the outsides of their vans defaced by the frauleins' affectionate messages, and were toughened for less demanding if more reputable tasks in Britain. As late as 1968, sending groups to Germany for a three-month stretch was still a foolproof method of separating the men from the boys. Black Sabbath's manager, Jim Simpson, reasoned that it was 'rather like training a thousand-metre runner by sending him on five-thousand metre courses'.

It wasn't compulsory to like it. Dave Berry 'hated every minute of it. I feel that every stage appearance should be special, but I failed to see how it could with repeating the same act six times a night.' His opinion was echoed by Twinkle: 'Hamburg was the first place I ever went to without an escort. I went on with a pick-up group, and it was a nightmare – mainly because I thought I'd have to do one set. I did several, doing the same numbers and wearing the same stage outfit. I gave up performing there and then.' It almost finished Harrow's Episode Six too. 'A month's club work turned into a terrible sweat shop thing', elucidated their Roger Glover. 'I contracted acute peritonitis there, and ended up in hospital.'[38]

Nevertheless, after a subsequent two months in the Lebanon 'playing background music to the clatter of one-armed bandits'[38] Episode Six had become, like every other act that spent lengthy sojourns abroad, an unknown quantity locally. Some groups did not remain so for long after casually cataclysmic performances that the spell away had forged – seeming as if, like Tony Sheridan, they couldn't give a cuss about the audience and were up there having fun amongst themselves. Whereas the customers might have Twisted to the other outfits on the bill, there'd be a spontaneous rippling towards the stage when the curtains swept back a few thundering and dramatic bars into the first number. It was food for thought for other local musicians who witnessed it. If they were appalled about the onstage cigarettes dangling from lower lips, and, of course, the horrible row, no-one could deny the impact on the crowd.

In the Bobby era, the homecoming groups often seemed like a throwback. Back at the Scala ballroom, Bern Elliott and the Fenmen had cut most of the previous niceties in favour of R & B and classic rock – partly because German teenagers, as Kingsize Taylor observed 'are a bit behind the times. They go for the old Little Richard gear and stuff like that.'[51] Nevertheless, a typical recollection of the Beatles' Freiheit period was of John and Paul composing in a backstage alcove while Pete and George downed steins of lager and socialized.

Few Lennon-McCartney efforts were then unveiled publicly, but the monotony of stretching out a short British palais repertoire was sufficient impetus to rehearse strenuously the most obscure material, the hoariest old chestnuts that could be dug up from a common unconscious. 'We played everything,' said Ace Kefford, 'Rock 'n' roll, blues, making things up, with Carl, Johnny Mann [guitarist] and me sharing lead vocals, just to fill in the time.'

The hours dragged more slowly between one night's stint on stage and the next. Up and about by mid-afternoon, players became anonymous wanderers anywhere beyond the immediate vicinities of their places of work. On outings to art galleries, taking pot-luck on whatever amusement an unknown part of the city might hold, and trips to the seaside on hot days, they could recharge their batteries for the night's toil. In Germany, sausages, *Appfle Kuchen* and like foodstuffs may have been recommended but most Britishers made more of a meal of 'Cornflakes *mit Milch*', something-with-chips and tea that was served in many cafes.

Ex-grammar schoolboys might have had some French and German already, but most UK musicians picked up enough to get by, despite that insular arrogance peculiar to certain Britons abroad that would come to a head in the soccer hooliganism of the 1980s.

Mention of UK pop musicians in Europe during the early to mid-1960s still brings out strange stories of what folk claim they saw and heard. During one unhinged evening at the Paris Olympia, Vince Taylor floated onstage in atypical white vestments to preach a repent-ye-your-sins sermon to a mystified and then furious *yé-yé* audience. There are also authenticated tales of shoplifting sprees, attempts to mug drunken marines and mock-Hitlerian speeches and jibes about the war to German audiences, uncomprehending, disbelieving or shocked into laughter. With eyes like catherine-wheels after winding-up for the night, groups would be ripe for mischief, which might begin with five-in-the-morning bar-hopping and end twenty minutes before showtime with everyone sleeping like the dead, until a club envoy bursts in, jabbing at his watch.

Yet, however much certain outfits made themselves out to be frightful desperados, many of the incidents attributed to them were improved with age, took place under the alibi of a stage act, or else were originated by others. More shocking than a Beatle farting loudly in a dressing room was a member of the Big Three stepping onto a club stage in nothing but a pinafore; one of the Undertakers donning a gorilla suit and emptying several Freiheit bars, and one hard-living Midlands combo getting on the outside of a whole month's allocation of *gratis* beer in the space of an evening.

Many a middle-aged British father had wartime memories of the flesh-pots of Europe, and knew that the travellers' tales about them were hard fact. As guardian of his daughter's innocence, Cilla White's dad wouldn't hear of her going to Hamburg as featured singer with Rory Storm and the Hurricanes. A trip there by Hemel Hempstead's Barry Edwards and the Semitones was cancelled too because the bass player's Jewish mother wouldn't countenance him setting foot on German soil.

By 1962, however, incentives for working in Hamburg had grown more powerful. A far cry from the dungeons of 1960 were the skylit bunkrooms of the Top Ten club and the crowded but homely Pacific Hotel. Certain individuals were able to demand even more. The Top Ten's proprietor, Peter Eckhorn, didn't quibble when Rory Storm's drummer, Ringo Starr, asked for thirty pounds a week – a huge fee for the time – and the use of a flat and car to transfer to Tony Sheridan's backing group.

Though the undisputed Presley of the Reeperbahn, Tony faced tough opposition whenever Lord Sutch, Johnny Kidd and other UK stars of the same calibre were brought over. France too was hurling down gauntlets with *yé-yé* entertainers such as Les Chats Sauvages, Les Chausettes Noires and a Parisian Elvis in Johnny Hallyday.

Stiffer competition followed when the Star-Club gave no quarter during a ruthless if costly campaign to outflank the Top Ten and the Blue Peter as the Reeperbahn's premier night spot. Initially starstruck British groups booked at the Star-Club would support and proudly mix with visiting US idols – Ray Charles, Little Richard, Pat Boone, Fats Domino and, yes, Gene Vincent – who were now plugging gaps in their European itineraries with nights there and at associated engagements in Stuttgart and Hanover. The British and American musicians had no way of knowing then to what extent many of their careers would interweave. As far as the UK contingent was concerned, they were only likely to meet again if the Yanks found themselves either on a UK tour or back *sur le continent*.

Europe seemed the better financial bet. Some British musicians preferred virtual foreign citizenship to spending a lifetime at home trying to become stars. Tony Sheridan, Kingsize Taylor, Adrian Barber of the Big Three, the Nashville Teens' Terry Crow, *Drumbeat* refugee Roy Young and an otherwise unsung Liverpudlian unit called the Georgians all opted for the security of Hamburg. Young, allegedly, preferred his Star-Club wage to an offer to play keyboards in the Beatles, whose first bass guitarist, Stuart Sutcliffe, would quit to recommence his art studies at the city's State School of Art.

Ken Levy settled in Karlstad with his Scandinavian wife. With the sundering of the Phantoms, drummer Robin Bailey joined Sven-Ingvars, and room was found for guitarist Mike Wallace in another Swedish group, the Caretakers, whose biggest domestic hit was with a 1963 cover of Skeeter Davis' 'The End of the World', her only UK chart entry.

Three years later, Neil Christian – who'd become a veritable expatriate Presley in Germany – would have his sole British success with 'That's Nice'. No further record successes at home were forthcoming, so Neil, with the Crusaders in constant flux, concentrated on the possible, and racked up more Teutonic smashes of which 'Two at a Time' – all oompah brass and quasi-military drumming – was typical.

The commercial discographies of many other Britons began in overseas markets — and ended there too, as did that of Tony Jackson and the Vibrations — with a Portuguese EP after a long series of European one-nighters. You'd have been hard-pressed to find any in their own land, but Ken Levy and the Phantoms released many records in Scandinavia, and the Deejays recorded an in-concert LP at Stockholm's Kingside Club as the Searchers tried to at the Star-Club in 1962.

The previous spring, the Beatles, Rory Storm's Hurricanes and Notting-ham's Jaybirds had been in Tony the Teacher's class at the Top Ten. The star pupils were the Beatles, who were selected by Bert Kaempfert, orchestra leader and a power on Polydor, Deutsche Grammophon's pop subsidiary, to cut tracks with Sheridan for an LP, *My Bonnie*. The title song rose to Number Five in the German chart, but, unhappily for them, the Beatles had settled on a standard session rate rather than a stake in Sheridan's royalties.

'My Bonnie' and its album were intended purely for foreign consumption originally, and so was Van Morrison's vinyl debut as one of Georgie and the Monarchs in 1963 with 'Boo-Zooh (Hully Gully)', taped while the group was working at a club in Cologne. 'It was a really bad song,' confessed Van, 'but we gave it a dynamite instrumental track. We needed the session money; you do when you're drinking your pay every night.'[52] Later, the Spencer Davis Group were to make use of their leader's German degree when he sang lead on a 1966 medley single of the bawdy *'Det War In Schoneberg'* ('He was in Schoneberg') and *'Madel Ruck-Ruck-Ruck'* ('Maiden, come closer'). Graham Bonney — an Englishman of similar standing to Neil Christian — *und die Jive Five* also scored in Germany with *'Das Girl Mit Dem La La La'* and *'Aber Nein Nein Nein'*.

Half the dialects of Britain resounded round the Freiheit from the Cornish burr of Dave Lee and the Staggerlees to the Jaybirds' flat vowels to the countrified cockney of south-east Kent's Loving Kind to Isabelle Bond's Hibernian trill. Carlisle was represented by the VIPs, while Kidderminster furnished the Shades Five — minus their guitarist Stan Webb who was too young — and Weybridge provided the Nashville Teens (with no less than *three* gyrating lead vocalists). The Rockin' Berries, Wayne Fontana, Cliff Bennett and his Rebel Rousers, the Warriors (with singers Anthony and Jon Anderson), the Krew Kats (later the Moody Blues) won their spurs there too.

In August 1964, the Hellions blew into the Star-Club from Worcestershire with lead guitarist Dave Mason from the disbanded Jaguars, drummer Jim Capaldi from Evesham's Sapphires, and, to satisfy a contractual stipulation about a female vocalist, Tanya Day, a Walsall lass with a Polydor single and attendant TV appearances to her credit.

The Searchers had been almost as much of a pot-pourri when an offer of a well-paid season in Germany had come their way in 1962. The hesitation of the guitarists John McNally and Mike Pender over going so fully professional had led Tony Jackson and drummer Chris Curtis to line up two replacements. 'There was Johnny Guitar from Rory Storm and the Hurricanes,' Tony recalled, 'and Howie Casey, sax player with Derry Wilkie and the Seniors, but, virtually at the last minute, John and Mike said they'd come.'

They discovered that Liverpool groups were so rife in Hamburg that bar staffs' pidgin English was infused with Scouse slang, and that there were rumblings that once you'd heard one 'Merseybeat' group, you'd heard the lot. The Beatles were expected back at the Star-Club to replace Dave Dee and the Bostons. On receiving this news, Dee inquired, '"And what are they called?" ... The Beatles ... "What a bloody silly name that is." You make a statement like that and you always remember it – then, of course, we ended up with a name like Dave Dee, Dozy, Beaky, Mick and Tich.'[48]

7 DANCE ON!

On his mother's instructions, a younger member of a group might have to leave after the first set to get to bed at a reasonable hour. As well as Wee Willie Winkie's apoplexy, there was also concern as the late nights took their toll on homework – though what did the Diet of Worms or compound interest in pounds, shilling and pence matter when a booking at the Co-Op Hall tonight would coin more for him than a month of paper rounds? He was famous, wasn't he? He was round here. At the district sports day, the school's head of PE, shirtsleeved in the heat, had been distracted from watching the high jump by a crowd movement in the terraces. It was a coterie of girls from another school elbowing towards – yes, you might have guessed – that long-haired boy in the fourth. No doubt they'd seen him doing his Tommy Steele impressions at some Teddy Boys' gala and were fishing autograph books from their satchels.

Inevitably, clashing educational, artistic and vocational priorities would become so disordered and unhealthy that the only solution was to give up one of them. The head teacher would have to discuss the boys's academic future with his parents. Were they truly convinced that this pop music would be a lucrative career for their child?

The ones who were convinced were the sort who supported any glamorous aspirations in their children with a zest that other mums and dads may have considered excessive. When I was sitting my eleven-plus, Steve Winwood had been in the third year at his Birmingham comprehensive. Yet, rather than being steered towards the sixth form as I was, his already recognizable talent was seized upon and exploited almost as soon as his voice broke. No cute showbusiness brat with top-hat and cane, he was in the Spencer Davis Group while envious boys of the same age pored over Euclid and the inner waterways of Latvia.

To the consternation of neighbours, Joe Cocker's parents had let him and the Cavaliers rehearse in the living room, just as they'd allowed their elder boy Vic with his Headlanders skiffle group. Because of the space required for electronic paraphernalia and Joe's drums, Cavaliers bashes spilled into the hall too. In Liverpool, it was the same in the basement coffee bar of the fifteen-room property owned by the mother of Pete Best.

When a group took a serious turn, other mums and dads raised quizzical eyebrows and groused about the opportunities in a blue-collar apprenticeship or job-with-a-suit that their son was wasting. Unlike his big brother on National Service, he wouldn't find them waiting for him when he got back to the real world. In alliance with her parents-in-law-to-be, his fiancée would prevail upon him to be sensible and withdraw from the group. Ex-Country Gentleman Jim McCarty's post as a trainee financial analyst was an honourable vocational option for a Home Counties grammar schoolboy. However, his evenings were not being spent thwacking a Young Conservative tennis-ball but thwacking drums in a semi-professional edition of what would become the Yardbirds.

Ledgers and slide-rules swam before budgerigar eyes the morning after a musician like Jim had got home as the small hours chimed. On the bus by 7.45 a.m., he couldn't think straight and would struggle through the day on automatic, greeting with a snarl anyone below him who approached his desk or work-bench. During the lunch hour, he'd make use of the office telephone for group business, whilst glancing over his shoulder for nosier working-day colleagues.

Earnings from the group weren't quite enough to jack in a day job or school until something came up like a residency in a foreign club – or a Butlin's season. Then either the outfit's leader with its manager (if any) or one of its more liberal parents might call round to affirm their faith in an immediate future which was like a working holiday. You couldn't argue with twenty-five pounds a week, could you, not when eight was then considered an ample wage for a young executive? Butlin's even had its own record label which, in 1960, had issued a 45 by the Trebletones, its Bognor Regis combo.

Sensing that their man needed only courage to hold out against his mum and dad and dump the predatory girlfriend, the supplicants invoked spicy *sotto voce* imagery of the saucy, fancy-free 'birds' at the camp, even in an age when a *nice* girl would tolerate no more than a fumble at her bra-strap whilst still unwed, and when Butlin's rules forbade staff from entertaining anyone with a different set of hormones in assigned chalets that, admittedly, were shabbier than those of the holidaymakers.

The ballroom where the group would play, however, had fluorescent lighting that made everyone look suntanned and fit. It was a hunting ground, see, for souls aching for romance. The procurement of this was easy for a musician. A tryst during a beer break could be sealed with a beatific smile, a flood of libido and an, 'All right then: I'll see you later.' Then it was back to the chalet for a few press-ups in a haze of cheap perfume and grubby bedsheets. Sounds marvellous, eh?

There are people for whom Butlin's is a vision of hell. Working mostly in the evenings, groups would groan expletives and be surly over breakfast after the camp Tannoy system crackled at seven with 'Zip-A-Dee-Doo-Dah', 'Oh What a Beautiful Morning', the Trebletones' 'Butlin Holiday' or another tune as oppressively perky.

The camps reflected Billy Butlin's personality which, before his knighthood, was that of an ex-fairground hoop-la huckster. His scheme had been for a radical alternative to turnstiled Victorian piers; fish-and-chips eaten from last week's *Daily Sketch*, and the lonely hours between boarding house cream teas and opening time. With borrowed capital, there grew an empire of knobbly-knees contests; good-natured cheers from entire sittings of diners if a butter-fingered waitress let fall crockery; 'Olympic-sized' swimming pools; noisy team games with Redcoats jollying everybody along; children lining up for ride after ride on the deliciously terrifying Wild Mouse, and campers determined to enjoy themselves, but complaining about the food, the chalets, the meteorological whims of British Augusts – and the house band.

As Saturday was changeover day, the ballroom would be at its most untamed on the preceding night, the laughter shriller, the eyes brighter. Friday evenings were frequently enlivened with fighting too. The Wars of the Roses weren't forgotten during 1962's summer in Pwllheli when two gangs of young millworkers from Wigan and Wakefield scrapped with each other on every possible pretext for the entire week they were there. At the same camp a year earlier, Rory Storm had been forced to pick his way across a railway line to throw off some hard cases riled by his stage antics. On the horns of a similar dilemma, Hurricane Johnny Guitar elected to take his medicine and be swung in full stage gear into the swimming pool in which an Indian elephant had lately expired; the carcass bobbing about in the chlorinated water for three days until a crane could be found to shift it.

Among a group's duties was accompanying the competitors in the camp's 'pop singing' and jiving contests – frequently sponsored by tobacco firms – as well as delivering the music night after night. Such an outfit's rise to a formidable level of professionalism was as assured as if it had been working in Hamburg – and they'd be rebooked for next summer. Ringo Starr would claim to have been 'educated' at Butlin's in that he 'couldn't have had better practice for a stage career. Those [Butlin's] audiences really used to heckle us, and when they wanted requests, it was usually for some square song that we'd hardly heard of before – so it was up to us to keep things going. We simply had to ad-lib and try not to take any notice of the remarks they slung at us – and, more important, play without any arrangement most of the time.'[53]

Butlin-bred 1960s musicians also included Status Quo's Rick Parfitt; Georgie Fame and, with Billy Gray and the Stormers at Filey, Chas Hodges of the Outlaws; Cliff Bennett's Rebel Rousers and, later, Chas and Dave. Cliff

Richard had got his break in the Rock and Roll Ballroom at the Clacton camp, while Joe Brown had twanged guitar for Clay Nicholls and the Blue Flames at Filey before his discovery by Larry Parnes and subsequent elevation to *Boy Meets Girls*. Brian Poole and the Tremeloes had 'gone pro' at the Ayr camp; Brian giving up a place at the University of Leeds to so do.

A lot of acts had moved up higher than Butlin's. The leader of Paul Russell and the Rebels, toast of Hillingdon Youth Club, had gone quickly to a Decca recording contract as 'Paul Raven' and a near-hit in 1961 with 'Tower of Strength'. Even without a record deal, many groups, if not above the odd engagement back at the youth club where they'd started, were now being booked at more salubrious venues with plush curtains and dressing room mirrors bordered by light bulbs (not all of them working). There were now journeys into surrounding shires for, say, a golf club dance or an engagement around the middle of the bill at a theatre with tiered seating. No more were they changing in the toilets or being paid in loose change. When supporting a hit parade entrant, their manager would ensure that they appeared second-to-last as if to imply that they were but one rung below Shane Fenton – and half a rung below Paul Raven.

Once in a blue moon, there'd occur an even less run-of-the-mill event like a broadcast on regional radio or television magazines like *Know the North*, *Midlands at Six*, Tyne Tees' *Rehearsal Room*, *Day By Day* on Southern ITV, Westward Television's *Launch Train* or, broadcast from Glasgow, *Come Thursday*. Johnny Kidd and the Pirates had made their TV debut on nothing less than ITV's *Disc Break*, and – nationally networked too – the Joe Gordon Four on BBC's *The White Heather Club* with a try at Bobby Darin's 'Dream Lover' that sleepwalked into Scotland's own Top 20.

It was, however, *The White Heather Club* one day and back on the road the next.

Hissing hi-hat cymbals and suspensory finger-snaps *à la West Side Story* would be almost perceptible as the exhausted van bumps off the early evening high street onto the gravel next to the Municipal Hall. From the vehicle, an unexpectedly large number of shadowy human shapes emerge, numb from bearing amplifiers and drums on their laps. 'Don't go in empty handed!' a voice shouts, causing someone to haul further gear from the overloaded van before shuffling from the midwinter neon towards the Hall's front steps. A janitor answers their banging but does not help lug the careworn equipment into the darkened hall with its chilly essence of disinfectant and echo of alcohol, tobacco and food intake from that afternoon's wedding reception.

The Federals travelled forty thousand miles in 1963 in a converted bus, complete with kitchen and bathtub, just like the one in *Summer Holiday*, Cliff Richard and the Shadows' film. Though Birkenhead's equally enterprising Steve Bennett and the Syndicate had spent much of 1961 in a tent in rural London in order to sniff round record companies, the next step up for most groups was to long-term contracts on ballroom circuits controlled by Top Rank, Mecca, Jaycee, or smaller leisure corporations like the Disc A-Go-Go clubs in Paignton (Saturdays), Brixham (Mondays and Wednesdays) and Totnes (Tuesdays and Fridays). Some clasped rock 'n' roll to their bosoms rather belatedly; the Silver Blades Ice Rink management only capitulating in July 1964. Catering more professionally for older teenagers than soft-drinks-only youth clubs, they had little in the way of seating – to encourage dancing – and it was incumbent upon groups to exude a happy, inoffensive onstage atmosphere as well as action-packed music to defuse potential unrest amongst over-excited adolescents. 'You've got to work your arse off to play to the same audience three hours a night, four nights a week,' advised Dave Clark. 'You had to change your repertoire and your songs to keep the thing interesting.'[4]

Local constabulary had started paying routine calls towards the end of what archaic posters billed as 'swing sessions'. Fists often swung harder than groups who kept smiling as their music soundtracked someone being half-killed out there.

The police didn't bother when, for half-a-crown, adult dancers savoured evenings with, as some advertisements stressed, 'No Jiving! No Rock and Roll! No Teenagers!' Yet it would be these undesirables that would give profit graphs a sharp upward turn when, grudgingly, elderly promoters turned a hard-nosed penny with 'jive and rock specialists', despite the danger of events degenerating into rough-houses with delegations from enemy gangs showing up, and youths pushing their way in straight after pub closing time. Narrow-eyed bouncers – security officers – were hired to keep order, but there was at least the threat of an incident like those resulting in the near-total wreckage of a palais in Stoke the night the Arapahos were on, and the Nashville Teens engaging in prolonged fisticuffs with a local rabble from the moment they arrived at Margate's Dreamland.

Certain agents used stink-bombs and strippers to disrupt proceedings at a rival venue, thus blackening its reputation with local burghers, and causing newspaper exposés and the resumption of the old policy of strict-tempo only. Maybe such mischief was excused by its perpetrators as a moral campaign to bring the 'swing session' scum to the surface to dissipate so that 'decent music' could reign once more.

In a prudish Britain that had obliged Billy Fury to tone down his sub-Elvisness, Gloucester town councillors had barred the Sapphires from ever defiling its guild hall again because of the tightness of singer Rodney Dawes' trousers. As if this sort of scandal and the rowdiness of patrons wasn't enough, what wasn't reported in local journals was groups either not turning up altogether or coming with only half their equipment, a player short and a slovenly onstage turn-out.

Newer venues were sometimes more understanding about awkward talent. Many were run by young entrepreneurs who were not self-depreciating about their knowledge and love of pop. Among the most successful was Peter Stringfellow who was to rise from *éminence grise* of Sheffield beat's first flickerings to a likeable notoriety as an international playboy and night club owner. Formerly a disc-jockey at Nottingham's Dungeon, he opened the Steel City's Black Cat – St Aidan's Church Hall – where one florin (10p) would buy an evening there. Pocking the city, too, would be similar clubs like the Blue Moon, the Club 60 – where The Small Faces would make their debut in 1965 – and King Mojo. The unlicenced Esquire, which opened in September 1962, was converted from factory premises with assistance from a team of art students. Its decor included huge stuffed reptiles.

Those Birmingham musicians that didn't have to be at an office or factory the next morning would gradually forsake Alex's Pie Stand for the Rum Runner and Club Cedar which each served drinks until 2 a.m. Both the nationally famous and those unknown beyond the Black Country would unwind on small stages in these new watering holes, in often unlikely *ad hoc* combinations as an escape valve from the less off-beat presumptions of a selfish public. For more sordid amusement, there was the Las Vegas, a haven for prostitutes, their pimps and – then liable to prosecution – practising homosexuals. Even there, the groups played on.

In London, Johnny Dankworth – the man who'd bellowed 'What about playing some jazz!' at Lionel Hampton – must have felt like King Canute when England's oldest jazz club, Studio 51, closed to reopen as the 51 Club with a new guideline that enabled rock 'n' roll groups and trad bands to share the same bill. This cautious readjustment was reflected on celluloid in Dick Lester's *It's Trad Dad!* in which performances by Gene Vincent, Chubby Checker and Helen Shapiro were juxtaposed with those of Acker Bilk, Chris Barber and other jazzmen.

With queues round the block whenever the Temperance Seven – a pop group by any other name – appeared, it made financial sense for more and more jazz strongholds to slip in a little out-and-out pop between the trad. From Worcester's Pierpont Street Jazz Club to even Victor Sylvester's Dance Club in Chelsea, the most unlikely venues 'went pop' too – and Mark Stone and the Questors left their mark on posterity by being the first beat group to play at Sheffield City Hall.

Mark and his boys' working area did not broaden far beyond South Yorkshire, unlike that of the more fortunate Jimmy Crawford and the Ravens who were able to compare notes with other proficient units that had likewise broken free of parochial orbits, among them Sounds Incorporated, the Beatles, Cliff Bennett and the Rebel-Rousers, the Federals, the Bobby Patrick Big Six, Wayne Fontana and the Jets and Leighton Buzzard's Barron-Knights. All were becoming dependable draws throughout the land. Fontana, for example, was so popular in the north that the single word WAYNE! plus the place, date and time on a newspaper's entertainments page was sufficient to fill a venue.

On terms of fluctuating equality, they'd brag of imminent tours of outlandish countries and even record contracts when paths crossed in dressing room or transport cafe. A more realistic measure of achievement were letters of undying love to a singer or instrumentalist for whom screams were already reverberating. Some nights, bouncers would have to rescue him as he lost tufts of hair to clawing females while the rest of the group bought their escapes with mere autographs.

The lads in the audience were more inclined to like what they heard rather than saw. The core of the average group's set was drawn from the current Top 20 and classic rock: anything that the mob knew and wanted to dance to. However, braver outfits surprised patrons with items from pop's remoter trackways: US smashes that had failed everywhere else, and items buried on B-sides and side two track four of LPs.

If they didn't make the British charts, certain 45s *mostly* from black America were as well-known as some that did. The Miracles' 'Shop Around' was one that warranted worthy versions by Johnny Kidd and Helen Shapiro. 'You Really Got a Hold On Me', also by the Miracles, was a 'sleeper' in this respect – and so were 'Please Mr Postman' by the Marvelettes, the Contours' 'Do You Love Me', 'Spanish Harlem' by Ben E. King and, issued on Parlophone in 1960, James Brown's 'Think'/'You Got The Power'. UK Top 40 entries that couldn't be resisted included Ben E. King's 'Stand By Me', 'Stay' by Maurice Williams and the Zodiacs – in the repertoire of innumerable British groups – 'Sea of Heartbreak' from Lorne Gibson, Marv Johnson's 'You Got What It Takes', covered by Johnny Kidd and a Janet Richmond, and 'I'm Gonna Knock On Your Door' sung originally in the 'kiddie' counter-tenor of Eddie Hodges.

Dance hall groups also latched into items by cult celebrities like Dr Feelgood and the Interns ('Mr Moonlight'), Richie Barrett ('Some Other Guy)', Teddy Randazzo ('Just a Little Bit', 'Let the Sun Shine In'), Barrett Strong ('Money'), James Ray ('If You Gotta Make a Fool of Somebody'), the Clovers ('Love Potion Number Nine'), Don and Dewey ('Farmer John') and Chan Romero ('Hippy Hippy Shake'). The songs might be familiar today, but how many of the artists are just as obscure now as they were then?

The hipper combos were also rifling the catalogues of Benny Spellman, Lee Dorsey, the Donays, Barbara George and other comparatively unknown Americans. Unobtainable from high street retailers, such discs would wend their way from a more exotic continent after collectors went directly to source. Some were on the mailing lists of untold US independent labels like Aladdin, Chess, Imperial and Cameo-Parkway who would export the sacred sounds to be filtered through British regional accents. Kingsize Taylor and the Dominoes prided themselves on being able to perform selections 'before anybody else had heard the records. We had them sent over from the States'[51] but Brian Poole and the Tremeloes actually made direct contact with the late Buddy Holly's producer, Norman Petty, who gave them unreleased Holly demos.

Other rare recordings were borrowed from ballroom disc jockeys such as Jimmy Savile at Manchester's Three Coins and Spinnin' John who presided over Basildon's Locarno, as well as non-performing lay experts like Roger Eagle of Manchester and Birmingham schoolboy Andy Dunkley (later a well-known radio presenter).

Along less exclusive avenues, you might tune in to some static-ridden gem on the American Forces Network, the BBC's overseas services or, more often, Radio Luxembourg. Sometimes a song like 'Up a Lazy River' or Brook Benton's 'Hurtin' Inside' would be heard all over the kingdom before being dropped quite inexplicably, never to be played again. In the air rather than exactly popular too were 'Everybody's Doing It', 'Michael Row the Boat Ashore' and 'My Bonnie' (which I was forced to pipe out in an uncertain treble at a primary school concert in the very month that Tony Sheridan and the Beatles recorded it).

Songs came and went, but Chuck Berry rode roughshod over them all with UK groups turning to his Chess LPs as regularly as monks to the Bible. Ray Charles still cropped up on every point on the map too. Mild-mannered interpreters like Marty Wilde and Johnny Gentle had given way to the tougher beat groups like Dave Curtiss and the Tremors in Clacton – who released a six-eight arrangement of Ray's 'What Kind of Girl Are You' in 1963 – or Newcastle's Alan Price Combo whose 'Hit the Road Jack' was rasped out by vocalist Eric Burdon with the rest on the skittish responses. It and many other Charles numbers were highlights of the Combo's all-nighters at the Downbeat, a club above a dockland warehouse. Before serving as Charles' interval band in Frankfurt, the Beatles had united with Tony Sheridan's Jets at Hamburg's Top Ten for a ninety-minute 'What'd I Say'. Shorter renderings were dared on stage – and later on vinyl – by the Searchers, Gerry and the Pacemakers and ex-youth club leader John Mayall of Manchester's Blues Syndicate.

Most British singers, however, were not capable of taking on Ray Charles without affectation or losing the overriding passion. The few who were up to it included Cliff Bennett, Eric Burdon, Joe Cocker, Gary Brooker, Van Morrison and Steve Winwood, whose brother Muff would 'remember us listening to "Hit the Road Jack" and the [*At Newport*] LP. Around that time [1961], Steve's voice started to break [and] he was consciously trying to sing like Ray Charles with a child's voice. After six months, it came out like a black voice and it was quite natural.'[54]

When the Twist *et al* came in, not only were certain group members thrust to the front for abashed dancing demonstrations, but even Berry and Charles were elbowed aside for numbers like 'Twist and Shout' (and just plain 'Shout') by the Isley Brothers, Dee Dee Sharp's 'Mashed Potato Time' and, from the Orlons, 'Shimmy Shimmy' and 'The Wah-Watusi' plus numbers in which the subject matter was less directly to do with Twist mobility but the beat essentially the same.

Though form sometimes overruled content, the usual order of the day was not the Orlons, Benny Spellman, James Brown, Don and Dewey and Barbara George but the passing joys of the Marcels' mauling of 'Blue Moon' and Bruce Channel's 'Hey Baby'. Every other request from the dance floor seemed to be for Pat Boone's 'Speedy Gonzales' and, when some idiot's girl wanted it, the much-covered 'Sucu Sucu'.

If a group got as far as a recording test, they were scrutinized for versatility and overall competence rather than any individuality. After half a day of being jolted shoulder-to-shoulder in the van, they ran through their stage set for a tardy and supercilious recording manager and his engineer, who issued orders from glass-fronted booths. Crippled with nerves, the musicians would be too eager to please with misjudged extemporizations and a solemn sterility far removed from their fervour on the boards.

The playback – if they were permitted to hear it – would seem precise if hesitant at most. Morever, whilst fright muted the rest, the most garrulous member might come across to the man in charge as having the most 'personality', and, therefore, become a prime candidate for election, however undeserved, as the unit's figurehead, its Cliff Richard.

Yet Jimmy Crawford showed what was possible in 1960 when he landed that elusive record contract – with Cliff's Columbia label. It did not cover his Ravens. After a couple of false starts, his version of The Paris Sisters' 'I Love How You Loved Me' peaked at Number Eighteen around Christmas 1961. Sadly, follow-up, 'I Shoulda Listened To Mama', didn't leave the runway – and that, as far as the British record-buying public was concerned was that for Jimmy Crawford. Yet he was able to cling on in the ballrooms for many years on the strength of his little 'I Love How You Love Me'.

8 LUNCH BOX

Not the most experienced of travellers, he wouldn't be reckless enough to get out and stretch his legs on the platform during the painfully slow departures *en route* to the Hook of Holland. Dutch jabber penetrated from outside as he gazed moodily at a flat landscape which the cold from the North Sea hit like a hammer. The pallor of dawn afforded light as, from the ship, he walked creakily with his cumbersome burden -- suitcase, guitar and amp – across the concrete desolation at Newhaven. After the train connection jogged forward, he slipped into an uneasy slumber now that he was more assured of getting home. Hours later, he climbed down onto the platform. Everything was the same as he'd left it. Near the taxi rank, a pipe-smoking road sweeper was still pushing a broom along the gutter. A newspaper vendor barked the headline of the afternoon edition of the *Evening Standard*. 'Never again,' the guitarist mumbled to himself, adding an unspoken 'until the next time'.

He wondered whether twenty-two wasn't a good age for a steady job, a mortgage, maybe wedding bells. Too long had he stared at the drummer tunnelling into egg and chips across a wayside cafe's formica table with 'Johnny Remember Me' always on the jukebox but overshadowed by the bickering, the twittering and the bass player's perpetual badgering to sing a number in the set.

As his parents would often remind him, it wasn't too late to resume his apprenticeship or go to college. These choices might be beckoning still, but, back in Hamburg or Butlin's for another three months, and, therefore, removed from domestic pressures, a decision – that most noxious of phenomena – could be held at arm's length for a while longer as he drifted from pillar to post, from group to unsatisfactory group, all arriving at the same commercial impasse.

Tired of imitating Hank Marvin in the Crescents, Jeff Beck had moved on to Him and the Others, the Bandits and then back to Kerry Rapid and the Blue Stars. Meanwhile, he'd got married. For the all-blond Fair Set from South Shields, the last straw might have been the engine freezing up over the mountains from Munich, and having to shiver the night away until the sun rose and warmed the radiator. Those that didn't leave reformed the group as the Caesars, and recommenced the drive round the trunk-roads of Britain and Europe.

The vehicle in which such a party huddled would attract dull watchfulness at lonely petrol stations. In the grim digs where they'd repair late at night, the leader would dictate who slept where, making certain that he had the least crowded bedroom; one of the others could kip on the floor if ever they were a bed short. Rumbustious repartee had become desultory as the spurious thrill of 'going professional' gave way to stoic cynicism as each man's few pounds for the week dwindled.

If welcomed back with the anticipated warmth, there were sometimes signs of fading popularity in a group's home town. Second-billed to acts that had once looked up to them, they'd make up for long absences abroad or in the holiday camps by packing in as many local engagements as the traffic would allow before they had to vanish again. Predictable as the set had become – even down to the syllables of the vocalist's patter – few could gripe about any falling off in quality. It was like expecting a racing bike for Christmas and getting one. In a month underscored with run-of-the-mill club dates, there'd be some prestigious presentation like a 'Rock and Trad Extravaganza' in Middle Wallop Village Institute or a 'St Patrick's Night Twist Gala' at Gainsborough Drill Hall.

Rather than modestly coming into their own on foreign soil like Doug Fowlkes and the Airdales, the Georgians or, all over Germany for two years, the Rockin' Berries, some groups favoured banging their heads against a brick wall at home. In demand as a reliable support act, they'd press contact addresses and songs they'd written on visiting recording artistes like Adam Faith and Julie Grant. Cumulatively, all this hustling sometimes got results, but there was a strong argument that self-contained groups were, indeed, on the wane. Had they ever been off it? Look at outstanding showmen like Dave Dee, Alex Harvey, Dave Berry, Zoot Money – Bournemouth's answer to The Big Bopper – Freddie Starr (formerly Freddie Fowell of *Violent Playground*), and another Liverpudlian, Bill 'Faron' Russley dubbed 'The Panda-Footed Prince of Prance' for his penchant for knee-drops and scissor-kicks. All they needed was to be in the right place at the right time, and, as with Jimmy Crawford, it'd be goodbye backing combo, hello stardom.

On the plus side, groups left behind might still be enormous locally – and, in cities like Cardiff or Leeds, that could be enormous enough if you'd gone beyond the back room of the Cat-and-Paintbrush to regular Saturday nights at the Majestic. Younger outfits would copy your repertoire and off-hand stagecraft, and envy your multitude of fans, some with no qualms about telephoning you to request numbers to be played at the next Cavalcade of Rock and Twist. George Harrison's earliest remark to the national music press was, 'You know, we've hardly done any touring in England. Working in and around Liverpool keeps you busy throughout the whole year.'[56] A typical night's work for his Beatles was an arrival at the Jive Hive at 8.15 for a half-hour set; on to the Cavern to do forty-five minutes; back to the Jive Hive to play last, and either home by midnight or on to, say, the Zodiac where a jam session with other off-duty musicians might still be dinning as milk-floats confronted daybreak.

If you still cared, how did you get up to the next level? The bigger ballrooms could be a link to nationwide 'scream circuit' theatre tours. These, however, weren't all they were cracked up to be. Uncertain whether you'd be sleeping in beds that night, you'd be first act on – with just enough time to play the A-side of your single (if you had one) plus one other number – in a show with, say, a US headliner, a mahogany-toned interlocutor, a stand-up comedian, a balladeer, a Larry Parnes cipher, a baby-voiced female singer and an all-styles-served-here unit like the Terry Young Six or the Mike Cotton Sound. In a clutter of cables, guitar cases and unassembled drum kits, a US legend looks on from the dusty half-light beyond footlights still being tested, as a squeak of feedback from a nervous amplifier launches you into a harrowing 'warm-up' (later referred to as a 'soundcheck').

Occasionally, he was impressed enough to take you on. Gene Vincent, then domiciled in Kent, had Sounds Incorporated constantly on the move round Britain and Europe. On another front, Steve Bennett and his Syndicate had struck their tents after netting lucrative engagements on the US air base circuit. They'd given up getting a record out as a bad job after failing a try-out with Pye because their diction was 'too northern'. Howie Casey and the Seniors, however, were about to issue another 45 from *Twist at the Top* – and, with the leverage of their *Saturday Club* spots, Shane Fenton and the Fentones had pinned down a Parlophone recording contract with a rider permitting the Fentones separate instrumental singles à la Shadows. With their Light Programme renown and scrupulous television plugs, Shane and the group accrued a modest stack of Top 30 hits by 1963. Their opposite numbers at Decca, Brian Poole and the Tremeloes, who were then less illustrious, began as accompanists on such masterpieces of song as 'Ahab the Arab' by Jimmy Savile and a Vernons Girls cover of 'The Locomotion'. Other groups hired to back solo stars and tape demos included the Hellions who were heard on a Oriele single by one Eddie Curtis.

For Oriele too, Dave Lee and the Staggerlees recorded 'Dance Dance Dance' and the self-composed 'Love Me'. Ember, another label of no great merit, issued 'Chaquita', a one-shot instrumental by the Dave Clark Five before they shifted slightly up-market to Pye's off-shoot, Piccadilly, for two more leaps in the dark. The Jaybirds gained a record contract of sorts with Embassy, and there were plenty of other budget labels: Record Club, Summit, Rhythm Records, Hit Parade, Pop Parade, Top Six, Crossbow, Cannon and, 'the nation's finest cover versions', Top Pops with space for bargain-bin groups to run off carbon-copy singles and squeeze up to eight tracks onto low-fi EPs.

Even on these second-rate terms, a record release under its own name was still a far-fetched afterthought for most outfits. Yet there'd been a marked increase in opportunities for considerable regional exposure. Dozens of ITV programmes were now being broadcast from Birmingham via Sutton Coldfield's transmitter, the first to be built outside London. The jewel in ITV's pop crown was *Thank Your Lucky Stars* – hosted by Brian Matthew, in pullover and *sans* tie – as 'swinging' as a man in his thirties could be without being called to task by stuffier superiors. As well as some elaborate stage sets, local flavour was injected by a Wednesbury teenager with a half-beehive, Janice Nicholls, who passed judgement on the latest discs like the panellists did on the other side's *Jukebox Jury*. Her over-used catch-phrase, 'I wouldn't buy it but I'll give it five' – the maximum score – delivered in a vile Brummie monotone, was to form the basis of an expedient single by her on Decca.

Given the advantage of proximity to ITV studios, some Midlands musicians known to Janice were transformed from boys-next-door to nine-day wonders. Denying his daytime occupation as a department store trainee, one Brian Hines made his TV debut as 'Denny Laine' with his backing Diplomats on *Midlands at Six*. Because they toed a clean, amiable line, ITV had Denny's group in matching suits and peroxided hair on two sub-*Lucky Stars* weekday pop showcases, *For Teenagers Only* and *Pop Shop*, and – at the bitter end – as intermission music on *Lunch Box*, lightest of light entertainment, hosted by Noele Gordon, future mainstay of ITV soap opera, *Crossroads*. Ultimately, nothing came of it apart from EMI convening Denny and his group at Abbey Road to tape a few demos.

Disturbed that the fish weren't also ostensibly biting for them, musicians too frequently on the dole took it out on their leaders, managers, van drivers and whoever else seemed likely to rise to it. Such an unfortunate might shake a frustrated fist in the direction of London – because it was going to be too late for him and the lads unless he pulled a more effective stroke than spray-painting the group's name on a railway station wall and being caught in the act by a porter.

An obtuse speculation is that if, in a parallel universe, the Beatles, Rolling Stones *et al* hadn't gained record company interest, they might have been superceded in parochial popularity stakes by younger acts such as the Mojos or the Downliners Sect. By late 1961, some groups must have been aware that they were either the same age or older than those already famous like all those Bobbies and Cliff Richard, who'd been just seventeen when first he donned his pop star mantle.

Indeed, it looked as if the likes of Norrie Paramor and Dick Rowe were correct; there really wasn't much future in groups after all. Fontana's patience with Howie Casey's lot was snapping as neither of their singles had had enough airplay to get near the charts – and no one knew anyone who'd got anywhere with studio auditions. Maybe pop music in general was on its way out. The studio audience on *Thank Your Lucky Stars* still screamed indiscriminately at male pop idols, but as much pin-ups as they were nowadays TV and film actors like Ed Byrnes – jive-talking 'Kookie' of *77 Sunset Strip* – Sean Connery in his first Bond movie, and Robert Horton, forever Flint McCullough, scout of ITV's *Wagon Train*, who was star enough to appear last on an edition of *Sunday Night at the London Palladium*.

It occurred to many backing players that they stood more chance of a livelihood as a musician than any two-bit front man. You didn't have to like what you did but, if you knew the right people and were sufficiently versatile and coldly professional, you were better off with London session work in the employ of whoever called the shots, with no extra time or favours done. The Outlaws, some of Lord Sutch's Savages, the Kestrels and, similar in style and motivation, Carter-Lewis and the Southerners were among those who were cashing in there.

Sheffield guitarist Chris Spedding had his head screwed on too as he marked time in blazer and tuxedo, churning out light orchestral slop under the batons of middle-aged bandleaders on luxury liners and at debutante balls. From just as far away from the kernel of UK pop, Allan Buck, drummer with Blackburn's Lionel Morton Four, had worked with both Joe Brown and Johnny Kidd, and Bobby Elliott was now in Shane Fenton's Fentones, having distinguished himself on a short-list that included Keith Moon of Wembley's Beachcombers.

Other percussive contemporaries had, like Chris Spedding, roamed beyond rock 'n' roll. Having taught himself to read the relevant dots, Jimmy Nicol from the New Orleans Rockers had been in the ranks of David Ede and the Rabin Rock whose upbeat musak had been featured on the Light Programme's now-forgotten *Go Man Go Show* in 1960. It was an apt prelude to his next post in the Cyril Stapleton Orchestra. Nicol was also hired for a session with Cleo Laine who was as much of a *grande dame* of jazz as Noele Gordon was on *Lunch Box* – in whose studio band Pete York played for the money he could not yet earn in various Midlands pop and jazz outfits. Pete was provident enough to keep up with a business studies course and not lose his touch on the drums.

Players of even more sober disposition threw in the towel altogether; some made to by whining parents with elbow-grease values. Both Tony 'Top' Topham – the Yardbirds' first lead guitarist – and (though reinstated later)

John Lodge, bass guitarist with what mutated into The Moody Blues, quit their respective outfits in the interests of higher education. Others were lumbered with wives and brats who wanted them home in the evenings or were freshly-qualified college graduates who now had to *work* to keep alive.

In the offices and factories of Britain today, how many fifty-somethings took the then wise course of leaving 1960s pop groups that later Made It? Exemplified by his pumping Buddy Holly's 'Peggy Sue' with one hand in his pocket, Paul Arnold's condescension towards the Zombies had become intolerable by 1963. Jim Rodford, Rod Argent's bass-playing cousin, was well-placed to replace him, but when Jim joined the Mike Cotton Sound, the Zombies settled for Chris White whose grocer father allowed them use of a room above the shop for rehearsals and equipment storage.

White's predecessor was to become Dr P. Arnold, MD. Perhaps solicitor Jim Spencer too had been well-advised to cease blowing sax for the Dave Clark Five in 1961, but maybe kicking themselves now are teacher Geoff Mott who turned down Pink Floyd, and Victor Farrell who bid farewell to the Hollies in 1962 and was dwelling in a house called 'The Hollies' thirty years later.

9 'LONDON, TAKE A LOOK UP NORTH!'

As unaware as his interviewers of the distant thunder, Roy Orbison in London in 1962 conjectured, 'You don't seem to have the kind of rhythm groups that we have in the States – and I'm sure that is what the kids want: strong, beaty rhythms that make them jump.'[55] Nobody at Roy's press conference could predict that soon British 'rhythm groups' would be jumping up the hit parade in abundance with discs as competent and attractive as anything American, but played with guts, like.

On Merseyside, guts were personified by Johnny Hutchinson, the Big Three's ambidextrous drummer, who wielded reversed sticks so that the heavier ends battered his kit. Not to his taste was the lighter touch that framed vocal harmony in units such as Ian and the Zodiacs, who were Kingsize Taylor and the Dominoes' rivals as north Liverpool's boss group.

From Ian and the Zodiacs to the Pathfinders in Birkenhead, each vicinity in the area seemed to have a group enjoying local fame. Either active or in formation were outfits of every variety and size including sextets and octets. Some were all female, others all black. A couple were even all female *and* black. For every one that threw in the towel, a dozen sprang up in its place. Most were in it for beer money and a laugh. Yet, as their hire purchase debts demonstrated, quite a few meant business.

Though Gerry and the Pacemakers prided themselves on embracing everything in each week's Top 20 in their act, they were as competitive as any other professional Merseyside group in seeking out more stimulating material. 'If a rhythm and blues record, say, something by Chuck Berry, was issued,' recollected Gerry, 'then I'd rush down to the shop and buy it straight away, and chances are I'd see somebody like Paul Lennon [sic] of the Beatles in the same queue. Then there'd be a big rush to see who could get their version of it out first.'[57]

Tony Sheridan praised the Beatles' 'great talent for finding unusual records', as *Merseybeat* editor Bill Harry did Chris Curtis of the Searchers. Both quartets were particularly adept at adapting songs by US girl groups of ingenuously fragile conviction. Each, for example, tried 'Please Mr Postman', 'Shimmy Shimmy' and the Shirelles' 'Boys'.

Such idiosyncrasies were symptomatic of both the regional isolation of parochial pop and its inward-looking nature. As a solo by some New Orleans dotard would be revered as definitive by trad dads, so a certain song might be so worthily executed by this or that local rock outfit that it would be shunned by all others. Few were assured long enough to take on 'You'll Never Walk Alone' after Gerry and the Pacemakers had brought the house down with it when they and other Liverpool acts supported Gene Vincent at a six-thousand-capacity stadium near Prince's Dock on 3 May 1960. Similar criteria applied to such diverse items as the Merseybeats' gaucherly sentimental 'Hello Young Lovers' and the Chants, an all-vocal quartet, with their arrangement of the Stereos' 'I Really Love You' in which street-corner harmony, complete with *basso profundo* 'fool' grumblings, conveyed the required despondency.

Purportedly, it wasn't until they noticed Earl Preston and the TTs performing a self-penned ditty that the Beatles risked any Lennon-McCartney numbers on stage. Of course, Liverpool pop composers were not unprecedented – Russ Hamilton had been one – and other beat musicians such as Stuart Slater of the Mojos and the Zephyrs' Jeff Taggart also came up with items superior to some of their respective groups' non-originals, while the Big Three were to knock together 'Cavern Stomp' after the inner city club where they were virtually resident.

This sodden oven in a ravine of lofty warehouses would become as far-famed a Liverpool landmark as the Pier Head. All manner of future worthies from Tory MP Edwina Currie to television actress Sue Johnson would relate proudly how they'd been amongst the massed humanity bobbing up and down in its choking rankness as the Big Three, Gerry, the Beatles *et al* entertained on its wooden stage beneath stark white light.

Partly because of their 'arty' mannerisms, and Lennon and McCartney's pretensions as composers, the Beatles had been derided as unprofessional posers by no-nonsense musicians like Johnny Hutchinson. A pop fan of Cilla White's discernment 'couldn't bear them. I thought they were scruffy and untidy. I didn't want to know.'[58] The tragedy of the Beatles was that they didn't care how awful they were – in fact, they revelled in it. 'It seemed an incredible time before they actually started a number,' averred Keith Hartley, a novice Merseyside drummer, 'as if they were just messing about.'[59]

They weren't even considered when a smattering of Liverpool groups were chosen to be interspersed with some of Larry Parnes' lesser creatures at the Gene Vincent extravaganza. Bigoted old Teds threw contemptuous pennies at them, but Gene in Liverpool only just upstaged the local boys whether plaintive Gerry with 'You'll Never Walk Alone' – soon to be Anfield football ground's 'Kop Choir' anthem – or Rory Storm, dazzling 'em with 'What'd I Say.'

A tape recording of yet one more Greatest Night Anyone Could Ever

Remember was erased but the impact of the Scouse groups on Mr Parnes was sufficient for him to charge local impresario Allan Williams with the hurried task of assembling a selection from which could be chosen a combo to back Parnes' signings who'd been earmarked to tour Scotland.

In a photograph taken at the auditions, Billy Fury – who'd strung along with his manager to provide a second opinion – appeared unimposing next to flamboyant Rory Storm, who had somehow acquired a tan during a wet spring. It was because Rory looked such a pop star of a man and Fury – whose Top 10 success was not yet consolidated – didn't that Larry threatened to call off the Scottish undertaking if a single copy of the snap was published. God knows what might have transpired had Storm and his Hurricanes bothered to play for Parnes that day, and he'd been foolish enough to select them. What could have prevented Rory in Aberdeen or Inverness from shoving the main attraction into the wings, and seizing the central mike himself?

Though the Beatles had no specially-designated front man, the greater emphasis was not on instrumentals but vocal selections which ranged from merry 'Sheik of Araby' to torchy 'September in the Rain' to the blood-curdling dementia of one in the throes of a fit whenever John Lennon attacked an elongated 'Money'. At least it wasn't weak; neither were they faking it. The anarchic inverse of Cliff and the Shadows, the Beatles walked a highly-strung artistic tightrope without a safety net, and had endured a baptism of taunts and slow hand-claps. Dauntlessly, they'd retaliated, and so rapidly had a common touch of turmoil accumulated between them and their antagonists that ugly moments were by-passed as all tuned in to their awry absurdity – especially as the group themselves conveyed the impression that they too were aware of it.

Much of the Beatles' attitude rubbed off on other Liverpool units who would also see nothing amiss in, say, serially consuming beer and food between numbers. The Merseybeats, the Moths, the all-girl Cockroaches, the Beatcombers (formerly the Beachcombers), the Keenbeats and others who'd worked the word 'beat' into their titles or used insectile appelations did so to be more like the Beatles who, with Gerry and the Pacemakers, the Remo Four, the Big Three, the Undertakers, Mark Peters and the Silhouettes, and Faron's Flamingos were among the area's most popular attractions by 1961. Which would play at the optimum moment when any combination of them were on the same bill was still a matter of conjecture. However, when looking back on the year in *Merseybeat*, Bill Harry – admittedly an old art school chum of Lennon – tipped the Beatles, Mark Peters and new face Karl Terry for national acclaim.

Yet Liverpool pop was an unknown quantity to the rest of the country's teenagers, apart from those who'd seen the few outfits who'd got on the national ballroom circuit or played at the Beachcomber in Bolton, Aldershot's Queen's Palais, Cardigan's Black Lion and other scattered venues that would have them. Nevertheless, the bacillus of Merseybeat spread down river. The Hollies, a quintet built round Ricky and Dane, were touted as 'Manchester's Beatles' – though Allan 'Ricky' Clarke was keener on the Big Three – and the more light-hearted elements of the Beatles' Cavern act were to have a beneficial effect upon a certain Peter Noone, who also travelled regularly from Manchester to catch this Scouse group everyone was talking about.

Before he became the 'Herman' in Herman's Hermits, young Noone had been a television actor. One of his parts was as Len Fairclough's son in ITV's *Coronation Street*. An episode in late 1961 had Eddie, a local rock 'n' roller, onstage at a social club. Besotted, teenager Lucille Hewitt incurred parental wrath by having 'Eddie' tattooed on her forearm.

How aware were the scriptwriters of locally-produced pop? Even before the storm broke, there were signs of strong domestic resistance to chart Americana. Owing less to the US than the Bobbyish Mark Wynters and Jess Conrads, Joe Brown, with his Bruvvers, swept to Number Two in 1962 with 'A Picture of You', a blend of rock 'n' roll's country end and cockney music hall. Even more gorblimey was 'Come Outside', a 1962 Number One for Mike Sarne and 'dumb blonde' actress Wendy Richard.

Striking back harder was British television. Shutting down *Wyatt Earp* and *77 Sunset Strip* in the ratings war were serials like *Emergency Ward Ten*, a *Casualty* prototype, after its producer grasped that kidney machines in action made better drama than stolen corridor kisses. More popular were *Coronation Street* and the BBC police series *Z-Cars*, also as ingrained with oop north 'kitchen sink' grit as censorship would allow.

Such programmes emphasized the dead-end destiny that awaited most northern teenagers. From the same environment rose playwrights such as Stan Barstow and Shelagh Delaney, novelists John Braine and Keith Waterhouse and others with names as stark. On celluloid, Delaney's *A Taste of Honey* was shot on location in Merseyside dockland while the new young turk of British cinema was Liverpudlian Tom Courtenay who'd moved from *Mrs Brown and her Lovely Daughter* to the title role in the film adaptation of Waterhouse's urban comedy, *Billy Liar*.

Charming some and sickening others with his 'swinging/dodgy' thumb-sign mannerisms, another Scouser, Norman Vaughan, had taken over as compere on *Sunday Night At The London Palladium* in 1962. His '*Swinging in the Rain*' in 1962 would tie with the Vernon Girls' You Know What I Mean' as the first Liverpool-accented record to make the Top 40.

The early 1960s also brought to the nation Yorkshire painter David Hockney, sculptor and professional Liverpudlian Arthur Dooley and Richard Hamilton's Pop Art school of Newcastle – plus a 'Liverpool Scene' of poets and *nouvelle vague* artists. With them came the realization that, as Royal College of Art student Vivian Stanshall commented, 'Clever people could have Geordie and Mancunian accents.' Liverpool ones too. To crown it all, why not a northern pop group?

By then, however, a lot of northern pop groups had taken parochial impact to its limit. In a rut of local bookings and trips to Germany, the Beatles were becoming as peculiar to Liverpool alone as Mickey Finn, a comedian unknown nationally but guaranteed well-paid work for as long as he could stand up on a Merseyside stage. As the Undertakers were to Orrell Park Ballroom, the Beatcombers to Kirby's Westvale Youth Club, and the Swinging Blue Jeans to their manager's Downbeat club, so the Beatles were a fixture at the Cavern after it had put the last vestiges of its jazz dignity into booking trad acts to warm up for the beatniks, schoolchildren, shop assistants and office employees milling about down there during the newly implemented lunchtime sessions. In Cilla White's revised assessment, 'The Beatles were just as scruffy as ever. They were sort of clean and scruffy if you know what I mean. Then I started listening to their sound; they were better than I thought.'[58]

Not everyone adhered to this view. For the Remo Four's Colin Manley, 'They really weren't very good.'[60] Yet, 'They were loud,' admitted a Swinging Blue Jean, 'they had presence.'[60] They were airing more Lennon-McCartney items too, but 'We preferred them to belt out old Everly Brothers numbers,' moaned Helena Joyce, a longtime fan.[61]

The Beatles had recently acquired a *bona fide* manager who was more than just a bloke with a phone. Though he wasn't especially enamoured with pop *per se*, twenty-seven-year-old Brian Epstein, nicely-spoken and soberly attired, had an instinct for a hit as shown by his bold requisitioning of 250 copies of 'Johnny Remember Me' when rival record dealers, hearing a flop, didn't order any. He'd also been intrigued enough by the spectacle of pop to pay exploratory visits to two or three 'scream circuit' shows.

As well as prodding his contacts in the business on their behalf, Brian sank hard cash into the Beatles during his struggle to get them off the Liverpool-Hamburg treadmill. He also spruced up both their behaviour and appearance as they forsook Hamburg leathers and the grosser extremities of *mach schau* for mohair suits, playing to a fixed programme and not cursing or horsing around onstage half as much. In other words, Brian was reshaping them into what a respectable record company executive in naive 1962 assumed a good pop group to be.

Like Steve Bennett and the Syndicate and the Swinging Blues Jeans before them, the Beatles got a London recording test, with Decca, but *Merseybeat*'s demand, 'London, Take a Look Up North'[62] was unheeded until the wheels of the universe finally came together when they landed a contract that summer with Parlophone, the one EMI subsidiary that hadn't given them a 'dodgy' thumbs-down. Then trading in comedy and variety more than outright pop, Parlophone was, consequently, less impeded by fixed ideas about what teenagers would buy than other labels.

More than the Beatles' music, George Martin had been won over by their humour – which was not unlike the ex-undergraduate satire on the LP-Martin had lately recorded with the team of BBC's *That Was The Week That Was*, a late evening topical series that nurtured such future pillars of British comedy as John Cleese and Bill Oddie.

Mr Martin decided to try the Beatles for an initial two singles with an option on further releases if these gave cause for hope. All the numbers on their tape had been fairly mordant and at odds with a hilarious corporate personality. Therefore, he'd have to grub round Denmark Street for a vehicle to project this. Dismissed, however, was the notion of creating a 'leader' from either the Beatles' own ranks or by rowing in an outsider to be their Cliff Richard.

When they returned to record their debut 45 in September 1962, they'd done some structural tampering on their own account in the replacement of Pete Best with Ringo Starr, a Beatle for girls to love more as a brother than demon lover. The Beatles had tempted him with a fractionally higher wage than that offered by Kingsize Taylor to join the Dominoes. Earlier that year, Ringo had re-enlisted as a Hurricane for a tour of US military bases in France, followed by another few weeks with, so Rory Storm assured *Merseybeat*, 'the only group to make the grade at Butlin's for three years in succession.'[63]

Rory, however, wasn't for Brian Epstein. Like Pete Best with the Beatles, he had a mother who still regarded herself as patroness of the group. Devoid of any such entanglements, Gerry and the Pacemakers, Cilla White – renamed Cilla *Black*, the Big Three, Billy J. Kramer and the Fourmost became clients of Mr Epstein's management company, NEMS Enterprises – after his North End Music Stores.

On a first-come-first-served basis, Brian did not attend to the recording careers of his new charges until the Beatles had got off the ground with theirs; ensuring that *Merseybeat* knew that they'd been genuinely and importantly airborne when they went from Liverpool to tape Lennon and McCartney's 'Love Me Do' as a debut A-side in preference to the brighter and more 'professional' 'How Do You Do It' that, though written by Mitch Murray with Adam Faith in mind, George Martin had thought tailor-made for them.

Nonetheless, John Lennon would admit later that, 'We all owe a great deal of our success to George, especially for his patient guidance of our enthusiasm in the right direction.'[64]

As some English history primers start with the battle of Hastings, so the pivotal date in the saga of British beat is 11 October 1962 when, propelled by a sprinkling of spins on Radio Luxembourg as well as the buzz from the north-west, 'Love Me Do' first penetrated the UK charts. With nothing on file about this 'vocal-instrumental group', the *NME* made much of their hailing 'from Liverpool, birthplace of such stars as Billy Fury, Frankie Vaughan, Norman Vaughan and Ken Dodd.'[65] They'd done well for first-timers, yes, but who would assume that the Beatles were anything other than a classic local group who'd got lucky and had already 'failed to please'[66] in a mismatched support spot in Peterborough to Frank Ifield, the yodelling country-tinged balladeer at the height of his fame with no less than three singles concurrently in the Top 20, and the inspiration for a spoof 45, 'I've Lost the End of My Yodel' by Charlie Drake. Responding to a request, the Beatles had approximated Ifield's 'I Remember You' Number One when, under protest, they honoured two short seasons outstanding at the Star-Club as 'Love Me Do' dropped from its high of Number Seventeen.

Nevertheless, Parlophone now had 'a male Shirelles',[67] reckoned George Martin, and though Helen Shapiro was the headlining lure when the Beatles embarked on their first national tour, considered ovations unfurled into screams as they fanned the embers of excitement rather too briskly. As a result, audience reaction was far quieter for Helen than she'd come to expect. Dispiriting press articles discussing whether she was 'A Has-Been At Sixteen'[61] were fuelled by her last two 45s flopping badly while the Beatles with their 'clipped Negro sound'[68] were, said Barry Booth of the Terry Young Six, 'very new news. They'd just appeared from Hamburg. There were animated conversations about this new quartet. The unusual spelling of "Beatles" was causing comment.'

Their second single, 'Please Please Me' was then scudding up the charts after they'd mimed it on *Thank Your Lucky Stars*, an ignition point for continued progress rather than being claimed back by the regional shades of Merseyside. The change of colour from red to black of Parlophone labels at this point was an apt herald of a new pop era.

Viewers, cocooned at home during a harsh winter, would gauge more objectively than the screeching studio audience that the Beatles weren't as other groups. Barry Booth would recall that, 'One of the novel aspects of the Beatles was that each member was required to present a different identity, and they didn't have choreographed movements on stage. Each man's persona was different so that John's movement would be up and down; Paul used to shake his head from side to side, and George was a bit more still than the other two. Ringo was a law unto himself. There was a complete absence of any organized footwork and patter.'

In Sheffield, Peter Stringfellow had given in to repeated demands to book the Beatles. After wringing his hands over the seemingly extortionate fee demanded, a show was pencilled in for the Black Cat but, on police advice, this was moved to the more capacious Azena to limit the danger of riot.

While still fuddled by their sudden fame, the lads seemed their old, selectively amiable selves. Yet when the momentous news that 'Please Please Me' had tied with Frank Ifield's 'The Wayward Wind' at Number One in the *NME* chart was announced down the Cavern, the crowd – and therefore all of the Beatles' possessive Liverpool fan base – had not been particularly thrilled. After February 1963, 'the newest British group to challenge the Shadows'[68] would never play another Cavern lunchtime as they were spirited further away from their Liverpool home.

Exacerbating Pete Best's dismayed bewilderment, 'Somehow, I – and a lot of other people up in Liverpool – had a feeling they would make it, nationally at any rate.'[69] A sure sign that they *were*, indeed, going places, was sour grapes from people like Joe Meek for whom the Beatles 'have nothing new about their sound. Cliff Bennett and the Rebel Rousers have been doing the same thing for a year, and so has Joe Brown.'[70] With no axe to grind, Dave Berry told *Top Star Special*, 'We've been singing in this so-called Merseyside way since we started.'[71]

George Harrison agreed that the Beatles were 'typical of a hundred groups in our area. We were lucky. We got away with it first.'[56] What made the difference, of course, was the formidable commerciality of John and Paul's songwriting union. 'Love Me Do' had been only the tip of the iceberg. As well as inserting further creations into the stage act, they had started canvassing others to perform and even record their numbers. First refusal of the newly-concocted 'Misery' was given to Helen Shapiro, but it was to appear in the shops by Kenny Lynch, a former vocalist with Bob Miller's Millermen, who was fresh from a solo Top 10 entry. 'Misery' was not to be another, but 'The song is very attractive,' declared the *NME*, 'with a medium-paced beat.'[72] It was something else: the first ever cover of a Beatles composition.

After Gerry and the Pacemakers, the next act in Epstein's 'stable' to reach the Top 10, Billy J. Kramer *with* the Dakotas, made a better job than the Beatles had of 'Do You Want To Know a Secret', from *Please Please Me*, their LP debut. Lennon and McCartney's bank balances swelled from a shoal of unsolicited versions, both on stage and vinyl, of other *Please Please Me* songs by groups such as the Viscounts, the Kestrels and the Brook Brothers – rather less than Britain's ace vocal groups now.

10 WHERE EXACTLY IS LIVERPOOL?

On 11 April 1963, Gerry and the Pacemakers – with 'How Do You Do It' – were the first Liverpool outfit to unarguably top all UK singles charts, but that figment of publicists' imagination, the 'Mersey Sound' or 'Liverpool Beat', would germinate the following month when the Beatles' 'From Me to You' eased 'How Do You Do It' from Number One. The Mojos' 'Everything's Alright' was about to leave the Top 40 then, but on their way in were debut 45s by the Big Three and Billy J. Kramer. Waiting in the wings were the Merseybeats who had needed police protection against killing with kindness by fans at Manchester's Oasis.

For the rest of 1963, Gerry, the Beatles, Billy J. and then the Searchers slugged it out for chart suzerainty, interrupted only by 'Do You Love Me' by Brian Poole and the Tremeloes who, partly through the implications of Brian's surname, would be promoted, like Bern Elliott and the Fenmen, as the southern wing of the movement.

Brian and his boys also earned a debatable footnote in history as the ones Decca chose instead of the Beatles. One consolation for the company's high command after the Scousers they'd rejected were grabbed to teeth-gnashing effect by arch-rival EMI would be the continued licensing arrangement it had with key North American labels.

Only Americans could possibly headline over the Beatles now. Negotiations for their second UK tour with Duane Eddy and the Four Seasons had begun but the more perishable Chris Montez and Tommy Roe were sent instead. As both had Bobby-like singles currently in the UK Top 20, their names were in bigger type on the posters than the Beatles'. Assuming they'd have a walkover, each went through the motions when the tour opened in London with stock wonderful-to-be-here vapourings and, snapped one reviewer, 'No semblance of a stage act.'[72] What was a minor sales territory like England to them? Who needed its cold and the snow still on the ground in mid-March? Worse still, right from the first night, the running order had been mercilessly reshuffled as audience response had dictated that the home-grown Beatles play last.

Six weeks after the last date with Roe and Montez, the Beatles were thrust into another such trek. Like his poorly-received compatriots, Roy Orbison would embark on a long-awaited British tour with the Beatles – and Gerry and the Pacemakers too – understanding that he would be its foremost attraction, but a jet-lagged Roy had barely sat down in his dressing room when John Lennon and Brian Epstein asked if he had a minute. It was like this: 'John said, "How shall we bill this? Who should close the show? Look, you're getting all the money, so why don't we [The Beatles] close the show?" I didn't know if that was true or not, whether I was getting that much more than they were. It wasn't that much – and the tour had sold out in one afternoon.'[73]

The Beatles' 'From Me To You' was a Number One fixture for the duration of the tour during which screaming pandemonium greeted even the compere's attempts to keep order. Roy was, however, to be no lamb to the slaughter. Though aware of the chasm into which he might fall, Orbison – at twenty-seven rather an elder statesman of pop – stood his ground to sustained cheering and attentive silences.

As *de facto* bill-toppers, the Beatles and Gerry were relieved that they could still whip up screams that were getting louder every time they played. A-twitter with excitement, they stopped short of open insolence towards others in the cast, and were ready to join in the laugh-a-minute ambience of the tour coach as it hurtled up the spine of England. If not household names yet, they were recognized in roadside cafes and corner shops.

The one-nighters that were still Merseybeat groups' bread-and-butter had become quick ticklish operations. A Pacemakers show in Bristol was halted by Authority after repeated warnings about rushing the stage. A girl crushed her spectacles in her fist because her view of the Searchers was blocked. Queues formed outside a Lincoln box-office a week before Beatles tickets went on sale, and it already made sense for the last scream-rent major sixth of 'Twist and Shout', by now the four's signature tune, to signal the final curtain – and their pell-mell bolt to a ticking limousine in the back alley.

Raising a few screams by association, the Viscounts – with Johnny Gentle in their ranks – popped up on prime-time TV with a mildly choreographed 'I Saw Her Standing There' but otherwise they couldn't get arrested these days. Neither could the Kestrels, the Brook Brothers (even with their hastily-assembled Rhythm and Blues Quartet) and all the rest of them now that the Beatles and Merseybeat had set the ball rolling for self-created beat groups.

Ripping page upon page from the Beatles' book, musicians in other outfits were giving this songwriting lark a whirl. A personal triumph for Gerry Marsden was when his own 'I'm the One' was prevented from topping the hit parade only by the Searchers' 'Needles and Pins'. Merseybeat had brought with it, too, the confidence to submit compositions to other artists as Stuart Slater did to Faron's Flamingos, and Lee Curtis – albeit in vain – to *Billy Cotton Band Show* pianist Russ Conway.

Meanwhile, Lennon and McCartney continued slinging spare smashes hither and thither. Billy J. Kramer and the Fourmost caught a few, and one was promised to Beryl Marsden, perhaps the most vocally talented female representative of Merseybeat, until Brian Epstein insisted that it go to Cilla Black – who gave a supple if rather nasal richness to 'Love of the Loved', the first of her many chart entries.

A real 'wacker', Cilla thrived on presenting herself publicly as self-assured but unpretentious. They all did. The Beatles in particular were loved, explained Jenny Walden, an Exeter teenager, as 'the most natural of the groups because they have not got big-headed and are just themselves. If they feel like putting their feet up, they do.'[31] Bereft of the practised 'sincerity' of a Bobby, their light-comedy irreverence towards both fans and record industry bigwigs was as winsomely irrepressible as that of moptopped Jimmy Tarbuck, quite an established young comedian after succeeding Norman Vaughan on *Sunday Night at the London Palladium* in 1963.

Principally because of its unforced urbanity, the unforeseen new wave of Liverpudlia was to be superimposed upon a media that was being swamped with a surfeit of indiscretion in high places. Throughout the summer of 1963 a flow chart of immorality had unfolded via Fleet Street's intricate investigation of the unhappy Cabinet minister who gave his name to the Profumo scandal, and whose disgrace rocked the Tory government. His 'sex romps' with a call girl who also enlivened the bedtimes of an official of the Russian Embassy in Park Lane led to another tearsheet and her upper crust clientele being winkled out. Soon anyone in politics or the aristocracy was suspected of sundry vices from organized crime to a Pandora's box of 'kinky' sex.

Next came rioters ransacking the British Embassy in Leopoldville and, into autumn, racial unrest in Alabama, the nuclear test ban, and the Great Train Robbery by a gang romanticized as twentieth-century highwaymen. To cap it all, the West Indies were beating us at cricket.

Come September, adults were no longer falling over themselves from bedroom to doormat for first grabs at the morning paper and its pungent disclosures. Saturated with England's shame and more east-west-black-white tension than usual, only a different kind of news could reactivate their interest. Anything would do providing it could hit.

On cue, the Light Programme had emitted the sinless strains of 'From Me To You', Gerry's 'I Like It' and 'Sweets For My Sweet' from the Searchers, and the Beatles' much-copied mid-air leap on their *Twist and Shout* EP sleeve depicted them as innocent scamps like Just Williams' Outlaws. 'They were regarded as clean-living lads during the time they were getting established,' confirmed the late Harold Wilson, leader of Her Majesty's Opposition in 1963, 'whatever may have gone on later.'[61] Or before.

From their pop columnists, editors finally got to hear of Merseybeat just as teenagers were wondering if records by its groups, though still catchy, were starting to sound alike. All the same, during this high summer, theatres shook with healthy, good-natured screams as uninhibited and contagious as those that had hailed Johnnie Ray back in the 1950s. All pop music is rubbish, granted, but, by God, Merseybeat was *British* rubbish. There were plenty of human interest stories too – Poor Honest Northern Lads Who'd Bettered Themselves. Furthermore, most of them oozed 'good copy': plain speaking delivered in thickened scouse as well as quirky wit and unofficial comedy, developed as a diversion from the daily grind of road, dressing room, stage and hotel.

A stooge-announcer was provided to indulge the Beatles' capers in *Pop Goes the Beatles*, a BBC radio series in which they held sway over such 'special guests' as Johnny Kidd, the Searchers and Brian Poole and the Tremeloes, whose follow-up to 'Do You Love Me' had trickled miserably to Number Thirty-one for Decca who, with every other label outside EMI, was alighting with nitpicking hope on the remotest indication of the Beatles' fall. They'd surely had enough revenge on those who'd spurned them when at last they agreed to star on *Sunday Night at the London Palladium*. Could anyone get more famous than that?

Viewing figures were at their highest ever when, straight after the prescribed hour of religious programmes that October evening, the Beatles kicked off the next hour with a teasing burst of 'I Saw Her Standing There' during a single rotation of the Palladium's revolving stage. Before the four reappeared for five numbers that they could hardly hear themselves, the seated majority of teenagers fidgeted through endless centuries of formation dancing, an American crooner and the 'Beat the Clock' interlude in which a woman was scolded by Jimmy Tarbuck for producing a large toy beetle from her handbag, thereby setting off another orgy of screaming.

Middle-class parents in living rooms may have scoffed at it all but their eyes were still glued to the set for the traditional *finale* when the cast lined up to wave a cheery goodbye as the platform once more turned slowly while the pit orchestra sight-read the show's 'Startime' theme. Whenever the Beatles hoved into view, 'Startime' would be swamped in screams that would ebb abruptly as the group were carried off to the back of the stage.

The next day, the media was full of the 'overnight sensation'. One pressured journalist came up with 'Beatlemania'. The phrase stuck, but Beatlemania was to have less to do with the group itself than the behaviour of a nation who, once convinced of something incredible, would believe it with an enthusiasm never displayed for mundane fact.

As it had been for Tommy Steele, an appearance on the Royal Variety

Show lurched the weather-vane of adult toleration if not approval in the direction of the Beatles' (and, by inference, other beat groups). Short hair would still be imposed upon sons of provincial Britain, but after John Lennon's merry 'rattle yer jewellery' *ad lib*, the *Socialist Worker* might have vilified them, but, overall, a wider cross-section of the populace 'knows how fab they are' – as the Vernons Girls sang in their tribute single, 'We Love the Beatles'.

The rest, as they often say, is history. The last months of 1963 completed the Beatles' conquest of Britain. In the *NME*'s popularity poll, they won the 'British Vocal Group' section with more votes than everyone else put together. Succeeding 'From Me To You', 'She Loves You' shifted a million in Britain alone, and 'I Wanna Hold Your Hand' had enough advance orders to slam it straight in at Number One. The Beatles occupied the first two places in the LP charts too, and had no less than three EPs in the singles Top 50. Even a repromotion of 'My Bonnie' sold well – though Tony Sheridan did not then capitalize on his Beatle link as others less qualified would.

Such was anticipation for the group's second album, *With the Beatles*, that an ITV public information flash warned of black market copies under counters a week prior to release. The EMI plant from where they'd been stolen could barely cope with demand anyway. During that fat December, 'All I Want For Christmas Is a Beatle', a Top 20 yuk-for-a-buck by comedienne Dora Bryan, set the seal on the national obsession.

Before it had been given a name, the madness had rebounded on Liverpool where those too young to have spent lunchtimes with the so-called 'Fab Four' would huddle in blankets for days outside the Cavern to be sure of being first inside when the group came home. The Beatles' old schools passed comment when, in an article devoted to the doings of old boys, the Liverpool Institute's termly magazine had included a 'less serious note' that 'Mr G. Harrison (1956) and Mr P. McCartney (1956) have found success as members of "The Beatles" singing group and have made a number of television and local stage appearances. They recently made their second record to top the national Hit Parade.'

In the same publication, another prim compiler mentioned that 'C.W. Manley and D.M. Andrew are displaying versatility in the realm of music too.'[74] The innuendo that the Beatles were more nationally conspicuous but no better artistically than the Remo Four (of whom C.W. and D.M. were members) was also acknowledged by those Merseyside musicians who hadn't forgotten a callow skiffle group called the Quarry Men. Geoff Taggart of the Zephyrs had burrowed his way backstage at the Manchester Odeon to demonstrate some of his songs to Roy Orbison. Afterwards, he handed his camera to Paul McCartney to take a souvenir photograph of himself with the great American. He didn't think to ask Roy to snap one of him with Paul.

What then was so fantastic about the Beatles? There were at least five other Liverpool outfits that Geoff considered superior to them. Among them were the Swinging Blue Jeans who, matching *Pop Go the Beatles*, had their own Radio Luxembourg showcase every Sunday. The Searchers – second in the *NME* poll – were causing the Beatles nervous backward glances too. After closing the gap on Gerry and the Pacemakers as leading pretenders to the Beatle crown, the Searchers were the first group to be honoured with a gala reception by Merseyside civic council, and a track from their aborted Star-Club LP generated enough interest as a single to reach Number Forty-Eight: the same position attained by 'My Bonnie'.

After an all-Merseybeat *Thank Your Lucky Stars* and the weekly broadcast of *Sunday Night at the Cavern* by Radio Luxembourg, commercial expediency had sent even the densest London talent scout up north to plunder the musical gold. It was likely that this 'Mersey Sound' would be as transitory as any other fad, and as much of it as the traffic would allow ought to be exploited while the going was good. Hadn't a Beatle once said that they were 'typical of a hundred groups in our area'?[56] If so, why bother with positioning research? All you did was shell other peas from the same pod, get them to exaggerate their Scouseness, tape a raver from their stage set in a few takes and smack it out on 45. Why shouldn't it catch on like all the others? Let's sign as many as we can, see whose racket catches on and hammer it hard. Make a fortune, eh? (Pause) Where exactly is Liverpool?

In the rush to the Holy City, unheeded was George Martin's cry, 'In my trips to Liverpool, I haven't discovered any groups with a similar sound.'[57] Nevertheless, preference was given to those with either a variation on the two-guitar-bass-drums format – like the Undertakers and Mojos who substituted, respectively, saxophone and piano for lead guitar – a passing resemblance to the Beatles or a more direct affinity. With Ringo's cousin at the drums, the Escorts were one up on scrimmaging rivals envious too of their winning of a contract with Fontana in the first Lancashire and Cheshire beat contest.

Most Merseybeat acts with the faintest tang of star quality would have a moment of glory as London – with little notion how to project them – got in on the act. Some visitors behaved as if on another planet, but most A & R reps were discriminating enough to leave their scotch-and-cokes half-drunk in clubs after eliminating such-and-such a group or vocalist from the running. Tony Hatch, Pye's freelance musical director, exemplified the breed. More at home with light orchestral outings, he was to mitigate an ill-judged choice of recorded repertoire for the Undertakers by his propagation of the Searchers' international hit parade run, and, less so, by a novel arrangement of 'I Could

Write a Book' (from the 1957 film musical *Pal Joey*) for the Chants. That it was a flop had less to do with quality than the group's black skin colour which, in 1963, still meant marketing problems. Through Hatch, Pye also signed Tommy Quickly and the Remo Four, and Dominic Behan – brother of Irish playwright Brendan, for a crafty 'Liverpool Lou'.

With the disbandment of the Eagles denoting that there was to be no offsetting 'Avonbeat' yet, some shyster from Bristol had wanted to contract *every* group in Liverpool in hopes that one might be a New Beatles who would lord it over the rest like a baron over villeins. In a single month, the more cautious Decca had made off with the Big Three, the Mojos, Kingsize Taylor, the Long and the Short and, chiefly because their drummer was Pete Best, the Lee Curtis All-Stars.

Before the Beatles-with-Ringo had transcended Liverpool's scruffier jive hives, there had been excruciating backstage moments when they and Pete Best affected not to recognize each other. Such awkward junctures were not unique on Merseyside by the middle of 1963. 'The friendliness and comradeship between different groups seems to have lessened. Groups don't help each other now. If one group suffers misfortune, others are glad.'[75] Thus spake Johnny Sandon, long parted from his backing unit, the hitmaking Searchers. At the root of many such schisms was Brian Epstein who had divided outfits by giving, say, only the vocalist the security of a fixed wage – as he did with Billy J. Kramer and his old accompanists, the Coasters – and berating the Beatles for obligingly backing the Chants for one Cavern bash.

It was hardly their fault that it was no longer safe for the 'Hit Parade Scousers!', frontpaged by *Merseybeat*, to appear at local clubs. Yet 'those of us who'd hoped for their success now resented it,' grimaced Helena Joyce, 'since we could no longer see them at the Cavern. What a sense of betrayal!'[61] Because the Beatles, Gerry *et al* had once paced it, the Cavern's very stage was to be sawn up and sold at five shillings a chunk. The first coachloads of Merseybeat and Beatle worshippers from outside the city had pulled up in May 1963. Next came camera crews stockpiling footage for documentaries like ITV's *Beat City* and, commissioned by the production body of *Tonight*, BBC's *The Mersey Sound*.

Rolls-Royces disgorged famous sightseers – Ken Dodd, Chet Atkins, Lionel Bart, Nancy Spain – outside, say, the Searchers Fan Club Convention at the Iron Door in January 1964. You couldn't move either in the Mandolin, the Peppermint Lounge, the Sink and all the other new venues that had sprung up along with the London-type boutiques now operational in the city centre. At the opening night at Warrington's Heaven and Hell, you got the Mersey Monsters, Rory Storm and the Hurricanes and Pete Best's new group for half-a-crown (12½p) – less than half the cost and discomfort of seeing Hit

Parade Scousers whenever they condescended to appear in Liverpool nowadays.

Thanks to them, Scouse was now the most romantic dialect in the country. Words such as 'fab', 'gear' and even obscurities like 'duff gen' (false information) spread from the asinine fan letters and poems published in glossy monthly magazines devoted solely to the Beatles and, briefly, Gerry and the Pacemakers, to girls' comics like *Mirabelle* and *Jackie*. Such was the glamour of all things Liverpudlian that *Mirabelle* appointed as feature writer a Pete Lennon, largely on the strength of his talismanic surname.

Merseyside slang also fell from the mouths of more refined young Britons like former Deb of the Year, Judy Huxtable, who was snapped clamouring for Ringo's autograph. She and other 'society' Londoners were intrigued to meet real 'wackers' now that Liverpool was where more happened than dock strikes. An additional fascination was that some of these wackers were suddenly rich enough to drive Ferraris and holiday in faraway places. Used to pushovers with stage-door scrubbers or openly tilting for the downfall of the knickers of female entertainers on the same tour, a lad from the Dingle was not quite so sure of himself with more ladylike judies more likely to be won over by a chap who dropped names like Segovia or limp and tasteful Stan Getz than anything as coarse as the Isley Brothers or Gene Vincent.

Hardly a week would go by without another gawky Merseybeat act being brought down to London to be thrust forward as a New Beatles. Someone who'd cadged cigarettes off you the previous month would be seen in a music paper with his or her outfit, posing round a fire-escape or on brick-strewn wasteland. From nowhere, Jeannie and the Big Guys (formerly the Tall Boys, it says here) were in *Record Mirror*'s review column with a version of 'Boys' – and so was the Remo Four's restoration of 'Peter Gunn' (with an unscripted 'bloody hell!' over its cadence). Their separate recording life from that of Tommy Quickly was less an emulation of the Cliff-Shadows set-up than that of Billy J. Kramer's Dakotas – who hit the Top 20 with 'The Cruel Sea', and sold enough copies of a second 45 without Billy to warrant an EP, *Meet the Dakotas*.

A Big Three EP, *At the Cavern*, was issued after their second single, Mitch Murray's 'By the Way', had seized up just outside the Top 20. It seemed to be onwards and upwards for others too. The Fourmost had been on *Ready Steady Go*, a new pop showcase on ITV (though not transmitted up north), while a *Look at Life* cinema newsreel had been devoted to Billy J. Kramer. Cilla opened for Gerry on his latest UK tour, and the Swinging Blue Jeans were featured in an edition of *Z-Cars*.

Plugging their definitive 'Hippy Hippy Shake' on another new programme, *Top of the Pops*, the Jeans had had an altercation in a BBC canteen with the

Rolling Stones who, believed *Merseybeat*, were 'a London group with the Liverpool sound'[76] – like Brian Poole and the Tremeloes maybe? Some recording managers, see, were sparing themselves a trip up north by getting outfits closer to London to steal a march on their Scouse counterparts by taking first grabs at the R & B motherlode; hence Brian and the Tremeloes' and, at Number Thirty, the Dave Clark Five's vanquishings of Faron's Flamingos' version of 'Do You Love Me'.

Bern Elliott and the Fenmen's stab at 'Do You Love Me' was rejected by Decca so that the Poole interpretation could have a clearer run. Nonetheless, by way of compensation, Bern and the Fenmen's 'Money' scrambled to Number Fourteen, partly because, Barrett Strong's original apart, it was the first. It was also the climax of the group's chart career.

A guitars-bass-drums quartet from Muswell Hill, the Kinks, attempted to catch the lightning with two Merseybeat-flavoured singles for Pye. As much of a shot-in-the-dark for Columbia was Brian Cassar – once the 'Cass' in Cass and the Casanovas – who actually moved from Liverpool to London where, as 'Casey Jones', he assembled a short-lived backing group, the Engineers, to promote the single, 'One Way Ticket', that had resulted from him scouse-talking his way into a one-shot deal.

As production exercises only, Joe Meek spiced a couple of other London-based units – including a Jimmy Lennon and the Atlantics – with Liverpudlia, but it was only when he did the same for the Dowlands that they had their only hit. While the Hampshire brothers' A-sides, 'Wishin' and Hopin' and 'Don't Make Me Over', would be overtaken by respective versions from the Merseybeats and the Swinging Blue Jeans, a disinclined 'All My Loving' (from *With the Beatles*) spent seven weeks in the Top 50 in early 1964 – and crushed a version by Liverpool's own Trends.

Striking while the iron was lukewarm too, other producers set up mobile recording equipment in hired Liverpool ballrooms to tape as many groups from the region as could be crammed onto a compilation LP with a title like *This Is Merseybeat, It's the Gear!* or the more generalized *Group Beat '63*. Others cheated by using London session players who probably bitched about the Beatles during tea breaks as they tossed out the likes of *The Mersey Sound* (with a vocalist who was a dead ringer for David Bowie) and the Embassy EP, *Liverpool Beat*.

All these cheapskate products ended up in the bargain bin, mostly because that was what they deserved, but also because, by spring 1964, there were perceptible signs that the Merseybeat ferryboat was grounding on a mudbank. Accordingly, having been stripped of nearly all its major talents, Liverpool was left to rot as, like pillaging Vikings of old, the contract-waving host moved on. . . .

11 ANGLO-BEATMINT (A REAL COOL CHEW)

... To Manchester where there were also groups with sheepdog fringes who could play 'Twist and Shout'. Again, EMI hooked the biggest fish in the Hollies and a radical departure from the formula in Freddie and the Dreamers, fronted by a kind of Norman Wisdom of pop, who figured that, 'We definitely succeeded on our visual appeal. We were on *Thank your Lucky Stars* and just did a routine to take the mickey out of the Shadows. Next week, the record went to Number Three. We reckoned it must have been the dance, kicking our legs forward – so for our next record, we did a routine kicking our legs back.'[77]

Manchester was later to relinquish Wayne Fontana and the Mindbenders, Herman's Hermits and non-starters like the Toggery Five whose recording career ended soon after it started with a death disc, 'I'm Gonna Jump'. On the outermost reaches of Greater Manchester, the Warriors in Accrington went the same way with the Beatle-esque 'You Came Along'. In Stockport, the Stowaways were all set for Hollies-sized fame just as the issue of 1964's *Sounds of a Swinging City*, an in-concert LP of local groups, was cancelled because the Manchester scene had 'finished' and, with the promptness of vultures, London talent scouts began pouncing arbitrarily on other northern regions.

A law of diminishing returns seemed to apply as each scout's successive sphere of operation yielded fewer and fewer rough diamonds to be processed for the charts. Knocking 'em dead in Newcastle were the Animals and the Gamblers, both of whom would make money for somebody: the former breathing down the necks of the Beatles and Rolling Stones by 1965, and the latter replacing the Tornados as Billy Fury's backing group. Yet Cheshire's Lancastrians (!) fizzled out after a fortnight in the Top 50 with twist-in-the-tale 'We'll Sing in the Sunshine', and Bolton's boss group, the Statesmen, were bypassed altogether.

What happened in Sheffield summarizes the frenzied search for a new Liverpool. Cumbersome BBC televison cameras were hauled into the Esquire in November 1963 for a pop documentary styled on *The Mersey Sound*. This had been provoked by Peter Stringfellow's City Hall showcases for local pop talent. London A & R people showed up but left disappointed: they wanted to sign the next Beatles, but they also wanted to keep their jobs. In January 1964, another tack was tried with a concert starring the Hollies plus a handful of city acts who'd ensure that claques of supporters would reinforce the tacit suggestion that, though the Hollies had scored a hat-trick of hit parade strikes by then, we Sheffield groups have everything it takes to do the same.

Wanting to believe them, EMI snatched Knives and Forks – whose Chris Stainton was to earn more by custom-building a PA system for Stringfellow than through co-writing the group's only 45, 1964's 'Being With You'. The Square Circles were left similarly short of cash after a fusion of Latin-American, comedy and Merseybeat on another ill-fated single, 'Coconut Woman'. Then there were Mickey's Monkeys, Ye Thimbleriggers, Small Paul and his Young Ones, the sober-suited Citizens, the Male Set and, theoretically top of the heap, the Staggerlees, voted 1964's 'Top Local Group' in *Top Stars Special*. Ironically, the only Sheffield beat group that did actually make it, Dave Berry and the Cruisers, got their break when scrutinized by freelance producer Mickie Most miles away at a Doncaster Baths booking in 1963 with Freddie and the Dreamers.

Freddie was then on the wings of his first hit, 'If You Gotta Make A Fool of Somebody.' He was fortunate in that there was only one rival attempt at this – by Buddy Britten and the Regents on Oriele – as there were many for 'Twist and Shout', 'Shout', 'Money', the Coasters' 'Poison Ivy' and other longtime rhythm-and-blues stage standards. The battle for 'Twist and Shout' ended in a draw between the self-possessed precision of Brian Poole and the Tremeloes, and the Beatles' frantic work-out, just one step from chaos; Lennon rupturing his throat with a surfeit of passion on what was only doggerel about an already outmoded dance (which the Dave Clark Five were to rewrite as 'No Time To Lose', and Kenny Lynch as 'Shake and Scream'). Morally, 'Shout' belonged to Birmingham's Redcaps' for a more exciting race through it than that of the better-known Lulu and the Luvvers from Glasgow.

The Paramounts' 'Poison Ivy' was challenged by EP versions from the Dave Clark Five and the Rolling Stones – as Bern Elliott's 'Money' was by the Searchers, Buddy Britten, the Beatles, the Undertakers, Kingsize Taylor and the Dominoes (as 'the Shakers'), the Rolling Stones and, on a flexi-disc free with *Jackie*, the Leroys. The Undertakers won a pyrrhic victory against the jazzier Voomins over the Drifters' tale of lovesick insanity, 'If You Don't Come Back', via a *Thank Your Lucky Stars* plug gained only after they'd mothballed their aptly macabre costumery and abbreviated their name to just the 'Takers. Though the Swinging Blue Jeans cornered 'The Hippy Hippy Shake', there was also a go on Pye by Pat Harris and her Blackjacks. The Sundowners' shot at Arthur Alexander's 'Shot of Rhythm and Blues' suffered too from a simultaneous cover by Johnny Kidd and the Pirates.

By mid-1963, the swing towards acephalous vocal-instrumental – or 'beat' – groups with overlapping repertoires was complete. Separate singles by Adam Faith's Roulettes and Billy Fury's Gamblers all featured vocals (with one Roulettes 45, 'The Long Cigarette', dogged by a BBC ban, not on health grounds but because it was seen as advertising). The Federals taped their first sung 45 – as did the Tornados who, after 'Telstar', had placed three more singles in the Top 10 before the exit of Heinz Burt and, with him, most of the group's teen appeal. Suddenly rendered old-fashioned, they soldiered on with a still-brimming workload whilst largely repeating earlier ideas in the studio.

In Solihull, the Jaguars with their Electronic Organist had dropped 'Telstar' and the rest of the instrumentals, added a singer and resurfaced as the Applejacks. By contrast, after the Stringbeats came second in the Devon heat of a National Band Competition, vocalist Mervyn Gratton quit the group who then 'decided to see how we fare without a separate vocalist, just doing group vocals.'[31] An alternative policy was that of Brighton's Mighty Atoms who pushed forward bass guitarist Stuart Hobday as lead singer.

Younger groups moulded themselves in the Merseybeat image from the onset. After Kevin Manning spent a school holiday in Liverpool, his path became clear after an evening at the Cavern. Back at his Hampshire comprehensive, he was going to form his own group. They'd call themselves the E-Types because it wouldn't be just him and backing musicians but a proper one like the Beatles.

The Olympic torch of Merseybeat had been carried to every nook and cranny of Britain, and you didn't have to look far for the principal blueprint. The Grasshoppers were 'Meridian's answer to the Beatles'[11] while Church Crookham had the Termites. Three Birmingham outfits called themselves the Brumbeats. There were also Beat Ltd., The Beatstalkers, The Counterbeats, The Beat-Chics, The Big Beats and so on. Hundreds of groups were 'pinching our arrangements,' griped John Lennon, 'and down to the last note at that.'[78] In an era when the Beatles could have topped the charts with 'Knees Up Mother Brown', youth club combos in the sticks wore collarless suits and *pilzen kopfs* that resembled spun dishmops whenever they shook their heads and went 'oooooo'. Instead of the Hank B. Marvin lookalike of yore, there'd be an unsmiling guitarist who, in imagination at least, played a black Rickenbacker through a Marshal amplifier, just like George Harrison.

According to Lennon, Gerry and the Pacemakers suffered 'terrible copying'[78] too. When Neville 'Noddy' Holder was in Wolverhampton's Memphis Cut-Outs in 1963, he performed Gerry's 'You'll Never Walk Alone' which he was to resuscitate as a showstopper with Slade. By 1964, there were a few combos that seemed to be modelling themselves on the Dave Clark Five: the Migil Five (who took over the Clark residency at the Tottenham Royal), Me and Them, Jimmy Nicol's Shub-Dubs (who depped for the Five after Dave went under with a stomach ulcer), the Saville Row Rhythm Unit (with a Paul Carrack rattling the traps), the Lynch Mob and Bob Vickers and the Debonaires – though, to be fair, Vickers had drummed with the group for at least three years.

From the north, the latter three acts were in the wrong place at the right time, because the record industry's focus had shifted to the Midlands – which, as *Midland Beat*'s widening catchment area indicated, sprawled into East Anglia, mid-Wales and as far south as Beaconsfield. There'd been signs of life since August 1963 when the Marauders lived up to the journal's 'pride of the Potteries'[79] citation by irritating the bottom of the Top 50 with their Decca 45, 'That's What I Want'. The Cheetahs from Erdington would bring off this feat later with 'Mecca' and a faintly ludicrous 'Soldier Boy' from the respective catalogues of Gene Pitney and the Shirelles.

The Four Aces were 'Hereford's Beatles', while the likes of the Farinas and the Broodly Hoo were the top groups in Leicester. The Fourbeats were still going strong in Oxford with a debut EP on Alpha Records. Winners of a 'Midland Search For Tomorrow's Stars', Ken Jackson and his Strangers, hailed from olde worlde Henley-in-Arden – while Pinkerton's (Assorted) Colours brought greater honour to Rugby when their 'Mirror Mirror', shimmering with electric autoharp, got a look in at Number Nine. Trentside Beat would be represented by Tony D and the Shakeouts, Jet Wayne and his Cavaliers, and, still in the running, the Jaybirds whose high-speed guitarist Alvin Dean was 'considered by many the best in the Midlands.'[80]

Over in Solihull, the Applejacks had graduated to a Monday night residency in the civic hall and bookings a year into the future elsewhere. Because three members were still at school, the group rejected a lucrative offer by a London impressario who also happened to be related to the civic centre's manager. This made national newspapers and got the Applejacks a spot on *Midlands at Six* and a subsequent signing to Decca. The Rinki-Dinks too were visualized as harbingers of a 'Solihull Sound', especially after the Applejacks ventured into the Top 10 with 'Tell Me When', a disc debut distinguished by doorbell-toned organ riffing.

In Coventry, groups who cracked the Top 50 could be counted on the fingers of one offensive gesture. The most successful was the Sorrows with 1965's atmospheric 'Take a Heart'. Lady Godiva's city also held Formula One, the Peeps, the Sabres, the Sovereigns and Peter's Faces, of whose 'Why Did You Bring Him to the Dance' no less an authority than Roy Orbison said, 'I don't know who Peter is – or his Faces – but they sure sound good to me.'[81] Despite its vocal ebullience and beefy horn scoring, 1964's rocked-up 'Acupulco 22' from another local outfit, Johnny B. Great and the Quotations, missed, possibly because the tune had been preempted two years earlier by Kenny Ball's trad jazz version. Nonetheless, Johnny and the lads were as unfailing a backing band on scream circuit tours as Sounds Incorporated and the Terry Young Six.

Midway between Liverpool and London, Birmingham was high on a grasping A & R man's hit list – especially after the *TV Times* predicted that it was the most likely source of the next Titans of Teen; an opinion formed when the Moody Blues' 'Go Now' got to Number One in January 1965. Sounder argument for this judgement was more deeply rooted. In 1962, the Beatles had taken part in a 'Battle of the Bands' promotion with Gerry Levene and the Avengers, a quintet of comparable popularity in Birmingham. In March that same year, Decca released what came to be regarded as the first 'Brumbeat' record, 'Sugar Babe' by Jimmy Powell (though his backing Five Dimensions in 1963 were actually Londoners just as Billy J. Kramer's Dakotas were Mancunians). Decca also put together a *Brumbeat* compilation LP *à la Sounds of a Swinging City*.

The main feature of the first *Midland Beat* had been an interview with John Lennon, 'of The Beatles, but otherwise the entire content is restricted to Midland items. Liverpool started the ball rolling. Now the Midlands is ready to take over!'[11] Uneasily tracing the Merseybeat scent, a slang compendium of Brum's riposte to Scouse was made up by a bored publicist.[82] This informed users that 'weird' meant 'strange', and 'face it' 'to examine the facts and accept them'. More peculiar was 'fluid chariot' for 'a car with a full engine' and 'blow your jets' for 'to get mad, upset'. How many of these tortuous expressions ever reached the lips of any Brummie – or anyone at all, I wonder?

December's *Midland Beat* editorial blew its jets, crying, 'Why has the Brum Beat failed to gain a place in the Top Twenty!?'[79] Perhaps it was because editor Dennis Detheridge had overestimated its cohesion and depth. His was an easy mistake. After all, most of its groups were less than a year old. Bloxwich, for instance, was ruled by 'the Midlands' youngest group', the Jaguars.

For all its laudable aims, *Midland Beat* was not, perhaps, the barometer of taste it imagined itself to be. Its poll in 1964 to find the region's most popular group showed the Talismen from Cheltenham on top. Not canvassing so hard, more likely aspirants the Rockin' Berries – who, despite carrying a throbbing sob-story, 'He's in Town' to Number Three months before 'Go Now' – made Number Eight. Swallowing dust way behind were Carl Wayne and the Vikings and other leading palais draws. The chart-riding Applejacks didn't rate at all. Next year's nine-day-wonders would be the Moonrakers who, by fair means or foul, presided over a tabulation that slotted the Moody Blues and Spencer Davis Group – both with records in the national Top 50 – between ten and twenty.

The apogee of the first flush of Brumbeat came when both the Rockin' Berries and the Moody Blues appeared on the same edition of *Ready Steady Go*. Nineteen-sixty-five was also a big year for one of at least three groups from the area called the Fortunes. As the Cliftons, a vocal trio, they'd been a sort of white Birmingham Chants until they broadened their scope by investing in electric guitars and adding a rhythm section. Renamed, they were complimented on their neat, besuited turnout after they gained the day at a beat contest at Edgbaston's Gay Tower Ballroom. After pirate Radio Caroline had adopted the Fortunes' second 45 as its theme tune in 1964, it was merely a matter of fifteen months before a hat-trick of Top 20 entries began with 'You've Got Your Troubles'.

The Fortunes were as dissimilar to the Moody Blues as the Moody Blues were to the Rockin' Berries. At a time when pop entertainers were only as good as their last single, each of them, without exception, faded within a year, though the Moody Blues and the Fortunes were to be granted a second bite of the Top 20 cherry later. Almost all that the three had in common was that they were groups from the same city – a city with room for the musical extremities of popped-up country-and-western from Dave Lacey's Corvettes and Steve Brett and the Mavericks, to the Second City Sound's mangling of Tchaikovsky's First Piano Concerto – which, following their slot on *Opportunity Knocks* in 1966, made Number Twenty-two. Not blessed with even modest hits but adored locally, Mike Sheridan and the Nightriders had an unusual stylistic determination that embraced Californian surf music as few other beat groups – notably Tony Rivers and the Castaways, and the Bystanders – then did.

There had been inevitable differences between all the pre-eminent Liverpool outfits too, but these were all variations within prescribed limits: Billy J. Kramer was the ballad merchant; the Swinging Blue Jeans wore denim; the Beatles combed their hair across their foreheads; the Merseybeats looked like gigolos; the Fourmost were the comedians; Gerry and the Pacemakers substituted electric piano for lead guitar.

Mike Pinder hammered the eighty-eights too but, to many watching his Moody Blues miming 'Go Now' on television, the group seemed lopsided, what with Denny Laine monopolizing the lead vocal and guitar spotlight, while general factotum Ray Thomas merely wailed 'waaaaaah' into a shared microphone and rattled a tambourine – as did Clive Lea on 'He's In Town', taking an atypical back seat to rhythm guitarist Geoff Turton's more suitable tenor. At a time when fans needed to identify clearly with a group before committing themselves, the Fortunes were on a losing wicket too, smothered by orchestration.

After 'Go Now' fell from the Top 40, no matter how much poetic licence Dennis Detheridge could wring from, say, an encore by Andy's Clappers at Bilston Town Hall, the naked truth was that, though the beat boom was an unstoppable as the Black Death, it had mushroomed in most regions – even in Liverpool – *after* rather than *with* Merseybeat. Back from Germany in November 1963, Ray Thomas, still a Krew Cat, had been astonished to discover Birmingham 'in total chaos. There were about two hundred and fifty groups, half thought they were Cliff Richard and the Shadows and the other half thought they were the Beatles.'[38] This was why, after Manchester had been picked clean, Birmingham, like every-where else, gave scavenging recording managers precious few enduring hitmakers from amongst its competent but generally derivative groups.

Issuing from a landlocked conurbation twice the size of Liverpool, Midlands pop was also short on regional individuality. The Rockin' Berries on their first two singles, 'Wah Wah Woo' and 'Itty Bitty Pieces' could be mistaken for Freddie and the Dreamers as 'Tell Me When' for Gerry and the Pacemakers.

If inclined to exhibit a certain insular superiority towards its Black Country neighbours, Worcestershire's pot-shots at the national charts were less impressive. The Cherokees had their fifteen minutes when their trudging 'Seven Daffodils' at Number Thirty-three nearly outpaced an almost identical version by the better-known Mojos. However, the Sundowners, from Malvern, did a reading of 'House of the Rising Sun' – the old skiffle stand-by – which was totally eclipsed by Mickie Most's chart-topping melodrama with the Animals.

B.P. Finch was the county's Bill Harry. As such, he found much to report in his *Worcester Whisperings*. At Malvern's Rock Group Contest in January 1964, for instance, the Seminoles brushed aside all opposition, but it was the Hellions who topped the bill at the town's Beat Week two months later. Though an unprepossessing bunch, they were, estimated B.P., 'Quietly becoming a most important force on the local beat scene more by personal recommendation than force of personality.'[83]

The Hellions had had to break into London clubland to obtain a record deal in late 1964 after A & R outriders had been instructed to fan out beyond the northern and midland regions of England. In Glasgow, they checked out clubs like the Picasso where Dean Ford and the Gaylords and the mordant Poets shared the limelight with the Alex Harvey Soul Band – led by an ex-'Tommy Steele of Scotland' – the Golden Crusaders, the Prowlers, the Chris McClure Section and other performers with strong reputations within Strathclyde. Of the two newer acts to appear there, acclaim was more immediate for the Poets with their one hit, the extraordinary 'Now We're Thru'', but Ford and the Gaylords were destined in time to soar much higher. They began humbly enough with a Butlin's season in Ayr, but were so hungry to succeed that they undertook terrible journeys to loss-making bookings in London pubs. The outcome was a toehold on the ballroom circuit of England where they often shared bills with Brian Poole and the Tremeloes, whose manager Peter Walsh took them on too.

While Dean and the Gaylords' battered van was rattling south, Horsham's Beat Merchants vanished as mysteriously as they had appeared on *Thank Your Lucky Stars*, miming frenziedly to 'Pretty Face'. In the Medway towns, only Bern Elliott and his Fenmen brought the area such prestige during this maiden flush of British Beat's Golden Age. True there was Erkey Grant and the Tonettes who opened the show on a Beatles tour as well as Terry Lee and the Checkers, toast of Orpington, but neither had been to Hamburg and knew the Beatles. After 'Money' left the Top 20, Elliott and his group almost returned with a try at Gary US Bonds' 'New Orleans'. Then came respectable sales for an EP of Star-Club show-stoppers, plugged on *Ready Steady Go*, and, quite a compliment for southern boys, a couple of tracks on an *At the Cavern* LP.

Beyond the opposite bank of the Thames, you could sample 'Hertsbeat' from Unit 4, now '+2' (a bass player and drummer), the Roulettes and especially the minor-key Zombies after their victory (with 'Summertime' as the clincher) in a contest sponsored by London's *Evening Post*. With a 'scholarly' gimmick of fifty GCE 'O'-level passes between them, the St Alban's teenagers also gained a Decca contract, and a London manager who dealt with another local lad, Cliff Richard.

Surprisingly, the Zombies' assigned producer, Ken Jones, was so charmed by 'She's Not There', an eleventh-hour creation by Rod Argent, that plans to release 'Summertime' as the debut 45 were scrapped. The week that 'She's Not There' penetrated the Top 20, the Zombies took the plunge and went professional – though they, the Nashville Teens, the Moody Blues and others were to discover that Decca, having saturated itself with beat groups, tended to be excessively thrifty over all but its most consistently best-selling artists.

Yet, having rejected the Beatles, a chastened and cynical Dick Rowe had had the foresight to sign the Rolling Stones in May 1963. The Big Three, Dave Berry and the Cruisers, the Nashville Teens, John Mayall's Bluesbreakers, Twinkle, Them, Tom Jones, Unit 4 + 2, the Moody Blues, the Applejacks and the Zombies were among further acquisitions, but for each chartbuster, there was a Beat Six, a Pete MacLaine and the Clan, a Fairies, a Gerry Levene and the Avengers, a Warriors, a Bobby Cristo and the Rebels, a Rockin' Vickers, a Mark Four, a Dawnbreakers, a Gonks, a Falling Leaves, a Wishful Thinking . . .

Once the Emeralds, the Wishful Thinking, if hitless, lasted until well into the 1970s. Another Decca act, Middlesex's Bo Street Runners had won ITV's *Ready Steady Win* beat group contest in 1964 (the Falling Leaves were runners-up) with 'Bo Street Runner' – about trying to park a car – which, apart from not being a hit, was not unlike Manfred Mann's similarly self-referential '54321'.

Nothing to do with either the Runners, Manfred Mann or Bradford's Quiet Three, the Quiet Five had backed Bournemoth singer Patrick Dane before bass guitarist Richard Barnes assumed lead vocals that were encased in smooth harmonies reminiscent of the Searchers and Unit 4 + 2. Between them, the Five's 'When the Morning Sun Dries the Dew' and its follow-up (a cover of US songwriter Paul Simon's 'Homeward Bound') spent three weeks in the Top 50.

Further along the coast in Paignton, the defiantly short-back-and-sides Rustiks came first in a Westward Television beat contest and gained the services of Brian Epstein. They made much of their cleanliness and decency – so different from certain other outfits they could mention – on their only *Ready Steady Go* appearance.

A *Ready Steady Go* in late 1964 was the first Britain at large saw of Dave Dee, Dozy, Beaky, Mick and Tich, whose first single, 'No Time' went straight in at Number Five – Number Five in the *Salisbury Journal*'s chart, that is, with advance orders of seventy-five at Messrs. J.F. Sutton in the high street. This compared well with one hundred for the Beatles' 'I Feel Fine'. An interview with Dave Dee on *Day By Day* a fortnight later guaranteed a rise to the very top. The Stringbeats had become big fish in the West Country pond too. 'They certainly get around,' gasped *South-West Scene*, 'One night they played the Drill Hall, Heavitree [Exeter]; the next at the Regal Ballroom, Minehead!'[31]

Continuing what has become a geographically illogical round-up of the south's bastions of beat, we arrive back in Oxford where the Troggs triumphed in a Battle of the Bands tournament. As a prize, the organizers paid the cost of the group's petrol money back to their home town of Andover. Cash from the Troggs' own pockets took them and a primitively exuberant three-song demo to the Denmark Street office of Larry Page, no longer the Teenage Rage but one of London's most supplicated pop entrepreneurs. Rubbing his chin, he decided to keep the Troggs on ice for nearly two years before unleasing them in 1966 as the unthinking man's pop group. Initially, Page secured a one-shot CBS single, 'Lost Girl'. He'd also given singer Reg Ball and drummer Ronnie Bullis the respective stage surnames of 'Presley' and 'Bond' during the campaign that put the group's second 45, 'Wild Thing', at Number Two in the UK. Under the same lease deal with Fontana, the follow-up, 'With A Girl Like You', would go one better.

The Troggs were brand-leaders of the non-existent 'Andover Sound' as Page snared the Loot, the Nerve and other local combos. After all, each area within these islands was now supposed to have a 'Sound' or a 'Beat', wasn't it? The Tewkesbury Sound was propagated by the Severnbeats (formerly the Vampires) as 'Blarney Beat' was by Penny and the Skyrockets, another Four Aces and Dublin's Green Beats, once hired to back Dusty Springfield. The Wheels stepped closer to the heat too with a long season in Blackpool that prompted a newspaper headline in their native Belfast to cry 'They're Ours and We Want Them Back!'

The Celtic ray also shone on Roy Denver and the Commancheros who reached the semi-finals of an Embassy beat contest. Nevertheless, local Swansea rivals, the Jets, were 'screamed' into first place. Also from the Gower peninsula, the Bystanders, after a lot of messing about and the involvement of Joe Meek, had their first national release, 'Girl You're Gonna Hurt Yourself'. Packing out South Wales clubs too were Lot 13, Tommy Scott and the Senators, the Human Beans and outfits that would metamorphose into Amen Corner and Love Sculpture.

Virtually every settlement in Britain put forward some local oiks who enjoyed a qualified fame – fame as qualified as that of Bristol's Force West with their huge hits. What the . . .? I'll do that bit again. Fame as qualified as that of Bristol's Force West with their placings in pirate Radio London's chart, based not on sales but disc-jockeys' choice.

Many such acts had been sounded out in the semi-darkness of venues like Redhill Market Hall's bi-weekly Teenbeat Rock Club – which featured records and 'live' groups – profits from which were ploughed back into bigger events like the 'Fab Big Beat Ball' on 10 October 1963 with the Hunters, Blues Syndicate, Sundowners and Confederates.

Some clubs had been hastily renamed – the Manchester Cavern, Brum

Beat Cavern, the Kavern, the Dungeon and so on – and lent an authentic sheen by dim lighting, arched ceilings and a Liverpool group at their inaugurations. More pubs began offering beat evenings and rehearsal facilities in function rooms that assumed a separate life from the main building. Local groups also claimed a stronger right to play for church youth organizations who, accepting that God would not cast out this Beatle pestilence as He had skiffle, had embraced regular beat sessions. I went to one such function in Farnham where the set was interrupted by a 'spontaneous' on-mike dialogue between the swingin' vicar – who had little idea how teenagers really talked – and the group's born-again drummer. They chatted about sin. His Reverence seemed to be against it.

This sort of engagement was a necessary evil in a quest for any exposure that might attract a big-shot prowling the provinces. Beat groups vied for the attention not of Larry Parnes – who had moved from pop to the theatre – but newer operators such as Page, Epstein, Mickie Most, Andrew Oldham, and Ken Howard and Alan Blaikley. Many of these had a more pronounced stake in musical output than those of the old school. Howard and Blaikley were a songwriting team while Aldershot-born Most, after resigning as South Africa's Elvis, had returned to England to front Mickie Most and the Gear, but proved unable to work that Transvaal magic on home ground. After a flop with 'Money Honey' in 1963, he put knowledge acquired at the console to better effect the following year as producer of smashes by the Animals, Nashville Teens, Lulu and her Luvvers, and Herman's Hermits. Dave Berry and the Cruisers, however, had slipped through his fingers because Decca had considered his plans for them unviable – so it had been A & R lieutenant Mike Smith who'd taken charge of the group in the label's West Hampstead studio.

On the payroll too, ex-Shadow Tony Meehan cajoled Decca into sign the Emeralds as potential harbingers of a 'Farnborough Sound'. Earlier in 1965, Kenneth – later Jonathan – King, a Cambridge undergraduate, had brought the company a production of his own composition, 'Gotta Tell' by Terry Ward and the Bumblies, but Decca elected to put more promotional muscle behind King's own latent pop star inclinations, getting him a hit with 'Everyone's Gone to the Moon'.

Many a middle-aged man lured by the financial possibilities inherent in the beat boom felt like he'd gone to the moon too as he merged into the shadows of teenage clubs in the same puzzled, timorous position as his late 1970s counterpart would be when looking for a New Sex Pistols. Torn between the sordid thrill of being out-of-bounds and a desire to flee the enveloping fug and prickly heat, never to go there again, he'd be studied by gaggles of girls as were all male newcomers. Assessing that he was a bit mature, they'd resume their jabber until four louts with Beatle haircuts sauntered onto the boards. Hitting all their instruments at once with a staccato 'Right!' the group would barge into an onslaught of pulsating bass, dranging guitars, crashing drums and ranted vocals. What would strike the adult intruder first would be the volume that precluded conversation and the ragged dissimilarity to any other pop presentation he'd ever seen. Cliff and the Shadows indulged in a little scripted playfulness, yes, but this lot were downright uncouth in the way they addressed the crowd. They said things like 'fuck' and burped into the microphone.

After the initial shock, he'd tune in to the situation's epic vulgarity and he'd ponder. The next day, he'd be drawn back to another sweatbath, and struggle through the crowd to suggest a formal meeting. The group might pretend to be nonchalantly indifferent to his overtures but would be willing to do anything to get away from the treadmill of local engagements. As Larry Parnes and Brian Epstein would have advised him, his first task was to make the group altogether smoother pop 'entertainers'. They had to be compelled to wear stylish but not too way-out uniform suits. Playing to a fixed programme, punctuality and back projection was all-important. Stage patter must not include swearing. The oldest member might have to lose up to five years from his age when annotating his life history for the press kit.

If he didn't lose heart, the new manager might bamboozle them a record deal. Before it died its death, the first single might crackle from the crowded late night wavelengths of Luxembourg and the new pirate stations (suffocating under bedclothes was the condition under which I first heard 'You Really Got Me' on my transistor). Some more radio plugs throughout the next month might net a *Saturday Club* session and possibly opening a *Thank Your Lucky Stars*. The 45 may then inch up to a tantalizing high somewhere between fifty and thirty in the charts. This would be either a vantage point for further advancement or a zenith signalling a drift back to obscurity.

It was like a lottery – because, as Shane Fenton would admit, 'some got the breaks and some didn't, but none of us could sing'[73] – not 'real singing' as sonorous as that of Roy Orbison or Elvis when he did hymns. Some singers could have been faceless anybodies. Among the few exceptions were Cliff Bennett and Zombie Colin Blunstone; Ray Phillips of the Nashville Teens, who'd won frauleins' hearts at the Star-Club with his note-for-note copies of Orbison's 'Cryin'' and 'In Dreams'; Geoff Turton singing 'He's In Town' almost entirely in pleading falsetto. All were all deprived of the acclaim they deserved because they belonged to outfits that lacked 'image'.

Another tremendous *chanteur* was Tom Jones, formerly Tommy Scott – 'the Twisting Vocalist from Pontypridd', who was blessed with a most professional demeanor, flexible vocal command, a liking for big-voiced ballads and a certain steady consistency – 'squareness' some might say – that wasn't effeminate or subversive like some of these other beat group front men. As a solo singer in a group age, the same could be said of Peter Lee Stirling – an embryonic Steve McQueen run to fat – who, unlike Tom, couldn't find a niche, despite commercial records such as 'Sad Lonely and Blue' which he performed on *Thank Your Lucky Stars*.

A Caruso-loving fly might well have blocked its ears during many a recording date, but inability to pitch far beyond a central octave was not always a disadvantage to certain 1960s vocalists who warped an intrinsically limited range to their own devices. With his Long John Silver burr, Reg Presley of the Troggs was in this oligarchy as were androgenous-sounding Adam Faith, wobbly Ray Davies of the Kinks, asthmatic Yardbird Keith Relf – and numb James Tamplin. Whatever became of him after a most memorable *Ready Steady Go* appearance miming to his 1965 single, 'Is There Time'?

Tamplin's vocal shortcomings were outweighed by a charisma that still wasn't sufficient to sell many records. However, Dave Berry's combination of a laconic delivery and fascinating stage presence ensured that loyal *Top Stars Special* readers voted his first Top 10 entry, 'The Crying Game', as 'Best Disc of 1964', tailor-made as it was for Dave's now fully-fledged antithesis of the usual hectic cavorting. A vague and surreal slant on Gene Vincent's crippled melodrama, it would begin on a stage lit only by tiny amplifier bulbs and a searchlight veering fitfully before homing in on the yet-unseen singer's digits curling round a flat in the wings. Clothed in black, the man variously described as 'Mr Slocomotion', 'The Human Sloth' and – by Ken Dodd – 'England's own Herman Munster', makes his Grand Entrance over the Cruisers' introduction to the first number.

With the deliberation and slow motion of a dream, and toying with a lead a full thirty feet long, he reaches the microphone stand by the last chord. He might then glower furtively behind an upturned leather collar, indulge in abstract hand ballets and, over an entire instrumental interlude, slide a pedantic handmike over a shoulder to the small of his back. What was also unusual among mid-1960 groups was the supplementing of the Cruisers' road crew with a lighting engineer whose task was to synchronize the peculiarities of each auditorium's *son et lumiere* to Dave's predetermined twisting and turning. It might have been sinister without the merriment in the eyes of one responsible for perhaps the most original stage concept of the era.

November 1959: Durrington Youth Hall thrills to the sound of the Boppers: (left to right) Phil Ball (note the Mohican haircut), Roy Jarvis (with one of the first stand-up electric basses in the country), David 'Dave Dee' Harman and Bernard Bevis. *(Ron Cooper)*

The late Johnny Kidd swashbuckles with the Pirates. *(Jackie Ryan)*

During his tour in 1960 with Eddie Cochran, Gene Vincent (far right) holds court at Sheffield Gaumont to Dave Berry (centre) and three Cruisers: (left to right) Frank Miles (lead guitar), John Fleet (bass) and Alan Taylor (rhythm guitar). *(Dave Berry)*

Inset Backstage at the Sheffield Gaumont in1960, a
teenage Dave Berry (centre) and three Cruisers: (left to
right) Brian Gee (drums), John Fleet (bass) and Alan
Taylor (guitar) pose with the visiting Cliff Richard.
Like role model Elvis, Cliff was to become an
altogether smoother pop 'entertainer'. *(Dave Berry)*

'King of Skiffle' Lonnie Donegan, a more likely British 'answer' to Elvis in his vivacious processing of
North American folk music for a UK audience. Many 1960's stars began in groups formed in the Donegan
image.

At Camberley's Agincourt in 1961, (left to right) impresario Bob Potter poses with Bert Weedon and local pop stars Cal Danger and Kerry Rapid – whose shared backing group contained Jeff Beck. *(Alan Hope)*

Rolf Harris (second from right) jams with The Tornadoes – (left to right) Alan Caddy (guitar), Clem Cattini (drums), Roger Lavern (keyboards), George Bellamy (guitar) and Heinz Burt (bass) – at the Windmill Theatre, Great Yarmouth in summer 1963. *(John Repsch)*

Geronimo and the Apaches: (second left to right) Pete Breslin (drums), Barry Allmark (vocals) and Kevin Bewley (bass) with Calamity Jane (Don Craine, far left). *Circa 1961-2,* they functioned simultaneously as the Downliners Sect. *(Don Craine)*

The Federals relax behind the curtain at the Wallington Public Hall. *(Jackie Ryan)*

Below Bruisers' guitarist Peter Lee Stirling and Tommy Bruce goof around backstage. *(Jackie Ryan)*

The camera catches Shane Fenton in a hot situation with one of his admirers. *(Jackie Ryan)*

The Outlaws – with guitarist Ritchie Blackmore (far right), later a founder member of Deep Purple – between soundcheck and showtime. *(Jackie Ryan)*

Shane and the Shane Gang ghast it up at Guildford Plaza. *(Jackie Ryan)*

The Downliners Sect – Kevin Bewley, Barry Allmark, Don Craine (Michael O'Donnell), Pete Maggs and Pete Breslin – hear the call of nature beside the Thames at Richmond, 1962. *(Don Craine)*

The Nashville Teens – (left to right) Ray Phillips, Art Sharp, John Allen, Barry Jenkins and Pete Shannon (pianist John Hawken is obscured) – fresh from Germany where they left behind Terry Crowe, a third lead singer. *(Jackie Ryan)*

On his first visit to Britain, Del Shannon (centre) was backed by the Eagles, who released a remarkable version of the Cornish Floral Dance in 1963. *(Jackie Ryan)*

Cliff Bennett and the Rebel Rousers – (left to right) Sid Phillips, Moss Groves, drummer Mick Burt (obscured), Cliff, Frank Allen and Dave Wendells – star at Hamburg's Star-Club in 1963. *(Frank Allen)*

Billy J. Kramer and the Dakotas
slay 'em down south, June 1963.
(Jackie Ryan)

Cliff Bennett and Rebel Rouser (and
future Searcher) Frank Allen in action.
(Frank Allen)

Right Gerry Marsden in ebullient form
with his Pacemakers at Botwell Pop
Festival, June 1963. *(Jackie Ryan)*

The lucky winners of a competition run by *Midland Beat* meet the Beatles at Wolverhampton Gaumont, 19 November 1963. *(Jim Simpson/ Big Bear Music Group)*

Black Merseyside vocal group, the Chants with their backing outfit, the Harlems. The Chants would re-surface as the mid-1970's chartbusters, the Real Thing. *(Jackie Ryan)*

Meet the Searchers: (left to right) Mike Pender (guitar), John McNally (guitar), Tony Jackson (bass), fan, Chris Curtis (drums) and fan, 13 August 1963. *(Jackie Ryan)*

The Swinging Blue Jeans – Ray Ennis (guitar), Les Braid (bass), Norman Kuhlke (drums) and Ralph Ellis (guitar) – exchange persecution complexes with a couple of interested parties. *(Jackie Ryan)*

The Undertakers and music lovers in affectionate mood. *(Jackie Ryan)*

Bill Hatton of the Fourmost feels the first symptoms of writer's cramp. *(Jackie Ryan)*

The future editor of *Trogg Times* socializes with Wayne Fontana (finger in mouth) and his Mindbenders – (left to right) Bob Land, Ric Rothwell and Eric Stewart. *(Jackie Ryan)*

The Merseybeats: (left to right) Aaron Williams (guitar), Tony Crane (guitar), Billy Kinsley (bass) and John Banks (drums). *(Tony Crane/Billy Kinsley)*

Left The 'L. Ransford' songwriting team – (left to right) Graham Nash, Allan Clarke and Tony Hicks – front the Hollies at Weymouth Gaumont, 1 August 1964. *(Jackie Ryan)*

Above Paul Jones, Manfred Mann's singer and mouth-organist, gives it some showbiz. *(Jackie Ryan)*

March 1964: the Trekkers – (left to right) Pete Sanderson, Charlie Sharpe, John Bloomfield and David Priestley – at Stowe School theatre. The Beatles played this venue one month later. With Twinkle as featured singer, the Trekkers were resident at London's Esmeralda's Barn (part owned by the Krays). *(John Bloomfield)*

Far right
Like Lennon and
McCartney, Stu
James (Stuart Slater)
of the Mojos had
the confidence to
submit his compo-
sitions to other
artists, notably
Faron's Flamingos.
(Jackie Ryan)

Tony Crane prepares
to meet his public.
(Jackie Ryan)

With Brumbeat forecast as the next big 'sound', Freddie (centre) and two Dreamers, drummer Bernie Dwyer (left) and guitarist Roy Crewsdon, peruse some instructive literature. *(Jim Simpson/Big Bear Music Group)*

Gary Kane and the Tornadoes, one of the West Country's leading groups, midway between quiffs and moptops. With only one personnel change in thirty-five years, they were still operational in 1994.

Finale of Birmingham Town Hall R & B concert on 28 January 1964 with (left to right) Keith Relf (tambourine), Chris Dreja (guitar), drummer Jim McCarty (obscured), Paul Samwell-Smith (bass), Art Themen (saxophone), Eric 'Slowhand' Clapton (guitar) and, at the microphones, Long John Baldry, Sonny Boy Williamson and Spencer Davis. *(Jim Simpson/Big Bear Music Group)*

Dave Clark in Guildford during the Five's only UK tour. *(Jackie Ryan)*

July 1964: awaiting his destiny as a civil servant, Chris Curtis stands up to be counted between John McNally and Mike Pender (Michael Pendergast). *(Jackie Ryan)*

Between 1969 and 1971, Procol Harum was essentially a regrouping of the Paramounts, (left to right) Chris Copping (bass), Gary Brooker (vocals, keyboards), Robin Trower (guitar) and B. J. Wilson (drums). *(Jackie Ryan)*

Dave Davies, the youngest Kink, takes a lead vocal at Redhill Town Hall. *(Jackie Ryan)*

Pictured with Eric Clapton (left) and Jim McCarty (obscured), Mick O'Neill of the Authentics at the central microphone with the Yardbirds when the group's usual singer, Keith Relf, was laid low with a collapsed lung in late 1964. *(Jackie Ryan)*

Keith Richards and bouncer, 1964. *(Jackie Ryan)*

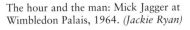

Allan Clarke and wife Jenny relax at the seaside during the Hollies' national tour with Shane Fenton and the Fentones in 1964. *(Jackie Ryan)*

The hour and the man: Mick Jagger at Wimbledon Palais, 1964. *(Jackie Ryan)*

Dave is but one artist who will be forever associated with British pop's most buoyant period. Until 1967, beat groups continued to beg for bookings in church halls, scout huts, youth clubs and pubs. Even riverboats offered beat sessions, and, after tussles with municipal park committees, open air events featuring up to thirty groups catered for pop too. I first saw Kevin Manning's E-Types on an open day at his school one afternoon in 1965. Until then, I'd only known him as a Beatle-fringed, barrel-shaped patrol leader in the scout troop and, of course, I had no idea then how many groups there were in my town – Fleet, Hampshire – alone. Even our next-door neighbours' quiet elder son, Chris Wilkinson, turned out to be rhythm guitarist in a band that had named itself the Rotations in order to be allowed to play on the Rotary Club float on Guy Fawkes' Night.

Waiting at a bus stop near Aldershot swimming pool, I heard another outfit in a garage opposite running through what sounded like one of its own songs. At any rate, it was bad. It was round that time that I formed my first group, Ace and the Crescents. After mastering one number, 'Pretty Face' by the Beat Merchants, we disbanded when the guitarist's mother denied us the use of his bedroom for rehearsals because she heard a Crescent swear.

Then came a fourth-form outfit that dare not speak its name. We only knew three numbers: 'Reelin' and Rockin'', 'Money' and 'For Your Love'. We broke up after a row. So far, I hadn't made a solitary public appearance with a group – and I wasn't to do so until 1969 at Hartley Wintney Kiln Hall – and even then we were booed off within ten minutes.

When they grew older, certain musicians of lost and long-disbanded outfits like mine began to believe that they had once Hit the Big Time, and it gave them deep and lasting pleasure to go around saying so. This is a silly analogy, but you could reason that Ace and the Crescents were as much the embodiment of the beat boom as the Beatles. All units merged together as one, all-powerful and immortal. With a certain logical blindness and readjustment of fact, I too could brag to my two sons of being in a 'legendary' 1960s beat group.

It might not have been that profitable if I had been – because skinflint promoters had smelt the money to be made from all these young bands happy just to have somewhere to make their noise for the many daft enough to pay to hear them. The average turnover per week for a semi-professional beat musician in the provinces was a couple of quid. Of sixty-six pounds net takings one midsummer evening at St Mark's Rooms in North Camp, only eighteen were split between four groups.

It was a boom time all right, but you had to be truly committed to go the distance. Back from school or work, you'd dive into a bath. Afterwards, with your sister's drier, you'd restyle your hair from the combed-back flatness required to avoid persecution in daytime surroundings where even Elvis was not yet a yardstick of masculinity. Bolting down a meal, you'd wait for an overloaded van one hour later to transport you to some musty hall where, through latticed windows dim with grime, you and the others would be perceived setting up little amplifiers to power voices – many yet to spit out the plums – and never-never guitars. Unaided by microphones, the drummer would position his kit which had the group name painted on the big front skin.

Unless you'd already done so, now was the time to change into stage suits in whatever alcove had been set aside for this – kitchen, toilet, store cupboard, maybe a dressing room. There'd be rare cranks like the Rolling Stones, who all dressed differently, but few did not adhere to prevalent fashion several steps behind Carnaby Street. This esplanade of outfitters off Oxford Circus was soon to dictate a male 'Mod' conformity, based loosely on Cuban-heeled 'Beatle boots', high-buttoned jackets with narrow lapels or none at all, thigh-hugging hipsters in Billy Bunter check and either roll-necked pullover or shirt with button-down collar and tie. The latter, being the cheapest, was the most variable, ranging from knitted plain to op-art slim-jim and, later, to eye-torturing kipper. Heads might be covered with a denim cap like the one John Lennon had been wearing lately in emulation of Bob Dylan.

Before barbers' mirrors, the hipper wielders of the scissors sculpted *pilzen kopfs* from the most stubborn quiff or Bobby blow-wave. As it neared completion, the customer's eyes would widen and jaws cease chewing their Anglo-Beatmint (a Real Cool Chew). If such a style was forbidden by parent or employer, the most determined could troop down to Woolworth's where moptop wigs were on sale along with Sayer's guitar-shaped cakes – 'the Cake for SWINGING Parties!'

There was also merchandise related directly to particular acts. The bigger chain stores were stocking Beatle wallpaper, 'Fab Four' powder compacts and twenty-two carat 'Beetle' bracelets while a pattern derived from the Beatles' collarless jackets was obtainable via an order form in *Fabulous* or *Rave!* for 'the Liverpool Look for you to knit for the man in your life' as a cardigan. Learning that the manufacturers of NEMS-sanctioned Beatle boots could barely cope with demand, an enterprising Sussex firm marketed 'Ringo the new Beat Boot' which also boasted elastic gussets in the sides and rounded toes. Less prosperously opportunist were the makers of shirts designed by Dave Clark, and Applejack red smocks.

Mark Wynter patterned braces, anyone? When confronted with the rearing monster of these upstart beat groups, the old guard attempted to protect their hit parade careers by paying heed. In August 1962, Shane

Fenton had headlined over the Beatles at the Cavern. Not quite a year later, he was supporting them at a *Swinging '63* extravaganza at London's Royal Albert Hall. He may have weathered the storm – especially as he was offered a management contract by Brian Epstein who had used an acetate of 'Do You Want To Know a Secret' as bait. Instead, Shane beat a calculated retreat as a song-and-dance act with his wife Iris, sister of Rory Storm. Rendered as square as Shane by the craze for groups, Paul Raven had gladly accepted a post as floor manager on *Ready Steady Go*.

Joe Brown didn't throw in the towel with the same force. If struggling in the charts, he was much in demand as a session musician, and was a talented comedy actor – as demonstrated by his part as Cockney layabout Alfred Higgins in 1963's *What a Crazy World* movie, and then as male lead in the West End musical, *Charlie Girl*. Another participant in *What a Crazy World*, Marty Wilde decided that if he couldn't beat 'em, he'd join 'em – by immersing himself in a group, the Wilde Three, with his missus and singing guitarist Justin Hayward, for a morose recitation with sung chorus, 'I Cried' in 1965.

Having also sustained their first flops in 1962, both Eden Kane and Adam Faith had switched without a pause to ersatz Merseybeat, and were accompanied on television by visible beat groups — Kane with Earl Preston's TTs and then the Downbeats, and Faith with his Roulettes. Their respective comebacks were one in the eye for some of these bloody bands that had got on *Top of the Pops* just because they had the right accent and hairstyles.

Johnny Kidd too had long seen what was coming and had been back in vogue, and the Top 10, with jaunty 'I'll Never Get Over You' – though the follow-up, 'Hungry For Love', ran aground at Number Twenty, much sales potential being drained by a version from the Searchers.

Old timers like Johnny, Adam, even Alma Cogan had been regulars on early editions of the epoch-making *Ready Steady Go* which, when it began in August 1963, had had a besuited interlocutor in his thirties called Keith Fordyce and occasional send-ups of current hits by comics of the same age. The pruning of these unhip distractions paralleled the series' elevation to the most vital pop show of the decade (despite the impression newcomers were to get from Channel Four's edited re-runs in the 1980s).

Yearning for the days before *Ready Steady Go*, a Cliff Richard enthusiast had asked of *NME* readers, 'Are you going to let Britain's king of talent be beaten by a flash-in-the pan group like the Beatles?'[84] Apparently, they were. Yet, Cliff didn't bother to compete, and, like Elvis, simply shovelled out a greater proportion of potboiling ballads until the danger had passed. It was more or less business as usual too for the King Brothers with 1964's waltz-time 'Real Live Girls' from the West End musical *Little Me*.

Fifteen-year-old Steve Marriott had made a West End theatre debut as the Artful Dodger in Lionel Bart's *Oliver!* in 1962. Like 'Herman' Noone, he was no stranger to TV cameras, having appeared *The Famous Five* series in the late fifties and episodes of *Dixon of Dock Green* and *Citizen James*. Not liking to see this public exposure going to waste, Decca put Steve through two singles as an Adam Faith soundalike as soon as his voice had broken. When groups came in, he formed the Moments with another former child actor, Jimmy Winston, on bass. After Steve Marriott and the Frantics missed the mark too, he was behind the counter at the J60 Music Box equipment shop in East Ham. One afternoon, this geezer, Ronnie Lane, comes in looking for a bass guitar. One thing led to another, and the Small Faces were conceived with Steve on guitar, Ronnie on bass, Jimmy on organ and Kenney Jones, a drummer from a Stepney pub duo.

Other members of Equity moved in on the beat boom too – with the Decca label gushing with most affection towards them. Some had been there before the beginning. Hayley Mills, a pert, snub-nosed young film star, had even been high up the US Hot 100 in 1961 with 'Let's Get Together'. She was considered when a romantic sub-plot was on the cards briefly for the Beatles' first movie, *A Hard Day's Night*, until it was realized how much the group's female following might resent it.

Like Hayley, Freddie Starr had been in films in the late 1950s, but he was more to the point, having served time in Hamburg and sung on Howie Casey's *Twist at the Top* before he was teamed up with the Midnighters for three flop 45s. To the chagrin of Starr and other neglected Decca acts, the identical twin sons of Marion Ryan, Paul and Barry, were handed a Decca recording deal on a plate, given the whole works by the publicity department, and some orchestrated slop that kept them in middling hits, on and off, until 1967. However, the company gave up on Michael Chaplin – son of Charlie – after the failure in 1965 of his 'I Am What I Am', a harmonica-led single, produced by Larry Page.

Paying fractionally more dues than the Ryans and Chaplin, two London flatmates, Gregory Phillips and Mark Feld, had had roles on children's TV before beginning recording careers – Phillips with a Beatles cover and Feld as 'Marc Bolan' with three solo singles before recruitment as lead guitarist with Leatherhead's John's Children. Preferring to drum rather than sing, John 'Mitch' Mitchell's most celebrated bit-part as a young thespian was in *Emergency Ward Ten* before he went on to beat the skins with latter-day editions of Johnny Kidd's Pirates and the Tornados.

Older luvvies that crossed over to pop included a Scouse operatic tenor who, calling himself 'David Garrick', was to twice enter the UK Top 30 in 1966, and was backed for a while by the Iveys, a Liverpool-Welsh unit noticeably influenced by the Hollies. Chris Sandford – who'd played rock 'n' roller Eddie in *Coronation Street* – also hired himself a beat group, the Coronets. His 1964 single, 'Don't Leave Me Now', renewed Anthony Newley's pseudo-cockney vocal style – which would also be taken up by David Bowie when he linked up with Margate's Lower Third.

This simulation was also evident on tracks like 'I Know You're Gonna Be Mine' by the Cockneys who – you guessed it – were from London. An infinitely more convincing sign that the 'power' might be returning more conveniently to the capital was when a challenger from another EMI subsidiary, Columbia, seemed to have brought the Beatles to their knees and signalled a finish to traipsing up north for pop news. 'At my home ground, a place called the Tottenham Royal, we were packing 'em in six thousand a night, four nights a week,' Dave Clark would reminisce with quiet pride. 'We even got a gold cup for pulling in the biggest amount of business at the chain of dance halls we worked.'[4]

The Dave Clark Five had gone for the jugular in January 1964 when their sixth single, 'Glad All Over', unseated the Beatles' unbroken seven weeks at Number One, and sparked off an unfair if jubilant Fleet Street field day in which *Has the Five Jive Crushed the Beatle Beat*? was a typical headline. In Britain anyway, the spring of 1964 was the Dave Clark Five moment, never to quite return. Another glorious racket, 'Bits and Pieces', splintered the charts a few weeks after 'Glad All Over', and even the enigmatically-titled *Dave Clark Five* EP sidled in.

A reason given for the Five's rapid dethronement was, 'If you're off Dave, you're off the group.'[85] With the Beatles, you could be fickle towards individuals whilst maintaining overall allegiance to the group as a whole. The coherence of their image presented what had seemed at first glance to be a sole focus of adoration but, by 1964, this Midwich Cuckoo uniformity was balanced by the realization of differences between them – Ringo's homely wit, for instance, being especially contributory to the eventual North American breakthrough. When Ringo wed his girl from back home, John Lennon alone knew that 'there might be a shuffling of fans from one Beatle to another – at least that's what happened when news I was married was "revealed".'[86]

Marriage did not maim beat groups as it had soloists like Marty Wilde, but, by 1964, being from Liverpool did. Shortly after 'Glad All Over', the Rolling Stones, Manfred Mann, the Honeycombs and the Kinks – Londoners all – had chart-toppers. With talent scouts not coming round any more, and their very accents millstones round their necks, some Scousers even tried passing themselves off as southerners, enlisting the same when vacancies occurred, as the Riot Squad did with Mitch Mitchell.

The more far-sighted provincials uprooted themselves to become London-based outfits. These included the Beatles, the Animals, Them, Dean Ford and the Gaylords, the Moody Blues and the Irish Four Aces. Until then, they'd attended to recording and broadcasting duties there by commuting from wherever their concert itinerary found them. If benighted in the capital, they'd bed down in hotels or avail themselves of the hospitality of new acquaintances. Generally, a London domicile would begin with a *pied à terre*, sometimes a target for graffiti and marathon vigils by fans, but handy for West End nightclubbing. Actually resident at the Pickwick would be Paddy, Klaus and Gibson, i.e. ex-Big Three guitarist Paddy Chambers, bass player Klaus Voorman (who'd join Manfred Mann in 1966) and Gibson Kemp, Ringo's replacement in Rory Storm's Hurricanes.

Though the Searchers, Gerry and the Pacemakers, the Hollies and a few more Merseyside outfits were still able to take chart placings for granted, Freddie and his Dreamers discovered 'there's only three ways you can kick your legs, and we never had another hit.'[77] Back in Liverpool, there was a sense of impending hangover. As a beehive can thrive for a while after losing its progenitive queen, so did groups with fab shiny suits, winsome grins and Lennon-like small ads in *Merseybeat*, the luckiest gaining a slot on *Sunday Night at the Cavern*.

Former likely lads, the Big Three, had been forced to record material that bore small relation to their own musical inclinations. 'By the Way' was pleasant enough but the slick exactitudes of the studio had made even the mighty Big Three sound uncannily like any other group, particularly when compared to the *au naturel At the Cavern* EP that was to stand as their testament. They hadn't needed a second guitarist to be one of the most popular acts on Merseyside. Yet another reason given for the Three's failure to maintain national success was that, lacking a fourth part of the standard beat group's two-guitars-bass-drums, people thought there was a bit missing from their music too. It was rumoured that the Hollies showed their understanding of this prerequisite by insisting that, onstage, vocalist Graham Nash should continue hacking an inaudible rhythm guitar unconnected to any power point.

The Big Three weren't the only ones with problems. According to the *Herald of Wales*, Bystanders releases disappointed many fans. The journal added, 'The Bystanders have been fobbed off with poor material. I can't understand why these groups don't push their own sound and ideas'.[44] It's all very well saying that. Fresh-faced outfits for the provinces were usually too much in awe of the condescending voice calling them to order via the control room intercom to splutter, 'We'd rather not, sir.' 'We decided a beat number would be a better first disc,' said Fritz Fryer of Blackburn's Four Pennies (formerly the Lionel Morton Four), 'but in our second recording session, Johnny Franz [producer] fell for "Juliet". 'And what's good enough for Johnny Franz,' interrupted drummer Allan Buck, 'is good enough for us.'[87]

'Juliet' wended its way to the top of the Top 50 by May 1964, and set up the Four Pennies for another three Top 20 excursions and two LPs. In most cases, a beat group album was a rushed affair by what was assumed to be a perishable commodity. Centred on The Hit and its follow-up, it generally played it safe with concessions to current taste. Indeed, more than a touch of Frank Ifield prevailed on the Beatles debut LP – notably in the 'I'm in love with yooooo' hookline in 'Do You Want to Know a Secret', and the melody of its selling-point single, 'Please Please Me', was not unlike that of 'Charmaine', revived in 1962 by the Bachelors.

Nevertheless, over half of the *Please Please Me* album was self-composed, a production choice extraordinary at the time. A fourteen-hour day was regarded as quite adequate for the Beatles to tape it. Mike Smith, therefore, had been aghast at the eight it had taken Dave Berry and his anxious Cruisers to make their first *single*. In future, he told them, they'd be replaced – with the obvious exception of X-factor Dave – with hired hands quicker off the mark. The Cruisers could then learn the song off the record. Apart from hurt pride, it wouldn't matter. No one would be any the wiser. OK, lads?

The use of session players was, if anything, more widespread than in the 1950s. Of all beat instrumentalists, drummers were most prone to ghosting by more technically-accomplished timekeepers, because groups on stage were inclined to accelerate and slow down *en bloc* to inconsistencies of tempo caused by the mood of the hour. In the early 1960s, among those earning Musicians Union-regulated tea-breaks in this fashion were ex-Kenny Ball Jazzman Ron Bowden, Laurie Jay from Nero and the Gladiators, Sounds Incorporated's Tony Newman, Jimmy Nicol – a temporary Beatle when Ringo was taken ill in 1964 – Bobbie Graham, Clem Cattini of the Tornados, and Andy White from the Vic Lewis Orchestra – who George Martin had brought in, with no slight intended on Pete Best (and, next the untried Starr), for 'Love Me Do' – though Jackie Lomax of the Undertakers reckoned that, 'Pete could only play one drum beat, slowed down or speeded up. The others called it "Pete's tango."'[88]

He was a proficient enough drummer in concert, but there was press tittle-tattle that Dave Clark didn't play on his own records. The Lower Third's Phil Lancaster was alleged to be one Clark changeling but to his investors, Dave was the epitome of a proficient beat group leader. He had been permitted more studio freedom than any other British pop artist of the day, and, if substitutes were ever needed, it might have been because he was busy at the mixing desk, head-to-head with co-producer Adrian Kerridge. Like Sly and the Family Stone after him, he may have employed another sticksman for the backing track; layering his own drumming only after the rhythm had been invested into a given item.

Derided for the attention-seeking ploy that it was, an allegation that the Beatles had used a substitute lead guitarist was made by an expatriate Texan entertainer. The changeling was even named as Jimmy Page – who was unarguably twanging the wires on Them's Top 10 smash, 'Baby Please Don't Go', during an embarrassing three hours at West Hampstead studios where one more member of the group was replaced by a session player with every succeeding take. Guitarist Russ Ballard and drummer Robert Henrit from the Roulettes were called in to help pep up Unit 4 + 2's third 45, 'Concrete and Clay', from a slow, semi-acoustic number into a snappy, uptempo chart-topper.

In essence, it scarcely mattered what went on behind the scenes as long as the disc sounded OK, but the Fortunes, Hedgehoppers Anonymous and, later, Love Affair were each damaged by unwelcome publicity after choosing to divulge that vocalists were the only group personnel actually heard on their A-sides. Fans didn't want these mystique-depleting details any more than a musician wanted to know about what sharp practice and under-the-bedclothes fixing might have manoeuvred his group's records into the Top 30.

Almost despite himself sometimes, he was becoming a star. A typical working day might begin in the afternoon with lip-synching for the boys and girls on *Crackerjack*. Then would follow a booking in, say, Basingstoke, and back to the recording studio till gone dawn. Sleeping through an alarm call, he'd be late for Friday's *Ready Steady Go* rehearsal. As he couldn't hurry unmolested to the underground station, he'd bomb over to Wembley in his new 'fluid chariot'.

Driving, driving, driving to strange towns, strange venues and strange beds, groups riding a hit led what the economist would call a 'full life'. Though still centred on clubs, colleges and ballrooms, there were suddenly more dates booked than they could possibly keep. Most burdensome were contracts signed when the Local Boys Made Good had been only semi-famous – though the backstage lionizing was often quite satisfying: I always knew you'd make it, lads. 'It's funny, since the hit, they all come running to us,' remarked Steve Winwood of the Spencer Davis Group, 'the people who have ignored us in the past.'[89] Local bookings weren't so frequent now but – in the teeth of partisan fears of defection to London with record success – grassroots devotion might remain strong for a while longer.

Exhilarated by unexpected applause from the house technicians during an afternoon rehearsal for *For Teenagers Only*, even the most reticent members of the outfit would forget themselves in the sweep of events as the record crept into the Top 30 while the van zigzagged from Smethwick baths to Alloa Town Hall to Margate's Dreamland to the Rock Garden Pavilion in Llandrindod Wells to Farnborough Technical College to Plymouth's Bird Cage to the Palace Ballroom on the Isle of Man via a matinee with Herman's Hermits at the Floral Hall in Southport.

Often the group would have to drop everything to fit in *Saturday Club*, a trip to the deconsecrated church in Manchester where *Top of the Pops* was shot, or a return to London for *Ready Steady Go*. They might also have photo calls, interviews, fittings for new stage outfits – and crass publicity stunts as exemplified by circulated pictures of Manfred Mann dragging their most hirsute mann into a barber's; the Classmates sporting a fez apiece for their 'In Morocco' 45; the Kinks wielding whips, and the Rockin' Berries copying the Beatles' mid-air jump.

A *Pathé* news item's tight close-ups of Gerry and Megan of the Applejacks tying the knot was followed by the happy pair, still in wedding attire, being airlifted to the BBC's London studios for *Juke Box Jury*, but this fuss did not elevate the group's latest 45, 'Three Little Words', above Number Twenty-four. Just as gormless had been Dave Clark's 'apology' to Prince Philip over some dance step popularized by his Five called 'the Duke', and the otherwise unsung Primitives having their girlish tresses cut on a TV chat show. Hoping to halt their 'Leaving Here' 45's exodus after a mere week in the Top 50, Middlesex's Birds served a publicity-earning breach of copyright writ on the Byrds as soon as this more illustrious US combo came through customs at Heathrow.

There were plenty of volunteers when beat group slants started being imposed on everything from ITV commercials to episodes of *Mrs Dale's Diary* on the Home Service. The Zephyrs turned up in a *Look At Life* newsreel in Rank cinemas. The Swinging Blue Jeans had a cameo in *Z-Cars* while a murder in the ITVs detective series *No Hiding Place* involved the all-blond By-Boys. A plot in the BBC's *Taxi!* was structured round awful Beatles copyists with several bookings in the course of an evening. In the same month – September 1963 – that the Rolling Stones featured in a music journal advertisement for Vox amplifiers, the Fourbeats performed on the wireless in the rural soap-opera *The Archers*. Other desperate outfits were talked into topical singles like 'We Love the Pirates' from the Roaring Sixties – formerly the Farinas – and, urging 'beat the ban/And join the clan/On station 242', 'Radio Scotland' on Thistle Records by the Carrick Four.

The most famous acts didn't have to demean themselves with any dubious diversions. They would now be travelling separately from stage hardware that might include a PA system capable of punching out 100 watts – pretty loud for the mid-1960s. This and the rest of the gear would travel in a Transit driven by a two-man crew answerable to a head road manager who, when dignified with the umbrella rank of 'production manager', might glide through the countryside with the musicians in their fancy Dormobile with fitted record-player and radio.

With the M1 still only half-completed, a road manager coped with the tactical problem of moving the operation from A to B. All part of a day's work were flat batteries, jammed starter motors, snapped towropes, overcharging alternators and long waits for an Automobile Association patrolman. Anticipating him shaking his head, a call might be put through to B where equipment would be borrowed from the support group who'd be valiantly over-running as the main act reeled into the dressing room after a frightening two-hour dash in a hired car. Hot and bothered, they'd shamble on only a few minutes later.

However the entourage got to B, the road manager would buttonhole promoters, organize security, shoo unwanted visitors from dressing rooms, sign chits and bills, and, like an army batman without the uniform, attend to the group's dietary, accommodation, and health requirements – particularly the singer's. Unaccustomed to singing so frequently, vocal cords would often weaken to a tortured rasp, bubbling with catarrh, and curable only with medication and enforced silence.

This was before the group had played a note. When they did, the fun really began. If an amplifier or microphone fell silent, a road manager would have to scramble on with a replacement – though on the scream circuit, it wasn't worth trying to change or fix faulty equipment *in situ*, so when the Dave Clark Five's organ packed up one night at Liverpool Odeon, their Mike Smith (not the Decca producer) was compelled to unclip the mike and front the band, centre stage.

Unhappy supporting turns fought on as the howls for the headliners welled up to a pitch where you drowned in noise. The beat boom was pop hysteria at its most intense. Somehow, the ear-stinging decibels would climb higher– as if they'd all sat on tin-tacks – when the top group, still outwardly enjoying their work, started playing as the girls went crazy, tearing at their hair, wiping their eyes, rocking foetally and flapping scarves and programmes in the air.

They'd go into pretend faints like some of them had practised in the queue; their friends catching them under the armpits, but no one was seriously hurt as the havoc – in the beginning – was tinged with good nature and British reserve. At the Wolverhampton stop on what would be the Dave Clark Five's only UK tour, a boy wriggled through the barrier of stewards to leap onstage for no other purpose than to dance self-consciously for a few seconds before meekly stepping down again. Somewhere further south at a Beatles bash, another joker had yelled 'Down with the Beatles!' during a sudden lull. His portly girlfriend swiped him with her handbag, and everybody laughed.

Though there were instances of performers being yanked offstage by rampaging fans and chased in the streets, groups were still able to take national celebrity in their stride. Now and then, the new motorway service stations would cook mixed grills on the house in exchange for autographs. There would be amusement rather than annoyance when musicians came across schoolchildren who'd hidden themselves in a hotel room for hours just to chat with them when they flopped in from the show. That morning, the hideout in the previous town had been rumbled, and a hundred or so fans – mostly truants – collected in its lobby. The group smiled and signed books while checking out.

Taking the air after breakfast and stopping at traffic lights would also attract the start of a crowd now, and certain factions desired more than autographs. Sheffield students planned to kidnap the Beatles for a rag week stunt. If unwilling to play along, the group cheerfully compromised with a donation to funds, and the following day the students actually succeeded in capturing Dave Berry.

Days before box offices opened, hundreds ringed themselves round theatres, cinemas and city halls to ensure admission. Those lacking such clubbable stamina recoursed to buying tickets from touts at up to eight times their market price. Streets surrounding the venue were closed to traffic as police, linked with walkie-talkies, co-ordinated the stars' admittance. Entrances weren't always grand as groups smuggled themselves to backstage destinations by climbing scaffolding, lowering themselves through lofts and, if in Plymouth, by groping along underground tunnels leading from the Westward TV building two blocks away to a narrow lane beside the ABC cinema. At a given signal, a fire exit was flung open and a support act ambled out to divert attention from the main attractions' dash across the passageway. Often, they were still spotted, and girls' fingers were crushed in the slammed door.

Once inside, chart groups would be incarcerated until, with the final chord of the last number yet reverberating, they'd be halfway down the road by the end of the National Anthem when the crowd realized that there wasn't to be an encore. Maverick souvenir hunters might then be able to scour the stage for discarded drum sticks and plectrums. Some wanted more. After a date in Birmingham, Wayne Fontana and the Mindbenders' van was stripped of wing mirrors, windscreen wipers, number plates and door handles. Another Manchester group, Lorraine Gray and her Chaperones, had stage clothes stolen from their vehicle whilst appearing at Bradford's Arts Ball.

The hours awaiting escape might have been passed carousing in the artists' bar, if there was one, or relaxing in an often Spartan dressing room. To palates coarsened by chips-with-everything in wayside snack bars, any comestibles laid on by theatre management were usually edible enough not to have to resort to using the toaster and electric kettle packed as insurance against their ever being needed. Babbling like an idiot relation in the corner, *Take Your Pick*, *Dixon of Dock Green* or other early evening television might be switched off and the portable record-player plugged in. A singer might preen himself in front of a looking-glass, perhaps applying lacto-calomine to spots that no hit record could prevent from erupting on an adolescent complexion. He and the rest had become practised at forging each others' signatures – as had the road crew – to more rapidly dispose of the hundreds of autograph books left at stage doors for their attention.

Perhaps the saga of a lot of acts should have ended there because, debatably, they were as good as they'd ever get. Indolence engendered aversion to venturing far beyond the boundaries of an existing style. Consolidation rather than development was the watchword. Why bother doing otherwise? Always, they expected it to end – even the Beatles. One of Epstein's underlings, Alistair Taylor, recalled that the party line was, 'If we can last three years, it would be marvellous.'[90]

By 1964, preceding them on a British stage was less demanding 'now that the Beatles have found their own level,' so said the most frequent of their guest stars, Kenny Lynch, in a *Melody Maker* article headlined 'Is the Beatle Frenzy Cooling Down?'[91] No one was so dazzled to think that pop stars were immortal. 'A couple of Number Ones, and then out eighteen months later won't make you rich,' Ringo Starr said philosophically, 'you'll be back on the buses'.[92]

12 CUCKOO PATROL

You didn't get many laughs from, say, the Poets, the Joystrings, the Zombies or Them, but, for the likes of Freddie and the Dreamers, the Barron-Knights, the Fourmost and the Rockin' Berries plus amplified yokels such as Adge Cutler and the Wurzels and Rockin' Henri and the Hayseeds, audience anticipation became such that to cut the cackle invited professional suicide. This was either the product of a general plan, a gradual evolution or a pure accident, such as that which changed conjuror Tommy Cooper into a buffoon. Yet it was noticeable that, for all their clowning on the boards, most of the comedy beat groups did not have hits with songs specifically designed to be funny.

Naturally, the first business of any pop group is simply to be liked. Though many believed that they needed no sweetener to make their act more palatable, a lot of 1960s groups sugared their concert sets with varying degrees of conscious comic relief. An obvious example is Dave Dee, Dozy, Beaky, Mick and Tich – and, lest we forget, Roy Wood served as both lead guitarist and bewigged Dusty Springfield impersonator in Mike Sheridan and the Nightriders. There were moments of levity from other groups too such as the time when Manfred Mann performed 'Dashing Away with a Smoothing Iron' as a slow blues or when the Jeff Beck Group, responding to a sardonic shouted request, struck up a deadpan rendition of Frank Sinatra's 'Strangers in the Night'. A reviewer of the Beatles' second national tour mentioned that 'Misery' was 'led into with some good comedy'.[93] On the horizon then were smart alec press conferences, non-musical sketches during *The Beatles' Christmas Show* and scousetalk fan club flexi-discs.

The Hollies tried to be amusing on vinyl too with the 1966 film theme, 'After the Fox', with comedy actor Peter Sellers, and a dull instrumental belied the promise in the title of the Artwoods' B-side from 1966, 'I'm Looking for a Saxophonist Doubling French Horn and Wearing Size 37 Boots'. Another 'serious' group, the Yardbirds, went in for facetious sleeve notes, courtesy of their Jim McCarty – who once disturbed another outfit's set at Bournemouth Winter Gardens by wandering across the stage muttering.[94] The Rolling Stones yukked it up on the LP track 'Something Happened to Me Yesterday' with its colliery brass band and Mick Jagger's jocular valediction. The Kinks, the Small Faces and the Who walked a more subtle tightrope, and even John Mayall was a very funny man in every sense.

When they arrived in London, Zoot Money and the Big Roll Band were not accorded the same respect as Mayall's Bluesbreakers, mostly through Zoot's penchant for face-pulling, dressing-up (for example in army uniform to promote 1965's 'Let's Run For Cover') and Freddie Garrity-like trouser-dropping. The outrage also extended to B-sides like 'Zoot's Sermon' and 'Self Discipline', and Money ritually hurling hundreds of pounds' worth of equipment off the end of the pier after one gremlin-infested recital at the Bournemouth Pavilion.

Working the same metropolitan club circuit as Zoot, the Downliners Sect betrayed a jokey line too with 'Leader of the Sect' (a spoof of the Shangri-Las' motorbike epic) and similarly clannish flip-sides in 'In*sect*icide', 'Sect Appeal', 'Sect Maniac' and a respectful take-off of Hank Williams' 'When God Comes to Gather His Jewels'. A 1965 'concept' EP was a compulsory purchase for any 'death disc' connoisseur worthy of the name. *The Sect Sing Sick Songs* lived up to its title with the inclusion of repulsively entertaining ditties like 'Now She's Dead' (which also embraces a send-up of the Bachelors) and 'I Want My Baby Back' – in which the singer and his dead lover are reunited *à la* Edgar Allen Poe in the departed one's coffin.

Behind closed doors, there was the notorious 'Troggs Tape': a muddled endeavour to tape a number entitled 'Tranquillity'. A quick-witted engineer left the tape running during a studio discussion riddled with swearing as the musicians and their entourage argued at cross purposes about hiring an independent producer before trying to tidy up the mess themselves. The high point of this inadvertent humour is when Ronnie Bond almost comes to blows with Reg Presley over a percussion fill a child could do. A more self-controlled drummer, Dave Clark, was prominent on an unreleased alternate take by his Five of a B-side, 'Concentration Baby', which he sings in an exaggerated Yorkshire intonation, and is barely able to conceal his mirth amid the severe march tempo and a cacaphony of kazoos and screeching violins.

These, nevertheless, were tangential to weightier artistic and financial motivations. In 1963 Dave Curtiss and the Tremors had played it for laughs on 'You Don't Love Me Any More' – about an infatuated dimwit and a deadly virago of a girlfriend – and Me and Them's 'Everything I Do Is Wrong' was in the same vein, but both Dave's lot and Me and Them reverted to 'sensible' items for subsequent 45s – because there was space on the scene then for only one Freddie and the Dreamers.

For aspiring popstars, Freddie's was an odd bunch with their podgy bass player, a drummer with the oily charm of a door-to-door salesman, and two guitarists, one in dour sunglasses and the other prematurely bald. Finally, there was Freddie, four-eyed and spindly, the geek who got sand kicked in his face in Charles Atlas advertisements. He was blessed, nevertheless, with a singular onstage vitality, a catch-phrase ('just a minute!') and a dash of that lip-trembling pathos that some find endearing. He was also a fair composer, co-writing the medium-paced Merseybeat exercise, 'I'm Telling You Now', the first of two singles that each fell one position short of topping the charts in 1963.

Over the next year, Freddie and his boys faded from the UK Top 20 – partly because, though their 45s still sounded like hits, it became possible to predict precisely when the half-verse guitar break would occur. Significantly, their best-selling disc during this fidgety retreat was the funereal 'I Understand' which, with 'Auld Lang Syne' quoted in melodic counterpoint, restored Freddie to the Top 10 as Britain slept off its Christmas dinner.

It had been presented without a trace of any characteristic high-stepping on *Ready Steady Go*. As the countdown to 1965 crept closer, the group mimed an earlier smash in silly hats. Without warning, Freddie ceased pretending to sing, and began cramming paper streamers into his mouth. A more appropriate setting for this imbecility was in pantomime where the lads made their debut in 1963 as court jesters in Chester Royalty Theatre's *Cinderella* – a highlight of which was a 'Teddy Bear's Picnic' more suited to Uncle Mac than a nascent heavy metal version released by Jackie Lynton a few months later. After the dignified 'Thou Shalt Not Steal' terminated their Top 50 tenure in 1965, Freddie and the Dreamers delved deeper into their natural element by recording a larger proportion of humorous material such as Ronnie Hilton's 'Windmill In Old Amsterdam' and an entire album of Disney film songs.

The Barron-Knights had long arrived at a similarly expedient juncture. With the exception of marginal latecomers like the Scaffold and the Bonzo Dog Doo-Dah Band, they were the only group to score in the Top 20 with comedy, namely four medleys that mocked current favourites. Deviations from this – such as a revival of Sinatra's 'It Was a Very Good Year' – sold poorly, even though the Knights could always guarantee a thoroughly diverting evening's entertainment far beyond the dictates of passing fads. A testimonial to this came from Bill Wyman of the Rolling Stones who had been inspired to 'get a worthwhile guitar and really work at it'[95] after a Knights' bash in Aylesbury.

Groups of the stature of the Stones and the Beatles were happy to have them as support act because, as with Freddie – 'the sort of pop star you didn't mind your girlfriend liking'[96] – and other units that made monkeys of themselves, the Knights weren't likely to steal female fans. Despite valiant attempts, the Knights could not free themselves from the stylistic straitjacket fastened to them by those who bought the medleys and fell about to the in-concert antics and patter. Eventually, the group stopped keeping an occasional straight face and laughed too – all the way to the bank.

Not laughing quite so loud were the Rockin' Berries whose chart run ended when 'The Water Is Over My Head' flowed out of the Top 50 in 1966. Their bread-and-butter hadn't always been comedy, and an opportunity to ditch it might have been taken when 'He's In Town' had cruised into the Top 10. Instead, they treated *Ready Steady Go* viewers to a 'hilarious' version of Elvis Presley's latest hit with one member in drag. A reliable indicator of future direction was also evident on their LPs where numbers from the songbooks of Benny Hill, George Formby and 'Laughing Policeman' Charles Penrose nestled uneasily amongst the Vincent-Lewis-Richard-Presley rockers dragged up from their German days, and concessions to the latest trends. By late 1966, the transformation was complete with the temporary plucking of the 'Rockin'' adjective from their name pledging them symbolically to a family audience.

Like 'The Berries', the Fourmost's recorded output was earnest enough before the hits dried up – and they had more than their share of tragedy as the declining health of guitarist Mike Millward condemned him to an early grave in 1966. In common with the Zombies, they'd got by on the 'intellectual' ticket with loads of GCEs and Millward's swot spectacles, and they used their brains in provident preparation for a life outside the charts. Being Liverpudlian, comedy rather than tap-dancing or the flying trapeze seemed the path to take.

Slick parodies of other pop stars, clever vocal mimicking of instruments, and singer Billy Hatton's arms growing longer and longer during 'With These Hands' were amongst factors that led to eight months at the London Palladium with Cilla Black in 1964, and attempts to reach record buyers with 1965's 'Girls Girls Girls' with its unashamed Donald Duck lead vocal. Having thus exhausted their borderline teen appeal, they teetered on the edge of the cabaret circuit that would keep them busy until every original member had left in one way or another by 1982.

Never mind, the Fourmost had come out of the beat boom with a backlog of hits and a degree of credibility not enjoyed by transient gimmick groups like Solihull's Batman and his Wonderboys (formerly the Crowin' Codas) who, costumed accordingly, made the front cover of *Midland Beat*, lapsed from transatlantic drawls to Black Country in heated moments, and played the same stuff as everyone else.

Of more considered substance were mixed-media aggregations like the Liverpool Scene, founded by artist Adrian Henri and ex-members of the Roadrunners and the Clayton Squares. Bringing satire as well as pop music to an audience prejudiced against one or the other, the Liverpool Scene drank from the same pool as fellow Cavern regulars, the Scaffold, who, with Paul McCartney's brother in their ranks were to agitate the Top 10 with the vexing catchiness of 'Thank U Very Much', 'Lily the Pink' and, years after Dominic Behan, 'Liverpool Lou'.

If light years from Freddie and the Dreamers too, the Bonzo Dog Doo-Dah Band's *raison d'être* also hinged on getting belters. Emerging from London's Goldsmith Art College in 1962, they created a pop-Dada musical junk sculpture that was less satire than conveying in pop terms that strain of fringe-derived comedy that would culminate in *Monty Python's Flying Circus*. The Bonzos eventual modicom of chart success was secondary to an alarming stage presentation that had been 'a little bit trad,' said co-founder Neil Innes, 'but that was too rigid. What we played turned out to be wonderful drinking music. We ended up doing five pubs a week with landlords paying us twenty-five pounds a night plus what we got in the hat – very good money for the time. We bought all these gangster suits and dreadful ties whilst Viv [Stanshall, vocals and euphonium] wore a gold lamé suit – that was the "look". We cut out speaking balloons, introduced silly gags, and Roger [Ruskin-Spear] made an exploding robot.

'The Easter before college was finished, Kenny Ball saw us at the Tiger's Head in Clapham, and his brother-in-law became our first manager – though we were pretty unmanageable. He booked us on the cabaret circuit in the north-east, two clubs a night per week. It was such a success that we got six more weeks' solid work immediately afterwards.'

Fun for all the family, the Beatles' TV appearances were as special after their fashion as a Bonzos *tour de force* in a Wallsend pub – and Christmas wouldn't be Christmas without the 'Fab Four' at Number One. Hell, they were an institution, weren't they? Yet, 'Who'd want to be an eighty-year-old Beatle,' chuckled John Lennon.[97] Like Tommy and Cliff before them, and Freddie and the Dreamers, they'd be ideal for pantomime, charity football matches and children's TV when they were overtaken – as they surely would be – by a newer sensation.

Anyone could see that in *A Hard Day's Night*. Movies were the thing, you see. 'To retain the attention of the public,' concurred Pete Townshend, guitarist with the Who, 'every pop star has to make the transition to films at some time. It's the only way to last.'

Without incurring financial risk themselves, the Eagles, Billy J. Kramer, the Rolling Stones and Ireland's Four Aces were among those thought worthy subjects for cinema newsreels. Another cheap way forward was climbing on a celluloid conveyor belt of diversified lip-synched ephemera connected by some vacuous story-line or narrative in the tradition of *It's Trad Dad*. Still in circulation as late as 1966, *Just For You* was an excuse for the Merseybeats, the Applejacks, the Bachelors, Peter and Gordon, Freddie and the Dreamers, Millie, A Band of Angels, the Warriors, Mark Wynter and the rest of a 'parade of top-pop singers' to project their latest releases between discourses by reclining media 'personality' Sam Costa, controlling an array of projectors and audio equipment from a bedside control panel.

B-featured in summer 1965, the seventy-minute *Pop Gear* did not extend the frontiers of the avant-garde either, though it dispensed with an interlocking theme altogether in favour of blink-and-you'll-miss-'em clips that paraded the Rockin' Berries, Nashville Teens and crooner Matt Monro; the fading Fourmost and Billy J. Kramer; hitless but popular Sounds Incorporated; Herman's Hermits and the Four Pennies, plus many other weavers of the rich tapestry of British pop.

As well as plugging records, the silver screen was an outlet for an assortment of pop stars who fancied themselves as actors. In some cases, adolescent afternoons gawping at Hollywood wouldn't be wasted. For others, however, enthusiasm for this film acting lark would evaporate as the memorizing of lines, longterm commitments and demanding schedules with their early mornings became onerous.

Cliff Richard's two movies of 1959, *Serious Charge* and *Expresso Bongo*, had been quite tough for the time, but with a weather eye on Elvis, he went soft with *The Young Ones, Summer Holiday* and 1964's *It's A Wonderful Life*: shopworn ideas but better-attended 'teenpics' about 'good kids' making wholesome and purposeful whoopee. Billy Fury and Adam Faith also trod the same backwards path from taut drama to the shallow 'fun' of *I Gotta Horse* (Fury) and *What a Whopper* (Faith).

A missing link between these and the more realistic pop movie commentary of *A Hard Day's Night* was 1963's *Live It Up* with Heinz as singer with a unit that included Steve Marriott as drummer Ricky. Gene Vincent, Sounds Incorporated and Kenny Ball's Jazzmen were passers-by in a yarn about the sunshine and showers of the group's pursuit of a record contract. For example, media exposure of the guitarist's industrial injury in his daytime job as a delivery boy leads to the outfit's appearance on an early evening TV magazine but a newsflash nixes this at the last minute.

Nearly all the action in *A Hard Day's Night* built up in behind-the-scenes situations too. This zany farce was produced by Walter Shenson, a Californian whose past had included *A Band of Thieves*, a vehicle for the 'economic' thespian abilities of Acker Bilk's Paramount Jazz Band. Though *A Hard Day's Night* was also a neo-musical about a gang of happy-go-lucky funsters, its bluff lyricism brought the curtain down on the old regime in a fictionalized account of the Beatles' eventful preparation for a television show. *Help!*, the group's second film, was less challenging with the more vitriolic reviews glooming that the Beatles had been overshadowed by distinguished support from Leo McKern, Victor Spinetti, Eleanor Bron and other 'real' actors.

More dated than either Beatle offering was *Ferry Across the Mersey*, a belated period film whose evocative title song was Gerry and the Pacemakers' UK Top 10 farewell. Drawing attention to their compromising Merseybeat origins too were the Fourmost, the bleached-blond Blackwells and the Koobas who, having insult added to injury, were losers in a Battle of the Bands contest that constitutes the main thrust of a plot which concludes with the triumphant Gerry and the Pacemakers launching into 'It's Gonna Be All right' (their first serious miss in real life), with Gerry's screen Mum foremost among fans cheering them on.

When faced with musicians with thick accents, it was common for directors to make them wear ear-plugs – thereby obliging them to speak more loudly and pronounce their lines more clearly. This was certainly the case with the Dave Clark Five – *norf* Londoners to a man – in John Boorman's directorial debut, the sombre *Catch Us If You Can* (US title: *Having a Wild Weekend*) which only allows Dave Clark (as 'Steve') any character development. The rest of the Five play themselves as Wonderful Young People fleeing from sordid commercialism.

Most post-*Hard Day's Night* UK pop flicks, however, lacked Boorman's highbrow pretensions. *The Ghost Goes Gear*, released in 1966, was carried by Carol White (as 'Polly') and Nicholas Parsons with musical intervals by the Spencer Davis Group, Dave Berry and St Louis Union – with diverting sequences such as Carol-Polly's cavortings in a musical sequence in the ghost's mansion, and Pete York being very Lennonesque in swimming trunks and admiral's greatcoat, holding a bottle to his ear in comic dialogue with a hotel's room service.

Hardly any beat groups received top billing in more than one major feature film – though quite a few turned up serially on celluloid as often as the Twist did earlier in the decade. Not surprisingly for such a visual act, Freddie and the Dreamers accepted more such work than many of their contemporaries. As well as *Just For You*, they performed (as 'Frantic Freddie and His Screaming Dreamers') 'Sally Ann' and the Hollywood Argyles' 'Short Shorts' – with inevitable downfall of same – in *What a Crazy World*. They were given more to do in *Everyday's A Holiday* (US title: *Seaside Swingers*) as holiday camp chefs with 'What's Cooking', a six-minute mini-opera anticipating the Who's 'A Quick One' by three years. A short from 1965, *Cuckoo Patrol*, was banned in some US states for, allegedly, belittling the Boy Scouts.

Generally, however, pop groups were required not 'to other be', but simply to stand up before the cameras and do a number without fuss. The Searchers had been promised acting parts in1964's *The System* (US title: *The Girl-Getters*), but recalled Mike Pender, 'All it was was appearing on a stage in a night club.' The Eagles had, likewise, come in handy for *Some People* in 1962 – propaganda for the Duke of Edinburgh's Award scheme – the Hollies for *It's All Over Town*, and, after the Who and the Animals passed on it, Jeff Beck smashed up a guitar when the Yardbirds played a thinly-disguised 'Train Kept A-Rolling' in Antonioni's drawn-out *Blow Up*, set in Swinging London.

In 1965, the Small Faces had performed at a concert sponsored by a pirate radio ship in a modern-day smuggling saga, *Dateline For Diamonds*, while the Pretty Things were token reprobate pop group in *What's Good for the Goose* the following year. As it became more obvious that its star, Norman Wisdom, was failing in his attempt to mutate from the cloth-capped 'little man' of British cinema comedy to a second Rudolph Valentino, the Pretty Things' contribution was increased beyond that of the sideshow originally required.

The Zombies' had a flash of celluloid immortality too – as a pub combo in a 1965 psycho-thriller *Bunny Lake Is Missing*. Its cast embraced the likes of Noel Coward, Laurence Olivier and Finlay Currie, but the Zombies' fifteen seconds in the full-length film were extended for the trailer to suck in the teenage market because, aware of the publicity value, directors and producers in the Swinging Sixties felt that any old rubbish would do as long as a pop name could be used to spice up the credits and guarantee a movie some added interest.

13 HOWLIN' WOLVES ON MOCKIN' BIRD HILL

Pop stars are two-a-penny. Much rarer is the diehard fan who can reel off at a second's notice, say, the matrix number of the Ceylonese pressing of 'I'm Telling You Now'. Perhaps being mad about a pop group is a more socially acceptable pastime – even obsession – than accumulating information about donkeys' false teeth. How did yours start? Was it because your first bout of snogging at a party was soundtracked by *Session with the Dave Clark Five*? Maybe a patrol leader you liked at Guides said she liked Adam Faith.

The worst aspects of of idolatry are exemplified by deed-poll Presleys, the lethal actions of Mark David Chapman and a lady from Sunderland who is clinically mad about the late cowboy singer Jim Reeves. Milder ritualists are represented by a fellow from King's Lynn whose entire record collection consists of the works of Joe Meek. On the other side of the coin, however, are those who, from a comparably single-minded root, are motivated by quasi-evangelical zeal to further the cause of one favoured musical form rather than a particular act, irrespective of personal popularity or financial gain. In the 1960s, the most vital of these interests was the blues – a word that Eric Burdon inked in his own blood across the cover of an exercise book in which he'd compiled lyrics of the same.

Though elderly Mississippi blues grandee Big Bill Broonzy's London concert in September 1951 has been accepted generally as British blues' sluggish conception, it was actually pre-empted by seventeen-year-old John Mayall, who, having painstakingly taught himself boogie-woogie piano, guitar and harmonica, made a debut with his blues trio at Manchester's Bogeda Jazz Club in 1950. Nevertheless, its growth as a bohemian cult only truly gained ground ten years later, partly through scorn for the hit parade toot-tooting of trad jazz.

Epitomizing this was *It's Trad, Dad!* and, playing over the closing credits, Chris Barber's Jazz Band seemed to have sold out too. Even so, though like Bilk and Kenny Ball he'd had a chart entry, Barber was a major catalyst in the development of British blues – for, unlike others who merely acted as agents for tours, Chris financed the conservation of the form. In the teeth of frequent advice to the contrary from the National Jazz Federation, and monetary losses such as that suffered on a Muddy Waters recital at St Pancras Town Hall, he had underwritten tours by many leading US blues and gospel artists including Little Walter, Sister Rosetta Tharpe, Roosevelt Sykes and the multi-instrumental duo Sonny Terry and Brownie McGhee.

Blues and 'rhythm-and-blues', as it became, infiltrated the Barber band repertoire. They were possibly the first British act to try Muddy's 'I Got My Mojo Working', which became the movement's anthem – though among close seconds were Ma Rainey's 'See See Rider' (recorded by Barber in 1957), 'Hoochie Coochie Man', John Lee Hooker's 'Boom Boom', and 'Baby Please Don't Go', erroneously credited to Ottilie Patterson, the band's vocalist (and Barber's wife), and augmented by a visiting Sonny Boy Williamson's harmonica. Another contender was Bobby Troupe's '(Get Your Kicks On) Route 66'. My friend Kevin ruined a school atlas, trying to figure exactly how 'it winds from Chicago to LA' – though the only version I've ever heard on which you could make out all the words was by Bing Crosby and the Andrews Sisters.

The earthier sounds of the blues attracted more jazzers, but possibly they'd always played it. 'A lot of horns and top-speed bass lines,' Jimi Hendrix would perceive. 'Most of those cats are playing nothing but blues.'[98] It was two disgruntled ex-Barber sidemen, Cyril Davis and Alexis Korner, who, in 1957, established the poorly-subscribed Blues and Barrelhouse club in a Soho pub.

More encouraging were the attendance figures five years later at their G Club in Ealing, which was patronized immediately by zealots from Middlesex and beyond, as earnestly devoted to blues as other cliques were to yachting and donkeys' false teeth. Most of them were students, weekend dropouts and middle-class bohemians who might have 'dressed down' for the occasion – frayed jeans, Jesus sandals, holey pullover, carefully tousled hair and CND badge – while *Jimmy Reed at Carnegie Hall* or Bob Dylan's second LP, *Freewheelin'*, warmed up the Dansette. Alternatively, if in highbrow mood they'd dry their hair to Mingus, Coltrane or Charlie 'Yardbird' Parker.

Some listeners were players themselves who were responsible for a fair number of musical assassinations, having got up from the audience to thrash guitars and holler gutbucket exorcisms with the club's resident band, Blues Incorporated, presided over by Korner and Davis. Among those who came forth were Paul Jones and Steve Marriott – pending respective enrolments in Manfred Mann and the Small Faces – Long John Baldry, Ronnie Jones and Herbie Goins, and a nervous economics student called Mike Jagger who, with another future Rolling Stone, drummer Charlie Watts, would be – like Baldry, Goins and Ronnie Jones – a semi-permanent member of Blues Incorporated.

Finding the rapid turnover of personnel prohibitive during these loosely-structured evenings, some musicians searched amongst themselves for the nucleus of a more fixed set-up. In the G Club's watching throng were subsequent Kinks, Yardbirds, and Pretty Things, as well as Manfred *Menn*, all poised to appear on *Top of the Pops* within a year of the Stones doing so, yet sticking as far as they were able to their erudite musical guns. Running in the same pack, the Downliners Sect were well-placed to do likewise, but they didn't quite fit.

Whether participants or spectators, blues enthusiasts – like the skifflers of old – frequented Dobell's, Carey's Swing Shop in Streatham and rare provincial stores like Violet May's in Sheffield that also dealt in a wide spectrum of vinyl goods from black America whether the rural stumblings of Snooks Eaglin, Robert Johnson or Champion Jack Dupree,[99] Chicago and New Orleans R & B or, via the likes of Chuck Berry and Screaming Jay Hawkins, its rock 'n' roll derivation.

Before they knew it, fans were rolling out of bed at 5 a.m. to catch a half-hour blues show on the American Forces network, and making expensive expeditions to Manchester, Birmingham and London for blues packages – such as the American Folk, Blues and Gospel Caravan of April 1964 which presented Muddy Waters, his Mississippi pianist cousin Otis Spann and testifying Sister Rosetta Tharpe. The following year, it diversified with the inclusion of Red Indian singer-songwriter Buffy St Marie and our own Ian Campbell Folk Group. 'I remember a blues show in Manchester,' said Dave Berry, 'with John Lee Hooker, Memphis Slim and T-Bone Walker. A large percentage of the audience consisted of musicians.'

Where did these musicians play if more regular journeys to the G Club and the Bogeda were impractical? An increasing number of provincial venues became blues strongholds on off-peak evenings. Off-the-cuff examples are Reading's Olympia (where the first hundred girls were admitted free), the Wooden Bridge Hotel in Guildford, the R & B Club above Andover's Copper Kettle restaurant (where the Troggs would debut), and of course, Uncle Bonnie's Chinese Jazz Club in Brighton. Further afield were the Rhythm and Blues Club (later, Club Rado) in the Old Sailors' Maritime Dance Hall in Belfast, Swansea's R & B Cellar, the dingy Downbeat in Newcastle's dockland, and St Andrew's Hall in Norwich which elicited the *Midland Beat* headline 'R and B Ousts Rock In East Anglia!'[100] after an initial blast starring the Pretty Things.

One foggy October Monday in 1963, beneath the shadow of Birmingham Town Hall, the art deco interior of the Golden Eagle framed 'the unusual sight of prominent jazz instrumentalists playing alongside members of the Renegades and other beat exponents'[11] Rhythm-and-blues hit the Midlands in the form of the Rhythm Unlimited weekly club, which complemented the pub's Wednesday jazz sessions. Spencer Davis then a mainstay of Rhythm

Unlimited, had 'been wanting to experiment with this type of music for some time. This club has provided me with the opportunity. I think it is a shot in the arm for the music scene in Birmingham.'[11] It was, indeed, a howling success. Within an hour of its 7.30 start, over eighty latecomers had been turned away. 'The packed crowd at the opening session and subsequent evenings make it quite clear,' crowed co-promoter Brian Allen, 'that there is a tremendous following for R & B in the city.'[11]

In Sheffield, groups whose R & B policy had barred them from other places started their own 'Bluesville' club in the back room of the Foresters in Division Street. Response was sufficiently encouraging for the opening of a similar club in the Leeds Arms. Much in evidence at these gatherings had been Dave Berry, then vocalist – in the languid manner of Slim Harpo – with the Chuck Fowler R and B Band, the city's own Blues Incorporated, before they became the Cruisers in 1960.

Greater London boasted by far the highest concentration of blues venues like St Mary's Parish Hall, L'Auberge, the Crawdaddy, Eel Pie Island hotel and the Crown – all dotted round Richmond and Twickenham. Foremost amongst those in the inner city were specified evenings at Studio 51 in Great Newport Street and the Marquee – which by 1963 had moved from Oxford Street to Wardour Street, and was still hosting 'an evening with the blues' in 1966. By the time Blues Incorporated's debut album, *R & B from the Marquee*, was released in 1962, Cyril Davis had left, preferring a narrower, Chicago-style interpretation of the music rather than Korner's 'everything from Louis Jordan to Martha and the Vandellas'. With Long John Baldry, David had formed a splinter group, the All-Stars, and founded a suitably purist club in Harrow-on-the-Hill that faded away following his death in January 1964.

As well as working the clubs, groups also had chances of one-nighters and even tours as accompanists to US incomers. One of the most frequent was Arkansas blues balladeer Jimmy Witherspoon, who was once backed by the Spencer Davis Group for a total fee of £40: seven for Witherspoon, eight for each of the group, and a pound for petrol. This wasn't a bad deal in 1964. A fond memory of that year for thrifty Muff Winwood was, 'You could make money while you were still semi-pro. This meant that you could take your time developing.'[101]

Ace Kefford recalled 1964 in a haze less rosy: 'Carl Wayne and the Vikings backed Screaming Jay Hawkins. He travelled in the van with us. He was a lovely fellow, and I felt sorry for him because he was getting paid less than we were, even though he was the star. Another case of a talent being ripped off by managers and promoters – same old story.'

The then-struggling Troggs supported John Lee Hooker with 'the excellent but little known John Mayall's Bluesbreakers',[102] though the Groundhogs, a group started in 1963 by guitarists Tony McPhee and Peter Cruikshank, were to become a more regular appendage to Hooker on later treks round Europe. Jimmy Reed was 'drunk for breakfast' according to Mike Cooper of Reading's Blues Committee who, with little time to rehearse with him, entertained at the Olympia with mutually familiar standards of the 'Boom Boom' – 'I Got My Mojo Working' variety during which the customers, dignified by the presence of undergraduates from the university, blamed errors on the Blues Committee rather than the befuddled gentleman fronting them. He was the genuine article, wasn't he? What did the town boys behind him know about blues?

Far from the speakeasies and juke joints of black America, British R & B outfits tried to emulate the Jimmy Reeds, Slim Harpos, Muddy Waters and Howlin' Wolves of black America, but the results – especially vocal – were generally nothing like. Praise indeed for Jimmy Powell and his Five Dimensions was entered in Mike Cooper's diary in which, after dismissing the Pretty Things as 'atrocious', he gives his opinion of Powell's ensemble at the same concert at London's 100 Club: 'Powell is a reasonable harmonica player and vocalist. His rhythm guitarist is quite good too. The rest of the group are mediocre but produce a competent sound which does at least sound like R and B and not rock.'

Cooper also liked former Larry Parnes' protégé Duffy Power, reborn with a black soul in a white skin, and credited with 'vocal and harmonica' on 1964's 'I Don't Care', a rewrite of 'Hoochie Coochie Man'. Give him credit too, Tommy Bruce leered audially with the expertise of a John Lee Hooker on a 1964 version of 'Boom Boom' – which was coupled with an equally strong stab at Rufus Thomas's 'Can Your Monkey Do the Dog'. That year too, Billy Fury stood as tall with Jimmy Reed's 'Baby What You Want Me To Do', B-side of 'It's Only Make Believe', his penultimate Top 10 entry.

Of the newer beat group singers, Colin Blunstone, David Bowie and Syd Barrett of The Pink Floyd Sound – named in 1965 by amalgamating the forenames of two black Georgia songsters – contended well enough with the feverish lechery but couldn't really hack it as blue-eyed bluesmen. Though the spirit was willing, other British voices were raucous not passionate when they extemporized from wolf howl to close-miked *sotto voce* over a thuggish copy of an original arrangement.

Yet some showed that you didn't have to come from the chain gang or the ghettos of southside Chicago to sound world-weary, cynical and knowing beyond your years. As well as grizzled, bearded types like John Mayall, there were spotty herberts like Eric Burdon, Steve Winwood, Mick Jagger, Steve Marriott, Phil May and Rod Stewart. Pop-eyed at the microphone, they were barely even the Mannish Boys that Muddy Waters bragged about being, but if you half-closed your eyes, with delicate suspension of logic, these striplings' lived-in, aged rasps would seem believable as, from a reserve of compounded passion, however unsubstantiated, they slipped comfortably from suppressed lust through lazy insinuation to intimate anguish, silencing Marquee drinkers like a mass bell in Madrid.

It is instructive to compare each rendering of a song that opens both the Pretty Things' debut LP and *The Zombies Begin Here*: Bo Diddley's 'Roadrunner'. The Zombies' more stilted approach pales beside the lean and hungry drive of the Pretty Things; Colin Blunstone being technically more proficient but less 'authentic' than the frail, straining attack of Phil May. Also, though Rod Argent could crush notes with the best of them, another crucial factor was his keyboard's purer tone and fixed tuning at odds with the rough guitar heart of the blues.

The solos and riffs of players such as George Harrison, the Dave Clark Five's Lenny Davidson, Tony Hicks of the Hollies and other lead guitarists in mainstream pop groups were constructed to integrate with the melodic and lyrical intent of a given number. Depending upon your point of view, they seemed either bland or attractively unfussed against those in 1964's sudden crop of blues groups. The main difference was that, unlike Harrison, Hicks *et al*, a guitarist would step forward into the spotlight to react with grimacing and intellectual flash to underlying chord patterns rather than the more obviously melodic aesthetics of the song. His eyes would fix on the neck of the instrument as if stupified by his own note-bending dexterity. A few such exquisites – like Syd Barrett and crew-cut Eric 'Slowhand' Clapton of the Yardbirds – also shared the self-immolatory tendencies of some of their black icons.

Of the same standing as Clapton in his neck of the woods was Stan Webb of Sounds of Blue who, with a line-up that included vocalist Christine Perfect and saxophonist Chris Wood, worked three nights a week in the Kidderminster-Dudley-Wolverhampton triangle. That male onlookers focused on him as much as tall, blonde Miss Perfect was reflective on the growing respect felt for instrumental virtuosity. This fostered improvisations that extended beyond the one verse at most that was the norm on pop singles. Though a Rolling Stones' blues jam, 'Goin' Home' filled twelve minutes of an LP in 1966, the 'rave-ups' on *Five Live Yardbirds* and Them's neo-instrumental 'Mystic Eyes' each streamlined an open-ended blue-wailing design that could run on and on and on on the boards at the Marquee and Club Rado.

This came to a head in the later 1960s with the deification of guitar heroes like Alvin Lee (once Alvin Dean of the Jaybirds), the outstanding Jeff Beck, and Clapton who, after a stint with John Mayall's Bluesbreakers was not 'Slowhand' any more but 'God'. For only as long as Beck, Webb, Clapton,

Lee, Raymond Williams of the Mustangs – 'one of the fastest I've seen,' gulped a *Herald of Wales* newshound[103] – and other would-be virtuosi fermented hitless in the specialist clubs and college circuit, would George Harrison continue to win polls as the kingdom's top guitarist.

Much later, George was to develop a kind of 'country-and-eastern' style on bottleneck (or slide) guitar. An inappreciable novelty in mainstream pop, bottleneck was, musically, as distinctive a signature as the mark of Zorro for some British R & B musicians – notably Brian Jones, Alexis Korner and John Mayall – though it was difficult to play creatively and well. With no *Play in a Day* published for slide, you were in virgin territory and, as they did, you had to learn what you could from records and trial-and-error. Tuned to a open chord, the guitar's strings were fretted with a finger-sized glass or metal cylinder, say, a test-tube or bit of piping. From sustained shiver to undulating *legato*, the resonant effects were most commonly heard in the contrasting spheres of Hawaiian music and ethnic blues.

Brian Jones and John Mayall were also recognized masters of blues harmonica (or 'mouth-organ' as Larry Adler would have it), as were Cyril Davis, Paul Jones, Keith Relf and the Downliners Sect's Ray Sone. Rod Stewart and Steve Marriot had both coveted Sone's job – and so did Van Morrison when first he encountered the group: 'It was at the Ken Colyer club. They were really doing it then. I heard the Pretty Things, but the Downliners Sect were *it*.'

The Sect were, if nothing else, multifaceted and, arguably, Britain's foremost Bo Diddley interpreters, with a typical set swerving from Diddley to rural blues to Chuck Berry to 'I Want My Baby Back'. You'd even hear skiffle and country-and-western in there. It did not reconcile easily on disc, however, and the Sect, acclaimed as they were within the walls of Studio 51 and the Crawdaddy, found themselves scrabbling around for a record deal the same as all other also-rans.

Moreover, you could have the most extensive R & B repertoire in the world, sing like a half-caste nightingale or make a guitar talk, but if, like Alexis Korner and Cyril Davis, you suffered from middle age, obesity or baldness, you'd never get more than a cult following. Whatever your popularity, booking fees would remain at best static because, then as now, most promoters took no account of inflation[104].

Not that this bothered the Rolling Stones, who could offer both R & B credibility and teen appeal, with Mick Jagger's grotesque beauty and Brian Jones' exaggerated blond moptop. Moreover, cash flow was such that Bill Wyman, now with a wife and child, was able to think seriously of packing in his day job as a storekeeper. No more a Blues Incorporated splinter group by 1963, they had secured a season at the Crawdaddy where they entertained an increasingly tighter jam of 'youths' and, half a class up, 'young people' whose liberal-minded parents collected them afterwards in Morris Minor 'woody' estate cars.

Through knowing Brian Epstein, club promoter Georgio Gomelsky engineered a visit to the Crawdaddy by the Beatles after they'd recorded a *Thank Your Lucky Stars* at nearby Teddington studios. It would be a fillip for the Stones if they impressed an act who, in April 1963, were bigger than Frank Ifield. As Georgio had foreseen, the Beatles took a shine to the Stones who were exciting their Crawdaddy audiences as much as John, Paul *et al* had theirs at the Cavern. On George Harrison's recommendation, soul-tortured Dick Rowe would appropriate the Stones for Decca, still gorging itself with beat groups in hopes that one of them might have Beatle-sized potential.

Many rungs below the Stones then were groups like the Cheynes, the Others, Gary Farr and the T-Bones – who introduced the tambour to British pop – and Hereford's Shakedown Sound (who would mutate into Mott the Hoople). For these outfits, the aim was for one engagement per week to net the same as that pocketed by, say, Paul Samwell-Smith for five days as a daytime electrical engineer since his Yardbirds took over the Stones' residency at the Crawdaddy in spring 1963, and Jim McCarty dared to tell his mother that he was about to chuck in his soul-destroying job in the City to become a full-time Yardbird.

One of the quintet's first professional tasks was a tour in February 1964 with Sonny Boy Williamson, bowler-hatted and vulture-like in posture. This included a remarkable yet not untypical date at Birmingham Town Hall, where master of ceremonies Bob Wooler – imported from Liverpool's Cavern – completed a well-modulated build-up for the first act who were 'at a sort of turning point in their career because they have decided that following the show tonight, they will turn pro' – like all the other poor sods – 'and we'll have them on television and nationwide tours' – some hope. The Spencer Davis Group's brief spot enabled adjustments to be made to the stage sound, the better to tape on a fancy Ampex reel-to-reel the more important artistes who'd be on later.

The Group weren't so unnerved that they couldn't join in the assembled cast's 'I Got My Mojo Working' finale. Even so, they'd been eclipsed, not surprisingly, by participants other than that repulsive old Mississippi legend whose spot had climaxed with 'harmonica contortions in which he even played the instrument with his nose'.[104]

On Wooler's insistence, second on had been Cavern regulars the Roadrunners, and carrying the torch for the late Cyril Davis, Long John Baldry's All-Stars had had in their ranks Humphrey Lyttelton's pianist and Ottilie Patterson who'd belted out the first 'I Got My Mojo Working' of the evening. Sending the Ampex's recording level off the dial had been 'the powerful rocking singing of young Rod Stuart' (*sic*),[104] once one of Jimmy Powell's Five Dimensions. Within the audience was another who was to trouble the world further into the decade: a certain Robert Plant of Bloxwich who'd be among those picking up the pieces when the Yardbirds fragmented in an unimagined future.

When Sonny Boy's bass harmonica was stolen afterwards, Plant was a prime suspect. Presumably, the best opportunity for larceny was when a caretaker, anxious to lock up, pulled the main electricity switch when all that awful din ran over by half an hour and turned into 'a late-night Twist session'[104] – 'late' in that innocent era meaning 9.30 p.m.

Both the Spencer Davis Group and 'the much improved Moody Blues Five'[100] performed at the next Town Hall R & B concert. Each operated in a parallel dimension to the denizens of the dance halls. In a way, being mentioned in the same *Midland Beat* paragraphs as the ordinary pop groups glad to festoon such newspapers' pages may have been detrimental to an outfit held in awe by people like the discerning Noddy Holder. The fifteen-year-old's gut reaction when he came across the Spencer Davis Group in 1964 is worth quoting at length: 'Of all the bands I saw in those days, they were the ones who impressed me most musically. They were very unassuming onstage . . . and then they launched into that old John Lee Hooker number, 'Dimples' . . . gosh, my mouth fell open and I felt a chill down my spine. That was the night I discovered rhythm-and-blues for the first time.'[105]

Earning similar approval further north, the Sheffields – like London's Mark Leeman Five and Artwoods – were exactly eighteen years ahead of 1983's brief jazz craze, spearheaded by Carmel and Animal Nightlife. The Sheffields' best-remembered release was an ambitious beat group treatment of vibraphonist Milt Jackson's 'Bag's Groove' which they retitled 'Skat Walking', commensurate with its wordless vocal duet. First recorded by the Miles Davis All-Stars in 1954, this brave updating had no precedent in a pop context. Too clever for the charts, the Sheffields were to be commended for overlooking outright commercial concerns, but such an uncompromising stance provoked a tailing off of engagements, and this promising group disintegrated in 1965.

Straighter groups had traced that R & B scent less closely by ditching stage suits and fab-gear winsomeness for longer hair and scruffy aloofness. The Mustangs took what the *Herald of Wales* described as a 'big gamble'[103] by replacing all the Top 20 pop with R & B. No longer milking their audiences either, Warwick's Tony and the Talons became the Original Roadrunners. 'There were two factions in the band', remembered their Edgar Broughton, 'one for the rural stuff, and one for Chicago blues.'[106]

Keith Hartley and Aynsley Dunbar, successive drummers with Rory Storm and the Hurricanes, would each garner a greater celebrity with John Mayall's Bluesbreakers and then as leaders of their own blues-based ensembles. Likewise, guitarist Roger Dean quit Russ Sainty's Nu-Notes for Mayall, and, after Rolling Stone Ian Stewart had lent him relevant R & B import albums, Jeff Beck formed Nightshift with Kerry Rapid's drummer, Dave Elridge. The Troggs' less direct indoctrination came from a long haul to Basildon to catch the Kinks and the gradual incorporation of the London group's R & B influences into the Troggian *oeuvre*.

The Atlantix of open-all-night Burton-on-Trent made a cleaner break by playing a farewell engagement before reforming the next week as denim-clad Rhythm and Blues Incorporated. Just as prosaic in name and style were the Beaconsfield Rhythm and Blues Group, Blues By Six, Leeds' Blue Sounds and, all the way from Grantham, the Rhythm and Blues Group. All Hohner Bluesvampers and 'Hoochie Coochie Man' too were Southampton's Howlin' Wolves, the Boll Weevils from dem ole cottonfields of Erdington, Sam Spade's Gravediggers from Coventry, two groups called the King Bees (one led by David Bowie) and the Primitives whose debut 45 was Sonny Boy Williamson's 'Help Me' with the original as a most helpful demo.

The Primitives made the mistake of the televised haircuts, and Vance Arnold and the Avengers (formerly Joe Cocker's Cavaliers) were to head in the same forlorn direction. During a Saturday night residency at Sheffield's Minerva, they'd phased out bow-tied copies of current hits on noticing that the wildest applause was saved for the blues numbers that Joe Cocker had insisted on sticking in from the beginning. The admittedly biased *Sheffield Telegraph* opined that Joe-Vance 'is surely a star of the future'[42] after he and the Avengers had held their own whilst supporting the Rolling Stones at the City Hall.

A one-shot 45 for Decca, however, was a routine race through 'I'll Cry Instead' from *A Hard Day's Night*, after plans for Cocker and the Avengers to release 'I Got My Mojo Working' were scrapped because of too many rival covers (including one by the Sheffields). 'I'll Cry Instead' was heckled during a tour with the Merseybeats, which was interrupted by an out-of-character spot on the ITV variety show, *Stars and Garters*. The horror passed, Decca washed its hands of them, and Cocker and Co. went back to whatever local venues would have them after they metamorphosed into Joe Cocker's Big Blues – which was all they played by then.

Them's first 45, Slim Harpo's 'Don't Start Crying Now', was also bound for deletion, giving little indication that they were superior to any other victims of the same passion. Attention to the *Muddy Waters at Newport* LP resulted in sound readings of 'Hoochie Coochie Man' by Dave Berry,

Manfred Mann and Long John Baldry. This, 'Help Me', 'I Got My Mojo Working' and all the others went down a storm onstage but on vinyl, their blunt lyrics and stylized chord cycles did not merit inclusion even in a 1964 Top 50 that had welcomed Howlin' Wolf's 'Smokestack Lightning' and, aided by a photo call outside Twickenham Girls Grammar, the Yardbirds' 'Good Morning Little Schoolgirl'.

Appealing to a similar bohemian market, Bob Dylan's first four albums had been bestsellers, so the calculated risk of releasing an LP seemed a sensible stroke to pull after making only little or no headway in the singles charts. Reasonable sales for albums by John Mayall, the Yardbirds, Georgie Fame, the Downliners Sect and the Spencer Davis Group confirmed that mediocre sales on 45 were but a surface manifestation of regard by sixth formers, undergraduates and the art school mob. *Their First LP* by the Spencer Davis Group left its mark at a gratifying Number Five in the UK album list well before they finally cracked the Top 10 with 'Keep On Running', while Mayall albums performed similarly without him making even the smallest inroad into the UK singles charts.

Nevertheless, before the stronger budgetary commitment to albums peculiar to the later 1960s manifested itself, most R & B groups that wanted to stay in business remained geared for *Top of the Pops* – and, as 1965 got underway, there was cause for optimism. *Melody Maker*'s 'Pop 50' for January showed the Stones in retreat from Number One with an unrevised 'Little Red Rooster', whose blues pedigree could be traced through Sam Cooke to the Griffin Brothers' US hit of 1951 to the first recording by Howlin' Wolf. Colliding with the falling Stones were up-and-coming Them with their definitive 'Baby Please Don't Go'. Not far ahead was the Animals' Top 10 entry, 'Inside Looking Out' – originally recorded as 'My Rebirth'. Wilfully devoid of a whistleable tune to carry its harrowing prison narrative, it had first been tried by Eric Burdon during a 1965 jam with Blues Incorporated under the more genteel title of 'Rosie'.

Some groups also did well with black styles from the West Indies. Access to the raw material had been mainly via import shops in suburbs with a pronounced Caribbean immigrant population, and 'turntable hits' at exclusive discotheques in London and the bigger cities. Amid the holocaust of the Big Beat was the infiltration of 'bluebeat' – derived from the ska-mento-calypso melting pot – into the UK Top 50 in the spring of 1964. An example of the real McCoy – 'King of Kings' by Ezz Reco and his Launchers – had drifted into the lower marches in March, while soaring into the Top 10 was 'My Boy Lollipop' by Jamaica's own Millie, and a revival of 'Mockin' Bird Hill' from the 1940s, which had been invested with a hiccuping 'bluebeat' lope by the Migil Five. After 'Mockin' Bird Hill', they issued ersatz bluebeat deformations of numbers such as 'Long Ago and Far Away' and Johnnie Ray's 'Cry'.

Trying to cash-in too were the Bluebeaters, the Blue Beats, the Beazers (alias Chris Farlowe and the Thunderbirds) and, Gawd help us, the Mersey Blue Beats, a last-ditch merger of two scouse units, Lee Castle and the Barons and Adam and the Sinners. Then came 'I'm the Greatest' – after heavyweight champion Cassius Clay's slogan – by Ross McManus[107] with the Joe Loss Blue Beats. The unforgiving galumphing rhythm persisted on Light Programme bandleader Loss's 'March of the Mods', a record I hate as much as Sonny and Cher's 'I Got You Babe'.

Leeds' Crazy Tymes, however, claimed to 'have been performing in this particular style since 1960'[87], and, as well as anticipating jazz-rock by five years, Georgie Fame's *Live at the Flamingo* LP and the self-explanatory EP, *Rhythm and Bluebeat*, featured West Indian set-works that had been in his stage set since 1962.

Fame and most progressive R & B musicians kept more eagerly abreast with what was becoming known as 'soul music'. Along with 'classical', 'soul' is the most abused expression in music. Steve Winwood had become wary of praise for his soul-singing, especially 'when people say I can blow Wilson Pickett off the stage. No matter how hard you try, you can never sing the blues like a coloured person. That's their life they are singing about.'[108] The lyrics of Pickett's biggest UK hit, 'In the Midnight Hour', describe a situation not exclusive to black experience. Both Pickett and white Chris Farlowe – who covered the song, and was billed as 'the greatest Blues Singer in the world today'[109] – sound equally thrilled about the prospect of a tryst beneath the stars. How then do you make a value judgement like Winwood's? The argument about white incapacity to 'sing the blues like a coloured person' loses ground through Farlowe's version of T-Bone Walker's 'Stormy Monday Blues' which, released under the guise of 'Little Joe Cook', tricked most into believing Farlowe was an obscure negro blues singer.

What, therefore, is 'soul'? Is it someone who sounds as if he needs to clear his throat? Is is the West Indian next door lilting a never-ending 'Stand By Me' as he creosotes the toolshed – or is it the hammy ritualism that most of the Stax and Motown reviews demonstrated in the mid-1960s? Let me hear you say 'yeah'.

Along with soul 45s by James Brown, the Supremes, Marvin Gaye, Edwin Starr, Nina Simone and others that were saturation-plugged into the Top 50 by pirate radio, those in the know were also *au fait* with 'Harlem Shuffle' from Bob and Earl, the surrealism of Billy Stewart's versions of 'Summertime' and 'Secret Love' – all stammering and rrrolling rrr's – 'Mocking Bird' by Inez and Charlie Foxx, which enlivened two otherwise interminable *Ready*

Steady Go spots by the two in 1964, and Stax house band Booker T and the MGs' 'Green Onions', an instrumental adopted by, among others, the Downliners Sect, Georgie Fame (who added perfunctory lyrics) and the Brian Auger Trinity (on an EMI 45, 'Sixty-Five Green Onions'). Its riff was also reworked on B-sides by the Stones ('Stoned') and The Dave Clark Five ('Move On'), and both the Five and Georgie Fame did 'You Can't Sit Down' by the Phil Upchurch Combo, the MG's Chicago compeers, and Manfred Mann recorded 'Watermelon Man', a surprise US hit in 1962 for black jazz pianist Herbie Hancock.

There was also much hard listening to both the back catalogue and the latest by even old timers such as the Drifters, the Coasters, Chubby Checker and the Chiffons as well as newer entrants in the US soul charts like Chuck Jackson, Brenda Holloway, Kim Weston, Don Covay, Betty Everett, Doris Troy, Little Stevie Wonder and the Soul Sisters. This strapping duo's 'I Can't Stand It' and then Holloway's 'Every Little Bit Hurts' were quickly thrust out as consecutive singles by the Spencer Davis Group. Carl Wayne and the Vikings and the Small Faces each featured 'Every Little Bit Hurts' on stage, and Cliff Bennett stretched 'I Can't Stand It' into a five-minute piledriver by doubling its tempo.

Yet it was hip to say you preferred the black blueprints of these and the Hollies' 'Just One Look' (Doris Troy), the Untamed's 'I'll Go Crazy' (James Brown), the Roulettes' 'Tracks of My Tears' (Miracles), 'One Fine Day' by the Mindbenders (Chiffons), the Bo Street Runners' 'Tell Me What You're Gonna Do' (James Brown again), First Gear's 'The In Crowd' (Dobie Gray), Tony Jackson's 'Watch Your Step' (Bobby Parker), and the Fourmost's 'Baby I Need Your Loving' (Four Tops).

A murderous mood pervaded a UK package tour in 1966 because the Hollies and the Tremeloes were both playing the Four Tops' 'Reach Out I'll Be There' – a number that the former group were thinking of recording purely for the European market if the Tops version flopped – as Cliff Bennett was about to do with Sam and Dave's 'Hold On I'm Coming'. The Cherokees would not regain impetus long lost after 'Seven Daffodils' through procrastination about 'Land of 1,000 Dances', an error of judgement that finished them during a battle with the Action, another EMI act, over this Chris Kenner opus that was won, oddly enough, by an even later entrant, Wilson Pickett.

The Zombies acquitted themselves well on stage with cultivated choices like the Impressions' 'It's Alright', but, after three 45s made a depressingly familiar descent into the bargain bin, the group blocked off a rich seam of internal A-side songwriting resources for resigned copies of US soul. The last of these, Little Anthony's 'Goin' Out of My Head', arrived too late to prevent an inferior version by Dodie West stealing the risible Top 40 thunder.

Since gaining an EMI contract in 1964, Dean Ford and the Gaylords had confined themselves almost exclusively to A-side soul covers, whether Chubby Checker's 'Twenty Miles', the Coasters' 'Little Egypt' (issued six months after a Downliners Sect version) and a 1965 arrangement of 'The Name Game' from Shirley Ellis. To Scottish Mods – who tended to be more specialist about the music than the Sassenachs – nothing yet indicated that the Ford unit were more special than any other soul-influenced group to be found anywhere else on these islands.

With only their reputation at South Kensington's Crypt Youth Club to lose, the Little Boy Blues started again as the Soul System, while the Mighty Atoms, now resident at Brighton's Chatsfield Hotel, became the Mike Stuart Span, added a horn section, and 'were trying to play soul,' admitted Stuart. The Span met tough opposition from other south coast outfits like Southampton's Soul Agents – who shared Sandie Shaw's habit of performing in bare feet – and Eastleigh's Big T Show, runners-up in *Melody Maker*'s 1965 band competition, who were fronted by Penny, Jenny and Fran, once a Basingstoke folk club trio, as a Caucasian Supremes. Ruling the roost, however, were Simon Dupree and the Big Sound (formerly the Howlin' Wolves). 'We always left rude messages for them on dressing room walls,'[110] grinned Mike Stuart [Stuart Hobday].

In Leicester, the Farinas hadn't bothered yet with a name change, but their transition from R & B to soul still necessitated the incorporation of saxophonists James King and, from Danny Storm and the Strollers, Roger Chapman. Meanwhile, the journey to a Joe Cocker barely recognizable from the singer (and demonstrator) of 'Let's Twist Again' at the Minerva continued in autumn 1966 when he injected his ancient blues repertoire with a massive shot of Stax and Tamla preferences, and was lauded as 'Sheffield's king of soul' in Peter Stringfellow's sleeve notes to 1967's *Rag Goes Mad at the Mojo*, an in-concert EP that could scarcely be given away when first pressed.

Birmingham's Locomotive were to have a long wait for their first (and only) hit, too. They'd been the Kansas City Seven when in transition from mainstream jazz via R & B to is-everybody-havin'-a-good-time soul routines and matching stage outfits. Come 1966, it was decided that, as a name, Kansas City Seven was too Acker Bilk. More in keeping with the new style, Locomotive were 'full steam ahead for the charts'. This statement of intent was amplified by the group's rabble-rouser, Danny King: 'We like the crowd to really join in and feel they're actively participating. We try to create a happy party atmosphere.'[111] Danny – one of the city's best vocalists – was a prize acquisition on a par with Locomotive's sensational four-piece horn section.

Bookings flooded in from as far afield as Up the Junction in Crewe, Stoke-on-Trent's Golden Torch, and even from the clutch of new clubs in and around the capital like Blaises, the Pontiac, Annie's Place, Tiles and Woolwich's Location. There were about ten fashionable central London niteries and precious few regional ones from which a pop elite and their hangers-on – the 'in crowd' – could select a night out: 'night' defined as round midnight to dawn; 'fashionable' meaning that the supercool Ad-Lib near Leicester Square would be 'in' for a while before the inscrutable pack transferred allegiance to the Speakeasy or Great Newport Street's Pickwick before finishing up at either the Cromwellian in SW7 for the finals of the national 'Bend' competition – a dance devised by disc-jockey Mike Quinn – the Bag O' Nails off Carnaby Street, the Speakeasy, the Scotch of St James and maybe four other hangouts, attractive for their strict membership controls, tariffs too highly priced for the Average Joe, lighting more flattering than that in a Butlin's ballroom, and no photographers admitted.

Scrutinized through club spy-holes and not found wanting, pop *conquistadores* would hold court with only their equals contradicting them. Close at hand would be a whisky-and-coke and, depending on status, an abundance of skinny Quant-cropped dolly-birds with double-decker eyelashes. In the house discotheque's deafening dark, no one Twisted any more. The order of the day was now the Banana, the Monkey and other US dances that no Briton was supposed to have mastered yet – though the headache-inducing Shake was rife in the ballrooms.

An alternative to cutting a rug in the Speakeasy was to saunter down to the Revolution in Mayfair to hear Lee Dorsey or the Ike and Tina Turner Revue. Slumming it further, you might end up in Soho inside the Crazy Elephant, Roaring Twenties, Marquee or Flamingo, mingling with those up too late to pester anyone for autographs. Instead, they'd be grooving to Zoot Money's Big Roll Band, Georgie Fame and the Blue Flames, the Peddlers, Herbie Goins and the Nightimers, Chris Farlowe and the Thunderbirds, Jimmy James and the Vagabonds, the Graham Bond Organization, Cliff Bennett and the Rebel Rousers, the Brian Auger Trinity or Julian Covay and the Machine with its two drummers – all 'group's groups' that meant little in the Top 40 but were appreciated by other artists for their stylistic tenacity and exacting standards, and noted for those they employed who went on to greater success.

Teen appeal didn't come into it. The Peddlers, for instance, were a seated, short-haired trio with an ex-Tornado on bass, a drummer from Faron's Flamingos and the Dowlands' former guitarist Roy Phillips on organ and vocals. For much of 1964, their jazz-pop concoctions had been heard nightly in the Scotch of St James, and the following January, a treatment of 'Let The Sun Shine In', delivered by Roy in a sort of blues-tinged snort, slipped into – and quickly out of – the Top 50.

The Peddlers were a democratic exception, for most the 'in' bands sported 'somebody and the somebodies' names with the 'somebody' having the same all-powerful hold over the others as Lonnie Donegan had on his Skiffle Group. A firm believer in the virtues of punctuality and discipline, Cliff Bennett once fired a horn player for drunkenness on stage – and God help you if he caught you with drugs. Although he rated the Stones as musicians, Cliff was a vitriolic critic of long hair on men. With their neat coiffeur and suits, he and the Rebel Rousers resembled a Mafia hit squad. Yet, on rousing the interest of Brian Epstein in 1964, Cliff's seventh single, 'One Way Love', a Drifters item, received unexpected exposure when a peak-hour TV trailer for a pop series on the BBC's new second channel broadcast it in its entirety. After this left the Top 10, Bennett stuck to the Drifters for 'I'll Take You Home' which, at a paltry Number Forty-two, was his last chart strike until 'Got To Get You Into My Life', a James Brown pastiche, was presented to him backstage one night by its composers, Paul McCartney on vocal and acoustic guitar and John Lennon making horn section noises. This gave Cliff and his ever-changing Rebel Rousers their biggest and final hit.

A series of flop singles also heralded Georgie Fame and the Blue Flames' Number One in 1964 with Jon Hendricks' 'Yeah Yeah', which precipitated a sarcastically-titled album, *Fame At Last*, and erratic Top 40 placings spread over several years. These included another chart-topper in 'Get Away' before it was dragged down by Chris Farlowe's 'Out of Time', the only 45 of his to get past Number Thirty.

Graham Bond and Zoot Money had likewise looked chartwards with uncharacteristic material such as the respective muggy ballads, 'Tammy' and Burt Bacharach's 'Please Stay' – in complete contrast to Zoot's hard-hitting 'Big Time Operator' at Number Twenty-five in 1966, which was more like the singing organist who yelled his head off down the Flamingo during a sweat-soaked work-out of 'In the Midnight Hour'.

Though proclaiming itself 'the Swinging Club of Swinging London', the Flamingo wasn't the Harlem Apollo but it was the nearest to it you were ever likely to experience in Britain with first London appearances by luminaries such as Little Stevie Wonder, Rufus Thomas and sequinned Dionne Warwick – all backed by whatever band was resident that day. Certain musicians with adrenalin pumping would need little coaxing to 'sit in' with *ad hoc* onstage aggregations, sometimes involving US visitors like Thomas and Wonder. On a crowded stage one summer evening, Ringo Starr and and Denny Laine were the bedrock of, recalled Starr, 'one of the worst bands I've ever been in'.[112] Making a noise on another occasion at the Marquee were Laine, two of Manfred's men, skeletal London-Irish drummer Peter 'Ginger' Baker from the Graham Bond Organization, organist Brian Auger, the venerable Alexis

Korner, Ronnie Jones of the Nightimers; and ex-'Tommy Steele of Scotland' Alex Harvey on the make with his Soul Band.

At Knuckles, a newer place, ex-Pretty Thing Viv Prince, its reliably unreliable host, might be beastly drunk at the bar when the Spencer Davis Group arrived to be 'greeted by the Animals and P.J. Proby. Stevie Winwood was soon on stage jamming with Brian Auger, Long John Baldry and the VIPs while Eric Burdon bellowed for "Lucille" '.[113]

It was a more formal Spencer Davis Group booking at the Flamingo in 1964 that had so knocked out Decca's freelance recording manager Mike Vernon that the then-unsigned outfit were brought to RG Studio in Morden to cut a demo under his supervision. To intrigue one such as Vernon was a feather in any aspiring R & B combo's cap. For a start, he knew what he was talking about, having compiled *R & B Monthly*, perhaps the first 'fanzine' of its kind in Britain. His first essay as a producer had been an LP by Texas-born pianist Curtis Jones who – like another Vernon artist, Champion Jack Dupree – had made Britain his home.

As well as the *bona fide* US article, Mike searched our blues- and soul-derived British talent. Among his earlier discoveries were the Graham Bond Organization, the Artwoods and the Yardbirds. Nevertheless, it helped if, like the Beatles, groups wrote their own songs. This may have explained why Decca weren't keen on either Vernon's Spencer Davis tape or one of Howlin' Wolf's 'Smokestack Lightning' by the Who, traders in loud 'Maximum R & B'. Decca had reckoned that these two new groups weren't right for teenagers: we know these things, Mike.

14 NICE LADS WHEN YOU GET TO KNOW THEM

There was, apparently, no company in which the Beatles couldn't feel at home. The strangest booking of their career had taken place in 1963 at Stowe public school where 'Twist and Shout' *et al* precipitated only polite clapping from the seated young toffs and their swingin' headmaster. During high tea, it was pointed out to the group that school rules were so libertarian that you weren't marched directly to the barber's if your hair touched your ears.

Almost everywhere else, you'd risk suspension for cultivating a Beatle cut – though a boy who arrived at his secondary modern one morning in 1964 with a Yul Brynner all-off was sent home on the grounds that it was just as attention-seeking. Yet, as Ringo Starr pointed out, 'If you look at early pictures of us with long hair, we had nothing'.[114] But after his Beatles made the Australian Top 10, a starchy Sydney headmistress barred not only the wearing of *pilzen kopfs* but also membership of fan clubs and carrying pop star pin-ups in satchels.

Girls getting used to mini-skirts would trim their newly-cut fringes with nail-clippers, so a psychiatrist wrote, 'to identify with these characters as either other girls or as sexual neuters'. This may have been why all-boys' schools were specially strict about short hair as a mark of sobriety and masculinity. It also labelled those who didn't mind it as supportive of a kind of official malevolent neutrality towards intellectually-stultifying pop groups. Yardbirds bass player Paul Samwell-Smith would recall that, 'There was a lot of opposition at [Hampton Grammar] school. Our music master was quite good but the head put a stop to it straight away – because it was dirty. He thought that anyone in rock 'n' roll and R & B must be involved in sex and drugs.'

Torquay Grammar made history in 1963 by presenting a pop group at its annual concert – albeit the drummerless Vikings. 'We don't need one,' explained rhythm guitarist Margaret Hobley, whose schoolboy brother David played lead. 'We make up for it with a strong beat on rhythm.'[31] Treading warily at other seats of learning were Jazz Clubs that dared to devote perhaps one meeting a term to, say, 'Blues and Jazz-Influenced Pop Singers'. At Farnborough Grammar, there was even a Blues Club that folded when 'Trunky' Cotgreave, deputy head, realized that, beyond a sociological study of aspects of black America, members actually enjoyed listening to its 'screaming idiotic words and savage music' – as a US segregationist handbill put it.

In less rarified spheres, beat music was gaining ground. Led by a chocolate factory taster, Pete Budd and the Rebels – with a sax player who once strummed banjo for Acker Bilk – played before kick-off at Bristol Rovers' stadium. Top 20 selections were heard over the PA at Tottenham Hotspurs soccer pitch too; the Dave Clark Five's early hits were particularly popular there for the neo-military percussive hooks that the terraces stamped out on cue. Despite worries about the floorboards, the club committee tolerated these public spins of the Five's discs. Not only had local lad Dave called his publishing company 'Spurs Music', but he was also leader of a group with a sporty outlook as shown in the keep-fit scene that opened *Catch Us If You Can*.

This was much at odds with the effeminte aura radiating from the likes of the Rolling Stones – 'the Five Shaggy Dogs with a brand of "shake" all their own' – as one local rag had it.[115] A simple image – the cover of the Stones' first EP – could trigger a ten-year battle with Authority over hair. Depending on how long the metaphorical wool could be pulled over the eyes of parents and teachers, you might approximate a Stone feather-duster or, as he was the most androgynously hirsute Beatle, try to look like someone who looks like George. The hair-style of the Small Faces, the ultimate Mod group, emphasized the cult's solidarity in the mid-1960s as the moptop had earlier. It involved a centre parting to the crown and a bouffant back-combing the rest of the way with the sides brushed straight over the ears.

These beat groups visited the barber's more frequently than their detractors imagined. A statement that some took as vague defence had come from Mr Scowcroft, president of the National Hairdressers Federation: 'Men's hairdressers do not object to youth wanting to wear its hair long, provided it is shaped.' He objected, nevertheless, to 'bardic beatles who believe that masses of woolly, straggly hair are a sign of intellectualism'.[116]

Long hair wasn't a red rag to just adults. In a country town where the 1950s didn't really end until about 1966, youths might be relaxing over a game of darts in the pub:

'Mine's a Guinness. Double six to win, isn't it? What about that lot on at the town hall, eh? The band room's like a poufs' parlour.'

'Yeah – and they make a terrible racket into the bargain. Don't look now but three of 'em have just walked into the lounge bar.'

'Hello! The landlord's refused to serve 'em. I don't blame him. Get a load of that cissy heading for the gents. Wrong one, mate!'

Apart from a handful of followers cowering near the sanctuary of the stage, long-haired groups were often faced with onlookers determined to hate them. Within a minute of the first number, a roughneck, bold with beer, might have to be restrained physically from slamming his fist through a PA speaker, having decided to be a lion of justice, striking a blow for decent entertainment for decent folk. Yet such attention was not typical. Most of the audience would keep their distance – though howls of derision, sporadic barracking and slow handicapping would flare up.

What couldn't be admitted was finding the group's androgyny guiltily transfixing. By slightly overdoing the obnoxiousness, the musicians revelled in a repellent bewitchment – and under the stage lights, they certainly looked and sounded Big Time. The set would end with long seconds of silence before grudging applause from a shell-shocked crowd. Local burghers getting wind of this might ban further pop concerts, but immediately after the show, however, there'd be entranced converts who vanished into the night lost in wonder. A sea-change had occurred, and years of incomprehension, lamentation, deprivation, uproar assault and domestic 'atmospheres' would follow.

In Aldershot Magistrates Court in 1965, a man accused of beating up a complete stranger offered the plea, 'Well, he had long hair, hadn't he?' as a defence. Even when it became acceptable for studs to grow it longer than a crew-cut, you could still invite persecution from those whose brusque coiffeur was governed by work conditions. 'Peter's pride was his shoulder-length hair,' began an amused write-up in the *Daily Express* about the scalping of a teenager by British soldiers garrisoned in Cyprus. The *Express* also made much of the scream-rent heroes' welcome laid on by their womenfolk when the Greenjackets touched down in Gatwick after their peace-keeping chore in the Mediterranean was over.

Peter would have sympathized with a Farnborough Grammar pupil who was held fast while his nape-length locks were hacked off by some 'manly' types in safe assurance of leniency from Mr Cotgreave – for whom hair was as touchy a subject as it was for those he penalized.

Men don't have periods and can't get pregnant, but pillars of Women's Liberation might note how difficult the issue of hair could be for boys in the 1960s who had to fight every literal inch of the way. With much the same attitude as a Great War trench private resigned to a stray bullet on the Somme, I would practise being Mick Jagger before the bedroom mirror to the detriment of physics homework, and on the understanding that, within the hour, I could be eating my fourteen-year-old heart out in front of that same mirror after a enforced – and seemingly arbitrary – trip to the barber which would humiliate and degrade me, as it would a village elder in Tzarist Russia being punished – as was common – by the removal of his flowing patriarchal beard.

No amount of backcombing, pulling or applications of a thickening gel·called Dippety-Do could disguise my shearing, and I'd make the best of a bad job, sprucing up for another small death at a local hall, trying to pick up a girl to the music of either the Modern Art of Living, the Unadorned, Soulbucket or the Sound of Time: all the local pop stars. At a time when a leader in a tabloid newspaper advocated a law that made short-back-and-sides compulsory for men, it would make my day – actually, the whole month – when some Oscar Wilde bawled 'get yer 'air cut!' from a passing car while his grinning mates twisted round in the back seat to register the effect of this witticism on me. I wasn't insulted – I was proud. At last, it was long enough to show.

Attempts were made to evict the Pretty Things from their Belgravia flat. This was largely because of the bad name they'd given the place after they'd first flashed into respectable homes with a TV appearance in which their cascading tresses – longer than those of the Rolling Stones – had flickered across surly, blemished complexions. Many teenagers were just as aghast as their parents. While even the coolest mums and dads battled for control of their features, the effect was most keenly felt by acned, middle-class youths who had previously gazed with yearning at the cover of *With the Beatles*: if only Mum would let me have my hair like George's then I wouldn't go on about it any more.

The eviction was nipped in the bud following a *Checkpoint*-type investigation on ITV, but, on the road, the Things still suffered from eleventh-hour cancellations by hoteliers, punch-ups with provincial cowboys and some unpleasantness with a shotgun at one particular cultural backwater. There were God-slot TV discussions concerning the depth to which pop music had sunk with this championship of such degenerates. The Pretty Things themselves were once hauled in to answer clerical criticism, but their verbal contributions were hastily restricted when they began upsetting the programme's intentions by using long words, talking correct and generally acting intelligent. Still, the infamy increased turnout at their bookings, even if it became usual for venues to be filled with curiosity-seekers with only the foggiest notion about the music they had paid to hear.

After a spell with the Things and then Georgie Fame, Mitch Mitchell was to be one of the Jimi Hendrix Experience. A great-aunt of mine came to refer to Hendrix as 'that cannibal' for his brown skin and the wide shock of fuzzy corkscrews on his head. An edition of *Good Evening*, an ITV chat-show hosted by Jonathan King, would feature Mitch and his parents conversing about how much Mr and Mr Mitchell had become reconciled to the way their son earned a living in the employ of wildman Hendrix. The foreseeable conclusion was that the Experience were Nice Lads When You Got To Know

Them – just like every other pop group from the Rolling Stones to the Pretty Things to the Sex Pistols.

Back in the Crawdaddy era, the Stones and the Things had been blues outfits. These days, however much *aficionados* might refute the suggestion, many such units would sometimes start behaving dangerously like pop groups; the Downliners Sect once co-existing in war-paint and feather bonnets as Geronimo and the Apaches with Calamity Jane. Past 1962's knotted-brow 'appreciation' of Cyril Davis perspiring over his mouth-organ or burly Ian Stewart's boogie piano, an old blues trainspotter's view was now blocked by girls in paroxysms of ecstasy over frail Keith Relf who needed mothering, youngest Kink Dave Davies with his centre-parting and thigh-high cavalier boots, and serpentine Dave Berry whose Cruisers had adopted identical string ties and Italian suits – though, if South Yorkshire's most illustrious young adult, Berry was once asked to leave a Chesterfield lounge bar because he and his retinue 'looked like beatniks'.

Berry had assumed a 'man in black' look; the Spencer Davis Group costumed themselves in white woollen roll-necks – impractical under sweltering arc lights – while Manfred Mann's beard and Don Craine ('Calamity Jane') of the Downliners Sect's 'headcoat' (i.e. deerstalker) were each as distinctive a gimmick as Johnny Kidd's eyepatch and the perpetual sunglasses of the Roulettes' Russ Ballard.

R & B had regressed, sneered Kenny Ball, to 'rock 'n' roll with a mouth-organ' thanks to these superficially exciting groups who'd sucked Chuck Berry and Bo Diddley into their vortex, and were commercializing soul, gospel and every other black musical form going. 'The Group plays poppy R & B,' chirped Spencer Davis, 'and we aim for a good dancing beat.'[117] The Pretty Things took this further with a stage show that developed into a continuous performance underscored throughout by Diddley's incessant trademark 'shave-and-a-haircut-six-pence' rhythm.

'The best R & B bands I ever heard,' pronounced ex-Roadrunner Mike Hart, 'were the Beatles, the Big Three, the Bobby Patrick Big Six and the Alex Harvey Soul Band, but nobody ever thought of putting them on at these R & B extravaganzas. They weren't boring enough.' Instead, while 1963 was the Beatles' year, the rest were still scrimmaging round the more unsalubrious new venues that were littering British towns such as the Cubik, 'Rochdale's Biggest R & B Club', inaugurated by the Rolling Stones, the St Louis Checks and David John and the Mood.

In such haunts, the Downliners Sect were treading on thinner ice than ever with country-and-western novelties like 'May the Bird of Paradise Fly Up Your Nose'. They got away with it because British R & B, deduced Don Craine, was 'a very strange animal' – and who could argue when listening to the Sect? Their daring repertoire was among factors that earned them a signing to EMI in 1964 after the issue of an in-concert EP, *A Nite In Great Newport Street*, on an independent label.

Their first LP, *The Sect*, was as freighted with Bo Diddley and Chuck Berry covers as those of the Yardbirds who – with a vengeance – followed the Stones, Animals, Kinks and Pretty Things into the Top 10. Their 1965 Number One, 'For Your Love', was from Eric Clapton's last session. For several months, he'd been unhappy about Paul Samwell-Smith's increasing control of the group's destiny. 'Had we continued to play just blues,' argued Paul, 'we would, in the end, have broken through [but] at the time we were desperate for a hit because you suddenly get on television. Everything opens up for you.' This was absolutely true, but while the Yardbirds were to be remembered as one of the most innovative groups of the 1960s, they also acceded to all manner of dubious ploys such as members donning suits of armour for a film short of 'For Your Love', and performing 'Questa Volta', a typically schmaltzy entry in an Italian song festival.

Clapton had been superseded by Jeff Beck who was more willing to participate in the sillier publicity obligations. As a lead guitarist, he displayed eclecticism and unpredictability in compatible amounts, and was a much more visual performer than his predecessor. Among his strategies were picking the guitar behind his head like Joe Brown, and leaving it to feed back while he roved the stage.

Noticing LPs by the Four Seasons, Beach Boys and Julie London in Jeff's flat, the Yardbirds had concluded rightly that he was less committed to the blues than Eric. In Nightshift, he'd been prone to 'going off on a tangent, and everyone would laugh and say, "Play some proper blues." There wasn't much room for experiment.' Neither had there been in his next group, the Tridents – especially during a stint in 1963 backing Craig Douglas.

After '54321' and the comparable Top 20 performance of its follow-up, 'Hubble Bubble', Manfred Mann had also readjusted itself to be a more viable long term chart act. The cruellest necessity had been the replacement of a balding bass guitarist with youthful-looking Tom McGuinness who, like Eric Clapton, had been one of Casey Jones' Engineers. Then the Manfreds squeezed into stage uniforms, and Paul Jones went in for a lot of spasmodic crouching and leaping about.

R & B was their stylistic standing-point, but the group were versatile enough to span other idioms from modern jazz to showbiz evergreens to Bob Dylan to Tamla-Motown. The Animals and the Spencer Davis Group also veered further than Blues Incorporated had towards the modern black sounds of North America whilst making irresistible and danceable concessions to the good, honest trash of hardline pop.

On paper, there wasn't much difference between the Spencer Davis Group and the Troggs apart from the image – contrived or otherwise – that attracted fans to either outfit, be it the Troggs' rustic vigour or Davis lauded as the first Bachelor of Arts to top the charts. After winning strong local renown with an R & B repertoire, each had been signed to a Fontana lease deal. Patchy chart placings – either at home or abroad were accumulated by both quartets before 1966 yielded two fast British Number Ones each. On the world stage for two years, each left a wound in the USA before retreating almost immediately.

As the Group's 'Keep On Running' raced up French and German charts, the *Birmingham Mail* cobbled together a story to go with its headline, 'City Group Top of the Pops!' It also noted that at Number Two with 'The River' was Ken Dodd, currently starring in *Humpty Dumpty* at the Alexandra Theatre. All pop songs are the same, aren't they?

Though it had begun as a bouncy ska demo by Jamaican composer Jackie Edwards, 'Keep On Running' now sounded as American as the Troggs 'Wild Thing'. Containing similar qualities to both 'Keep On Running' and the Rolling Stones' '(I Can't Get No) Satisfaction' was 'Hold Tight' by Dave Dee, Dozy, Beaky, Mick and Tich, with its trendy fuzz guitar and catchy football chant beat. The Spencer Davis Group and before them the Stones, Animals, Kinks and Yardbirds, were pop stars now – just like the Troggs and Dave Dee's outfit – but perhaps they always had been. In any case, it was an end to whatever regard was still felt for them by blues purists and narrow-minded Jazzers.

Glancing up from *Melody Maker*'s jazz pages, an armchaired trad pianist who'd once rubbed shoulders with them at Studio 51, would notice on TV the Stones miming on *The Joe Loss Show*. That they'd done so without compromising their aggressively unkempt image, as they'd had to in 1963 to get on *Thank Your Lucky Stars*, proved that for a group to be a hit, it didn't have to be like the Applejacks, the Honeycombs and all the other butts for the scorn of pop's purported intelligentsia.

In 1965 the most surprising manifestation of R & B's new acceptability was when Alexis Korner, in the footsteps of Bert Weedon, led the house band on *Five O' Clock Club*, the ITV children's series where continuity was provided by Wally Whyton who, seven years earlier, had invited Alexis to join his chart-riding Vipers. The memory of Whyton's glove-puppet compere, Pussy Cat Willum, introducing Korner's gritty rendering of 'See See Rider' isn't easy to forget.

Bert Weedon, meanwhile, remained in the public eye with a spot on *Sunday Night at the London Palladium* where he showed that he could rock out on his Hofner 'cutaway' as well as anyone – and so did the Shadows in

1964 on the twelve-bar 'Rhythm and Greens', 'A raving great send-up of the R & B scene,' in their words.

By then, the Rolling Stones were not only the brightest stars in the R & B firmament, but were an even closer second to the Beatles than Gerry, the Searchers and the Dave Clark Five had been. For weeks in 1964, 'A Hard Day's Night' and the Stones' 'It's All Over Now' had monopolized the first two positions in the British charts (necessitating the avoidance of such revenue-draining clashes in future) until brought down by Manfred Mann's 'Do Wah Diddy Diddy' which in turn fell when 'Have I The Right' by the Honeycombs and the Kinks' 'You Really Got Me' tied at Number One.

The Kinks and the Honeycombs represented the new polarizations of the beat group. Born of the R & B scene rather than straight pop, the Kinks were built to last longest, and they notched up several more smashes by sticking largely to the same riff-based format and borrowing the Stones' angry scowls and sexual suggestiveness for their stage act. The Honeycombs, on the other hand, were all big smiles. Joe Meek's last big fling, 'Have I The Right' owed more to the Dave Clark Five's crude stomp than 'Telstar'. Yet it was Meek's backroom twiddling rather than the Honeycombs themselves that got it to the top. Light and instant with a gimmick female drummer, the group was soon back where they had started.

Lead singer Denis d'Ell was a closet bluesman, but this had no discernable effect on the Honeycombs' output. However, a few other mainstream beat groups flirted with blues on record. At their most rugged, the Four Pennies made a Top 20 killing with an update of Leadbelly's 'Black Girl'. Miming it on TV, Lionel Morton on lead vocals and rhythm guitar got so carried away that he abandoned his six-string altogether during the instrumental break, a display repeated during the Pennies' UK tour with Freddie and the Dreamers, that followed a flying promotional visit to France.

During television interviews and press conferences, musicians were now inclined to gesture with cigarettes and let loose the odd mild expletive like 'cra*p' and 'bl***y'. Antagonized by this, a Tory Member of Parliament, with specific reference to the Beatles, bleated that, 'We must offer teenagers something better.'[118] He did not say what, but causing comment in the House of Commons was the cost to ratepayers of the extra policing and stewardship at Beatle concerts.

That middle-class fathers disparaging them in breakfast rooms knew which one was which was an indication of how cosy Beatlemania had become. At a school speech day in Havant, Lady Nancy Bridge recommended that, 'If you feel you cannot do what is asked of you, think of the Beatles. They have got where they are by sheer hard work.'[119] With her parents' leave, a girl called Jill who lived two doors away from me rang the Champs

Elysees hotel where the Fab Four had checked in before their first concert in Paris. A photo of her gripping the telephone made the front page of the *Fleet Times*.[120]

Fan hysteria had been good-humoured at first. Police patrolling the round-the-block queues kept eyes peeled for the odd runaway, but no bother was expected from beneath the sleeping bags, transistor radios and comics lining the pavements. Once they might have wrung their heads, but now mums and dads would bring provisions to their waiting children. Well, it was only the Beatles.

Once the customers got inside, there were instances of fainting, sure, and heightened blood pressure brought on nose bleeds. The odd tip-up chair would snap off its spindle too – but afterwards the screeching would cease for the National Anthem, to resume half-heartedly before everyone filed quietly out.

Fire hoses, and arbitrary manhandling of fans by exultantly brutal bouncers, were needed to quell riots at shows by those sinister Rolling Stones. A judgement on them was that, after one such fiasco, their guitarist Keith Richards lay among the twenty-two unconscious, hit by a flying bottle. On the sodden carpeting, auditorium cleaners would come across soiled knickers among smashed rows of seating.

In a private prosecution by its manager and a local youth club organizer doing their bit for common decency, three of the Stones were fined in 1965 for pissing against a garage wall. 'Because you have reached exalted heights in your profession, it does not mean that you can behave in this manner,' barked the magistrate who'd never absorbed accelerating adulation throughout late adolescence, and was not under pressures that John Citizen couldn't begin to understand. One of Colchester's Fairies, another bunch of temperamental, long-haired reprobates, had caused death by dangerous driving, and some of the VIPs were in court for criminal damage to British Rail property.

After a particularly exhilarating one-nighter, musicians might storm back to their digs, ruining other guests' rest. Off-duty japes in a Bristol hotel culminated with one member of a well-known group in ripped trousers being knocked cold with an aspidistra pot. The police were called after another asked a vacuum-cleaner for directions to his room. A night porter looked up from the day's first edition of the *Daily Herald* and noticed that he had a woman with him. No, she wasn't his missus, but so what? Do you want to make something of it, mate?

Though 1960s pop musicians were frequently most admirable young men, they had their share of young men's vices. Some were outlined most graphically in Thom Keyes' novel, *All Night Stand*,[121] estimated by guest reviewers Alan Price (in *Disc*) and Bev Bevan (*Midland Beat*) to be a fair fictionalization of a working pop group's secret life. Yet dressing room scenes were sometimes just how susceptible fans might have imagined them: a card or board game on the middle table, the TV on, someone tuning a guitar, another shaving at the wash-basin. However, time which hung heavy between one concert and the next wasn't only killed with snakes-and-ladders and watching *Z-Cars*.

As *omerta* is to the Mafia, a vow of silence concerning illicit sex has always persisted among bands of roving minstrels. Feted wherever you went, a Roman emperor might never have had it so good, and they'd get quite accustomed to demure requests to meet a certain type of girl in, say, the romantic seclusion of a backstage broom cupboard. For such determinate purpose, there was a young lady known as 'The Torpedo', one of many female music-lovers notorious for evading the most stringent security barricades to impose themselves on famous beat groups. Conversely, a midnight raid on a girls' borstal was foiled when a warden woke up to find an Animal snuffling about her bedroom. Certain groups' procurement of sexual gratification was not brought to public notice by a press who judged any besmirching of their cheeky but innocent images as untimely: save the scandal for the Rolling Stones.

I know it's distasteful to carry on mentioning such things but, alas, it's true: members of 1960s pop groups took illegal drugs – but, if all too aware of 'Purple Hearts', 'Black Bombers' and other pep-pills, marijuana ('pot') was then a bit too cloak-and-dagger. Yet it was flattery of a kind if a musician looked disreputable enough for beatniks to ask if he'd care to partake of pot with them. See, it was a herb that was packed into a large cigarette called a 'reefer' and smoked communally in a hidey-hole like, say, an equipment van. After no less than the Beatles giggled through the shooting of *Help!* in a marijuana haze, the rest of the in-crowd sampled its short-lived magic.

Apart from the kicks, pot was used more and more as a narcotic handmaiden to creativity now that pop had started being taken semi-seriously. Newspapers no longer put sniffy inverted commas round the Beatles followed by 'the Liverpool "pop" group'. Hip vicars would slip the Rolling Stones into *Five to Ten*, an incongruous five-minute religious broadcast linking Uncle Mac and *Saturday Club*, and former choristers Muff and Steve Winwood were approached by the vicar to rearrange some hymns and canticles in a more modern style.

In the wake of releases like Fritz Spiegl's Mozart pastiche, 'Eine Kleine Beatlemusik' and 1965's *Beatle Flamenco* EP on Parlophone, a random Beatles B-side, 'Yes It Is,' was analyzed as if it was a Bach fugue in *Music and Musicians*. Yet this highbrow journal's endorsement 'meant they couldn't be any good'[122] to a pop consumer like David Cook (later pop idol David Essex but then an amateur drummer). There were many like Cook for whom the Beatles had 'matured' too quickly and, like Tommy Steele, would be soft-shoe shuffling before you could blink.

Though a concert at the Prince of Wales theatre – scene of the Royal Variety grand slam – had been standing-room-only, everyone on a bill which included the Chants, the Vernons Girls and the omnipresent Kenny Lynch 'went down very well without interruptions from people shouting "we want the Beatles!" like they used to.'[123] Mind you, this was London where Kenny calculated, 'The Rolling Stones may be just as big as the Beatles now.'[123] Nevertheless, innocent of metropolitan *sangfroid*, unabated screaming in the shires indicated that the Moptop Mersey Marvels were just as gear as ever.

15 ACE FACES

After Mod reached the masses – principally via *Ready Steady Go* and pirate radio – around the middle of 1964, most beat groups, even if olde tyme rock 'n' rollers at heart, projected themselves as at least cursory Mods, some giving themselves *de riguer* abstract non-pluralized names as necessary: the Accent, the End, the Static, the Frame, the Gass, the Cat, the Move, the Buzz, the Carnaby and so forth. With practical approbation from the Animals, Stafford's Hipster Image secured a one-shot 45 with Decca, and an Aston outfit called the Mods thumbed noses at a rash of other opportunists by topping a 'Local Group' poll in *Jackie*.

Being a Mod was a soft option because, long hair apart, your parents were less likely to moan about your turnout. They would even help pay for a motor-scooter as long as you didn't get into fights with rough boys in leather windcheaters or smoke those Purple Hearts that you read about in the papers. On the strength of appearance, so-called 'Mods' wouldn't get turned away from the parish dance. They'd even earn praise from the vicar for looking so smart. You could be a bank clerk and still look the part without inviting the sack. At the same time, you'd still be recognized by other initiates by signs as conspiratorial as a freemason's handshake. Some Mods identified themselves by simply leaving all coat buttons undone except the top one.

Back in 1962, prototype Mods were known for a clean pseudo-suavity and a dress sense in constant flux. Everything had to be just so: double-breasted bumfreezers with back vents precisely seven inches one week, exactly five the next. How wide are lapels now? This shirt's got a pointed tab collar which means I can never wear it again. At the Flamingo one Saturday, you had to be electric-blue Italian. Go back the following Thursday and it'd be Parisian. With middle class bohemians generally heading for the G Club in darkest Ealing, the clubs of inner London had worked up a sharper-dressed, principally male clientele, usually from a lower social caste. With their deepest musical roots in an alien US culture, groups like the Who and the Action were tolerated, and were regarded as Mods by yokels in Uxbridge and Staines where all the excesses in which metropolitan Mods allegedly indulged belonged to speculation while sharing a cigarette behind school bike sheds. I know someone whose sister's friend once touched Georgie Fame.

At weekends, 'Mod' clothes weren't much more than gang uniforms in which no pretence was made of keeping up with the on-the-spot Carnaby Street (and, later, King's Road) front-runners. By the time the gear hit provincial outfitters, it was probably 'out' anyway. You could be ostensibly 'in' as long as you had Chelsea boots, corduroy jacket, and hipsters – even if worn to every local hop until you outgrew them. Some followed Who vocalist Roger Daltrey's enterprise in customizing clothes to ersatz Mod standards on his mother's sewing machine.

Of corresponding uniformity were Rockers – later demeaningly called 'Greasers'. Males wore brilliantined ducktails, real or imitation leather jackets, jeans, motorbike boots and T-shirts. The girls sometimes dressed the same but more frequently it was flared skirts, stilettos and beehive hairdos. Their taste in music was similar to that of Teddy Boys. Their gormless hostility towards interlopers into their hang-outs was, too. Among leading Rocker outfits had been the Rockin' Berries. A few months before their formation in 1959, their Clive Lea had defied all comers in an 'Elvis of the Midlands' talent contest. The title was next assumed by Tipton's Nicky James who, backed by a group containing future Moody Blues and Move members, continued defiantly hip-shakin', smirking lop-sidedly like Elvis and oiling his gravity-defying cockade throughout the Mod-dominated beat boom.

On a national level, 'Terry' by Twinkle caught if not the mood, then *a* mood, of 1964. Peaking at Number Four in the charts, it was about a biker who, irked by his girl's infidelity, zooms off to a lonely end of mangled chrome, blood-splattered kerbstones and the oscillations of an ambulance siren. As well as distressing the BBC, it was also banned by *Ready Steady Go*, not for the death content so much as its non-conformity to the programme's Mod specifications. In the following week's *TV Times*, a letter suggested a special edition entitled *Ready* Teddy *Go* – for there was no doubt about Terry's identity.

There was, however, some speculation about Twinkle's: a London dolly-bird singing about a leather boy whose idea of a good time was perhaps an evening on the dodgems at some backdated funfair in the sticks. It was like *West Side Story*, wasn't it: a Mod loving a Rocker?

Actually, enmity between the two tribes was never as virulent as the newspapers made out. Usually, they'd just congregate at opposite ends of a café – though there were still ructions at dances, just like there'd been between rival factions of Teds. At set-piece clashes at seaside resorts during bank holidays, 'It wasn't so much violence as hordes of young people running around and looking for the excitement that others were committing,' expounded John Albon, an eighteen-year-old in Brighton in 1964. 'We were like a huge mobile audience though in fact we were the main act. There were fights but they were kind of hit-and-run. Nevertheless, the tradition of police manning-up for public holidays continued right the way through to the mid-1980s.'[22]

The Who's managers, Kit Lambert and Chris Stamp, were all too aware of the publicity inherent in booking the group to play Mod strongholds in Margate, Clacton, Hastings and anywhere else where there was likely to be newsworthy shoreline trouble with Rockers. Yet, though Chris and Kit made much of the four's sartorial extravagance, were the Who ever true Mods? If they were, they surely belonged to the greasiest end of the spectrum. A toothless movement anyway, Mod faded *circa* 1966, and the Who felt it was safe to insert old favourites like 'Shakin' All Over' and 'Summertime Blues' into the set. It was also cool for them to admit that they'd always liked classic rock.

For all their pillhead nightbird aura, the Who's background was, like the Yardbirds', mundane Greater London suburban. Individual members' musical antecedents embraced trad jazz, surf music and copying the Shadows and Johnny Kidd. Seeking work in local social clubs, the group marked time until one of their first managers, Pete Meadon, also publicist for the Pretty Things, found them engagements closer to the heart of the city and, boasting that they were the first authentic Mod group, negotiated a one-off 45 with Fontana.

Having phased out their Acton wedding reception repertoire, the Who gave Meadon's sales pitch a veneer of truth via a copious injection of Motown and James Brown to complement the urban blues mainstays. They also agreed to fulfil the Fontana contract as the High Numbers. Referring to self-appointed Mod leaders who wantonly redesigned the image from tailor to dance floor, 'I'm the Face' was Slim Harpo's 'Got Love If You Want It' grafted to Meadon's Modspeak lyrics. Despite a feature in *Fabulous*, this lumbering single fared badly, but the High Numbers themselves flourished as a flashy 'Maximum R & B' group; Pete Townshend's trademark windmill guitar pose (on permanent loan from Keith Richards) dating from this period.

After Lambert and Stamp's takeover, it was as the Who again that Decca, against its better judgement, signed them to its Brunswick subsidiary as the label's answer to Pye's Kinks. The Who turned out to be a sound investment. A chief advantage was songwriter Townshend's belief in the disposable nature of pop: 'It should be like the TV – something you can turn on and off and shouldn't disturb the mind.'

Terrific Top 10 singles – 'I Can't Explain', 'Anyway Anyhow Anywhere', 'Substitute' – made them the idols of would-be Mods everywhere when aligned to a stage act fraught with smoke bombs, flashing lights, and splintered instruments and amplifiers amid ear-splitting feedback. In what seemed an equal opportunities organization, drummer Keith Moon was as much the Who's Ace Face as any other member. A known exhibitionist, he would create mayhem from nothing, the most documented instance being his disruption of a party in Chertsey through steering a Rolls Royce Silver Cloud into the host's swimming pool. In lucid moments, Keith would confess that such pranks were all part of his job as the Who's newsmaker.

That he maintained his maniac persona throughout his short life infers a less sound motivation, as his tomfoolery would often deteriorate into a nonsensical frenzy of explosives in hotel bedrooms; parading round London's Jewish areas in Nazi attire; breaking into a aeroplane pilot's cabin to rap his sticks on the control panel, and razoring his wrists at the drop of a hat. This was balanced by Moon's chief asset: he drummed like a rhythmically-integrated octopus, but, if gratuitously busy, he still maintained a precise backbeat. Much of his technique – too quick for the eye to follow – had been learned from the Pretty Things' Viv Prince who deputized whenever Keith was indisposed.

While Moon had been born without brakes, ex-art student Townshend had a more considered approach, acknowledging auto-destructive artist Gustav Metzger as inspiration for the Who's expensive if occasional habit of closing the show by smashing up their equipment.

Many Mod outfits with intriguing stage presentations also contained at least one key musician who'd attended art school at a time when Pop Art, predicted by some to be the coming trend, was scorned by the establishment as a novelty. Pre-empting Andy Warhol's soup-cans, the goal was to bring humour and topicality back into Fine Art via an earnest fascination with the brashest of junk culture, a mannered relishing of advertising hoardings, comics, beach movies and other artefacts of this Coca-cola century, ridiculed as puerile, tasteless and fake. In the interests of research, Pop artists listened avidly to Top 40 radio which was, indeed, 'like the TV – something you can turn on and off and shouldn't disturb the mind'.

Both the Kinks (whose Ray Davies studied at Hornsey Art College) and the Who would record the 'Batman' theme. With ex-Moseley Art collegian Roy Wood at the creative helm, the Move first impinged on the nation's consciousness by refining the Who's 'auto-destruction'. Their Carl Wayne would charge onstage with a chopper to hack up effigies of notable world figures before destroying televisions – and if that's not Art, then I don't know what is. Among those insulted by the Move onstage and off was Prime Minister Harold Wilson who, after being caricatured in a rude publicity postcard, won a libel suit against the Move and their manager.

Earlier Who disciples, the Creation, describing their music as 'red with purple flashes', climaxed their act in more two-dimensional manner by splashing onto a canvas backdrop an action painting that owed less to

Jackson Pollock than to Tony Hancock – though one mischievous night singer Kenny Pickett, taking more time than usual, confronted onlookers with a messy exposition of the female nude. Perhaps the most striking of Mod groups, the Creation also pioneered the scraping of a violin bow across an electric guitar on a brace of 1966 chart entries, and an LP, *We Are Paintermen*.

Other Mod groups left well enough alone, and evolved few characteristics that set them apart – though I must add that the Action's standing in Mod circles was such that their van would be met on the outskirts of Brighton by a cavalcade of Parka-clad scooter-riders, who'd escort them to the venue.

No true Mod ever missed the Small Faces either. Though the 'real thing' in both appearance and attitude, this Cockney quartet hadn't anything very exceptional going for them during the brief preamble to their emergence as the best of the bunch. Their initial objective was to be like an English version of Booker T and the MGs with vocals. Nevertheless, within eight weeks of signing to Decca, they were secure in the Top 20 with 'Whatcha Gonna Do About It', with a title borrowed from Doris Troy and a chord pattern from Solomon Burke's 'Everybody Needs Somebody To Love'. As with all their 45s, the basic song was a foundation for a sterling studio performance. Over round-the-kit drum clatters and an accented two-note unison riff on organ and bass, Steve Marriott's half-strangled, knock-kneed passion matched an electrifyingly slipshod fretboard style lacquered with Who-ish feedback scrawl.

The downbeat follow-up, 'I Got Mine', took a dive, but the Small Faces bounced back with Kenny Lynch's 'Sha-La-La-La-Lee' at Number Three and a lesser smash, the self-composed 'Hey Girl' – though both might have better suited Herman's Hermits. After their only Number One, in 1966, 'All Or Nothing' and a slight hiccup with 'I Can't Make It' – which lived up to its name – the Small Faces were chart fixtures for three years when singles mattered most.

16 TRAINS AND BOATS AND 'PLANES

The only way should have been down. By definition, pop stars — especially British ones — weren't supposed to last. Yet Britain was about to become the world's prime purveyor of pop, and Liverpool, quoth post-beatnik bard Allen Ginsberg, 'centre of the consciousness of the entire universe'[124] after the Beatles topped the US Hot 100 with 'I Want to Hold Your Hand' prior to a messianic descent on Kennedy Airport in February 1964. Dismissed by an Italian radio broadcaster as 'a group without a future,'[125] the four deluged overseas Top Tens five or six singles at a time; the Indonesian Minister of Culture outlawed long hair on males, and *A Hard Day's Night* was screened in Warsaw.

Spearheaded by the Beatles, British beat's subjugation of the rest of the free world was a large-scale re-run of the hysteria known at home, but with even more presentations to civic heads, louder screams every stop of the way, and longer queues of handicapped unfortunates wheeled deludedly down backstage corridors for the Fab Four's curative blessing. Thousands of teenagers would converge on an airport whenever a new UK sensation shed the light of its countenance upon their land. On the aeroplane, baffled musicians would be greeted by what they'd mistaken for engine noise on touchdown.

In back street palais in Copenhagen or Hong Kong, you'd come across many an outfit that had reinvented itself as a post-Beatles beat group. The Librettos, once 'New Zealand's Shadows', had made such a transition, and even Soviet Russia threw down a gauntlet with what translates as 'The Candid Lads'. There were also instances of local talent checkmating UK originals. Another Kiwi ensemble, Ray Columbus and his Invaders, issued a version of 'I Wanna Be Your Man' which sold more than those by both the Stones and the Beatles. The same unit also copped another hit with 'She's a Mod' from Birmingham's Mods. In Scandinavia, the Who were especially prey to pre-emption. Stockholm alone came up with 'My Generation' by the Sunspots, 'I'm A Boy' from the Hi-Balls, and, with hilariously mispronounced lyrics, the Lunatics' 'Pictures Off Lily' (*sic*). Sweden also bred the Jackpots who were as fond of the Ivy League.

As it had been when British singers duplicated the Americans in the 1950s, US xeroxes of UK hits came to be better-remembered by some than the originals. 'Sha-La-La-Lee' and the Pretty Things' 'Don't Bring Me Down' were both regional hits when nabbed by the Jades of Fort Worth, and Chicago's Shadows of Knight scored nationally with both 'Gloria', which had begun life as a Them B-side, and 'Oh Yeah' from the Others, who had attended the same school as members of the Yardbirds.

Of course, North America was where it counted most. Until what has passed into myth as 1964's 'British Invasion', no UK pop act had ever made sustained headway there, nor was likely to if you agreed with the *New York Times*' rejection of Billy Fury in *Play It Cool* in 1963 as an Elvis duplicate 'without the stamp of an original personality'.[126] Helen Shapiro, also in the same film – and voted the *NME*'s most popular British female singer – attained the dubious distinction of peaking at Number One Hundred in US music trade paper *Billboard*'s Hot 100. To a taxi driver at Idlewild (soon to be Kennedy) airport, a British pop star setting foot on US soil was just another lift like any tourist – though professional interest might find him in record stores, thumbing through wares unreleased outside the States.

Domestic hits by UK beat groups had had, in the first instance, the impact of feathers on concrete in a continent whose wavelengths were overloaded with yapping disc-jockeys with lurid *noms de turntable* – Wolfman Jack, Murray The K, Magnificent Montague – who were mostly unmindful of whatever was gripping an outback like Britain.

Yet some of their countrymen were discovering it, albeit indirectly, even as Murray the K on New York's 1010 WINS was sliding the needle into the Beach Boys' 'Surfin' USA'. 'We learnt all the songs off the Beatles' first album,' recounted Dave Dee,' and all these American sailors were coming into the Top Ten [in Hamburg], and they came up to us and asked, "What is this music you are playing?" We told them it was Beatle music, and they said, "Gee, why don't you play it in America? It would go down really great." I guess they were the first Americans that had ever heard of the Beatles, and of Beatle-type music.'

'I don't know. What do you think?' had been the spirit that had surrounded the eventual unleashing of 'I Want To Hold Your Hand' by EMI's US outlet, Capitol. Though this ensured a better chance of airplay than earlier 45s had had with independent companies, none could assume the Beatles would be anything more than a strictly European phenomenon like Cliff Richard. Why should the USA want them, anyway?

Why should British beat groups want the USA? A lot of them loathed the glimpses they'd had of it. 'When The Dave Clark Five started,' said their drummer, 'we used to play the American air bases in England. It was hell because the American servicemen kept getting pissed. It was the only side of America I'd seen, and I didn't care for it.'[34]

Dave was made to care, however, after the British Invasion was predicted by Roy Orbison on returning to the States in 1963 with English screams still ringing in his ears: 'It seemed to me at first like it was just a rehash of rock 'n' roll, but it turned out to be very fresh and full of energy and vitality – so I recognized it at the time.'[127] Once upon a time, it *had* been a rehash of rock 'n' roll, every number a salaam to the trailblazing sounds created in studios in Memphis, Chicago and New York, but though Roy considered the Beatles pretty rough-and-ready, 'they had the magic there', and, as for Gerry, 'I think that monster grin would sell him before they even heard his voice.'[128]

As Albion had long been seen as merely a furbisher of nine-day wonders like Lonnie Donegan and the Tornados, few believed Orbison. Two that did were Del Shannon and Gene Pitney. Both had also had first-hand experience of the new British madness. A break in Shannon's UK itinerary had allowed him to book a studio to tape 'From Me to You', thereby hoping to steal a march on the Beatles before they hit the US. Moreover, Pitney became a confidant of the Rolling Stones, playing piano on their debut LP, and recording 1964's 'That Girl Belongs to Yesterday' the first Jagger-Richards composition to enter the Hot 100.

For all Dave Clark's initial dislike, his Five were the first British group to undertake a full-scale North American tour. Though 'Glad All Over' – 'the Mersey Sound with the Liverpool beat', according to Epic, their US label – had soared into *Billboard's* Top 20, the Five's reception at Idlewild, reported on BBC TV's *Six O' Clock News*, was muted by comparison to the Beatles' tumultous arrival a few weeks earlier for a handful of shows and, like the Five, to top the bill on the nationally networked *Ed Sullivan Show* – North America's *Sunday Night at the London Palladium*. How the Five dared to go on their US visit without getting the sack from their day jobs astounds me – because they only went cautiously professional after a homecoming appearance at the Palladium.

'I don't think anyone expected musicians playing rock 'n' roll to have any wit or repartee at all,'[129] reckoned the Five's Mike Smith. North Americans, you see, were used to their pop stars being more devoid of independent opinion than the most pliant Larry Parnes puppet. A Bobby would be set in motion by his manager as a walking digest of '*Twixt Twelve and Twenty*, Pat Boone's manual for wholesome boys and girls. 'We all have bad habits,' it read. 'Personally, I'm not too keen on getting up in the morning, and I happen to enjoy scrambled eggs for breakfast.'[130] When Boone moved into films, he paraded this dearth of private vices by refusing to kiss his leading ladies. Well, you never know where these things might lead . . .

With Uncle Pat in the background, Bobby would give gentle, uncontroversial replies about his favourite *color*, preferred foodstuffs and the age at which he hoped to marry to questions from *Sixteen, Datebook* and similar journals full of probing items about Tommy Roe's gorgeous smile. Having flexed their muscles with the European press, the Beatles, the Rolling Stones, Freddie and the Dreamers and, to a lesser degree, the Five and Herman's Hermits, trampled this bovine regimen as they cracked back at banal, ill-informed enquiries as repetitious as a stuck record from circling media hounds. If as pedestrian as their interrogators at times, it was the long-haired Britons' overall combination of zaniness, unsentimentality, unblinking self-assurance and the poker-faced, what-are-you-laughing-at way they said 'em that did it. Do you guys think they'll be another war soon? Yeah, Friday. How did you find America? We went to Greenland and made a left turn.

'Our appeal,' ruminated Ringo Starr at a press conference in Milwaukee, 'is that we're ordinary lads.'[131] This, as it had in Blighty, did the corrective trick in a another country depressed by recent traumas: vehement opposition to the Civil Rights amendment, the first boy-soldiers blown to bits in Indochina – and President Kennedy's assassination in Dallas on the same November day in 1963 that the Beatles' forthcoming US trip was proclaimed. John Lennon's more forthright theory was, 'Kids everywhere all go for the same stuff and, seeing we'd done it in England, there's no reason why we couldn't do it in America too.'[132]

What's more, the US Top 20 was sodden with Bobby-ballads, forgettable instrumentals and edifying anthems like the Beach Boy's 'Be True To Your School'. To the chagrin of the Beach Boys, Four Seasons and others on Capitol, the intruders were launched with one of the most far-reaching publicity blitzes hitherto known. As a result, 'I Want To Hold Your Hand' was stuck at Number One while clambering up were all Beatles discs that in 1963 had been aired to negligible listener reaction on those few US radio stations that could be bothered.

Beatle chewing gum alone netted millions of dollars within months – because, as is their wont, the Americans exhibited a fanaticism that left British Beatlemaniacs swallowing dust. Our colonial cousins were devouring the grass on which the group had trodden, and swooning on fingering a guitar autographed by all four and owned by some old idiot who'd declared himself 'the Beatles' Most Elderly Fan'. Whingeing from their children would cause well-off US parents to interrupt European holidays to fly to Liverpool where back copies of *Merseybeat* would fetch inflated prices, and the seat on which Ringo had, allegedly, always perched when in the Cavern bandroom was kissed like the Blarney Stone.

Demonstrating general adult acceptance of the Beatles was an episode of *The Lucy Show*, in which stooge Mr Mooney tries to book for a hundred dollars 'that English combo that everyone's talking about' for the bank's dinner-and-dance, settling instead for one of many outfits who'd found it paid to either grow their hair or acquire wigs, and rehearse tortuous Liverpool accents for onstage continuity during a set consisting wholly of yeah-yeah-yeah Beatles' imitations. There'd been swiftly-assembled tribute discs and soundalike studio combos such as the Bug Men, the Wackers, John and Paul, and the Merseyboys.

Backtracking to 'Love Me Do' and the Sheridan tracks, so insatiable – and uncritical – was demand for anything on which the Fab Four had ever breathed that for one week, they occupied nine places in the Canadian Top 10. A small US label – the first of many – got hold of poor old Pete Best. With his new group, he was brought across the ocean to milk his connection via a sell-out North American tour at odds with ebbing interest in him, even in Liverpool. 'Just about everyone is tired of the Beatles,' cried *Billboard*, 'except the buying public.'[133]

'Britain hasn't been so influential in American affairs since 1775,' read the same editorial as fascination with all things from our sceptred isle peaked when two-thirds of *Billboard's* Hot 100 was British in origin. Though one executive was overheard cawing, 'I tell ya, Elmer, you heard one Limey outfit, ya heard 'em all,' most of Britain's major pop acts made progress to varying extents in the uncharted States.

Some minor ones did too. Thanks to the printing of a photo of them in *Sixteen*, Force West acquired a New York fan club. Grander still, the Hullaballoos were high in the Hot 100 with 'I'm Gonna Love You Too', and so, by default, were the Beat Merchants when 'Pretty Face' B-sided a Freddie and the Dreamers million-seller. Former Dorset public schoolboy Ian Whitcomb enjoyed short-lived celebrity with an off-the-cuff falsetto blues shuffle. Titled 'You Turn Me On', it missed at home but, thanks to a dousing of publicity, reached the US Top 20. Two other nicely-spoken boys, Chad and Jeremy – 'as English as a cup of tea'[134], beamed their agent – did even better with three such entries, even though they too didn't mean a light at home. Less honourable attempts to crack the States at the expense of domestic success had been made by Steve Marriott's Moments who made a futile attempt to put one over on the Kinks by releasing 'You Really Got Me' in the US only. Dave Berry's 'Crying Game' was likewise abducted by Ian and the Zodiacs who took it to Number One in Texas whilst sliding towards poverty-stricken disbandment back at the Star-Club.

As engagement fees at home shrank too, the Zombies' undignified demise was held at arm's length with heftier triumphs over the Atlantic. After 'She's Not There' went to Number One in *Billboard's* rival music rag, *Cashbox* (news that Colin Blunstone's old headmaster saw as unworthy of mention in school assembly), the group's popularity throughout North America didn't vanish as speedily as it had in Britain. They'd invaded the continent at the optimum moment, just after it had lost its marbles over the Beatles. However, instead of coming on as rough, untamed scousers, the chaps from St Albans gave the impression that they probably whiled away idle hours on the road with chess tournaments rather than boozing and looking out for skirt.

Straight out of *Tom Brown's Schooldays*, the Zombies' genteel manners and girly enunciations were brought into play when interviewed during a ten-day New York season, hosted by Murray the K, with Ben E. King, the Shangri-Las, the Shirelles and another Limey unit with a world-wide smash ('Tobacco Road'), the Nashville Teens. The next visit was for six weeks' hard graft as the only British artists on a coast-to-coast *Caravan of Stars* package, organized by Dick Clark, presenter of TV's *American Bandstand*. Such tours were well-known for being hard on their acts: hundreds of miles a day, sleeping on the bus every other night, and peanuts to show for it at the end. Any subtlety packed into the Zombies' spot was lost on screaming mid-Western audiences who, nevertheless, put 'Tell Her No' into the Top 10. Two more US treks likewise assisted sales of 'She's Coming Home' and a jazz-tinged waltz, 'I Want You Back'; both less spectacular hits but hits all the same.

What American found so attractive about the Zombies was what might have exhausted their momentum at home. In corporate character, they adhered closely to a Hollywood movie idea of Britain, the mythical land of Good Queen Bess, Robin Hood, fish 'n' chips, Oxford-and-Cambridge, Beefeaters, monocled cads, kilted Scotsmen and hello-hello-hello policeman. A member of a British Invasion group could only be either a proper Lord Snooty or a Cockney barrow boy. A US cartoon strip about an outfit called 'the Beadles' had them using redundant East London colloquialisms like 'blimey, guv'nor' and 'blighter', and addressing each other as 'mate'. Frankie Avalon played it posh as 'the Potato Bug', an English pop-singing 'refugee from a haircut', in the film *Bikini Beach*. Similar in assumed character, former window-cleaner Screaming Lord Sutch put it about that he was 'the Sixth Earl of Harrow' when in the States during the fag-end of the British Invasion.

Though there were no serious signs of wavering, the impetus relaxed fractionally by late 1964. Nevertheless, as it had been after the fading of the Liverpool Sound, into the breach came Manchester. As their fortunes subsided at home, the New World went as nuts over Freddie and the Dreamers as it would over Benny Hill's saucy inanities years later. In the few months that were his, Freddie Garrity was king of North America. The twenty-month-old 'I'm Telling You Now' sliced to the top as a wire through cheese, and Chubby Checker weighed in with 'Do the Freddie' which the lad himself also took to the US Top 20. However, with the spread of the next

Mancunian pestilence, 'Hermania', the Dreamers and Freddie became as old hat as they'd long been back in Britain.

Herman could scarcely fail in a maternally-minded society that was later to surrender to Cabbage Patch Dolls. Exploited in a like fashion, he magnified the cheeky schoolboy persona he'd been developing since *Coronation Street*. What the Zombies merely hinted at, Herman's Hermits took to the limit by hammering home their Britishness with the same force that had caused Rolly Daniels to Twist like a lunatic on BBC television in 1961. On vinyl, Herman's Hermits reheated stone-cold pre-war musical repasts like 'Two Lovely Black Eyes', George Formby's 'Leaning on a Lamp-post', 'I'm Henry The Eighth I Am' (with Joe Brown's 1962 version as blueprint) and, most blatant of all, 'Je Suis Anglais'.

The British themselves wouldn't have worn it. Though a revival of Tom Courtenay's 'Mrs Brown You've got a Lovely Daughter' went down well in the *NME*'s pollwinners concert in 1965, Herman's musical flagwaving was seen by his own kind as a concession to the daft Yanks. Tellingly, no Herman's Hermits LP made much of a splash in Britain. The singles weren't guaranteed to chart either, especially if released in a heavy week. Yet Britain hardly mattered any more while Hermania filtered across the USA like bubonic plague.

There were others too who would be bigger in North America than they ever were at home. If Chad and Jeremy took some of the edge off it, another upper-class duo, Peter and Gordon, issued five US albums to every one in Britain. As a measure of their US eminence, Epic Records issued *Dave Clark Five Versus Peter and Gordon*, an LP on which both acts had one side.

Televised on *The Ed Sullivan Show* more times than any British act before or since, the Five, arguably, overtook the Beatles momentarily as the Union's top UK act. To British *cognoscenti*, *Session with the Dave Clark Five*, from 1964, was the only true Five album, because succeeding collections were all culled from dozens of US-only LPs. When studying the music papers, you'd often notice a Clark record you were never likely to hear in the UK, way up the *Billboard* list. To the further chagrin of their home following, the group's last UK concert appearance consisted of two numbers in the 1965 Royal Variety Show during a schedule of regular bi-annual voyages to take the USA for every cent they could get. Their box-office takings were astronomical and they left as little as six weeks' gap between some frankly sub-standard albums. Although they scrupulously plugged their 45s on British TV, this was only market research for the States. Flops at home could be recouped abroad by readjustment of emphasis. 'Look Before You Leap' floundered wretchedly at Number 50 for one week in Britain in 1966, but its flip, 'Please Tell me Why', promoted as the A-side in the US, sailed effortlessly up the Hot 100.

If children had to like British beat groups, reasoned adult America, let it be ones like the Dave Clark Five, more palatable than the Stones, Pretty Things, Kinks, Them and, with shoulder-length peroxide jobs, the Hullaballoos. 'You walk out of the Amphitheatre after watching the Rolling Stones perform,' exclaimed one Illinois newspaper, 'and suddenly the Chicago stockyards smell good and clean by comparison.' Derided by grown-ups as Elvis had been, the Stones were naturally as rabidly worshipped by the US young.

Immigration authorities temporarily refused visas for more Limey longhairs wishing to propagate their filth in Uncle Sam's fair land. After their third UK Number One, 'Tired of Waiting For You', reached a *Billboard* Number Six, further US advances by the Kinks were disadvantaged by a lengthy Musicians Union ban from North America for 'unprofessional conduct', and even the relatively short-maned Animals, who wanted to tape an in-concert LP at the Harlem Apollo, were thwarted by official obstruction – though it had been quite in order for the Beatles to record two of *their* US concerts.

Factions in the Deep South's 'Bible Belt' quoted I Corinthians xi. 14: 'Doth not even nature itself teach you that if a man have long hair, it is a shame unto him?' While some groups tried to make out that they were genuine Britons, those in redneck areas, like the Sir Douglas Quintet from San Antonio, dared not sport a *pilzen kopf* offstage for fear of disapproval expressed in a manner stronger than simply bellowing 'get yer 'air cut!' from a car window.

As Britain's overseas representatives, the Pretty Things' notoriety was stressed, via filmed TV snippets, to such a pitch that adolescent America and its exploiters anticipated a freak carnival of greater magnitude than had greeted even those depraved Rolling Stones. Dollars danced before the Things' eyes as their management dithered.

After the Yardbirds winged over to the States, Jim McCarty observed that, 'Either they thought we were The Beatles or else we got spat upon,' while Paul Samwell-Smith recalled an incident when, 'We had an interview with a disc-jockey in the middle of Disneyland – which was going out on the radio. The guard at the door said, "You can't come in. Your hair is too long." "But we're the Yardbirds." "Don't care. Those are the rules." Five years later, I went there independently, and the bloody guards had longer hair than I did.'

Nevertheless, alighting on mid-west towns even in the graveyard hours, a British group might be greeted by hundreds of hot-eyed teenagers, many chaperoned by parents who hadn't chastized them for squandering their allowances on a six-dollar can of 'Beatle Breath' or for shirking household chores to ogle a TV 'documentary' of Freddie and the Dreamers' first US press conference – with surreptitious hand-held studies of Freddie's ear lasting minutes on end.

It was also cool for the hippest of the hip to like British beat. Protest singer-in-transition Bob Dylan dug the Beatles; hung around with Brian Jones and Alan Price, and even strummed a Herman's Hermits number in an unguarded moment during *Don't Look Back*, a film record of his UK tour in 1965. In New York, Andy Warhol sneaked backstage at the Brooklyn Fox because 'I wanted to be in the presence of the Yardbirds'. To a more practical end, self-important Phil Spector said he'd like to apply his spent 'genius' to the Beatles. Years later they let him and found that his histrionics were more trouble than they were worth.

Symptomatic of such big shot preoccupation with British beat, a common complaint was that made by Frank Zappa then of Los Angeles' Soul Giants: 'If you didn't sound like the Beatles or Stones, you didn't get hired.'[135] It was no skin off the Supremes' comely noses to issue *With Love (From Us to You)*, an entire LP of British beat covers, but from the sub-cultural woodwork had crawled legion Anglophile 'garage bands' who'd been able to grow out their crew-cuts and seize upon whatever aspect of the new Limey idioms they felt most comfortable.

The Yardbirds outfitted the Count Five with the vestments of musical personality that propelled 'Psychotic Reaction' into the US Top 20. For the Byrds (formerly the Beefeaters), it was the Searchers' fusion of Merseybeat and contemporary folk, specifically their vocal harmonies and jingle-jangle finger-picking of two electric guitars. Listen consecutively to the Searchers 'When You Walk in the Room' and the Byrds' 'Don't Doubt Yourself Babe' (both by the same writer, Jackie de Shannon), and the sounds merge until they become interchangeable.

Moulded less successfully to breadwinning UK specifications were groups like the McCoys, the Standells, the Strangeloves, the Barbarians and, far behind all of them, the Sundowners, a Florida outfit formed by one Tom Petty whose style would be determined by assiduous attention to the Byrds imitating the Searchers. Though their debut 45, 'The Peppermint Beatle', was a miss, The Standells' Gary Leeds later worked with the Walker Brothers, who found greater rewards in Britain itself.

In contrast, Jack Good, the brains behind *Six-Five Special*, *Oh Boy!* et al, inflicted himself on US television after emigrating in 1962. Other Britons who were encroaching on North America via pop-associated professions included John Peel who, because he had been born near Liverpool – refined Heswall actually – was engaged as 'Beatle expert' by a Dallas radio network. London clothes designer Mary Quant, and top model Jean Shrimpton also 'arrived' in the States. In the same mini-skirted league as Shrimpton was George Harrison's fiancée, Patti Boyd, commissioned by *Sixteen* to write a regular 'Letter From London', while Jean's sister Chrissie was likewise persuaded to report for *Mod* on the activities of London's in-crowd in her capacity as Mick Jagger's girlfriend.

On the sidelines sat Gerry and the Pacemakers who, despite Roy Orbison's recommendation and their closeness to the Beatles, were slow to gain ground in the States. Eventually, 'Don't Let The Sun Catch You Crying' came to rest at Number Six in 1964, a giant step forward consolidated by repromotions of 'How Do You Do It' and 'I Like It'. With the movie on general release in the USA, 'Ferry Cross the Mersey' made the loftiest climb of all before a foreseeable downward spiral for subsequent records. Still, it had been a reasonable run.

US chart penetration by the Hollies was a long time coming too – possibly owing to their comparative facelessness, being neither hairy monsters nor as conservative as Herman' Hermits. Late in 1965, 'Look Through Any Window' probed the Hot 100 tentatively, but they had to wait a further year for 'Bus Stop' to place them in the Top 10. After this, they were always assured of a fair hearing.

The Small Faces and the Spencer Davis Group were both poleaxed by severe personnel problems just when they ought to have been capitalizing on their first US smashes. By the time the Small Faces finally played a first American date in 1968, their UK chart seniority did not prevent the Move from topping the bill. It had been all over for the Spencer Davis Group too when they'd got round to a US trip a year earlier.

For the Troggs, much momentum was lost through legal wrangles between Fontana and US label Atco. Nevertheless, though their Hot 100 standing dwindled after a Number One with 'Wild Thing', they accumulated crucial grassroots support during two nationwide tours. Their instrumental directness paired with Reg Presley's nasal vocals encouraged hundreds of minor US groups to borrow from them as the Count Five had from the Yardbirds.

Certain British groups that hadn't had much luck in the US made the best of it with covers for the domestic and European market. Brian Poole had his last hit with the Strangeloves' 'I Want Candy'. In 1965, too, Dave Berry was back in the UK Top 10 with ' Little Things' just after it had sold a million in North America for composer Bobby Goldsboro. To less effect, the Flies put a version of 'I'm Not Your Stepping Stone' into the shops and onto pirate radio before the original by the Monkees had even been heard in Britain, while Simon Dupree and the Big Sound did likewise with 'I See the Light' by the Five Americans, and the Wheels with Paul Revere and the Raiders' 'Kicks'.

Pop obeys no laws of natural justice – which is why the Merseybeats, Brian Poole, Dave Berry and Dave Dee, Dozy, Beaky, Mick and Tich didn't really Make It over the Atlantic. Visits there might have been on the cards and, provoked by US fan mail, a provisional tour route even mapped out. However, with no *Billboard* bullet for 'I Think of You', Brian's 'Twist and Shout', 'The Crying Game' and 'Hold Tight', it was decided to err on the side of caution and look elsewhere. If the States was off-limits, there were sustained chart strikes for British beat in New Zealand, Greenland and all other stops in between.

In Europe some groups famous in Britain could still go shopping unmolested on days off – though the pace was hectic. After going before the cameras for a Hilversum TV special, you'd then play an Amsterdam all-nighter. A televised concert to six thousand next morning was followed, after a few hours' respite, by a round-robin set back at the Star-Club before the breakfast flight back to Heathrow. Teutonic organizational efficiency was often absent in neighbouring territories. You'd find yourself in Italy at a humid outdoor event plagued by mosquitoes, gremlins and gleeful bouncers laying into an audience fighting drunk on local moonshine. On *Tele de Bois et Ages Tendres* in Paris, a group miming its latest release would be less prominent than a line of choreographed chorus girls.

To a degree, the French way had been paved by the exiled Vince Taylor; hit translations like Petula Clark's 'Please Please Me' and 'Concrete and Clay' by Richard Anthony (with accompaniment by the Roulettes, strangely enough), and the inclusion of 'Money', 'You'll Never Walk Alone' and further Merseybeat standards in the repertoires of Anthony, Johnny Hallyday, Eddy Mitchell and other Gallic pop icons. Yet matters got off to a bad start in 1964 on a late-running bill at the Paris Olympia, co-headlined by Hallyday, Sylvie Vartan (his singing wife), Trini Lopez – and the Beatles whose onstage banter grew less jovial as equipment persistently malfunctioned, sparking off the outbreaks of barracking to which the *yé-yé* were prone. A year later, however, after the Stones, Kinks, Honeycombs and Animals had done better in France, the Fab Four would be able to extort their accustomed pandemonium and justify closing the show two nights running at Le Palais de Sports.

Germany was the Beatles' for the taking – though visits there were curtailed between 1962 and 1966, owing to a worrying claim by a Hamburg *fraulein* that one of them had fathered her child. Consequently, the group were never booked for *Beat Club*, a TV showcase as vital in its way as *Ready Steady Go*. Transmitted from Hamburg, it was an essential inclusion in the European schedules of foreign outfits such as the Easybeats and Dave Dee, Dozy, Beaky, Mick and Tich, who were among many who became at least as acclaimed in the German record market – the third largest in the world – as they were at home through regular appearances on the programme. Indeed, in 1967, Dave Dee's unit were to beat the Beatles by over three thousand votes to win *Bravo* magazine's Golden Otto award – the equivalent of being Top Vocal Group in the *NME* poll (where Dee *et al* were always outside the leading ten).

Pop is an erratic business. John Mayall's Bluesbreakers got into the Belgian singles chart, and 'Lost Girl', the Troggs' first 45, which flopped in the UK, entered the Dutch Top 10 in 1965, the year that Dave Berry suddenly found himself the Presley of the Flatlands after performing 'This Strange Effect', a Top 30 failure in Britain, in customary cobra-like fashion at an international song festival. Dave himself attributed an arbitrary gesture with a cigarette butt someone had thrown onstage as ignition point for his continental success – though a German faction considered his act distasteful. 'This Strange Effect' was Holland's biggest-selling disc ever, and, for well over a year, Berry swamped the Dutch hit parade with up to three records at once. As a former Cruiser, I'm possibly the wrong person to cast judgement on his second-biggest Euro-smash, 1965's 'I'm Gonna Take You There', which still evokes a shudder because it dribbled mockingly from a transport café's Tannoy at hourly intervals during a long winter's night in 1986 after a broken-down Transit stranded us on the Belgian border.

Variables as bizarre as Dave's subjugation of the Netherlands had the Moontrekkers going out in a blaze of glory in 1963 with a single, 'Moondust', in Sweden's Top 10. The next year, the Downliners Sect was at Number One there with 'Little Egypt'. Further Scandinavian hits put the Sect on a par with the Beatles to the degree that an imposter calling himself 'Keith Grant' – after the Sect's singing bass player – based himself in Gothenburg where he demanded and received massive engagement fees as leader of his Sect-like R & B outfit, Train.

The Lizards' tour of Norway in 1966 was the summit of their career; the Renegades had a Finnish Number One with a cover of the Sorrows' 'Take a Heart', and Reading's Blueblood found themselves in Sweden's LP chart. The Zombies performed before the best part of a million Filipinos over ten days for fifteen quid each. 'Wake Up My Mind' by Birmingham's Ugly's (*sic*) topped charts throughout Australasia. Episode Six were as huge in Singapore as the Swinging Blue Jeans were in Denmark long after their British hits had frizzled out.

You'd be sucked into a vortex of events, places and situations that hadn't belonged even to speculation when your group was pleading for a booking at the youth club with as much notion of getting a hit record in some outlandish country as the drummer had of getting an MBE – and there you were on *Brisbane Tonight* playing across Queensland a number you'd composed with a leaky biro on a cardboard gasket during a lunch hour at the tractor factory only last year. Caught off-guard by an abrupt rise in sales in France in the middle of a tour of the Far East, you'd have to cancel a show in Bangkok to wearily mime the track that had done the trick on television in Paris on *Music Hall* – a sort of Gallic *Billy Cotton Band Show* – before jetting back to the interrupted campaign in Asia. After a while, you were devoid of will, past resistance to the circumstances that seemed to make it impossible to go back to the old life. If the tour bus had drawn up outside a ballroom on Pluto, it mightn't have seemed all that peculiar.

17 MY SHIP IS COMING IN

Garlanded with cameras, American tourists would mentally tick off a *gen-u-ine* British beat group from a list that also included the Changing of the Guard and Morris dancers. However, wanting more than just something to tell the folks back home, many US music business people, correctly anticipating further demand for Limey talent, became as wasps round the jam-jar of Albion, just as the nation's own entrepreneurs had lately been round Liverpool. Some wooed prospective customers by proxy, but the more dauntless actually crossed the Atlantic in person to stake claims in the musical diggings.

Among them were songwriters like Clint Ballard Jnr. who, following the Swinging Blue Jeans' Top 10 version of his 'You're No Good' (written originally for Betty Everett), began actively looking for further UK clients, eventually achieving much the same relationship with Wayne Fontana and the Mindbenders as Nashville tunesmith John D. Loudermilk did with the Nashville Teens, penning both of the Weybridge combo's only Top 10 entries, 'Tobacco Road' and 'Google Eye'. Though Ballard's 'Game of Love' was both Fontana and the Mindbenders' biggest UK smash and a US Number One, the follow-up, 'Just a Little Bit Too Late', barely made the British top 20. Doubtlessly, Wayne and the lads kicked themselves when another Ballard item, 'I'm Alive', on which they'd had first refusal, was picked by the Hollies and became a chart-topper.

The Hollies nearly repeated the feat with 'I Can't Let Go' by Chip Taylor, brother of Hollywood actor Jon Voight, who also placed 1965's 'On My Word' with Cliff Richard and 'Wild Thing' with Hedgehoppers Anonymous and then, more spectacularly, with the Troggs – for whom he also wrote the subdued 'Any Way You Want Me'. These triumphs mitigated other Taylor ditties that fell on stony ground such as 'Don't Do It Baby' by Linda Laine and the Sinners and Chip Fisher's quite dreadful 'An Ordinary Guy', which swiped at 'protest' songwriters like P.F. Sloan – who wrote in less caustic fashion for Herman's Hermits and the Searchers – and Buffy St Marie who likewise toned down the ills of the word in the much-covered 'Until It's Time For You To Go' which was first brought to the Top 20 by the Four Pennies in 1965.

In respective arrangements of Randy Newman's 'I've Been Wrong Before' and 'Simon Smith and His Amazing Dancing Bear', Cilla Black and the Alan Price Set did much to familiarize the British public with his songs, then barely known even in his own land. A staff writer at the same Los Angeles publishing company – and a recording artist in her own right – Jackie De Shannon set foot in England in 1964. On the crest of a wave with her 'When You Walk in the Room' smash for the Searchers, she was on the lookout for further vehicles for her compositions. London engagements by both the Paramounts and the Hellions were, therefore, graced by her presence. Squiring her was Jimmy Page, now British beat's foremost studio guitarist, who'd heard glowing reports about both groups. Astute enough to recognize their weathered stagecraft and now cooler professionalism, Jackie promised each of them a number.

Both the Paramounts' 'Blue Ribbons' and the Hellions' 'Daydreaming of You' fought shy of the Top 50, and Jackie returned to California to resume her singing career. 'Daydreaming of You' was produced by Hollywood jack-of-all-trades Kim Fowley who also supervised sessions for Noddy Holder's new group, the In-Betweens, which included a brutal 'Hold Tight' intended to nip in the bud the Dave Dee, Dozy, Beaky, Mick and Tich treatment in the USA. In 1966, Fowley created the Belfast Gypsies to cash in on the US breakthrough of Them, who were by then fragmenting.

Them's Latin-slanted ballad of lustful envy, 'Here Comes the Night', had cast its shadow at a UK Number Two in the UK in 1965. It was an opus by Bert Berns, a canny New Yorker with a fast mouth, who also wrote 'Twist and Shout', the Drifters' 'I Don't Want To Go On Without You' (later recorded by the Searchers and the Moody Blues), Solomon Burke's 'Cry To Me' (Pretty Things, Stones) and the Vibrations' 'My Girl Sloopy', which before its refurbishing by the McCoys as 'Hang on Sloopy', was one of the worst ever covers by the Yardbirds. Screaming Lord Sutch also dashed off a version whilst in New York.

Berns joined Them's movable feast of producers at Decca as well as contributing further songs to the Irish outfit's debut LP, *The Angry Young Them*. For their Top 20 finale, 'Someone Someone', an old Crickets B-side, Brian Poole and the Tremeloes acquired the services of Norman Petty the original co-writer and producer and surely the next best thing to the deceased Buddy. Petty tinkled the ivories on both 'Someone Someone' and other items from the same session.

With neither long association nor past reputation as leverage, Shel Talmy achieved his position as producer of the Bachelors, the Kinks, the Who and the Creation by pretending to British record executives that the work of others was his own. Jimmy Miller, another US producer who made his name in Britain, was once a would-be pop singer whose early ambition had been checked by a dismaying fistful of flop 45s for CBS. Accepting that he wasn't to be the Elvis of New York, 'I soon realized that the aspect of the business I liked best was being in the studio.'[136] When British beat broke on his native soil in 1964, 23-year-old Miller came over to London with a backing track of the feverish 'Incense', recorded with a session crew whom he named the Anglos to signify English connections. He contacted Chris Blackwell, head of Island Records, a West Indian label making inroads in Britain. Could Chris suggest a suitably fiery singer to ice the 'Incense' cake?

As manager of the Spencer Davis Group too, Blackwell had no hesitation in recommending an incognito Steve Winwood. He also asked Jimmy to sort out the Group's only unassisted A-side composition, 'Gimme Some Lovin'', which jumped into the Top 10 in late 1966, and stirred up some interest in the States. Identifying Steve as the main chance, the late Miller was to produce the Boy Wonder's next outfit, Traffic, before producing the Stones and buying a house near Newbury on the proceeds.

Closer to the periphery of the music industry, certain moneyed young Americans, glad to breathe the air round UK beat groups, were treated as unpaid and unrecompensed minions, but sometimes they had their uses. For example, the 'Go Now' blueprint by Bessie and Larry Banks came via B. Mitchell Reed, a New York disc-jockey, who 'went overboard for the Moody Blues whilst in Brum'.[137]

That was jolly decent of him but other of his countrymen expected more than a 'thank you' for their kindnesses. With a mouth that spewed forth estimates at a moment's notice, Allen Klein, a cigar-chewing accountant-manager from New Jersey – 'like the archetypal villain in a film'[138] said Ray Davies – hovered over British pop as a hawk over a partridge nest. Into his administative caress would melt Ray's Kinks, the Dave Clark Five and the uncut rubies – including the Animals, Herman's Hermits and Donovan – that had been processed for the charts by whizz-kid Mickie Most. After Allen underwent a crash course in their music to better butter them up, the Rolling Stones and, in 1969, most of the Beatles would also bite.

The fawning reverence of this go-getter's employees was tempered by innumerable derogatory *bon mots* from former clients. Yet Klein's blunt stance when wheedling an unprecedently high advance from Decca for the Stones in 1965 particularly impressed Paul McCartney – though, to Brian Epstein, such hard and unrelenting monetary killings were secondary to fair dealing and sound commodities. Furthermore, from being so pleased with Klein's bellicose interventions, Mick Jagger would take the trouble to call on the Beatles to try to dissuade them from getting involved with one he suspected of sharp practice. Allen, however, was already there, spieling in top gear.

Once, Klein and his sort wouldn't have spared Britain a second glance unless a king's ransom was offered for one of their artists to show his face over there. However, regarding the islands as a halfway house between non-English-speaking obscurity and the Hot 100, many acts from continental Europe had become semi-resident in London prior to the 1962 divide. Little Tony and his Brothers had been seen in Italy by a holidaying Jack Good in 1959. Despite profound language difficulties, the vocal group then wowed giddy females with their Latinate charm during a UK tour with Cliff Richard, and TV plugs for 'Foxy Little Mama', 'The Hippy Hippy Shake' and other 45s overseen by Good. Yet Tony was without his siblings when he grazed the UK Top 20 in 1960 with 'So Good'. The following year, Tony returned to Italy to be runner-up in the San Remo Song Festival with an item translated as '24,000 Kisses' when covered by Roy Young and by Liverpool's Paul Rogers.[139]

'The Hippy Hippy Shake' was also among the first recordings by the Rattles who, guided by Manfred Weissleder, proprietor of the Star-Club, were as near as you'd get to Teutonic Merseybeat. They often shared bills with the likes of Tony Sheridan, Cliff Bennett, the Beatles and Kingsize Taylor. After a successful fortnight's residency in Liverpool's Cavern, and appearances on British television, they waited years for one of their German singles, 'The Witch', remade with English lyrics, to fly into the UK Top 10 in 1970. They were, however, unable to secure a lasting place in overseas hearts.

Victory over England was not a priority for Sweden's Spotnicks – though they were frequent visitors to British shores before their disbandment in 1964. They came on like an interplanetary edition of the Shadows, with a complicated set-up of space-suits, remote-control stereo guitars and other technological gimmicks. On peaking in Britain with 'Hava Nagila' at Number Thirteen in early 1963, they were joined by Jimmy Nicol for a tour of Europe and the Far East.

Though the Spotnicks were as much vocal as instrumental, post-1962 British beat was a more acute stimulus to fellow Scandinavians like the Shanes whose lyrically nonsensical 'Chris Craft Number Nine' replicated Herman's Hermits' 'A Must To Avoid' melodically. This was recorded at Abbey Road like 'Daytime Nighttime' by Stockholm's Shamrocks was at Regent Sound – and produced by its composer, Mike Hugg, drummer with Manfred Mann, with whom the Shamrocks had worked in Germany and France. They were also recipients of 'Don't You Know She Mine' by the Ivy League. The Tages' try at cracking English-speaking regions was more fruitful if indirect when the Swinging Blue Jeans covered their 'Crazy 'Bout My Baby', a 'Tip for the Top' on *Top of the Pops* in 1965. Later, the Tages toured Britain, taping *en route* a 45 penned by the Herd.

No Stockholm Sound or Fjordbeat was to take over the planet, so Decca, still searching for the Next Big Thing, went beyond the Pyrenees for Los Bravos, formed in 1965 from ex-personnel of Los Sonors and Los Runaways. Though regarded as a Spanish group – like Los Brincos and Los Canarios who also came to London – they had a German lead vocalist, Mike Vogel, whose clipped precision gave his otherwise Americanized singing a distinctive edge. On the first all-live *Top of the Pops*, Los Bravos' formidable instrumental competence also gingered-up an otherwise nervously inept array of performers. Kept from Number One only by the Troggs' 'With a Girl Like You', the quintet's 'Black Is Black' contained a riff designed to stick in a listener's head to the grave.

'Bring a Little Lovin'', one of many Los Bravos misses in the wake of 'Black Is Black', was penned by guitarists George Young and Harry Vanda of the Easybeats – named after the Light Programme series. Ostensibly Australians, they were actually two parts Dutch and three parts English – with an ex-Mojo in drummer Snowy Fleet. When they crossed the Straits of Dover in 1966, the Easybeats were hardened professionals with five consecutive Oz chart-toppers to their credit. As Glasgow-born Young so evocatively put it, 'We could have gone on stage and picked our noses'.

Not in Britain they couldn't. Like Los Bravos, they had but one big smash there. Produced by Shel Talmy, the self-penned 'Friday On My Mind', a detailing of hedonistic escape from the bondage of the working week, electrified the Christmas Top 10 with its two-note instrumental shuffle and morse-code backing vocals.

The Easybeats may be seen as having tested the British water for the Bee Gees – the Brothers Gibb – who, recruiting a drummer and lead guitarist, growing their hair and wearing the latest swinging gear, were far removed from the brilliantined, Bugs Bunny-esque trio who'd appeared regularly on Down Under's *Bandstand* in the early 1960s. After a period as moptops, they'd found their own sound, had domestic hits and were brought over to London to be groomed for the Big Time by another Aussie, Robert Stigwood, whose agency had merged with NEMS.

Sepulchral echo down a recording complex's dark, twisting staircase, and news of schoolchildren buried alive by a shifting slag heap in Wales combined to inspire 'New York Mining Disaster 1941', which, aided by media build-up, catapulted the Bee Gees into the UK Top 20. They didn't then disappear with the haste of Los Bravos or the Easybeats. Very much the opposite, they were bigger than Frank Ifield – but, by 1970, internal squabbles had reduced them to a trio again.

Other musical Australians that came back to the Old Country were of more folky denomination. The Seekers were an update of the Springfields –

though there wasn't much to update – and one of the most popular non-beat groups in the world in the mid-1960s when Olivia Newton-John won a TV talent show. Her prize was a trip to London where she worked in a duo before recording in 1966 her first 45, 'Till You Say You'll Be Mine', an item left behind by Jackie de Shannon.

London provided more temporary accommodation for other commonwealth artistes like Tom, Dick and Harry, New Zealanders whose *Focus on Folk LP* was sold at the Muswell Hill coffee bar where they were resident in 1965. In Manfred Mann and Mickie Most's footsteps, the Woodpeckers blew in from South Africa – as did Beau Brummel, Esquire who was attired like his Georgian dandy namesake and backed by the Noblemen. He cut a dash on *Ready Steady Go*, bowing from the waist over Cathy McGowan's hand during the introduction to 'I Know, Know, Know', the failure of which effected his return to the Transvaal after the ungallant tactic of selling the story of his backstage love-life to the *News of the World*.

As Brummel departed in 1966, another Boer, singing multi-instrumentalist John Kongos, landed in England. After leading an outfit called Scrub through several dud records, and a few more on his own, he was to have two swift Top 10 strikes in 1971 before melting into the background just as rapidly.

Antedating the less dense 'township jive' of the late 1980s, Kongos injected aspects of his own musical culture into the bloodstream of British beat. This was far easier a task for GIs like Ronnie Jones and Herbie Goins who, awaiting demobilization, came to sing on Blues Incorporated's second LP, 1964's *Red Hot From Alex*. Encouraged by both Korner and customer reaction to their onstage efforts, they stayed on; Goins forming the Nightimers to accompany himself and Jones, who was very much the junior partner in the enterprise. Being a genuine black American lent Goins the confidence to record material that less assured British soul shouters would shun – notably a 'Knock On Wood' issued within weeks of Eddie Floyd's Stax original. This guaranteed work if not chart placings, and it must have been galling for Herbie and Ronnie when the inferior Geno Washington and the Ram Jam Band – fronted by another black ex-US serviceman – crept into the lower reaches of the Top 50, and even the album Top 20 in the mid-1960s.

Other US vocalists who sought their fortunes in Britain included Ben Carruthers, who led a group called the Deep into a void, and the incredible P.J. Proby whose career had started on a Houston radio station in 1949. His appearance – pony-tail, bat-winged blouson shirt, buckled shoes – influenced Beau Brummel, Esquire as his magnificent voice (minus the odd mannerism) did Tom Jones, whose big break came when he filled the gap in a package tour left after ol' P.J.'s fall from grace began when his too-tight trousers split from knee to crotch during a second house at the Luton Ritz.

Though the most insidious US *emigrés* in the UK charts, the Walker Brothers were not overnight sensations as all three unrelated siblings had been familiar faces in Los Angeles showbusiness circles for years before they made their collective vinyl debut in 1965 with 'Pretty Girls Everywhere'. Nevertheless, with Scott Engel's immaculate singing and the Nordic good looks of tall John Maus, they were made for success – particularly with the young ladies.

The least obviously gifted Brother, drummer Gary Leeds, had backed Proby on that fateful pant-ripping tour, and it was he who suggested to Maus and Engel that going to Britain was better than continuing to kick their heels round Hollywood. In London, the trio were soon signed to Philips by Johnny Franz, who'd already squeezed mileage from another predominantly ballad act, the Four Pennies. However, it was 'Love Her', an item taped back in the States, that, helped by a spot on *Thank Your Lucky Stars*, took the Brothers into the Top 20 for the first time.

This also set the style for every A-side until their dissolution in 1967. As it was with the Fortunes, orchestral scoring would augment basic beat group instrumentation – while Engel emoted and Maus waded in with high supporting harmonies. Touring incessantly throughout 1965, John, Scott and Gary became leading pin-ups in girls' periodicals and *Ready Steady Go* mainstays, once having a whole edition devoted to them. There were, however, very real difficulties when they came to promoting the product on the road. Initially, they had added only the keyboards of ex-Ugly Jimmy O'Neill to their guitar-bass-drums line-up, but as mauling by berserk females came to characterize their shows, Maus and Engel decided to shelve their instruments to concentrate on vocals – with Leeds and Johnny B. Great and the Quotations taking care of everything else.

Their first chart-topper, 'Make It Easy On Yourself' had extinguished totally a version by Bern Elliott. Next, 'My Ship Is Coming In' sailed to Number Three, and 'The Sun Ain't Gonna Shine Anymore' returned them to the top for all of April 1966. The going got harder largely because, as Eric Burdon pointed out on *Juke Box Jury*, all their singles started to sound the same, and, by 1967, the Brothers seemed archaic to younger listeners while being too long-haired to impress parents.

With their two most recent 45s relative flops, the Walkers commenced their final tour, trying to smile whenever the Jimi Hendrix Experience upstaged them with naked sensationalism. Taking the Who's auto-destruction a stage further, Hendrix had, on the very first date, sacrificed his guitar in an audacious *woomph* of petrol.

A black journeyman guitarist from Seattle, Jimi had been working in a half-empty New York club in the latter half of 1966 when he'd ascertained from an intangible buzz in the air that his time was about to come. It came in the stout form and Geordie accent of Chas Chandler, bass guitarist with the Animals. As the group was on its farewell tour of the States, Chas had decided to diversify into artist management – and there before him was Hendrix, a Wild Man of Borneo who happened to be a sublime guitar-picker and, if no Scott Engel, possessor of a droll, smoky husk of a voice that would do quite nicely. If Jimi agreed to come to England, Chas would build a group round him, and procure a recording deal. What had he to lose? Sinking into an uneasy oblivion on an evening flight to Heathrow, Hendrix let himself be pushed in whatever way fate and Chandler ordained.

First on the agenda were auditions for those who'd make up the rest of the Jimi Hendrix Experience. It was to be a three-piece with Jimi, a bass guitarist and a drummer. As the very name of the group suggested, the latter two had to be a fluid complement to Hendrix's playing and image, and were not to threaten any head-on rivalry.

Noel Redding, ex-lead guitarist with the Loving Kind, was persuaded to transfer to bass. He'd been under the delusion that the vacancy was for a New Animals, but, at a low ebb professionally, he was glad of whatever else was available. The only one of Noel's old groups to endure had been Screaming Lord Sutch and the Savages. Another who'd served under the godfather of British horror-rock was Mitch Mitchell. After a short spell in the Pretty Things, he'd joined Georgie Fame's Blue Flames who had just disbanded so that Fame could live out his jazz aspirations on 1966's plucky *Sound Venture* LP. Mitchell was, therefore, looking for another opening when he was asked to try out for Hendrix.

A TV appearance on the last edition of *Ready Steady Go* was conspicuous for the quality of the debut 45, 'Hey Joe', the visual effect of Jimi biting the strings of his Stratocaster during the solo, and the fuzzy-wuzzy halos sported by him and Noel. This was more than sufficient to lift 'Hey Joe' off the runway and start the group's climb to global stardom.

Hendrix and the Bee Gees were almost the last major attractions to come in from the outside of British beat. Time was when, fuelled by not entirely truthless tales of UK record companies contracting anyone who could hold a guitar, musicians from the Earth's most distant fastnesses had poured in for a piece of the action too.

Britain's own ethnic minorities came forth most discernibly in the shape of the Equals. As Them are now remembered principally as Van Morrison's old group, so some think of the Equals as the outfit in which Eddy Grant cut his teeth before achieving solo fame. After his family had emigrated from British Guiana to north-east London in 1960, Eddy formed the racially-mixed Equals at school with himself on lead guitar. 'The rest of us had to learn from scratch,' admitted Derv Gordon. 'We were each allocated an instrument to master although, as I couldn't afford a guitar, I was given the role of vocalist.'[45] Given Eddy, Derv and his brother Lincoln's Caribbean backgrounds, it was scarcely surprising that the music was undercut with elements of ska and bluebeat but, recalled Derv, 'It seemed that whatever we did would come out with our own particular sound stamped on it.'[45]

In 1965, the Equals were offered not so much a tour as a long run of one-nighters on the continent where they developed into a sought-after concert draw. A presenter on a West German radio station liked the loose-limbed drive of 'Baby Come Back' better than the A-side of their second single. Other disc-jockeys started spinning it too, and 'Baby Come Back' leapt to the top in both Germany and the Netherlands, and their *Unequalled Equals* blockaded Europe's LP charts for months. In 1968, 'Baby Come Back' was a 'sleeper' hit back home, and the Equals were to notch up six more UK Top 40 entries before Grant left them to fend for themselves in 1971.

More of a trace element in the crucible of British beat were outfits who sang exclusively and wilfully in Welsh, thus setting the ceiling of their ambition on discs issued on small labels to be plugged on BBC Wales' pop show, *Disc a Dawn*. Significantly, the final 45 by the most well-liked of such groups, Y Tepot Piws (The Purple Teapot), was 'Nid Ydym Ni Mynda'r Birmingham' ('We're Not Going To Birmingham').

Past regional identity, the prayers of a Salvation Army 'beat group', the Joystrings, had been answered by two Top 50 ascents in 1964. Not so blessed were Chinese Londoners the Etceteras and the Ying-Tongs. Though neither made a record, Nottingham's Latvian and Sheffield's Polish communities could each boast a group too in, respectively, Kaija and Tempo Four. The world will never know what it missed.

18 DO-RE-MI

A lingering critical prejudice of most A & R divisions was that the last thing anyone, from a teenager in a dance hall to the head of the Light Programme, wanted to hear was a home-made song. Composers have to start somewhere but, apart from B-sides, the possibility of a group developing composition to any great extent had been unheard of before 1962.

There were very special cases such as Johnny Gentle being permitted to write all four sides of his first two singles. His 'Wendy', a four-chord ballad that went 'Wendy, Wendy, when? Wendy, Wendy, when?' *ad nauseum* must have made John Lennon and Paul McCartney wonder what they were doing wrong when the Beatles backed him in 1960. Marty Wilde's only top 10 hit that wasn't a cover was 1959's self-penned 'Bad Boy'. In 1963, Nicky James composed 'My Colour Is Blue' as his first A-side, but with most of the new beat groups starting off with arrangements of non-originals, the Denmark Street demarcation line between composer and artiste persisted well into the 1960s.

After making scant headway as performers, Manchester's Graham Gouldman, Birmingham's Peter Lee Stirling and Philip Goodhand-Tait were three who found their feet as jobbing songwriters. Gouldman was one of British beat's great enigmas: composer of smashes for the Yardbirds, Hollies, Herman's Hermits, Dave Berry, Wayne Fontana and Jeff Beck, home and abroad, but unable to get anywhere with his own group, the Mockingbirds. Goodhand-Tait was in the same dilemma with the Stormsville Shakers but his time was to come later with three hits on the trot for Love Affair. Likewise, Stirling, sometimes with his uncle or another Midlands tunesmith Barry Mason, provided chart fodder for Kathy Kirby, Wayne Fontana, the Miami Showband (in Ireland), Tommy Bruce and/or the Bruisers – with whom he'd played guitar – and, the ultimate accolade, Elvis Presley.

John Carter and Ken Lewis had given up on Carter-Lewis and the Southerners to concentrate on the likes of 'Will I What?' and 'Is It True?' inquired respectively by Mike Sarne (with Billie Davis) and Brenda Lee. They teamed up as the Ivy League with Perry Ford who, as well as vamping keyboards for Bert Weedon, was also a composer; Adam Faith's 'Someone Else's Baby' being one of his crowning achievements.

The Ivy League began as session singers before trying some records under their own name, arguing that no one within the spectrum of the beat boom had capitalized on the Four Freshmen – Hi-Los close harmony sound as the Four Seasons and the Beach Boys had in the States. The League proved this judgement correct with 1965's 'Funny How Love Can Be' high in the charts. Two more chart entries followed before the three signed off with 'Willow Tree', another well-crafted melancholia that appealed to bedsit girls, grannies and those too tough to admit they liked it.

After the Kestrels threw in the towel, Roger Cook and Roger Greenaway's tenacity paid off in a similar fashion when they wrote 'You've Got Your Troubles' for the Fortunes in 1965 and established themselves as middle-of-the-road hitmen with a knack for hummable tunes. Like the Ivy League, the two Rogers themselves – as 'David and Jonathan' – scored twice in 1966's UK Top 20 wth 'Michelle' (the bi-lingual ballad from the Beatles' *Rubber Soul* LP) and their own 'Lovers of the World Unite'.

As well as performers with lost business innocence, producers and managers – and husbands – muscled in on songwriting too. Tony Hatch's 'Sugar and Spice' (under a pseudonym) was the Searchers' stabilizing second single. Harvey Lisberg (manager of Herman's Hermits, the Mockingbirds and Wayne Fontana), Gordon Mills (Tom Jones), Andrew Oldham (The Rolling Stones and founder of Immediate, Britain's first major independent label), Tommy Scott (Decca producer) and Bobby Willis (Mr Cilla Black) all foisted their creations on their charges too. Scott, for example, had a monopoly on all Twinkle's Decca B-sides, and Willis had a tally of eight amongst his wife's first fourteen hits.

It must be said that, like Hatch, Mills was actually quite an accomplished hit writer, delivering Top 20 goods for Johnny Kidd and Cliff Richard prior to coming up with Jones' first Number One, 1965's 'It's Not Unusual', a collaboration with Les Reed who had dashed off an Adam Faith flip-side when still one of the John Barry Seven. From this small beginning, it was, indeed, unusual if a UK Top 40 in the mid-1960s didn't list a Les Reed number (usually in alliance with Barry Mason). Acts indebted to Reed as writer and arranger were Jones, the Applejacks, Herman's Hermits, P.J. Proby and the Dave Clark Five.

Yet, with internal sources of new material and their own publishing companies, a lot of these blasted beat groups gave the business a nasty turn. The rules of the *Ready Steady Win* tournament had even insisted on at least one original per entrant. However, after the gift of a Lennon and McCartney opus became like a licence to print banknotes, the pair would still be damned in 1966 with such faint praise as 'reasonably good "amateur" composers, greatly assisted by the poverty of British composing standards';[140] this, three years after virtually every track on *With the Beatles* had been covered by another artist from 'Little Child' by a Billy Fonteyne to 'I Wanna Be Your Man' by the Rolling Stones to George Harrison's 'Don't Bother Me' – his first solo composition – rehashed by Gregory Phillips for Pye.

Formidable even before 1962, John and Paul's head start was a hard yardstick for other beat songwriters. Nevertheless, stirred when the two completed 'I Wanna Be Your Man' virtually to order while looking in at a Stones rehearsal in 1963, Mick Jagger and Keith Richards had a go too. A year after their first Stones A-side (1965's 'The Last Time'), they penned all fourteen tracks on their *Aftermath* LP. Such self-reliance had been born of both syndication of earlier material (such as 'Tell Me' by the Termites, and Herbie Goins' chancy 'Satisfaction' while an Otis Redding treatment was still thundering in London discotheques) and they had received commissions like Jimmy Tarbuck's 'Someday' 45, 'Blue Turns To Grey' for Cliff Richard, and, less unlikely, 'So Much In Love' with which the Mighty Avengers penetrated the Top 50 in 1964, though no such luck befell the Herd's version nor the second Jagger-Richards 45 for the Avengers, 'Walking Through the Sleepy City'.

Aftermath elicited as many covers as *With the Beatles* had done. 'Take It Or Leave It' gave the Searchers their final Top 40 entry, and, when under producer Jagger's wing, Chris Farlowe had his UK Number One with the since much-revived 'Out of Time'. Mick and Keith also earned pin-money from turntable hits on pirate radio like 'I Am Waiting' by the Quiet Five, Wayne Gibson's 'Under My Thumb' and 'Mother's Little Helper' from Gene Latter (who alleged that Jagger had stolen his stage act).

Meanwhile, after 'All Day and All of the Night', his second self-penned smash for the Kinks, the more prolific Ray Davies was to be courted for numbers he felt were unsuitable for the group – though an item submitted to the Seekers was considered 'too masculine', and the Honeycombs relegated his 'Emptiness' to fifth track, side one of their second LP. Davies also mailed demos to Elvis Presley, though the King did not deign to use them. Yet so far there have been around two hundred recorded non-Kinks versions of Davies compositions; among the more successful in the 1960s were Dave Berry's 'This Strange Effect' and 'Dandy' by Herman's Hermits – though for every bullseye there was a miss like 'King of the Whole Wide World' by comedian Leapy Lee, 'Little Man in a Little Box' by Ray's art school chum Barry Fantoni and 'I Go To Sleep' by the Applejacks in 1965. Quite a feather in Ray's cap, however, was when Peggy Lee, international entertainer since 1938, had been first in the queue for 'I Go To Sleep'.

Ray's credit rose even more when he forged a new, intrinsically English – and frequently unfashionable – pop form. Its first manifestation had been 'A Well-Respected Man', previewed on *Ready Steady Go* in October 1965. A literate, watchful lyricism was married to idiosyncratic reconstructions derived largely from outmoded musical genres, some dating back to Victorian traditions. Surrounded by pop star tumult, the endlessly inventive Davies was attracted, amused – even envious – of the culture that had produced monologues, tea dances and similarly stylized entertainments – even if its patrons' lives were far harsher than those of their Swinging Sixties descendants. While LPs like the transitional *Face to Face* and 1968's *Village Green Preservation Society* would not match the sales of earlier albums, the Kinks remained entrenched in the singles lists with tracks such as 'Sunny Afternoon', 'Dead End Street', 'Waterloo Sunset' and, as late as 1970, 'Lola'.

To the further detriment of Denmark Street's worker-ants, the LPs and demo tapes of the Who, Zombies, Small Faces, Hollies, Troggs and even Unit 4 + 2 were scrutinized for potential smashes. The Yardbirds found their feet as composers too after 'For Your Love' precipitated three years of increasingly more challenging hit singles. A disgruntled ex-manager, Simon Napier-Bel, would admit that 'there were four rock bands in the world that really counted – and the Yardbirds was one of them'.[141] In 1966 an *NME* reviewer called the *Yardbirds* LP 'a mini-*Revolver*' (The Beatles' latest). Such praise was all the more deserved because, unlike the Beatles, the Yardbirds' studio time was always limited, but though they were granted only five days off from a punishing concert schedule to record *Yardbirds*, any extension may have detracted from the proceedings' spontaneity and endearing imperfections. Certainly no cover – whether Paul and Barry Ryan's 'I Can't Make Your Way' or Al Stewart's 'Turn Into Earth' – ever surpassed the Yardbirds' original draft. No combination of Yardbirds, however, was a Lennon-McCartney, whose swelling stockpile could fulfil the Beatles' EMI contractual commitments many times over, and now included Number Ones for Peter and Gordon and the Overlanders.

Russ Ballard, who was to join Unit 4 + 2 full-time, and cast his net into their writing pool, had been the Lennon-McCartney of the Roulettes as James Hare was in the Static as Ron Wood in the Birds, and Colin Manley in the Remo Four. Many other groups also had either an individual or team that may or may not have been as talented as John and Paul. None, however, had the same resources. As sound an investment for EMI as Presley was for RCA, the Beatles could take as much time as they liked at Abbey Road, with the freedom to requisition all manner of auxiliary instrumentation and, later, musicians.

With the Beatles had been the first album to be taped on four-track equipment. Though this and other early Beatles LPs were conceived technologically during recorded sound's late medieval period, they heralded, nevertheless, a new attitude towards a product that had not been regarded hitherto as an artistically rounded entity but a cynical and clumsily-conceived patchwork of tracks hinged on a hit 45. Testaments to commercial realism rather than quality, these singles-chasers were targeted – especially in the States – at fans beglamoured by an artiste's good looks and personality, and happy to buy haphazardly-programmed output, short on needle-time and padded with previously-released B-sides, forgotten flops, hackeyed showbiz standards, unoriginal 'originals' and time-consuming stylized instrumentals, excused as an exhibition of 'versatility'.

The studio clock would dictate such short cuts as Mike Smith and Steve Winwood singing both the call and response sections of certain respective Dave Clark Five and Spencer Davis Group numbers – with the *accelerando* coda of 'It Hurts Me So' from *Their First LP* inducing visions of a console engineer's leg-crossing anxiety to visit the gents. Yet *Session with the Dave Clark Five* was surprisingly sophisticated when set against the crash-bang-wallop of the Five's best-known singles – as if proving that the group could hit you with the quality stuff too via a stylistic diversity then unexpressed by any of their contemporaries including the Beatles and the Rolling Stones. Ranging from jazz to pseudo-folk, items penned by co-producer Dave with and without other of his four colleagues went in harness with interpretations of numbers such as 'Rumble' in which the depth of sound exceeds that of the Link Wray original, thus insinuating that, but for the beat boom, the Five might have developed into one of the great British instrumental acts like the Tornados or Shadows.

Without as much capacity for self-promotion or as big a backlog of chart entries as the Five, the Zombies had been rushed by Decca through *Begin Here*, which contained as well as 'She's Not There', one-take stand-bys from their ballroom repertoire, a royalty-earning instrumental by producer Ken Jones, and some songs by Chris White and Rod Argent hinting at what might have been. Argent at least would be receiving Performing Rights Society cheques for years to come for 'She's Not There'. Propelled by his keyboard ramblings, Colin Blunstone's spellbinding vocal was supported by precise harmonies on critical lines in the restrained, haunted atmosphere of this minor-key classic that had no obvious precedent. This approach had prevailed on the follow-up, White's 'Leave Me Be'. Described as 'the ultimate teen angst melodrama' by one reviewer, it was thought too wantonly melancholy by most radio presenters at the time. Yet it might not be too presumptuous to intimate that the likes of 'Walk Away Renee', 'Bridge Over Troubled Waters' and Nilsson's 'Without You' might not have been envisaged as pop songs without the contradiction of enjoyable depression that was the frequent aftertaste of the Zombies' music.

Rod Argent was one of the few would-be Gershwins of the beat boom able to sight-read and write musical script. The majority that couldn't would dah-dah-dah as a 'proper' musician notated any scoring required. Therefore, a transistorized reel-to-reel tape machine – forerunner of the cassette recorder was often as much part of touring luggage as a change of socks. From flashes of inspiration thus noted, a song might grow, but sometimes a composer would tinker into the night, red-eyed and unshaven, on a guitar that might as well have been a coal shovel.

Many a group would walk into a studio session with nothing prepared beyond, say, a chord sequence, some half-finished lyrics or just a title. Though some of their pieces would be presented as a *fait accompli*, the Yardbirds' usual recording methodology seemed slap-dash to outsiders. 'We'd start with a basic rhythm and bass pattern,' elucidated Jim McCarty, 'and then sort of build it up.' While the backing track was being organized, someone – usually Keith Relf – would be elsewhere collating the words and little by little a number would surface. At Chess in Chicago, one of the group's biggest hits, 'Shapes of Things', was teased from nothing more than a riff.

As all artists do occasionally, composers borrowed from others, trying to disguise the source of inspiration in the hope that nothing would remain infuriatingly familiar. Ideally, such artistic appropriation added mere icing to what were already strong songs. Though it mutated into what Paul Samwell-Smith called 'happy Russian rock 'n' roll', the Yardbirds' 'Over Under Sideways Down' had started life as an unlikely kick in the direction of 'Rock Around the Clock'. From *Aftermath*, 'Stupid Girl' had an air of Manfred Mann about it, but not enough for anyone to consult a solicitor.

I wonder if a writ was dumped on Chris Farlowe, accredited writer of 'Treat Her Good', a B-side from 1965 that was a laughable theft of Roy Head's 'Treat Her Right'. While on the subject, the reason for bass guitarist Fritz Fryer's 'Juliet' being buried in the first instance on a Four Pennies' B-side may have been its close melodic affinity to a Ruby Murray hit of 1955. Then, of course, the resemblance of 'My Sweet Lord' to the Chiffons' 'She's So Fine' would make George Harrison guilty of 'subconscious plagiarism' in 1976 when he was ordered to pay the aggrieved party just over half a million greenbacks. This outcome of the best-known civil action of the 1970s led Little Richard's publisher to claim breach of copyright in a track from the twelve-year-old *Beatles For Sale*. Yet surely every combination of even the chromatic scale must have been used up by now. By rights, the inventor of the twelve-bar blues ought to be richer than Croesus. Should a plumber receive a royalty every time a toilet he has installed is flushed?

One potent advantage of pinching something from public domain – music deemed to be 'from time immemorial' or 'traditional' – was that the larcenist's publisher could cream off royalties. Well, who else ought to get them? God? A grafting of, say, a Chuck Berry backbeat onto such an item was seemingly enough for a group to claim it as their own composition (and probably Berry to put in for a cut too) – though many would have the honesty to put the abbreviation 'arr'. ('arranged by') in front of the bracketed names beneath the title on the record label.

Plundering our national heritage has always been an intermittent ploy of British pop. Off the top of my head, there's Clinton Ford's 'Nellie Dean Rock', the Packabeats' 'Gypsy Beat' (Raggle-Taggle Gypsies-O'), 'Greensleeves' by the Fabulous Fleerekkers (as 'Green Jeans') and the Country Gentlemen (a kind of staccato Gerry and the Pacemakers), 'Silver Dagger' from the Pentad, the Fleerekkers again with 'Early One Morning' (as 'Hangover') and 'Phil the Fluter's Ball' (as 'PFB'), and the Eagles' imaginative rocking-up of the Cornish Floral Dance (as 'Come On Baby') on Pye in 1963.

Another strategy is adapting the bits everybody knows from classical music – hence Sounds Incorporated's 'William Tell', and 'Peter and the Wolf' by the Clyde Valley Stompers. For the Cougars' 'Saturday Nite at the Duck Pond', a robust variation of his 'Swan Lake' tune, Tchaikovsky used the pseudonym 'Keith Owen'. The tortured Russian got his own back, however, on 1965's *Beatle Cracker Suite* EP by Arthur Wilkinson and his Orchestra which substituted Lennon-McCartney tunes for the interweaving *motifs* in the *Nutcracker* suite, thus bestowing on it a 'Lennon-McCartney-Tchaikovsky arr. Wilkinson' composing credit.

Among the reasons that the Beatles downed tools as a working band in 1966 was that their music was becoming harder to perform in concert using conventional beat group instrumentation – though some sections could be approximated by using Paul or John's skills on the Vox Continental organ that now travelled with the guitars and drums. While the backwards-running coda of the 1966 B-side, 'Rain', was yet to come, for 'Yesterday' from the *Help!* LP, Paul McCartney sang solely to his own guitar-strumming as there was little to be gained in taking to the road with the string quartet hired for the recording. Money was no object. It was just that the fans had bought tickets for a tribal gathering rather than a musical recital. Had it too been flung into the screams, 'You've Got To Hide Your Love Away', garnished with flutes, would have been almost as much like feeding a pig strawberries.

Hit records and increased van space meant that other groups could also take on the road a purring two-tier electric organ that cursing road crews would have to drag up and down backstage stairs. Like Roy Phillips of the Peddlers, Alan Haven swore by the Lowry that he pressed nightly at the Annie's Room niterie and when recording the theme to 1965's *The Knack*, yet another movie set in Swinging London. However, triggered by an article on Hammonds in *Midland Beat*, Dave Grounds of Ray Everett's Blueshounds, runners-up in *Melody Maker*'s national competiton in 1966, shelled out £825 for this trendy toy. Though Tommy Eyre of the Candies – led by ex-Fortune Glen Dale – got one for a knockdown £700, this was still a vast outlay for a teenage member of a struggling group.

The flute was a sound more peculiar to Brumbeat than any other area, employed as it was by the Moody Blues and the Falling Leaves. When Second City pop came belatedly of age, circa 1967, Traffic and Tea-and-Symphony featured flautists too, and after the Hellions had renamed themselves Deep Feeling in 1966, their drummer, John Palmer (later of Family) transferred to flute and vibraphone, yet to be of more than negligible significance in a pop context – likewise, the amplified squeeze-box employed by the Amazons, a Midlands girl group.

As well as 'Yesterday' (and, later, 'Eleanor Rigby'), orchestral string instruments fairy-dusted various Jagger-Richards' songs by other artists such as Marianne Faithfull, Twice As Much and Chris Farlowe – as well as caressing the Troggs' soft underbelly in 'Anyway You Want Me' and 'Love Is All Around'. With the opposite effect in mind, horn sections assumed parts that could have been allocated to lead guitar on Manfred Mann's chart-topping 'Pretty Flamingo', the Hollies' 'What Went Wrong', the Pretty Things' 'Death of a Socialite', the Beatles' 'Got To Get You Into My Life', the Stones' trumpeting 'Have You Seen Your Mother Baby, Standing in the Shadow', and the Dave Clark Five's revival in 1967 of 'You Got What It Takes'.

On records by what were still called 'beat groups', other more intriguing effects were now being heard, some of them courtesy of talented multi-instrumentalists like Brian Jones, Steve Winwood, Manfred Mann's Mike Vickers, Alan Blakely of the Tremeloes and Graham Bond, at ease playing sax and organ simultaneously. Open-minded about new instruments, he was seen patiently demonstrating the mellotron – an electro-mechanical key-board activating tapes of instrument sounds – to Cathy McGowan on *Ready Steady Go*.

Brian Jones was admired for his weaving of quainter instrumentation into the fabric of *Aftermath*, such as the dulcimer on Tudor-flavoured 'Lady Jane'. Of similar antiquity was the harpsichord that the Ugly's tried to push to pop prominence, while the autoharp of Pinkerton's (Assorted) Colours (and New York's Lovin' Spoonful) had been pre-empted by the Downliners Sect whose Don Craine had been stroking one on the boards since 1961. The Who featured John Entwistle's French horn on 'Disguises' and 'I'm A Boy', and the Hollies got Tony Hicks to pick electric banjo on 'Stop Stop Stop'.

A tape of marching feet from EMI's sound archives was grabbed by the

Hollies as rhythm track for a 1966 LP track, 'Crusader'. Other instances of similar experimentation are the Small Faces gulping down water when trying to tune a tumbler to A, and peeping a whistle on 'Understanding', one of their B-sides. A pot-pourri of polyrhythmic percussion supplemented Mick Wilson's drumming on Dave Dee, Dozy, Beaky, Mick and Tich's 'Save Me', and a bullwhip noise (an empty beer-bottle zoomed down a fretboard as two bits of plywood were smacked together) would punctuate their 'Legend of Xanadu', the most breathtaking of their arrangements of any Howard and Blaikley song. The hum of a faulty organ marked 'There's Always Work', a John Mayall instrumental, and an eerie vocal tremelo made the Hollies' 'Lullaby to Tim' seem as if there was fluff on the needle. A now-forgotten singer on *Five O' Clock Club* swivelled his head from side to side at the microphone regularly enough to convince me that it was for a deliberate vocal effect.

Along more orthodox lines, though Bert Weedon (on 1965's 'Twelve String Shuffle') and The Poets both used one, the Searchers were mainly responsible for introducing the twelve-string guitar to the common-or-garden beat group. While it was still a novelty at home, they had procured a semi-acoustic model from the States. Limited as a solo instrument, its uniquely circular sound, nevertheless, powered most of the group's later hits.

It might have been an irritating occupational hazard to the Searchers, but neither Jeff Beck, Dave Davies, the Creation's Eddie Phillips or Pete Townshend dismissed guitar feedback as such, pursuing it as a contrivance, and as a method of sustaining notes and reinforcing harmonics. The dentist's drill whine that began the Beatles' 'I Feel Fine' in 1964 echoed the in-concert use of feedback by the Yardbirds and Kinks. Rendering the circle unbroken, the Kinks would reiterate the 'I Feel Fine' introit on 'I Need You', a 1965 B-side.

When serving Craig Douglas, Beck's Tridents had been rejected as a recording entity in their own right because 'the guitar sounds distorted'. However, with the Yardbirds in 1965, Jeff drove his new Telecaster through a Marshall amplifier to actively create distortion, utilizing extra-light strings for unprecedented *legato*. 'You could never get him to tune up,' said Keith Relf. 'He'd go on stage with his guitar totally out of tune, and bend the strings. He never really played chords, just all bendy notes – but he never played out of tune.' 'Shapes of Things' and its B-side, 'You're a Better Man Than I', composed by Manfred Mann's Mike Hugg, are, perhaps, the best examples of Beck-as-Yardbird's aggressive passagework, lubricated with feedback.

Believing that guitar tone lay in the hands of the player, Beck was not a major advocate of the fuzz-box, a device intended to make a guitar sound like a saxophone but which assumed a character of its own after its blackboard-scratching hoarseness had electroplated 'Satisfaction'. Bass was fed through one to manufacture the searing trump on a Beatles LP track from 1965, 'Think For Yourself', but 1966 was the big year of the fuzz-box as it surfaced in the hit parade on 'Keep On Running', 'Hold Tight' and the Animals' 'Don't Bring Me Down'. In November, growling fuzz organ was a chief selling point on the Spencer Davis Group's 'Gimme Some Lovin''.

Mistaken in a *Music and Musicians* critique for a harmonica were the tearful guitar phrases achieved with a volume pedal on the Beatles' 'Yes It Is'. The precursor of the wah-wah effect, this artifice had been first employed more aptly by veteran session player Big Jim Sullivan the previous autumn on Dave Berry's 'The Crying Game' and its follow-up, 'One Heart Between Two'. This effect was refined by George Harrison on *Revolver* in 'I'm Only Sleeping' via the overdubbing of two backwards – and tuneful – lead guitar overdubs to create the necessary 'yawning' sequences. This appealingly enveloping sound was to be developed further by other guitarists, notably Jimi Hendrix on the title track of the 1967 album, *Are You Experienced*.

Over a year before Harrison's sitar lessons with Ravi Shankar, both the Kinks and the Yardbirds had invested respective singles with an Indian feel. A seated sitarist had been present on a Yardbirds session but the group preferred the exotic twang of Jeff Beck – given to tossing in Eastern *leitmotifs* during his stage solos – which was more like the real thing than the real thing. A few weeks later, the Kinks' 'See My Friends' – with, purportedly, an additional and braver intimation of bi-sexuality – exhaled a more pungent breath of the Orient. Overlooking the pibroch-like thrum of the Poets' 'Now We're Thru' of 1964, it was, estimated the Who's Pete Townshend, 'The first reasonable use of the drone – far, far better than anything the Beatles did and far, far earlier.'[138]

Soon after one was heard on the Beatles' 'Norwegian Wood', Brian Jones discharged a masterful sitar *obligato* on both *Aftermath*'s 'Mother's Little Helper' (with its 'oi!' cadence) and the Stones' third Number One, 'Paint It Black', while Mick Jagger's production of Chris Farlowe's 1967 version of 'Moanin'' had sitar where a busking sax might have been. With a seal of approval from the Stones and Beatles, this wiry-sounding nine-stringed instrument with bulging gourds, movable quarter-tone frets and 'sympathetic' under-strings became as essential an accessory as a fuzz-box or volume pedal for certain precursors of pop's fleeting classical period. Roy Wood, then of the Move, invented the 'banjar' which combined properties of sitar and banjo, and both Dave Mason, from the half-formed Traffic, and Donovan acquired a sitar after an exploratory hour or so on George Harrison's imported model. It was treated by most like some fancy guitar. Eventually it held less allure because of the fine line between its ear-catching extraneousness and sounding like a parody of 'Norwegian Wood' or 'Paint It Black'.

Beyond mere gadgetry, Eastern musical theories had long been a trace element in folk and modern jazz, becoming more pronounced in the mid-1960s through the work of British acoustic guitarist John Renbourne, John Mayer's Indo-Jazz Fusions and the 'trance-jazz' of Gabor Szabo. Yet it was Ravi Shankar, the Indian sitarist who brought about the most far-reaching popularization of Indian music, when, as he put it, 'There was a sitar explosion. All of a sudden, I become superstar (*sic*).'[142]

This was splendid news for stockists of Indian goods in the West. In provincial Britain now, a certain sort of teenager might waste hours outside a record shop debating whether to blow three weeks' paper-round savings on, say, Ravi's *Portrait of Genius* or Ustad Ali Akbar Khan's *Young Master of the Sarod*. Youths whose short hair broke their hearts would board trains to London to buy joss-sticks. One hippier-than-thou Hampshire schoolboy, Stephen Macdonald, even came home with a sitar.

Stephen was also the first at Farnborough Grammar with the debut album by the Velvet Underground, an arty New York combo in whom Brian Epstein was 'interested'. Some of the sleazy lyrical perspectives on this record were underlined not with a bass guitar throb but a noisy electronic whirr that made a melodrama out of what was merely implicit in Indian music. The lengthy screech-out of its final track, 'European Son', took the Who's studio simulation of auto-destruction a stage further. Like 'Anyway Anyhow Anywhere', 'European Son' seems milder now, but, in 1966, it was explosive, even on the cheapest monophonic hi-fi.

The Yardbirds did the Velvet Underground's 'I'm Waiting for the Man' during a stage act in which some of their own studio efforts had no serviceable place. Among these was 'Still I'm Sad' which, in 1965, had brought Gregorian chant to the Top 10. This was to be taken up by the Herd two years later in the lower register background cantillatings on 'From the Underworld' and 'Paradise Lost'. Symphonic tempo changes and other eruditions pioneered by the Yardbirds were also elaborated later by the similarly-motivated Pink Floyd, King Crimson, Yes and Zoot Money's new outfit, Dantalion's Chariot.

Like the Yardbirds, Brian Jones moved further from (though some would say nearer to) his blues core. As well as his investigations into the ethnic music of Morocco, further excursions into non-Western cultures by British beat musicians were exemplified by the careering coda of the Zombies' 'Indication' which conveyed a hint of Arabia, and Ian Amey's balalaika which decorated the quickening pace of Dave Dee, Dozy, Beaky, Mick and Tich's 'Bend It', their understanding of Paul Samwell-Smith's 'happy Russian rock 'n' roll'. Crude as they may seem now, the likes of 'Indication' and 'Bend It' were among the first creaks of a door that would open wider on a treasury of what would be termed 'world music'. From these caskets, Malcolm McLaren, Adam and the Ants, Monsoon, Peter Gabriel and other burglars in the 1980s charts would help themelves.

'Bend It' with the Troggs' 'I Can't Control Myself' and 1967's 'Let's Spend the Night Together' from the Stones were all excluded from prudish airwaves for sexual innuendo. Yet, casting Reg Presley as a sort of bumpkin Heathcliff, the rush-released 'Night of the Long Grass' suffered airplay restrictions in the States not because it might have been about something rude, but on the ridiculous premise that it referred to drugs ('grass' and all that).

Because it exposes a point of view, 'Night of the Long Grass' may be construed as political. In a more accepted sense, protest songs were the most political in all pop, and Bob Dylan their most famous singing composer, despite his offending folk purists by 'going electric', *circa* 1965. The in-crowd took to quoting Dylan lyrics as if they were proverbs, and beat groups dipped into his portfolio of songs: the Animals, Them, the Byrds, the Fairies and Watford's Cops and Robbers among them. Even a Dylan sleeve note was set to music in 1965 by Ben Carruthers and the Deep as 'Jack O Diamonds', but in Bob's view, Manfred Mann were the most effective interpreters of his songs, an opinion justified financially when their versions of 'If You Gotta Go, Go Now', 'Just Like a Woman' and 'Mighty Quinn' all became global smashes. He also liked an LP, *Songs of Bob Dylan*, by the Silkie, duffle-coated students from Hull who'd gained a management contract with Brian Epstein, and made the Top 30 with a limp rendering of 'You've Got To Hide Your Love Away'.

'It Ain't Me Babe' from 1964's *Another Side of Bob Dylan* was chosen as A-side when Decca allowed Dave Berry's Cruisers a single of their own in 1965. It was up against other versions, including one by Dave Helling, a nineteen-year-old who cut a sullen figure on Britain's folk club circuit.

Though it involved sweating a bit over words, both Denmark Street and composers in groups put their minds to Dylan-style creations. John Lennon put 'I'm a Loser' on *Beatles For Sale*, and Jonathan King gave 'It's Good News Week' to Hedgehoppers Anonymous. The Downliners Sect came up with 'Bad Storm Coming', a euphemism for impending nuclear holocaust, while 'Shapes of Things' and the Stones' '19th Nervous Breakdown' are two more that betrayed an absorption of Dylan through constant replay of his LPs.

Dylan was already one jump ahead when 1965 became the golden year of all-purpose protest songs like P.F. Sloan's 'Eve of Destruction' for Barry McGuire. Whereas Bob used to go on about war being wrong and fairer shares for all, he was now singing through his nose about myriad less wistful topics; his rapid-fire stream-of-consciousness literariness revealing infinitely greater possibilities beyond protest and boy-girl relationships. For British composers, looking beyond fifth-form sermons and the old moon-June travesties of love, a vista to a wider canon was opened, containing more than what was almost said in the lewd middle eight of 'I Can't Control Myself'. Subjects like dead end streets, nervous breakdowns, gender confusion (as in the Who's 'I'm a Boy') and – with a sense of longing rather than self-loathing – drug addiction and sex for its own sake took tangible form as literary-musical wit from composers who were assumed by many to live the part.

On *Aftermath* alone, 'Under My Thumb' rode roughshod over mitherings about its sexism, and was still in the Stones' concert set fifteen years later. 'Mother's Little Helper' was about the habit-forming tablets which hasten a distraught housewife's 'busy dying day'. After Phil May and guitarist Dick Taylor of the Pretty Things found it fun to be composers too, 1966's 'Midnight to Six Man' concerned the Dracula hours kept by pop star nightclubbers, though the group's encounters with the clergy may have occasioned track's like 'Death of a Socialite' and – an essay in urban isolation – 'House of Ten', both from *Emotions*, an LP that, beneath its overdubbed strings and bandstand brass, uncovered a fading singles chart act in uncertain transition.

In the LP lists too, the Hollies' more interesting albums could not match sales of those packed with covers that went down well on stage, greatest hits and, long after the Silkie, *Hollies Sing Dylan*. Many of their most inspired moments were overlooked – the perverse non-rhyming couplets to 'Peculiar Situation', the medieval overtones in 'Crusader' and the eloquent time signature switches on 'Pay You Back With Interest'. In step with this growing musical complexity, Allan Clarke, Graham Nash and Tony Hicks had organized themselves as a composing team under the collective pseudonym 'L. Ransford'. Chancing their arms with an A-side, 'We're Through' followed 1964's 'Here I Go Again' into the Top 10. Though heedful EMI ordained a return to outside writers for the next six 45s, from autumn 1966 until Nash's exit three years later, almost all Hollies tracks dripped from Mr Ransford's pen.

Though the tune of 'Stop Stop Stop' had been unveiled on an earlier flip, 'Come On Back', its lyric revealed a maturer dexterity in a feverish account of unrequited desire for an erotic dancer. Another highlight was 'King Midas In Reverse', an ambitious production that belied its below-par Top 20 showing. Salt was rubbed into this wound when the Hollies' artistic nullity, 'Jennifer Eccles', tripped daintily into the Top 10 six months later. Nevertheless, other artists, notably the Fourmost and, flatteringly, the Everly Brothers, commissioned songs from the Hollies who, second to the Beatles, would survive Merseybeat's collapse as the most distinguished northern group.

Bidding goodbye to the Top 50 forever with L. Ransford's 'Have You Ever Loved Somebody' in 1966, the Searchers were, on the meritocratic basis of chart performance, third. Their own material had been confined to B-sides and album fillers except for 'He's Got No Love' which, if only a moderate hit, was a personal coup for Chris Curtis and Mike Pender, its writers. Other Merseybeat musicians that, however belatedly, boarded the songwriting gravy-train ranged from Gerry Marsden, whose creative parameters continued to be proficient if limited; the Fourmost's Brian O'Hara, who co-wrote the march tempo 'How Can I Tell Her'; and two of 1965's edition of the Dakotas, Robin McDonald and ex-Pirate Mick Green (albeit a southerner by birth), who penned 'Don't You Do It No More', B-side of Billy J. Kramer's first flop.

A quota of Wayne Fontana's own songs appeared on 1966's *Wayne One*, a solo LP, and Denny Laine and pianist Mike Pinder started taking care of most of the Moody Blues' output. Their 'From the Bottom of My Heart' was the group's entry into a 1965 ITV-sponsored song contest won by Kenny Lynch's 'I'll Stay By You'. Yet the Moody Blues emerged as chart victors at Number Twenty-two, eight places above Kenny. 'From the Bottom of My Heart', which built from a murmur to a wailing horror-movie coda, tied with the 1966 tango, 'Boulevard De La Madeleine' as the most exquisite 45 any incarnation of the Moody Blues ever made.

Pinder and Laine didn't produce enough to be able to put much in the way of other artists (though Julie Grant covered 'Stop' from the Moody Blues' first LP). Unless you were Lennon-McCartney, Jagger-Richards or Ray Davies, monetary rewards were generally meagre in this area. John Mayall entered the UK Top 30 in 1965 by proxy when his 'Something' was recorded by Georgie Fame and, after the Small Faces defected from Decca to Immediate, Steve Marriott and Ronnie Laine wrote smaller hits for Chris Farlowe and P.P. Arnold. Rod Argent provided a miss for the Mindbenders in 'I Want Her She Wants Me', and Reg Presley for the Loot and the Nerve. Undaunted by Jonathan King's *Juke Box Jury* remark that 'if you like "With a Girl Like You", you may consider yourself the very lowest common denominator in the pop audience,' Reg offered 'Cousin Jane' to the Spencer Davis Group.

Before the Honeybus had their only smash with 'I Can't Let Maggie Go', Pete Dello, their singing guitarist and the song's writer, had given 'I Don't Want You' to the Anteeeks (*sic*) who would be remembered more for their one-piece zip-up stage suits. Pete's 'Do I Figure In Your Life' would be as inexplicable a miss for Dave Berry in 1968 as it had been the previous year for the Honeybus.

A guitar-shaped swimming pool could not be ordered by Paul Jones and Tom McGuinness for supplying Tony Dangerfield and the Thrills with 'I've Seen Such Things', nor by Unit 4 + 2's Tommy Moeller and Brian Parker with amassed royalties from 'The Table's Turning' by the Senators – though they might have been able to afford a diving board from 'Baby Never Say Goodbye' for The Bo Street Runners, which was every bit as engaging as 'Concrete and Clay'.

Besides income for his work in the Who, Pete Townshend was not particularly prosperous as a mid-1960s composer either – though there were substantial cover versions of his Who songs by groups like the Merseys, the Fleur de Lys and the Untamed, and the Barron Knights' 'Lazy Fat People' and Oscar's 'Join My Gang' were among Townshend numbers unrecorded by the Who.

Bass player John Entwistle was the Who's second-string composer – and if you can't be first, be peculiar. A minority of listeners – me included – found his macabre offerings the group's most endearing aspect. Though John himself preferred Pete's paean to self-gratification, 'Pictures of Lily', Jimi Hendrix's favourite Who opus was Entwistle's 'Boris the Spider', squashed against the wall in 1966's *A Quick One* LP – in which the hallucinating alcoholic of John's 'Whisky Man' was condemned to a padded cell. You cannot easily disregard a man who penned pop songs too about miserliness ('Silas Stingy') and, later, voyeurism ('The Window Shopper') and an insurance swindle ('I Found Out'). That the boy had talent was emphasized further by his invention of a challenge to the Twist in 'Do the Dangle' – from the neck after you've kicked away the chair 'and you're dancing on air'.

Even before the release of his first solo record in 1969, Entwistle found it easier to get his pieces onto vinyl than other writers trying to penetrate a given group's caste-within-a-caste. Some found it unbearably frustrating to bask in a less dazzling spotlight than the ruling individuals who, championed by producer and manager, had hogged a near-monopoly of songwriting within the unit structure. Often, they were the quiet blokes. Toiling over his kit, Jim McCarty posed no limelight-threatening challenge to the Yardbirds' front line. Yet he co-wrote nearly all the ensemble's most enduring songs.

To a shy youth, attempting to get past his group's quality control was torturous. Like a travelling salesman with a foot in the door, he had to make a pitch with the most enticing wares. Clearing his throat, he'd start chugging chords; a deep breath and into the first line. When the song died, he'd blink at his feet before glancing up with enquiring eyebrow. Sometimes, he'd realize it was useless as soon as he opened his mouth. At other demonstrations, he couldn't comprehend his listeners' amused indifference to his little ditty.

Such was the predicament of George Harrison whose subsequent flowering as a composer would contribute to the Beatles' eventual self-destruction. Though Bill Wyman's recruitment by the Stones may have saved him too from a more mundane life, his stymied ambition as a writer deserves a measure of sympathy. Though 'In Another Land' entered the US Top 20 in 1967, only one more item penned solely by Bill would ever be issued by the group. Speculating in artist management and record production, he was, however, able to offload some of his remaindered numbers onto the End, Bobbie Miller and other unprofitable clients.

With his position as leader usurped, Brian Jones, like Bill, suffered from Jagger and Richards not being very receptive to the compositions of others. '[Brian] always made his songs too complicated,' was Mick's excuse, 'one hundred chords a minute, like a jazz progression. He was a reformed traddie, and, although he despised them, he was really one of them'.[114] Certainly Brian relocated eight-to-the-bar trad banjo to electric rhythm guitar on 'It's All Over Now' and '19th Nervous Breakdown'.

You might be as much the public face of the group as any other member – more so in Brian's case – but, the chemistry of its public persona apart, you were expendable. Under no commercial pressure to compose, your musical explorations would be of less value that the power you gave to the main writers' patterns of chords and rhymes. Through dogged persistence, however, you might get one composition per album and an odd B-side – even if less time was spent on these than ones from the chief fount of original material. They were further undermined by being used as a means to show off some new sound-effect or to immortalize an instrumentalist's arrogance as he took more than his fair share of *obligato* interjections and solo bars. It might have been simpler to have just moaned ineffectually before resigning yourself to being treated as a tool for the masterworks of a couple of fellows who'd once been your mates. Instead, the creative artist in you couldn't be suppressed, and a compounding of friction and muffled rancour manifested itself again in one of these flare-ups that had grown more frequent of late.

19 THE HARD WAY

'Progress' might have been in the air in 1966, but many preferred the old ways. Once when the Animals were on *Ready Steady Go*, Eric Burdon unbuttoned his jacket to reveal the shocking inscription, 'ROCK 'N' ROLL LIVES!', scrawled on cardboard across his front. The group felt privileged to warm up another audience, shrouded in leather and motorbikes, in a Jerry Lee Lewis – Gene Vincent – Little Richard TV spectacular directed by Jack Good during a flying visit to England. The Animals had also pulled through a UK tour in 1964 with Chuck Berry who, the following year, frequently joined them onstage during their maiden coast-to-coast trek across North America. With coat torn off and shirt hanging out, Burdon's orange-peel complexion poured sweat as the other Animals drove him through 'Around and Around', 'The Girl Can't Help It' and 'Shake Rattle and Roll' as well as their hits and the purer R & B.

The Hollies weren't yet above slipping in Berry's 'Sweet Little Sixteen' amongst titles like 'Oriental Sadness' and 'Fifi the Flea' on 1966's *Would You Believe* LP. The Dave Clark Five were to return to their primal repertoire right up to the end of their existence, even borrowing titles for their own compositions – the prime example being Carl Perkins' 'Glad All Over'. From 1965, they reverted to revivals of numbers like Berry's 'Reelin' and Rockin'' and Bobby Byrd's 'Over and Over' to try to redress the UK Top 40 balance after clever flops like 'Everybody Knows', with its abrupt dynamic shifts, and 'Try Too Hard'.

More overt rock 'n' roll acts were still in business. In 1966, Johnny Kidd was traversing the country with yet another new crew of Pirates. He'd listened to management advice about moderating his style towards country-and-western to suit clubs where easy-listening was the rule, attempting a third chart coming with a 1964 treatment of Hank Williams' 'Your Cheatin' Heart'. When a remake of 'Shakin' All Over' found no passage into the Top 50 either, Kidd was thinking aloud about an entire LP of Gene Vincent numbers. Moreover, he always had plenty of work assured with or without record success – and, for all anyone knew, a chance to hit the Big Time again was lurking just round the next bend.

For such a tireless tourer, the law of averages dictated a major transport mishap sooner or later, and for Kidd it came when the group's van collided with a skidding lorry near Radcliffe on 7 October 1966. On BBC TV's *Nine O' Clock News* the next day, it was reported that twenty-seven-year-old Johnny had been among the fatalities.

At a benefit concert for the widow, Lord Sutch underwent a temporary name change when, as 'Lord Caesar Sutch and his Roman Empire', he rode on stage in a chariot, resplendent in toga and laurel wreath. That year, he'd revived 'Purple People Eater' – *the* novelty hit of 1958 – by placing the wretched creature in Swinging London. His Lordship's itinerary was still mostly one-nighters and support spots to outfits who'd once supported him but he was still there, wasn't he? He was still transcending the slings and arrows of fashion, long after Dickie Pride, the Moontrekkers, Jet Harris, the Federals, Vince Eager, Don Charles and nearly every other early 1960s contemporary had faded away to insurance offices, painting-and-decorating, the civil service and, in Jet's case, back on the buses – as a conductor.

When Sutch's old mentor Joe Meek squeezed a fatal trigger on himself in February 1967, the interrelated disbandment of the Tornadoes was imminent. The next year, the Shadows were down to fifteen minutes in the first half of a Palladium variety show. Yet, as they and Cliff Richard had delved deeper into pantomine and evangelical Christianity, Adam Faith had had a surprise US smash with one of his B-sides, 'It's All Right'. Obliged to appear straight after the Rolling Stones at a *NME* Pollwinners concert, he'd also displayed an unprecedented and jaw-dropping flicker of sexy movements that almost out-Jaggered Jagger, the Roulettes bucking and cavorting around him. Nevertheless, it was back to ballads afterwards as he bid a restless farewell to the charts, 'Cheryl's Going Home' waving him out of sight in 1966. By then, he was ensconced in a repertory drama company, learning his new craft the hard way in the provinces.

Billy Fury left the Top 50 in 1966 too. As he steeled himself for cabaret, however, he was gratified to discover that up north at least, girls still screamed at him.

Nineteen-sixty-six also meant transition for the Nashville Teens. They'd registered their last hit parade entry – 'The Hard Way' – in February, and 'Revived 45 Time', the follow-up's B-side, was either hopelessly outdated or too far ahead of its time. If given the bird by small-minded Teds, they'd been proud to be on a UK tour headlined by Chuck Berry in 1964. Lower down the bill had been Kingsize Taylor and the Dominoes who, while growing fat on the Star-Club circuit of Hamburg, Kiel and Berlin, had, agreed Taylor, 'been out of the country at the wrong time'.[31] However, a Liverpool booking during one of their forays to Britain sparked off a commendatory write-up in *Melody Maker*, the Berry job, and the protraction of a sporadic recording career into 1967.

Back in Germany, Tony Sheridan was plucking jazz guitar as customers chattered in a Reeperbahn bar when one of his singles from 1964 with the Pete Best Beatles was re-issued. It spread itself thinly enough to sell a million without making much of a dent in most charts. Drawn from his exile by pragmatism, Tony released a new LP (*Just a Little Bit of . . .*), brushed his grey-flecked hair forward at last, was 'special guest' on a tour with the Searchers, and appeared on British TV again – on *Five O'Clock Club*. However, a hail-fellow-well-met reunion with the Beatles was not repeated a few months later when the group and Tony were benighted in the same Australian hotel.

The Beatles hadn't become so swollen-headed not to, say, drop in on a Merseybeats disc date or gravitate back to Liverpool's small-hours clubs – albeit with decreasing frequency – where chat would be peppered with anecdotes about what Gerry said to Sam Leach in 1961. The Fab Four were nobody's lions there. In the Blue Angel, George Harrison had greeted a Roadrunner with, 'Hi, Mike, how's the band?' 'Great, George,' began Mike Hart's crushing rejoinder, 'how's yours?'

While many of those who'd once enlivened its pages struggled, *Merseybeat* – now calling itself 'Britain's leading beat paper' – had died like a sun going nova; its final burst of energy unleashed in full-colour illustrations, articles on non-Merseyside acts and a circulation that straggled as far south as Leicester. This trod on the toes of *Midland Beat*, which had branched out into theatre, cabaret and selected book reviews as well as jazz. It outlived *Merseybeat* by almost three years – while *Top Stars Special* ended its run in 1970. Demonstrating an awesome contempt for historical and cultural interest, an executive decision caused the destruction of all unsold back copies.

More than any of them, *Merseybeat*'s saga had paralleled that of the buoyant local scene singled out as a pop centre, then desecrated and the culprits pardoned. In March 1965, the journal had been swallowed by *Music Echo* (itself to be consumed by *Disc*), and coverage of the Liverpool scene was confined to a solitary page commensurate with drooping interest in any more two-guitar-bass-drums groups who couldn't get record contracts, let alone hits, to save their lives nowadays.

Time had run out too for those who'd been there at the right time. Clint Ballard's 'It Isn't There' for the Swinging Blue Jeans was too *deja vu* but its tearjerking harmonica gave it such period charm that, as much as Gerry's 'Ferry Across the Mersey', it served as a requiem for Merseybeat's passing. Neither the Fourmost nor Billy J. Kramer were ever to be on *Top of the Pops* again while most of the rest had never been there in the first place. After the Big Three's first set at the Blue Angel one night, another drummer took over when Johnny Hutchinson collected his pay and went home. While his other

Mersey groups were cashing in what chips were left, Brian Epstein had overloaded himself with trendier non-Liverpool signings like the Moody Blues.

He'd also made a sole venture into record production with 'America' from *West Side Story* as rendered by Rory Storm and the Hurricanes. On the evening in 1965 that the Beatles performed before nearly sixty thousand (a new world record) at New York's Shea Stadium, the Hurricanes and Storm – as daredevil and hip-swivelling as ever – had been on at Orrell Park ballroom. Other engagements now stretched to the very edge of Swinging London – but no further.

20 INSIDE LOOKING OUT

With no Svengali or outside management behind them, the Dave Clark Five were probably the most successful self-contained business enterprise in British pop; their drummer being a man with an instinct for the manoeuvres that had given them the required pushes up the commercial ladder – all the way up when the time came. It was said that if anyone criticized his music, Dave would justify himself by pulling out a wad of bank-notes. Like other managers, he would study the hit parade as a stockbroker would the Dow Jones index because pop music was and is a commodity to be bought, sold and replaced when worn out, and, no matter how much their luck continued to hold while other groups came and went, even the Beatles expected it to run out at any second. 'It's been fun but it won't last,'[144] persisted John Lennon in 1964.

Financial schemes had long been afoot for the Beatles and other outfits to ensure that they'd recoup more than golden memories when the game was up. Usually, each member was given shares in budgetary receptacles for net income from records and concerts, and guarded if provident speculations in, say, chains of launderettes, building firms, land securities and property development – even if many would be credit-squeezed out of existence by a mid-1960s Labour government fighting a formidable balance-of-payments deficit. Perhaps not grasping that this had been inherited from the Tories, pop star hearts might have remained socialist, but, after supertax, their purses might not have been.

At meetings with accountants, some musicians would probe more than others about where this percentage came from or why so-and-so had been granted that franchise. Vocabularies swelled with phrases like 'tax concession' and 'convertible debenture' during natters about private investments like Chris Farlowe's military memorabilia shop, Merseybeat Tony Crane's stake in a Spanish night club, John Lennon's titular co-directorship of a Hayling Island supermarket, bass player Alan Howard's dry-cleaning business – for which he'd eventually quit the Tremeloes – and Dave Clark's buying up of the *Ready Steady Go* series and other film archives that he'd sit on for twenty years.

With most earnings tied up, your wallet would often hold little real capital – though you only had to phone the office whenever you wanted more than that with which your bank account might be regularly transfused. You became unaccustomed to actually paying for things in hard cash as you never had to prove your identity to sign bills for large amounts, and road managers and other menials took care of minor purchases. Small change was as unnecessary as eyesight to a monkfish – or so you'd think. Motoring home from a party in London, one of the Beatles let his car run out of petrol and, stranded without a sou, he was obliged to hitch a ride from one who chilled him with the information that he wrote for a national daily.

The tabloids were full of Dave Clark buying his mum and dad a ten thousand pound house – a veritable palace thirty inflationary years ago. Other pop star parents also enjoyed a dotage rich in material comforts. As with winning the Pools, they were able to retire early and wonder what to do between breakfast and bedtime. Some of them used their second-hand celebrity to open fetes, judge beauty contests and even attend fans' weddings. After all, who else was responsible for their present life of ease, if not the fans?

For other nearest and dearest, a pop star was the supplier of expensive birthday presents and, less directly, gifts that fans parcelled to the fan club. The home-made 'gonks', the honoric plaques, the childish daubs – most were less than ornaments, but from those with more money than sense came complete dinner services and even silverware.

What were the other siblings' feelings about Our Kid's popularity and wealth just because he'd sold a few gramophone records? The child they'd known all their lives was now influencing the minds of millions. Even whilst hurrying from doorway to taxi, it was sometimes necessary for him to scrawl an irritable autograph or two – and there were times when other members of the family couldn't go out either without nicotine-stained fingers jotting down something they said. The next morning, it might be in the papers, and their illustrious relation may or may not be annoyed.

Illustrious he might be, but habit still motivated collections of spittled books of trading stamps. Moreover, if he was an immature provincial who'd never signed a cheque or called room service before, his consumption might be more conspicuous than those born into wealth. There'd be the diamond rings, the gold watch, the champagne and newly-purchased clothes consigned to the dustbin because they hadn't looked as good in a full-length mirror at home as they had in the shop. Thanks to the instant fortune that had fallen into his lap since gatecrashing the Who in 1963, Keith Moon could afford to apply a cigarette lighter to his £150 pay packet for a day's film work.

For those who'd once pressed noses against showroom windows, the first big royalty pay-out might go on a Jaguar, a Ferrari, a Triumph Vitesse, an Aston Martin DB5 or – motorized embodiment of the 1960s – a Mini.

Freddie Garrity had spent most of his on a flash E–Type three times the price of his humble abode in Manchester. Next, much bowing and scraping would ensue as one such as Freddie paced up and down rows of gleaming Rolls-Royces and Mercedes with one-way windows, all the latest gadgetry and driving seat contours which could be adjusted to the shape of either his or the chauffeur's buttocks. With customized tailgate, Rolls-Royce parts, electric windows and walnut on fascia and doors, Ringo Starr's Mini Copper S had worked out five times dearer than an ordinary one.

Out on the highway, a grin and autographs might settle the matter if police pulled you over, but it was a red-letter day if you were allowed to eat a restaurant meal in solitude, without having to sign a napkin whilst masticating a sausage. Even a jazz jamboree in Richmond was no sanctuary as an excursion by various Beatles and Stones to see the Animals there fired an outbreak of fan mania and a hasty exit. Disguises, decoy tactics and secret destinations were as essential as spare underwear should you and the missus decide to go on holiday. Without these precautions, today's deserted beach would become tomorrow's media circus. Curtains in hotel rooms would be drawn to reveal an expanse of faces and camera lenses between the main entrance and the silver strand where palms nodded.

Back at your London *pied à terre*, you'd answer the phone to stifled giggles from fans who'd winkled out your ex-directory number. Tatty girls with laddered stockings and someone else's love-bites leaned against the wall opposite. Some would still be there in the dawn drizzle, sinking into a languid daze induced by the fixity of gazing up at your window. Even *boys* tried to kiss you as you came and went.

The antics of some fans were even more frightening as they dangled from ledges, gulped down poison, threw themselves under your car wheels and slashed wrists to simply be noticed by you. Others turned to breaking-and-entering. One well-known musician and his wife were startled awake one night when his arm dangled from the bed to touch one of two young ladies hidden under the mattress. As they'd already stolen items of clothing as souvenirs, instead of pulling autograph books from their handbags, the pair wisely took to their heels as their idol switched on the light and yelled.

With Billy J. Kramer and Spencer Davis letting slip their addresses to journalists to precipitate a fulsome avalanche of fan mail and nuisance callers, invasions of privacy were sometimes self-inflicted. Nevertheless, when Ringo Starr's tonsils were removed, he couldn't help the jamming of the hospital switchboard with requests for the gruesome excisions. In a Carl Giles newspaper cartoon, a schoolgirl off to join star-struck loiterers in the infirmary's car park was commanded, 'You're not bringing 'em back here!'[145] by her father.

City lights would lose their allure, and you'd start house-hunting in the Surrey stockbroker belt and the wooded rural quiet of Essex or Hertfordshire. Greedy estate agents with prejudices against long-haired pop stars would force up asking prices for those they assumed had wealth beyond calculation. One solution was to send a subordinate to look around and report on likely-looking properties that had caught your fancy in the pages of *Country Life*.

On purchase, an ivy-clung Plantagenet manor house that no son of a schoolteacher or corporation dustman had ever dreamt of owning would be fronted by Britain's first electronically-operated gates, and razor-sharp barbed wire would crown the outer walls. Even so, day trippers would say 'cheese' outside these forbidding borders, and American and Japanese tourists would train cine-cameras up the drive.

When people left you alone, it was a sweet life, much more restful than London with its unremitting churn of traffic – though late afternoon cornflakes might bring an onset of high spirits by dusk, and it was sad to sink them into a sofa when they cried out for diversions you could no longer enjoy because of the havoc that you'd accumulate. Therefore, the diversions would have to come to you.

With reckless indulgence, country estates were treated to all kinds of structural idiosyncracies. A hoop-shaped alcove might be converted into a bar, and a stable into a music room. Feature films and home movies would be screened in 'cinema rooms' with exposed rafters. Alien to a medieval baron too were swimming pools and – exotic even for the Home Counties – sauna cottages.

A lot of time was spent less on anything constructive than on just mucking about. Crazes would possess you and, hanging the expense, you'd have to have all the necessary top-of-the-range equipment. Because the bass player had had a pool table, cues and triangle of balls sent over after becoming hooked on the game in the States, the drummer felt obliged to do the same, and another snooker den would appear behind stained-glass windows. A go-kart track would weave in and out of tree-lined landscaping. On discovering words like 'field', 'gate' and 'aperture' as applied to a camera, the guitarist might create a dark-room so that he could develop and print his own films. In every nook were tape-recorders, cine-projectors, stereos, early colour televisions and Britain's first privately purchased cassette machines.

Some corners would be given to gold discs and mementoes of a past that, through its unbelievable outcome, had attained a certain romantic grandeur as, in orgies of maudlin reminiscence whilst switching from Scotch to bourbon, you'd get sentimental about the days when you could small-talk on the pavement while chomping a snack from Alex's Pie Stand.

Now that you were world famous, the past was never far away – especially when relatives and family friends that you hadn't realized existed knocked on stage doors. Fathers would roll up twenty years after deserting you, with hands open for any bounties that might trickle from your coffers; the most famous incident being that of Freddie Lennon, John's estranged dad, who was also signed up by Pye to record a single. Bogus half-brothers, step-sisters and cousins all appeared from nowhere to spin a likely tale to gain entry to a dressing room theoretically as protected as Fort Knox – though the very security guards paid to keep riff-raff out could often be bribed to let them in.

With countless hordes of special female admirers aspiring to an orgasm at a musicianly thrust, members of the road crew were not surprised when directed to bring the more personable up to one or other of their masters' hotel suites. If in more gregarious mood, members of the group would be seen in the bar holding court to a veritable bevy of dolly little darlings.

Sounds like hell, eh? Yet though there are worse ways of making a living, it became an onerous obligation for some. A man suddenly preoccupied with success is likely to be an inattentive swain. It was a trifle unsettling for wives and girlfriends back home to hear stray mutterings about amatory adventures on tour – particularly for those who had to keep up a 'just good friends' farce to protect the group's 'available' image.

Not everyone loved you. You'd thread through customs areas resounding with jack-in-office unpleasantness and beset with every fibre of red tape that bureaucracy could gather to hinder hairy foreigners. Priggish hoteliers would be at pains to stress that no minor was to be served alchohol, their faces falling when the youngest player produced his passport. As your voice shimmered over a sea of heads, you'd notice offensive placards and be victim on rare occasions of peltings with decayed fruit and more odious projectiles, thrown mostly by jealous boyfriends. Recalling a night in 1964 when 'a kid in Brisbane threw a tin on stage and it freaked George Harrison right out,' an eye-witness theorized that, 'George has an incredible fear of being killed.'[146] Who hasn't, sport?

In Tokyo, performances at the Nippon Budokan Hall took place with the disquieting knowledge that, outside, there were protest demonstrations about pop singing *ketos* polluting this temple of martial arts. This was nothing to the naked malignity that the Beatles endured during an agitated scuttle from the Phillipines where they had insulted unwittingly the hallowed person of President Marcos, and then in North America following a story of John Lennon 'boasting' that the group was more popular than Christ. The possible in-concert slaughter of the artistes by divine wrath – or someone acting on the Almighty's behalf – improved attendances but did not forestall public bonfires of Beatle records and the picketing of shows by Klu Klux Klansmen.

Deliberate danger apart, bolstering any misgivings about flying were some of the paint-peeling antiquities hired to lift you from here to there as you scanned the ocean for sharks. Often flying in the face of superstition, you were haunted by the ghosts of Buddy Holly, Patsy Cline and Jim Reeves. On the road, it was Eddie Cochran and Johnny Kidd. After a resigned silence, you'd drift back into the desultory chat that always supervened when the late-night radio went off the air. Even when too fatigued for conversation, you preferred not to nod off with the road buzzing in your ears.

The distinction between night and day had long been blurred, and the means of staying awake or falling asleep when you wished were generally obtainable from local narcotics dealers who'd been able to contrive access to sell you their goods. Sharpening paranoia as they did after they'd worked their dubious magic, drugs did not make touring any more bearable as, heartily fed up with it all, you braced yourself to deliver another unheard codswallop special.

From stadium dugouts, you and the others would slouch rather than dash towards the stage where you'd hear the relentless screaming no more than a mariner hears the sea. As far as guesswork and eye contact would allow, the group would adhere to recorded arrangements with only the snare-drum off-beat more a sound than a presence. Virtually gulping the microphone, the singing would strain against the bedlam. Some musicians might affect a customary exuberance while others would roar purgative off-mike obscenities during a half-hour no worse than any other dished out for ticket-holders that year.

Even in Britain now, bouncers had to be so rough with rampaging fans that reprimands would issue from the stage – as would vain pleas for discontinuance of the rain of votive offerings cascading from the audience. Nothing that thudded onto the boards – sweets, cake, toilet rolls, tubes of lipstick, binoculars, nails – surprised you any more.

The sound systems at some venues might have been loud and clear enough for you to pull yourself together if you'd taken the trouble to tune-up, but truly you couldn't care less about any wavering bars of bum notes. For devilment, the vocalist would mouth songs soundlessly, and the guitarist slam sickening dischords. For the wrong reasons, concerts could still be fun. Off-stage, who could keep a straight face in the madness? Socialites, civic dignitaries with their hoity-toity children – everyone who was anyone was doing anything to be presented to a plebeian British pop group. At a famous-names-in-good-cause Hollywood gala held in the Beatles' honour, you'd pass a dozen famous faces along a single staircase. Cassius Clay and Ringo would spar playfully. Zsa Zsa Gabor would have her photo taken with George, and Paul would unbutton himself in adjacent cubicles to Bing Crosby and Edward G. Robinson in the gents. Peculiar to Billy J. Kramer and the Dakotas was an incident on US television when a chief of the *Dakota* Sioux relinquished a headdress to Billy, who said he planned to write a song about it. Words are cheap.

For idle hours, you might take challenging reading matter. However, during bouts of self-loathing in this torpid bandroom or that chartered flight, it would occur to you that you'd scarcely peeked at a solitary page the entire trip, and that the highlight of the day wasn't the concert any more but the building-up, the winding-down and roguish pranks when other acts were on. In Stockton-on-Tees, Mick Jagger spread cold chips on the blind side of the microphone-bound Steve Winwood's piano – not that the effect was noticed amid the tumult. Somewhere in America, Keith Moon had sawed halfway through Ronnie Bond's drumsticks and wrapped tape round the cuts so that Ronnie ended up with only one stick with which to play three-quarters of the Troggs' set.

In common confinement in characterless dressing rooms, a Pretty Thing might tell the one about what Brian and Bill of the Stones had got up to in Adelaide; Del Shannon compliment Keith Richards on 'High and Dry' off *Aftermath*, and Bobby Elliott agree with Charlie Watts, jazzman to lapsed jazzman, that at least it paid the mortgage. Before Authority complained, two Easybeats, an Animal and the drummer with Johnny Hallyday's group had a blow in a Cannes hotel lounge. More interesting was a fracas between the two Kinks brothers: 'He [Dave] got very annoyed with me last week,' recounted Ray Davies. 'He picked up ash trays and things in the dressing room and threw them at me. Then he knocked me over and tried to kick me. He missed and kicked this iron table, and went hopping out of the room, holding his foot.'

Such activities passed time as you circled a globe less and less eye-stretching. Dishes with specious names – trepang soup, veal Hawaii, furst puckler – pampered stomachs yearning for the greasier satisfaction of fish-and-chips eaten with the fingers. A hotel in Belgium was just like one in Tennessee. The Coca-Cola tasted exactly the same. Everywhere was the same. If it's Monday, it must be Shoreview, Minnesota.

Where had all the good times gone? Waking up, you'd almost expect to yawn and stretch to a standing ovation so intrusive was the world's adoration. Where was the world? There were photos of you performing in every continent but, like a blinkered dray-horse, you'd only ever seen your immediate environment. You'd guess you were in Canada only by Mounties that patrolled the neon-lit perimeter of the besieged hotel. What had been the point of travelling so far and seeing nothing but what you could remember of, say, a stolen afternoon driving a borrowed car in the Dandenong mountains or a bleary-eyed glimpse of a sunrise in Indianapolis after an obliging state trooper sneaked you into a squad car for breakfast in an empty roadhouse out on the freeway? When asked what such-and-such a city had been like, you were damned if you could even find it on a map.

There was always the money to think about as you weighed up the cash benefits of churning out the same stale music night after artless night against your self-image as an artist. Box office receipts were still huge but there was, by 1966, a perceptible falling-off of attendances – sometimes as low as half capacity for even the Dave Clark Five in North America. Though the schedule had been whittled down for fear of over-exposure, you were becoming as over familiar on the world stage as you'd been locally in 1961. Like a high street bus, if fans missed a show, there'd be another one along if they waited.

No home venues could yet compare with overseas coliseums that could rake in the most loot with the least effort by accommodating thousands in one go. The management had cut down on press conferences too. These were now like a parody of some Hollywood B-feature: cameras click like type-writers at the stars' tardy arrival in a twenty-foot limousine; no autographs please; newshounds circle the group, thrusting stick-mikes at their mouths as, with bad grace, they'd deadpan the usual inane and impertinent questions.

These weren't interminable sessions of wry shallowness any more. Zany merriment about mini-skirts swung in seconds to two-line debates about inflammable issues. A certain surliness and even vulgar signs directed at photographers would anticipate the affectations of punk. Past caring, major groups became oblivious to the behaviour that would have been tantamount to commercial hara-kiri back in 1963.

Three years on, Brian Epstein had had to calm friction over an album cover showing his Beatles as butchers gleefully going about their grisly business. That limbs and heads of dolls were among the bloody wares hadn't mattered when this picture appeared in Britain. Such a scene was comic opera in a country that housed Madame Tussaud's Chamber of Horrors and David Edward Sutch. However, with the Vietnam war cranking into gear, the 'butcher sleeve' was hastily withdrawn from circulation in North America. 'All this means,' answered diplomatic McCartney, 'is that we're being a bit more careful about the sort of picture we do.' Lennon had no time for tact. 'Anyway, it's as valid as Vietnam,'[147] he quipped unfunnily as various toadies sniggered.

The concealment of the recording studio – where mistakes could be revoked – was agreeable to contemplate during the last weeks of the Beatles' most public journey. There wouldn't be any more after a showdown in San Francisco where they ran through their final thirty minutes with George fluffing his guitar runs, Ringo forgetting the words of 'I Wanna Be Your Man', and Paul trying to make a show of it.

If they only could, more groups might have followed suit. A shattered Spencer Davis on tranquillizers spoke of retirement to a Hebridean island and no one knew whether to believe him. For others too, up to three years of unbroken press visibility had given birth to new ambitions to be unphotographed stepping from a lift, unrecognized in a restaurant, unchased down the street, but these now seemed more far-fetched then getting rich and famous had been way back when.

Furthermore, as they'd been within earshot of each other for every working day since God knows when, how refreshing it was for members of groups to be able to undertake individual projects. Some outfits weren't especially mature about this. 'The band becomes a prison,' said Mike Pender. 'You can't do anything without the others. Someone asked if they could use me on an album and the rest of the lads didn't like it.' With 'Jennifer Eccles' a hard cross to bear, Graham Nash began talking openly about a solo LP. Dave Davies was on the verge of releasing 'Death of a Clown', the first – and biggest – of his two 1967 hits without the other Kinks, and Keith Relf had already edged into the Top 50 – just – with 'Mr Zero', a solo 45 produced by Paul Samwell-Smith in 1966.

Following Jeff Beck's sacking that year, the *NME* reporting incorrectly that it was to be Keith Relf *and* the Yardbirds now. Others had not become beings apart by choice. 'Is It Mick and the Stones Now?' asked *Melody Maker*, prompted perhaps by a televised Chelsea Rag Ball when the group was introduced by Jimmy Savile as 'Jagger M. and the Rolling Stones.' When the Move auditioned for a Marquee residency in 1966, an onlooker stated that Ace Kefford – all blond androgeny *à la* Brian Jones – ought to be the central figure. 'That's when the rot set in,' remembered Ace, 'because I had been separated from four other ego-maniacs who also wanted to be stars of the show. Later, there were requests from *Fabulous* and magazines like that for photos of me on my own. There was a big row, and I was cold-shouldered in the van, two hundred miles there, do the gig, two hundred miles back – not a word.'

Managers might pour oil on troubled waters by insisting that any such spotlighting 'Enriched the Group as a Whole' just as another cliche, 'Musical Differences', would be given as a reason for a person leaving – even a *de jure* leader like Brian Jones after he could no longer pretend that he held the Stones in the palm of his hand. Paranoia split his concentration, and he became more morose as Mick started handling the bulk of press calls and generally overshadowing him until the public realized that Brian wasn't The Man after all.

When Steve Winwood no longer hid his embarrassment when any of the Spencer Davis Group's early 45s shook the record-player at parties, Spencer too saw what was coming. He strained his ears to catch murmured intrigue as Winwood and Dave Mason, intermittently the Group's malcontented road manager, tinkered secretively on guitars backstage.

The two of them, see, had formed an unnamed unit with some fellows from Locomotive and the Hellions. Their objectives were understood to be no more than a bit of a lark, but they voyaged beyond Birmingham clubs and rural pubs to dare an unannounced bash at the Marquee. The atmosphere thickened, and Winwood was often missing minutes before showtime. 'Steve seems to have retired completely,' sighed Spencer indulgently. 'He roams the Berkshire Downs with his mates in a jeep.'[148] Three weeks later, *Melody Maker* announced Steve's 'amicable split' with the Spencer Davis Group, and the name of his new outfit, 'the Traffic', in which 'musicians expected to join him include Jim Capaldi (drums), Dave Mason (guitar) and Chris Wood (flute)'.[149]

The first major personnel change of the group era had been Tony Jackson's parting from the Searchers in 1964, likewise to start a new outfit, Tony Jackson and the Vibrations. Before that, Billy Kinsley had quit the Merseybeats to lead the Kinsleys, spilling the beans later: 'It was untrue to say that I left because I couldn't stand the pace. In actual fact, I left because of personal disagreements.'[150] When his eponymous unit came to nought, Billy reunited with Tony Crane as the Merseys for a 1966 version of a McCoys B-side, 'Sorrow'. This processed into the UK Top Five and, before the subsequent flops, the craziness of 1964 passed before Tony and Billy again as they packed auditoriums throughout the nation.

By then, Bern Elliott had swapped his Fenmen for the more malleable Klan on stage and the Mike Leander Orchestra on record in hopes of a new beginning as a Sinatra of the Medway. Meanwhile, Decca had compelled the Fenmen to cover the Four Seasons' 'Rag Doll' before they transferred to CBS in 1965 when they released the Zombies-like 'Rejected'. Though the single was aired frequently on pirate radio, the group disbanded after half their number was absorbed into the Pretty Things whose bass player had emigrated, rhythm guitarist gone from the face of the planet, and drummer headed ultimately to an unhappy association with the Hell's Angels.

From around the middle of 1966, such schisms seemed to occur about once a month. With no Top 10 entries for two years, Brian Poole and the Tremeloes started recording separately, but it wasn't until a Birmingham University booking in 1967 that they finally sundered; the group updating the beery, fun-packed spirit tinged with sentiment that they used to brew up at Butlin's, and Brian concentrating on ballads like 'Everything I Touch Turns To Tears', which was voted a hit on *Juke Box Jury* but didn't get so much as a sniff at the Top 50.

Wayne Fontana's casting aside of his Mindbenders had not been so smooth. Each faction blamed the other for a chart decline that had begun with 'She Needs Love' in 1965. 'All we've lost is our tambourine player,' snarled guitarist Eric Stewart as the group's 'A Groovy Kind of Love' became their first and last US hit. However, the UK charts were game for three more offerings before even a cameo role in the feature film *To Sir With Love* could not resuscitate them as Top 50 contenders after 1967. Wayne's oscillating chart performance included 'Pamela Pamela', written by future Mindbender Graham Gouldman. After the group wound things up in 1968, Gouldman and Stewart plunged into session work. Among their clients would be Wayne with whom Eric had buried the hatchet.

It was rumoured that Fontana had been considered when it was all change in Manfred Mann. Mike Vickers tired of a travelling life and his departure meant the transfer of Tom McGuinness to guitar and the enlistment of bass player Jack Bruce (who would be succeeded in turn by Klaus Voorman). More serious was the outfit taking formal leave of Paul Jones at the Marquee before the flash-bulbs of the press. Rallying, Manfred vacillated between Long John Baldry, Rod Stewart and, allegedly, Wayne before alighting on Michael d'Abo from a Band of Angels, whose gimmick had been straw boaters indicative of their public school education. There would be intense disagreement between d'Abo and Mann over the former's desire to pursue a parallel solo career, but the hits kept coming for the group with only Randy Newman's 'So Long Dad' faltering outside the Top 50.

Neither was no immediate harm done as the similarly atrophied Animals, Small Faces, Hollies, Yardbirds and Kinks continued to tramp, a well-trodden path up the Top 20. Of their former colleagues, for every Alan Price Set or Jeff Beck Group, there was a Pete Quaife's Maple Oak, a Jimmy Winston's Reflections and an Eric Haydock's Rockhouse.

Winston and Haydock had each left their respective groups under a cloud. Brian Jones was an emotional disaster area and his days as a Rolling Stone were numbered too. When he was finally squeezed out, it would be worthy of the *Nine O'Clock News*. More than just a pop group as transient and gimmicky as any other, the Stones were part of mid-1960s Britain's cultural furniture like Promenade Concerts, ITV's *Coronation Street*, BBC's *Till Death Us Do Part* – and the Beatles.

In the run-up to the post-Profumo general election, a *Daily Express* cartoon had the two main political leaders soliciting the Fab Four for their votes, thus lending credence to the homily, 'I care not who makes a nation's laws as long as I can write its songs.' A year later, the group would be invested as Members of the British Empire by the Queen on the advice of Prime Minister Wilson. No Honours List before or since has ever been as controversial. As well as jokes about the Stones getting the Order of the Bath, disgusted civil servants and retired admirals returned their medals to Her Majesty. In the *Daily Express* was a suggestion that the Fab Four ought to subject themselves to a 'decent' short-back-and-sides before setting off for the Palace.

Yet who could help but be impressed by British pop as generator of vast financial power? A *Daily Express* gossip columnist assured readers that, 'There's no harm these days in knowing a Rolling Stone. Some of their best friends, in fact, are fledglings from the upper classes.' A few became more than friends. Herman married well, as did Barry Ryan. Having won the hand of a Stuart, Phil May, Pretty Thing and, therefore, social pariah, would be among those privileged to attend the Prince of Wales' wedding. Back in 1965, the most signal celebrity to attend a celebration of the Things' first year as a hit group was actress-with-a-heart-of-gold Diana Dors.

Pop had started to move up in highbrow circles too. Through the Aeolian cadences and sub-mediant key switches he'd noticed on *With the Beatles*, Lennon and McCartney had been described as 'the greatest composers since Schubert' by Richard Buckle of the *Sunday Times*.[151] Less plausible was a gushing lady Juke Box Jurist who cited Alan Price as 'the best organist in the world.' Yet, beginning with Adam Faith's chain-smokingly intelligent *Face To Face* BBC television grilling in 1960, further 'articulate' pop spokesmen were found, including ex-Oxford undergraduate Paul Jones and the Who's Pete Townshend, the Derek Jamieson of British beat.

The notion of pop as a viable means of artistic expression had intensified by the middle of the decade. Musicians were invited to write books. John Lennon led the way by collating his verse, stories and messy cartoons for two immediate best-sellers, excerpts of which were adapted for stage presentation at the Old Vic in 1968. Another ex-art student turned author, Charlie Watts, did a more considered job on *Ode To a High-Flying Bird*, a eulogy to Charlie Parker.

There were painting exhibitions such as ex-Beatle Stuart Sutcliffe's posthumous retrospective in Liverpool's Walker Gallery in 1964. Pop musicians also featured in non-vacuous movies. Indeed, hardly an edition of *Melody Maker* went by in the mid- to late-1960s without something about another pop icon or other having a try at 'proper' film acting. Lennon was 'Private Gripweed' in *How I Won the War*, a curate's egg of a World War 2 satire; Paul Jones kept biting his lip as a pop star-turned-messiah in *Privilege*; Mick Jagger was in dreadful *Ned Kelly* and riveting *Performance*, and Cilla Black was in *Work is a Four Letter Word*. What did the world of drama lose when eternal Geordie Eric Burdon, supposedly, failed a screen test to star in a film treatment of Evelyn Waugh's *The Loved One* with Rod Steiger?

Marianne Faithfull joined the cast of Chekov's *Three Sisters* at the Chichester Festival in 1966. The previous year, Dave Berry had taken the Cliff Richard part in an Essex theatre production of *Expresso Bongo*. On BBC television, Ray Davies comported himself creditably in the title role of *The Long-Distance Piano Player*, one of the Wednesday Play series. Yet to come was Dave Dee as 'Caliban' in *The Tempest*.

Lucrative offers to turn out all-purpose incidental music for films and more concise material for ITV commercials were taken up by both the Pretty Things and Manfred Mann. Brian Jones would channel part of his artistic frustration into the soundtrack to the German movie, *Mort Und Totschlag*. Almost as soon as they were formed, Traffic were commissioned to do film music for *Here We Go Round the Mulberry Bush*, diplomatically padding it with contributions from the Spencer Davis Group. George Harrison would rope in Eric Clapton, mouth-organist Tommy Reilly (renowned for the *Dixon of Dock Green* theme) and the Remo Four to assist on an oddity of a film called *Wonderwall* after Paul McCartney had already had a go in 1966 with *The Family Way* starring Hayley Mills.

Newly and apprehensively involved in literature, film and the theatre, pop musicians often hadn't a clue how to go about what they'd taken on. Some baulked at the task like gymkhana ponies refusing a fence. Those that muddled on simply applied themselves to getting a clearer picture from the confusion, learning what they could *in situ* and unwittingly dismissing many preconceptions and introducing fresh ones. As if it was the most natural thing in the world, they'd be cursing their way through a manuscript's sub-editing, 'spotting' uncut film sequences with a stop-watch, arguing with a stage manager about lighting, fretting about character development or making suggestions about camera angles. A surprising number of reviews of the end results, if patronizing at times, testified to the presence of more intrinsic virtues than had been expected of participants in entertainment industries where sales figures and number of bums-on-seats were arbiters of success.

21 END OF THE SEASON

Now and then, certain areas in Britain that had been backwards fashion-wise would align exactly with the trendsetting capital. The junk shops of Aldershot thrived during a craze in 1966 for Victorian military uniforms. Experiments with dundreary side-whiskers, raffish moustaches and pointed imperials led a Manchester costumier to market fake ones with 'side-pieces' so those without the wherewithal to sprout their own could still 'Make the Scene With These Fantastic New Raves!'

Olde tyme whimsy prevailed in the hit parade too with 'Winchester Cathedral' and other hits by the New Vaudeville Band – all vicarage fete brass and megaphoned vocals – who were derived from Cops and Robbers, whose inspired R & B arrangement of 'I Could Have Danced All Night' from *My Fair Lady* brought them to *Ready Steady Go*. Now they had a new name and style – though much of the latter had been filched from the Temperance Seven and, more so, the Bonzo Dog Doo-Dah Band who 'were playing in South Shields,' reminisced Neil Innes, 'when Bob Kerr, our trumpeter, had a call from his mate Geoff Stephens who'd written "Winchester Cathedral". Geoff reckoned it was going to be a hit but, as it had been recorded with a session crew, he needed a band to promote it. Bob rushed in all excited with "how'd you like to be the New Vaudeville Band!?" We said no, and the next thing we saw was Bob on *Top of the Pops* in a New Vaudeville Band that looked pretty much like the Bonzos. Afterwards, people kept saying to us, "Hey, you're just like that New Vaudeville Band!"'

While it lasted, others were just like them too. As Whistling Jack Smith, Tommy Moeller's brother was at Number Five with 'I Was Kaiser Bill's Batman'. Howling ineffectually at his heels were the Ugly's with Ray Davies' nonchalant 'End of the Season'; 'Tea Lovely Tea' from Sir Sydney Saitheswaite and his Garbage Collectors, and the Marquis of Kensington's 'Changing of the Guards'. Though Ian Whitcomb tried to halt his Hot 100 decay with a revival of the ragtime novelty, 'Where Did Robinson Crusoe Go with Friday on Saturday Night', all post-British Invasion North America could cope with then was 'Winchester Cathedral'.

Yet, though the last All-Britain Best Contest had been held late in 1965, there were still beat groups as the Age of Aquarius dawned: doughty anachronisms unknown beyond their parish, battling through the old 'Dizzy

Miss Lizzy' and 'Poison Ivy' warhorses to those for whom even Mods and Rockers had become dim recollections. On a geography field week in the Peak District in the summer of 1966, another Farnborough Grammar fourth former and I sneaked out of the hostel one rainy evening to sample the flesh pots of Sheffield. The depths of depravity there turned out to be sitting in a cafe as a jukebox seemed to spin only the Small Faces' 'Hey Girl' and Dave Berry's chart valediction, the sentimental 'Mama', spun perhaps in rueful affection for a seldom-seen local hero. After revelling in our wickedness, we spent most of the next few hours gazing into space over cups of coffee, served by a gent in a battery-operated bow-tie that lit up with the words 'Swinging Sheffield'.

My own observations contradicted this. The impetus of Steel City pop – and that of other provinces – had certainly relaxed by the mid-1960s when record companies weren't coming round any more. Club 60 closed in 1966 through falling attendances and authority complaints about inadequate fire escapes and the stink of drains. It was to become a storeroom for the plumbing shop above. However, eavesdropping on small-talk down the Stonehouse, you might learn of local jazzer Tony Oxley drumming for Georgie Fame and, raising hardly a liberal eyebrow then, Jimmy Crawford's imminent tour of South Africa.

Before Traffic had been plotted in Birmingham's Elbow Room, the Hellions' poverty had compelled them to organize a jumble sale to cover accumulated parking fines. The final blow to this classic local group had been the liquidation of their fan club. Dominating B.P. Finch's *Worcester Whisperings* now were groups like New Sense, the Wavelengths, the Daleks, the Buzz, Censored! and the Banned. Also mentioned were the King Snakes who had none other than Robert Plant as lead singer.

Plant had once been a peanut-waged road manager to a group containing Noddy Holder who, by 1966, was adrift with Dave Holland – a bass guitarist destined to play alongside Miles Davis – in Steve Brett and the Mavericks, with whom he made several appearances in *For Teenagers Only*, notably with 'Sugar Shack', a US cover that fared well enough but didn't reach the charts.

Since their brushes with the Top 50, the Applejacks, with a new lead singer and Americanized sound, were in cabaret and ocean cruises after a final single, 'You've Been Cheating'. Of the same vintage, the Marauders had passed from Decca to Parlophone. On the way, they'd picked Ricky Ford from Bristol whose Cyclones had run out of puff after reaching their professional zenith – a UK tour support to Peter and Gordon.

An apogee of the Lynton Grae Sound's career was supporting the Spencer Davis Group at Northampton Technical College when both groups combined for an unsteady 'You've Lost That Lovin' Feeling'. A few miles away in Leicester, the Farinas, after living down the pirate radio 45 as the Roaring Sixties, had become Family and, with Roger Chapman centre stage as lead vocalist, migrated to an uncertain future in the Smoke.

The Mojos, meanwhile, had relocated to Romsey, Hampshire. During the 'Winchester Cathedral' era, they and the Fourmost drew out the agony with respective quaint revivals of 'Goodbye Dolly Gray' and George Formby's 'Aunt Maggie's Remedy'. In the United States, ex-Undertaker Jackie Lomax had immersed himself in the Lomax Alliance, despite advice from Brian Epstein that he'd fare better as a soloist.

Tellingly, the Beatles had been the only Merseybeat act in 1966's NME's Pollwinners Concert where they'd waved into the blackness and vanished from the British stage forever. That spring, too, it was entirely fitting that Rory Storm should headline at the Cavern hours before the bailiffs closed the place (for much the same reasons as Club 60). A telegram from the Beatles was read aloud when the place was re-opened with a facelift and proper sanitation, but it would never be the same. Beat groups still performed there, but the fact that it was also hosting poetry readings and similarly arty *soirées* exemplified the passing of the old order.

Over in Germany, Paul Raven fronted a soul outfit, Boston International, for three years in Kiel: 'After the bleak time I'd been experiencing since leaving *Ready Steady Go*, it seemed too good an opportunity to miss; plenty of women, plenty of booze and, most importantly, plenty of work.'[153] During Welsh combo Smokeless Zone's solitary month at Hamburg's Top Ten, 'We saw these cameras coming into the club,' exclaimed vocalist Plum Ellis, 'but didn't know they were there to film us. Then this character told us we were to be featured in a documentary about the Beatles. What a gas!'[152] Well, hadn't Kingsize Taylor said that 'they are a bit behind the times'? Yet the Remo Four were wowing the Star-Club with jazz-rock these days. Not so adaptable, however, Ian and the Zodiacs returned to England to await the end after turning down 'Even the Bad Times Are Good' which, picked up in 1967 by the Tremeloes, made the UK Top Five.

Kingsize Taylor had also reached the end of the line. Largely through the bad faith of the racketeers that controlled the venues where he worked, he'd been left destitute and had had to apply for an assisted repatriation. As the Beatles jetted overhead, Kingsize heaved his guitar, amplifier and suitcases into a second class compartment at Hamburg-Hauptbahnhof station. Miss the last train, and you'll be stuck on the platform forever.

As conspicuous a loser as Taylor, Rory Storm threw in the towel after an inglorious relaunch with two ex-Mojos and Karl Terry. 'He never wanted to make it nationally,' his sister, 'Mrs Shane Fenton, would insist when it became obvious that he wouldn't, 'as he was happy being King of Liverpool.' After former Nightrider Roy Wood cracked the Top 40 nut with the Move, Mike Sheridan would claim likewise that he'd 'never harboured any desires about becoming famous – although I'd have accepted it had it happened'.[154]

So would the Downliners Sect, but, after 'Glendora' missed in 1966 – even in Sweden – their booking fees were often a minus amount after deductions, and 'Do you know anywhere we can sleep tonight?' became a too-frequent question asked of hangers-on in frowzy dressing rooms. With the rest unwilling to face another night in the van, Keith Grant and Don Craine tried again as Don Craine's New Downliners Sect until Don himself packed it in, leaving Keith to soldier on with yet another new edition.

Certain musicians from groups like the Sect reappeared as semi-professionals at the parochial venues from whence they'd sprung. Some had never strayed that far from them. Jimmy Crawford, Mike Sheridan, Kerry Rapid, Rory Storm *et al* had flaunted their fame on home turf for all it was worth; perhaps consolidating parochial media connections so that, if the Big Time was to be denied to them, they could still cling on somehow or other. Despite a stutter, Storm was soon to be commuting as a disc-jockey between engagements in Benidorm, Amsterdam and the Silver Blades Ice Rink back on Merseyside. Don Craine ran a local folk club, and Jimmy Crawford played in his city's All-Star soccer XI, and was advocate of a celebrity swimming gala to likewise help the needy.

Time was when musicians were falling over themselves to work with you – until it became clear that being in your backing group was a springboard to better-paid, more prestigious employment. Wasn't Paul Dean, as he was then, from the same youth club just a few streets from the pub where you, the Federals and Cal Danger used to perform and you still did, in between recounting how it was playing with you that had got the Overlanders where they are today? Sometimes it was as if you'd never got those encores, had your shirt ripped off by girls at Ashford Tech or won that *South West Scene* popularity poll.

Once, you'd stood before kings: attending Herman's housewarming party, letting Chris Curtis sell you his stereo, calling on a jet-lagged Brian Jones minutes after he'd got back from the Stones' second US tour. Always over-valuing the goodwill of his peers – even those still struggling, Brian had banished sleep and had made you welcome in his way. 'Man, you should see the stuff we've got through,' he'd brag hours later, indicating the reefer stubs and empty bottles among the LP sleeves, fast-food leftovers and stoned layabouts all over his front room.

Never at ease in London, you'd gravitated back home whenever you weren't working to give it some showbiz in local social clubs. Reg Presley never left Andover, and Dave Berry and his Dutch wife, Marthy, settled near the market town of Chesterfield, ten minutes' drive from Sheffield. 'Mama' was a weighty cross to bear whenever he and old pals reminisced about Violet May's and Bluesville. Fuelling a growing disenchantment with Decca had been a session in which Dave found himself intoning a new but equally nauseating libretto over the 'Mama' backing track. The resulting 'Daddy' was rejected, thank God, during the company's usual Tuesday morning board meeting.

Another disgruntled Decca act, Unit 4 + 2, were still picking the bones from 'Concrete and Clay', and had considered themselves fortunate to land some dates on the Rolling Stones' fifth British tour, opening at Finsbury Park in September 1965. Replacing the Unit on three occasions, the Moody Blues seemed to have had their fifteen minutes too as the shrieking pandemonium was no barometer of their market standing. On the same jaunt, the Habits backed a low-billed vocalist, Charles Dickens (alias photographer David Anthony). That was their lot before crash-diving into oblivion – though their Geordie drummer Brian Davidson was to Make It in the end with the Nice.

Veterans of low-paid spots on round-Britain package tours had never been sure of eating even one square meal a day. Nevertheless, they'd been there, hadn't they? Others had had hits – but were they worth having? Though he'd had a few with the Pretty Things, Dick Taylor had once been a Rolling Stone, and was entitled to be bitter and twisted about missing the millions. Instead, he was attractive in his phlegmatic candour, assessing that if he'd stayed on, he, like Brian Jones, might have ended up drowned in a swimming pool.

Under no circumstances would some of the old school think that groups like the Stones were any better than they. The Stones had just met the right people in 1963, hit the jackpot and stayed lucky. If they hadn't, they'd probably be in jobs where they had to metaphorically touch their cap as everyone else did. Away from all this pot-smoking music they were playing these days, the Beatles were probably just the same as they ever were. This 'transcendental meditation' caper they'd cottoned onto now wouldn't have cut much ice in the fleshpots of Hamburg. Indeed, raising a derisive laugh among Reeperbahn club employees who had known him, Ringo found the yoga-ashram the group visited in India 'a bit like Butlin's'[155] – a remark that also inspired a *Sunday Express* cartoon in which the Maharishi inquires of John Lennon, 'This Butlin guru that Ringo speaks of: what's he got that I haven't?'[156]

Certain incorrigible old showmen that didn't Make It still made the famous groups topping the bill locally seem tame. Knocking 'em dead with a lot of the same material that had been in the set in 1959, they were so far behind, they were ahead of the first traces of 1968's rock 'n' roll revival but were too tired, indolent or out of touch with the business to do anything about it.

Most of them returned to secure anonymity, but real or imagined horrors about this outraged Mr Big from some European club or that unmarried mother still induced certain ex-beat group musicians to renege on their past and start at shadows. Some had good cause. A new-born baby was once held in front of the stage when the Kinks were performing, and, on two separate occasions, a Nashville Teen was to answer the door to a different German teenager, both claiming an irregular kinship.

Beat groups such as the Nashville Teens, the Downliners Sect and the Remo Four who hadn't yet had enough, had come to depend more and more on one-nighters for a living. Diners in these newish motorway service stations still stared at you occasionally as you stared fascinated as the bass player laid into a greasy but obviously satisfying fry-up while you picked at your plate with less enthusiasm. The other members of the group, old and new, were still good company, too – though their detailing of last night's carnal shenanigans and stimulant intake could prove monotonous.

The van nears a faraway soundcheck while back home, loved ones wonder in that ancient night until headlights signal one more deliverance from the treadmill of the road.

22 THE BEAT GOES 'OM'

A lot of groups stopped thinking of themselves as mere entertainers. Some had already become pseudo-mystics whose songs required repeated listening to comprehend what might be veiled but oracular messages. Though certain singers could attack the most oblique metaphysics without pretension, the more gaga lines seemed too much like pretty-but-nothing syllables strung together to carry the melody in an age when even the Troggs were singing about 'the bamboo butterflies of yer mind'. 'It wasn't really us though,' confessed Reg Presley. 'It's difficult if you weren't on drugs to write lyrics like that.'[157]

'I think you have to be on something to understand the words of that one,' said Reg of Traffic's 'Hole In My Shoe'.[158] Real or imagined extremes of drug experience beyond pills and reefers were also implicated in self-consciously 'weird' discs by groups such as The Pink Floyd, the Pretty Things – and the Small Faces whose 'phased' drumming gilded the surreal evocation of light and space that was 'Itchycoo Park'.

The spoof 'LS Bumble Bee' 45 by Peter Cook and Dudley Moore was symptomatic of a general knowledge if not use of lysergic acid diethylamide – LSD. A similar hallucinogen was known in the Middle Ages and was central to a 1956 episode of ITV's *The Adventures of Robin Hood* when the Merrie Men aid an apothecary in gathering herbs with which to fight its mental distortions. These were often too apparent as you crossed from reality into a wild dream, your psyche boggling with paranormal ('psychedelic') sensations.

Chemically-induced glimpses of the eternal had been 'turning on' factions within London's In Crowd for about a year before LSD was outlawed for recreational purposes in 1966. Pop stars began talking openly about psychedelic escapades to both the 'straight' press and 'underground' journals like the fortnightly *International Times* and *Oz*, its unofficial colour supplement. 'Dropping acid' had become so widespread that Dave Dee would insist to *Melody Maker* that, as far as his clean-minded lads were concerned, LSD still stood for pounds, shillings and pence. Moreover, the Troggs were confined to provincial bookings to minimize the chances of drug publicity sticking to them.

'We were on the threshold of this new thing,' Jeff Beck reflected, 'the Yardbirds were the first psychedelic band.' Yet the Moody Blues and Small

Faces were two outfits who'd known LSD since 1965. So did the Pretty Things if the worst was thought of titles like 'Trippin'' and 'LSD'. It was also implicit in 'My Friend Jack' by the Smoke, 'A Girl Named Sandoz' (where the stuff was originally manufactured) from Eric Burdon and the Animals, and the eerie omega that was the Beatles' 'Tomorrow Never Knows'. Standing little chance of superceding 'Yesterday' as the most recorded composition of all time, the latter was a supposed sound picture of LSD's inner landscapes in its fusion of half-understood Eastern mysticism with an electronically-warped vocal, a monotonous percussion rataplan and a slither of tape loops. 'Everyone from Brisbane to Bootle hates that daft song Lennon sang at the end of *Revolver*,' declared a horrified *Mirabelle* whose schoolgirl subscribers were mostly insensible to shifts in parameters of musical consciousness as another watershed year approached.

'Chapter 24', an LP track by The Pink Floyd – once a beat group just like any other – quoted directly from the *I Ching* as 'Tomorrow Never Knows' had from *The Tibetan Book of the Dead*. Both could be bought via the account that cool cats had at the Indica bookshop off Piccadilly where you'd thumb through further hardbacks on mysticism, religion and the fashionably airy-faerie. *Autobiography of a Yogi*, *The Golden Bough*, Tolkein, the Koran, even the Bible now had discreet places on hip student hostel bookshelves. Mostly this was just for show as a marijuana 'joint' was passed round during a conversation with words like 'karma' and 'cosmic' in it. Behind school bike sheds three years earlier, it had been 'gear' and 'grotty' over a Woodbine.

The music and underground press in 1967 was rife with statements such as this sweet flower from the lips of disc-jockey and *International Times* columnist John Peel: 'There are sparrows and fountains and roses in my head. Sometimes I don't have enough time to think of loving you. That is very wrong.'[159] To *Melody Maker*, Jim Capaldi spoke of trying to 'get as much colour into our lives as possible. We see movements and roam through the temples of our minds.'[149]

Before inanities like this were thought worth publishing, if the average guitarist in a beat group entreated God at all, it was as a sort of divine pimp with an amused tolerance of wenching, boozing and pill-popping – but with enough self-discipline to seldom indulge Himself. Piety had been considered a regrettable eccentricity in 1950s rockers like Elvis, Jerry Lee, Little Richard and our own Terry Dene and Cliff Richard, who were prone to vigorous bouts of evangelicism.

As devotional in its boy-girl way as sacred music, pop's contradictory merger with religion had reasserted itself. As early as 1964, Cliff Richard had undertaken his first gospel tour, and the Joystrings had used the Devil's music to Spread the Word. Doing the reverse, the Small Faces and the Zombies had in 1966 adapted the respective melodies of 'Ding Dong Merrily On High' ('My Mind's Eye'), and the *Nunc Dimittis* ('She's Coming Home') to secular purposes.

The Beatles, who had the time and money to take a deeper interest in theological matters, tried meditating under the Maharishi Mahesh Yogi. Like a Charles Atlas course for yer mind, his overall aim, he said, was to eradicate piecemeal all human vices and ego until a pure state of bliss was reached. Such washing of spiritual laundry was feasible without forsaking worldly possessions – bar his fee – and, within reason, worldly pleasures. This seemed a fine creed to anyone who'd viewed the world from the Olympus of stardom since 1963.

As more than pop stars now, the Beatles were under pressure from the world's youth to find 'the truth' and, judging by the hollow-eyed teenage derelicts that littered inner cities, it wasn't LSD. Many of them had only 'turned on' in the first place because they'd read that the Beatles had – but some, stuck as they were between the supposed dope-crazed sensuality of pop culture and their own stolid compliance to middle-aged values, were relieved when the Fab Four publicly repudiated using classified drugs (meaning that individually, they either continued or resumed the practice but never again made an issue of it).

These days, a Beatle or Rolling Stone could attend 'happenings' in the capital without someone shouting 'There's Mick Jagger! Ooo, 'e's lovely!' – though when Graham Nash was slipping unobstrusively out of a Mothers of Invention concert at the Albert Hall, his heart sank to his boots as an adolescent voice bawled, 'It's Graham Nash of the Hollies!' through the Kensington twilight. As the awestruck boy panted up to him, Graham's inbred professionalism caused him to listen politely to some tongue-tied utterances instead of telling me to get knotted.

Without any such annoyances, stars of the Top 20 would be seen at events where flickering strobes and ectoplasmic light projections on walls were among audio-visual aids that simulated psychedelic experience as 'bands' (not 'groups' any more) played on – and on and on and on – for tranced hippies and other updated beatniks, either cross-legged or 'idiot dancing'. At the Fourteen Hour Technicolour Dream at Alexandra Palace, the Move, the Pink Floyd, Tomorrow, John's Children, the Flies (who urinated over the front row), you name 'em, appeared one after another. During one of few intermissions, the promenading audience was treated to a turn by Yoko Ono, a Japanese American who, some felt, was living proof of her own conjecture that 'you don't need talent to be an artist'.[160]

The Pink Floyd, the Nice, the Soft Machine, Cream, Family and the Sam

Gopal Dream were the darlings of new psychedelic clubs like the Spontaneous Underground (held every Sunday afternoon at the Marquee from February 1966) and the Night Tripper (later the UFO and then Middle Earth). From their unsmiling 1967 publicity shots, Family looked, frankly, a nasty shower, but in a year when another son of Leicester, Engelbert Humperdinck, ruled British pop, their regular appearances at Middle Earth *et al* were supplemented with sessions on John Peel's *Top Gear* radio series, and their off-duty rollickings were chronicled in Johnny Byrne and Jenny Fabian's racy *roman à clef*, *Groupie*.

Family were one of many groups – sorry, *bands* – who performed at 'Sundays at the Saville' in an art deco auditorium where pop mitigated poor takings for the drama and dance productions during the week. Buried amid the sea, stars and naked flower girl on a foyer poster would be information about forthcoming attractions of such diversity as John Mayall's Bluesbreakers, the Four Tops and the Bee Gees. When their turn came, it seemed entirely appropriate for Traffic to play amidst the cardboard ramparts left from the weekday set of a Shakespeare play.

'Sundays at the Saville' and like presentations beyond the closed worlds of the psychedelic dungeons drew mixed gatherings of hippies, school-age fans, London's in-crowd and riff-raff from the provinces where sixth-form common rooms would fill with tinted smoke from joss sticks, thereby lending credence to their providers' self-generated tales of a groovy weekend among hippy friends in London – where nowadays a man wasn't necessarily asking to be beaten up for walking the streets with beads and bells round his neck, embroidered slippers and floral trousers. Well, the Beatles dressed like that so it must be OK.

The Beatles also dictated a new attitude about making records. The day spent taping their first LP was no longer considered adequate for one track now. Brisk finesse had deferred to late hours of console minutiae – stereo panning, editing, degrees of reverberation and so on. Close-miked vocals floated effortlessly over layers of treated sound, whether thunderclap aggression or feathery emanations. The increased artistic licence had been exemplified by a calculated muttered overdub on the coda of the Animals' 'Don't Bring Me Down', and a brass band inserted for two bars only on the children's song 'Yellow Submarine' off *Revolver*. Yet raw materials were frequently inconsequential and self-indulgent. It has to be said that the Beatles' *Sgt. Pepper's Lonely Hearts Club Band* couldn't hold a candle to *Revolver*: the music was better, the songs weren't.

Yet even the still formidable Yardbirds realized that, 'If you didn't have a hit single,' as Jim McCarty elucidated, 'you were a fading band.' With a weather eye on the hit parade, yet with enough sophistication still to be considered 'progressive', it was possible to operate ambiguously with 'musicianly' fancies on albums, and chart-directed 45s, often with the most trite cut like 'Yellow Submarine' (which nipped in the bud a cover by another Parlophone act, the She Trinity, fronted by Beryl Marsden), 'Over Under Sideways Down' from *Yardbirds* and the Soft Machine's 'Love Makes Sweet Music', as much soul music as psychedelia.

With members writing 'musician' on passport application forms less sheepishly, a working band's appeal was now reliant not so much on nice smiles and tight trousers as stamina to sustain incessant extrapolation of tracks from both its last LP and the unfamiliar successor being 'laid down' during a studio block-booking of weeks and months. As intuitive a guitarist as Jimi Hendrix, The Pink Floyd's Syd Barrett was also as prone to spontaneous improvisations onstage that went beyond key and time signature, mixing severe dissonance and serene melody. Like Hendrix too, he earned the esteem of Eric Clapton, Pete Townshend and others who wished that they had the nerve to be as adventurous.

Clapton's high-decibel Cream, a trio he formed with fellow ex-Bluesbreakers Jack Bruce and Ginger Baker, would soon be spinning out a three-verse blues for nigh on twenty po-faced minutes. This was as much a case of the Emperor's New Clothes as screaming at Herman had been. Yet groups like Cream didn't think that a quarter-hour spot between Erkey Grant and the Terry Young Six on something-for-everybody scream circuit packages was sufficient any more. If there was room for other acts on the same bill, it couldn't be someone who sang fiddly two-minute singles. A typical Saturday night spectacular at, say, Swansea's Top Rank, might now include the Bystanders, Love Sculpture, Eyes Of Blue and the Dream (formerly the Corncrackers) – all of the same progressive stamp – while the Jimi Hendrix Experience's next national tour after the one with the Walker Brothers would also feature the Move, Amen Corner and Pink Floyd.

A rival late autumn touring party showcased the Who, Traffic, the Tremeloes, the Herd and then hitless Hibernians, the Marmalade – formerly Dean Ford and the Gaylords, who were glad to be away from the grim Highgate flat they'd shared since migrating from Glasgow. 1967, nevertheless, ended optimistically with the climb up the Dutch hit parade of their psychedelic 'I See The Rain', and a weekly residency at the Marquee where they functioned with the unusual sound of two bass players after guitarist Pat Fairlie switched to a new six-string bass.

Instrumental proficiency mattered more now as outlines dissolved between rock and jazz. *Fresh Cream* and *Are You Experienced* thrived on 'meaningful' musical interplay between their respective protagonists. If titivated with vocal harmonies plus a pot-pourri of tambourines, handclaps and other percussion trifles, these and similar albums focused almost exclusively on guitar, bass, drums and lead singing. Among few special effects might be a octave-divider, a vari-speed or a wah-wah pedal, originally devised to make a guitar sound like a muted trumpet.

A real trumpet was to the fore in the Alan Bown Set's 'We Can Help You' which lifted its main *ostinato* from the 'Hallelujah Chorus' as 'Night of Fear' by the Move did that of the '1812 Overture', and Procol Harum's 'Whiter Shade of Pale' from J.S. Bach's 'Air on a G String'. Old habits die hard, but during pop's 'classical' season – approximately from late 1966 to the 1968 release of the Beatles' 'mock-rock' 'Lady Madonna' – as likely to blast from car stereos as Dylan or Shankar were the pioneering tonalities of Penderecki, Berio and Stockhausen. These affected, if not song structures, then certainly approaches to soloing as pop artists became aware of – even concerned about – the formal do's and don'ts that traditionally afflict creative flow, and the now debatable usefulness of the blues, jazz and rock 'n' roll cliches of old. Among valuable object lessons were records by the Mothers of Invention and, on 23 September 1967, their first British concert, the one attended by Graham Nash and my adolescent self.

With their maelstrom of rock, jazz, classical modernism and parody, the Mothers evoked a mixed response. Most 'progressive' musicians were enthusiastic, but the Tremeloes, who'd seen the Mothers in the States, weren't keen. The mind-expanding 'Here Comes My Baby' in spring 1967 triggered twice as many hits for the Tremeloes as they'd had with Brian Poole until an ill-fated bid to 'go progressive' in 1969.

Tastes were divided too over such disparate pop as a Beach Boys estranged from the surf, and the Incredible String Band's exotic Gaelic mysticism. A less conscious infiltration into the canon of progressive bands were beat groups such as the Zombies, the Poets and Unit 4 + 2. Sharing much the same vision were the 'Waterloo Sunset'-period Kinks and Procol Harum of ponderous majesty. Not for them either were the overdone pastiches of the Beatles or the funny noises of the Soft Machine and The Pink Floyd, who when no longer passive vehicles for the ground-breaking songwriting born of Syd Barrett's inner chaos, favoured creating musical moods through improvisation.

So did most of Traffic who, with the Move and a revitalized Moody Blues, were basking in Brumbeat's Indian Summer. Yet Traffic had 'got it together in the country' where, under a starry canopy, the rehearsing group could be perceived miles away as, bathed in swirling colour from a light show loaned from Dantalion's Chariot, they lost themselves in music till sunrise.

Far out, man! Too much! Traffic templated the stock angle of these beautiful guys, united by mutual respect, occupying an isolated rural retreat and devoting themselves to creating these beauteous sounds without any outside interference. Swallowing this, Humble Pie larked about in an Essex haystack for a *Disc* colour spread while, with former Searcher Chris Curtis in an unlikely role as lead singer, Roundabout – later, Deep Purple – were set up in a farmhouse by their manager. Another group who'd peak in the 1970s, Yes – with ex-Warrior Jon Anderson – honed their music down in Devon as the Ace Kefford Stand would in a Staffordshire hamlet. Over in the New Forest, future Yes drummer Alan White with Denny Laine, ex-Ugly Steve Gibbons and other Midlanders – calling themselves Balls – tested their stage act in a local village hall. Of similar genital nomenclature, Hard Meat thrashed it out in the wilds of Cornwall, fulfilling part of Ray Davies' hypothesis that, 'If I had all my own way and had a country cottage to get together in, I'd write lousy songs and make a lot of money.'[161]

Eric Burdon and the Animals, however, resided communally in San Francisco, now as vital a pop Mecca as Liverpool had been. Like the Big Three's homage to the Cavern, hit records in 1967 by Burdon and the Animals amongst others would pay vinyl tribute to the flower-power city's new eminence. Cashing in quickest in Britain with 'Let's Go To San Francisco' were the Flowerpot Men (the Ivy League by any other name) who, in chiffony robes, tossed dead chrysanthemums into the audience. In the eyes of the world, the apogee of the Summer of Love was reached on 25 June 1967 when the Beatles performed 'All You Need Is Love' as Britain's contribution to *Our World*, a satelite-link transmission with a global viewing figure of four hundred million.

British groups festooned in buttercups on picture sleeves epitomized pop's gingerbread castle hour with pixified musical scenarios like 'Hole In My Shoe', the Rolling Stones' 'Dandelion', Keith West's kiddie-chorused 'Excerpt from a Teenage Opera', Billy J. Kramer's 'Town of Tuxley Toymaker', David Bowie's 'Laughing Gnome' duet with a voice vari-speeded to Chipmunk pitch, and just plain 'Gnome' by The Pink Floyd. Simon Dupree and the Big Sound put their brassy soul on hold for 'Kites', a windswept evocation of mythical China.

The Beatles had stuck their oar in with 'Lucy in the Sky with Diamonds' on *Sgt. Pepper's Lonely Hearts Club Band*. Like 'Rock Around the Clock, this album was judged to be a pop milestone. 'It was a milestone and a millstone in music history,' qualified George Harrison. 'There are some good songs on it, but it's not our best album.' Certain Americans had already elevated the long-player to something more than a pig-in-a-poke, slopping with musical swill and a hit 45. Inspirational to *Sgt. Pepper* were 1966's *Pet Sounds* by the Beach Boys and *Freak Out* by the Mothers of Invention. Both hung on a specific and recurring mood – a 'concept', if you like – that was longer and more far-reaching than *Idol on Parade* or *The Sect Sing Sick Songs*.

The next step was a continuous 'work' with no gaps between tracks and teeming with interlocking themes, segues, 'second subjects', *leitmotivs* and all that. The Beatles' effort did, indeed, embrace a reprise plus various cross-fades and links via a mixing desk that would seem Heath Robinson by today's standards – but only at the start and near the end were you reminded that it was Sergeant Pepper's show.

Yet the Word had been made vinyl in the comfort of your own home. Many – especially in the States – listened to *Sgt. Pepper* in the dark, at the wrong speeds, backwards. Every inch of the cover and label was scrutinized for some hidden *communiqué* that would turn you into a more aware, more creative human being at one with the Beatles. In San Francisco, 'Beatle Readings' became as much a part of the pageant of its streets as mime troupes, dancers and vendors of journals like *The Psychedelic Oracle*. Listening to *Sgt. Pepper* now, you can almost smell the joss-sticks and see its fabled montage cover being used as a handy working surface for rolling a joint.

If *Sgt. Pepper* had been pirate Radio London's most plugged album during the summer, the 45 was surely 'A Whiter Shade of Pale' by what had once been the Paramounts. Group names with abstract leanings and lack of preceding article that stressed a collaborative ethos was very much *à la mode*; if you were the Hedgehogs, it was kinda groovy in 1967 to change to just Hedgehog. After Syd left, the 'The' was symbolically dropped by Pink Floyd as it was too by Soft Machine and Marmalade.

You were still, however, only as big as your last single – and so the Yardbirds were, indeed, 'a fading band' by the end of 1967. If able to continue in a recognizable form, the outfit would never recover from Paul Samwell-Smith's departure after a final straw at an Oxford University ball where Keith Relf had contrived to appear onstage roaring drunk. Jimmy Page was then brought in to play bass but wound up as joint lead guitarist with Beck whose fragments of speech and feedback imitation of a police siren were but one facet of 'Happenings Ten Years Time Ago', the disc that extinguished the Yardbirds' chart life. Some considered it an aural nightmare while others shared one pundit's view that it was 'possibly the greatest single ever released'.[162]

Of the same vintage, the Pretty Things' 'Defecting Grey' was aswarm with jarring vignettes of sound spliced together to coalesce beneath a half-sung narrative that lacked a discernable melody line as it darted from section to indissoluble section. Though it actually had a tune, Dantalion's Chariot's 'Madman Running through the Fields' was closer to 'Defecting Grey' than 'Love Is All Around'.

In retrospect, the chasm between the Troggs and the Pretty Things does not seem so great but, in 1967, Reg Presley *et al* were regarded by

International Times-type journals as perpetrators of vulgar 'pop' while the Things played 'rock' – which only the finest minds could appreciate. With *Sgt. Pepper*'s expensive and syncretic precedent, record companies found themselves underwriting further concept albums (e.g. *Their Satanic Majesties Request* from the Rolling Stones, John Mayall's *Bare Wires*), rock operas (the Pretty Things' *SF Sorrow*, *Arthur* from the Kinks and the Who's *Tommy* – all, technically, song-cycles) and other *magnum opi* (the Small Faces' *Ogden's Nut Gone Flake* in its circular sleeve) by groups entering realms even further removed from their beat origins. Some such outfits had been able to convince fans that *Top of the Pops* excursions were marginal to a main body of work on albums and in projects such as the Beatles' interesting-but-boring TV special, *Magical Mystery Tour*.

The Beatles – and the Dave Clark Five – had spared themselves from having to be 'real' musicians in front of non-screaming customers by retiring to the studio, but Manfred Mann carried on plugging their 45s on the still-running *Crackerjack* as part of a day's work. It had been business as usual for Cliff Bennett after his hits in 1966 with 'Got To Get You Into My Life' and *Drivin' You Wild*, the first pop album on EMI's low-budget Music for Pleasure label – both products that showcased Cliff's soul-rock crossover, though his let-me-hear-you-say-'yeah' stage routines were very behind the times.

When most of his Rebel-Rousers defected to Roy Young's leadership, Cliff formed 'progressive' Toe Fat, and finally gave his defiantly short hair its head as well as standing further from his razor. Around the same time, the Fortunes departed fundamentally from the orchestral slop that made them; one 45, 'The Idol', even being aired on *Top Gear*. Other groups adjusted too, often without getting the point, with a psychedelic or blues-derived set prolonged with endless soloing *à la* Cream.

After Dave Dee, Dozy, Beaky, Mick and Tich's 'Touch Me Touch Me' stalled at a mere Number Thirteen in 1967, they shifted to themed epics set in tropical islands ('Zabadak!'), ruined haciendas ('The Legend of Xanadu'), organized crime ('Last Night in Soho') and the high seas ('The Wreck of the Antoinette'). In all cases, these hits were promoted with costume drama rather than the old comic capers – the buccaneer spectre of Johnny Kidd an obvious starting point for 'The Wreck of the Antoinette' – and the group were augmented with all manner of orchestrations. Discs like these were in a different rather than lower league than those of Family, Jimi Hendrix *et al*: more *Hotspur* than *International Times* – and Hendrix wasn't yet so untouchable a guitarist that Beaky and Dave Dee couldn't join him in an after-hours jam in a Frankfurt auditorium.

In much the same style as the Dave Dee group, the Aristocrats (formerly the Bo Sneekers) left their mark on history not only for playing Freddie Mills' West End club the night before he killed himself, but also for being the last act to record for Joe Meek before he also died with the help of a rifle. Cue dimmers and creepy music. Nevertheless, the very presence of an outfit like the Aristocrats in 1967 was a validation of the persistence of other unreconstructed beat groups. Releases in 1967 like the Swinging Blue Jeans' 'Tremblin'' and the Riot Squad's final 45, 'Gotta Be a First Time', still sounded very Merseybeat, while the Quiet Five's 'Goodnight Sleep Tight' wouldn't have sounded unusual had it come out in 1964.

Even among the sitars, freak-outs and drug-dazed visions, melody lingered on. Of The Pink Floyd's 'See Emily Play', an *NME* reviewer wrote, 'It's crammed with weird oscillations, reverberations, electronic vibrations and fuzzy rumblings. Surprisingly, somewhere amid the happening, there's also a pleasant mid-tempo tune that's appealingly harmonized.'[163]

In March 1967, the Floyd had just left a British Top 20 in which the psychedelics of the Move and Jimi Hendrix sat awkwardly amid sweetcorn peddled by Engelbert Humperdinck and Tom Jones, thus demonstrating that the opposite of a prevailing trend is always represented to some degree – but which was actually the prevailing trend? Paradoxically, 1967 was also a boom year for schmaltz with ex-palais crooner Engelbert's 'Release Me' and 'The Last Waltz', respectively, keeping singles by the Beatles and Traffic from Number One. Down Under, Slim Whitman's 'China Doll' slung 'All You Need Is Love' from the top. Petula Clark, Harry Secombe, Des O'Connor and – you'd better believe it – Donald Peers all groped into the Top 20 during this period. After all his blues records had failed, Long John Baldry joined this syrupy elite with 'Let the Heartaches Begin'.

As they'd included cinema interlude slush on their first LPs, no one was surprised when the Dave Clark Five also attempted to Grow Old With Their Audience with two slop-ballads – both hits, mind – by Les Reed and Barry Mason, the same team who'd provisioned Engelbert with his Number Ones. Trusting Mickie Most, Jeff Beck clocked up three UK Top 40 entries with the singalong 'Hi Ho Silver Lining' – now a 1960s nostalgia circuit perennial – that shut down a version by the Attack (formerly the Soul System); Tallyman (a vocal duet with Rod Stewart) and 'Love Is Blue', a string-soaked instrumental, beaten in the Top 30 by the Paul Mauriat Orchestra.

Carl Wayne was campaigning for the Move to move into cabaret, and had been genuinely charmed to meet Donald Peers at the *Top of the Pops* studios. Jonathan King produced a 'Last Waltz'-esque arrangement of the Everly Brothers 'Let It Be Me' by the singer with the now-defunct Hedgehoppers Anonymous while the King Brothers looked and sounded just the same as ever on a 1967 EP advertising kitchenware.

This counter-revolution of 'decent music' was tacitly applauded by commentators like the *NME*'s 'Alley Cat' chatterbox who fawned over aging record business executives – 'Pye chief Little Louis Benjamin tips Number One for Long John Baldry' – whilst gloating, 'This year, Yardbirds absent from Top Thirty.'[164] It also made feline remarks about the demise of pirate radio after the Marine Offences Act became law in August 1967. Repentant ex-Radio London disc-jockey Simon Dee, anxious to keep his plum job on BBC television, stimulated headlines like *Weekend* magazine's 'Simon Axes Hippies On *Dee Time*!' – and the cautious programming and union-regulated employment of middle-of-the-road session bands on the BBC's two new national pop radio stations had certainly rendered *Top of the Pops* generally shallower in content.

Radio One Club at lunchtime was an updated *Workers' Playtime*, even using the same resident artists, Danny Street and Bob Miller and his Millermen, and crass duplicates of current hits; the Moody Blues' grand 'Nights in White Satin' with a trademan's knock ending, and a kind of squeak instead of the whip noise in 'Legend of Xanadu'. For the sake of decency, the word 'breast' in 'Lady Madonna' was sung *sotto voce*.

In view of the hippy sub-culture's supposed trafficking in promiscuity and drugs, you could understand the 'establishment' hoo-hah over the celebrated Rolling Stones bust in February 1967. Armed with a search warrant, police officers and a sniffer dog had reason to believe that the premises of both John Lennon and George Harrison were also being used for the consumption of controlled drugs contrary to the provision of the 1966 Dangerous Drugs Act, section forty-two. National treasures or no, even the Beatles weren't above the law any more – nor were Joe Cocker, Small Faces organist Ian McLaren and other pop stars who were to help various narcotics squads with their enquiries.

The Beatles compounded the us-and-them situation further with the 'controlled weirdness' of 'Apple Corps'. After moustaches, LSD and meditation, the Beatles hadn't suddenly latched onto bourgeois greed. No more qualified to run a business than the recently deceased Brian Epstein had been to play guitar, 'We had this mad idea of having Apple there,' said George Harrison, 'so that people could come and do artistic stuff and not have a hard time.'[165]

Advertisements appeared, therefore, in both national and underground outlets soliciting the public to bring artistic stuff to the new Apple Foundation for the Arts in London. Not a postal delivery would go by without a deluge of demo tapes and manuscripts thumping onto its doormat, begging for cases to be heard. I sent a bundle of my poems, and, after a few weeks, decided to pay a call to ask if the Beatle who'd read them had set a publication date yet. Wondering what I'd wear on the dust-jacket photograph, I approached what looked like a private residence in Savile Row where a few girls were loitering round the steps. The front door was open so, unchallenged, I entered and explained myself to a friendly receptionist on whose desk top was a tin marked 'Canned Heat'. She was sorry no one could see me right now, but promised I'd hear from Apple in due course. As the twenty-first century approaches, I should imagine my teenage verse must be quite near the top of the pile.

23 HALF AS NICE

The Summer of Love was no more the dawning of the Age of Aquarius than the Twist had been. In Britain, flower-power was supplanted by gangster *chic*, enabling Georgie Fame to revitalize a flagging career with 'The Ballad of Bonnie and Clyde', a Yuletide chart-topper and by far his biggest major North American smash. Yet an older strategy, also tried by Fame amongst others, was covering US chartbusters purely for home buyers. Mercilessly, Love Affair – formerly the Soul Survivors – heisted two consecutive 1968 releases by soul singer Robert Knight, serving him as Tommy Steele had Guy Mitchell in the 1950s. Almost as lucrative were similar time-honoured heists by Amen Corner, Marmalade – and the Dave Clark Five who also had a sneaky US smash (one of their last) with Amen Corner's only UK Number One, '(If Paradise Is) Half As Nice' – as did the ailing Yardbirds with Manfred Mann's 'Ha! Ha! Said the Clown'.

The Yardbirds' final A-sides were by external composers – though fleeting sparks of the old creative fire were shown on the odd B-side and *Little Games*, the group's farewell US-only LP. After the group's final booking – in Luton in 1968 – Keith Relf and Jim McCarty reunited as Together. Perhaps because Keith Relf had fought to be heard amidst the overwhelming volume of lead guitarists, Together's two 45s were imbued with the pastoral lyricism and acoustic emphasis that the two would bring to the more remunerative Renaissance with ex-Nashville Teen John Hawkden on keyboards, bass player Louis Cennamo (briefly with the Herd) and Relf's singing sister, Jane. A promising debut LP in 1969 left a vaguely 'classical music' after-effect. The group was then abandoned by its every member, though, with new personnel, it was to enjoy considerable acclaim later, especially in North America.

The Jeff Beck Group had already made an outstanding US debut after much picking and choosing from musicians of the stature of Jet Harris, Viv Prince and Aynsley Dunbar. Eventually, Beck had settled on Rod Stewart, Ron Wood (on bass) and drummer Mickey Waller, formerly of the Fabulous Fleerekkers. Waller had favoured Beck over the higher wages of Jimmy Page's new group who'd toured Scandinavia as the New Yardbirds before renaming itself Led Zeppelin at Keith Moon's suggestion.

Borrowing the Creation's violin bow idea, Page also recursed to *Little Games* and the Jeff Beck Group's *Truth* when planning Led Zeppelin's eponymous first album. Though half the group – ex-King Snakes drummer John Bonham and vocalist Robert Plant – were from the Band of Joy whose meat had been the flower-power pop wafting from California, the feature most associated with Led Zeppelin would be a blues-plagiarized brutality in which Plant's lung power was on a par with an instrumental sound-portrait of Genghis Khan on the rampage.

Other bands tore chapters from Led Zeppelin's book as 'heavy metal' bands of the same ilk popped up with almost the same frequency as beat groups had. Many had, indeed, descended from the beat boom. The doom-laden Black Sabbath, for example, originated in Erdington where once rehearsed the Rest, a soberly-attired 1965 four-piece containing Sabbath's future drummer Bill Ward and guitarist Tony Iommi.

Though lead guitar was as important as vocals in heavy metal, it was less of a hallmark in Joe Cocker and the Grease Band. A Chesterfield disc jockey had enticed Denny Cordell, producer of the Moody Blues and the Move, up the M1 for a Cocker pub performance. Reaction to the stage act – built round Joe's clammy bellyaching and spasmodic movements – was sufficiently encouraging for Cordell to supervise 'Marjorine' a group original, replacing the entire Grease Band except Chris Stainton with session players. 'Marjorine' spent a week in the Top 50.

This, however, wasn't enough for those Grease Bandsmen unheard on 'Marjorine' to hold on hoping. Only Chris and Joe were willing to uproot for the required migration to London. With them went Tommy Eyre, keyboard whizz-kid from the Candies who, on the boards, had xeroxed the Beatles' 'With a Little Help from My Friends'. This was taped in funereal waltz-time by Cocker, Stainton and Eyre with assistants that included Jimmy Page. Though a version by Joe Brown had made the Top 40 in 1967, 'With a Little Help from My Friends' by windmill-armed Cocker – the Surprise Hit of the Windsor Jazz and Blues Festival – wrenched Welsh soprano Mary Hopkin's 'Those Were the Days' from Number One.

Bearing the catalogue number Apple 2, Mary's 45 had succeeded the Beatles' own 'Hey Jude' at the top. Apple Records had wanted to sign Graham Nash's new group. Their warblings weren't everyone's cup of tea, but Nash ended up a sight richer than if he'd stayed with the Hollies. Styled a 'supergroup' by the music press, Crosby, Stills and Nash – an ex-Byrd and an ex-Buffalo Springfield-er and an ex-Holly – could not extricate themselves from existing contracts and the deal fell through. It was the same with Peter Green's Fleetwood Mac, made up mostly of ex-Bluesbreakers. David Bowie slipped through the Beatles' net too after an interview with Paul McCartney, but Grapefruit – nearly all from Tony Rivers' Castaways – and Jackie Lomax, back from the States, were both taken on.

The first photograph of (left to right) Ray Thomas, Denny Laine (Brian Hines), Clint Warwick (Clinton Eccles), Graeme Edge and Mike Pinder as the Moody Blues. The shot was taken by Jim Simpson, future trumpeter with Locomotive, at Erdington's Carlton Club (later, Mother's).

Eric Clapton, Chris Dreja and Jim McCarty wonder which one of them is the young lady's favourite Yardbird. *(Jackie Ryan)*

The Dave Clark Five, 1965: (left to right) Mike Smith (keyboards, lead singer), Denis West Payton (saxophone), Dave Clark (drums), Lenny Davidson (guitar) and Rick Huxley (bass). *(Herman Hamerpagt)*

The Animals on the set of *Get Yourself A College Girl* during the 'British Invasion' of the USA: (left to right) Alan Price, Hilton Valentine, Bryan 'Chas' Chandler, Eric Burdon and John Steele.

Guitarist Dick Taylor and vocalist Phil May were still leading the Pretty Things three decades after their chart debut with 'Rosalyn' in 1964. *(Jackie Ryan)*

The Migil Five ride the bluebeat craze: (left to right) Red Lambert, Gilbert Lucas, Mike Felix, Alan Watson and Lenny Blanche. *(Jackie Ryan)*

Ray Davies asleep on the job.
(Jackie Ryan)

Many listeners found bass guitarist John Entwhistle's macabre compositions the most attractive aspect of The Who.

ROBERT STIGWOOD ASSOCIATES LTD.
are proud to present the king of R & B

CHUCK ☆
☆ BERRY

IN PLACE OF P. J. PROBY ON THEIR AUTUMN TOUR AT

NOVEMBER

Fri. 6, EDMONTON, Regal
Sat. 7, SLOUGH, Granada
Sun. 8, ‡ * BIRMINGHAM, Hippodrome
Mon. 9, ● ‡ ‡ SUTTON, Granada
Tues. 10, LEICESTER, Odeon
Wed. 11, YORK, Rialto
Thur. 12, BOLTON, Odeon
Fri. 13, ‡ * NEWCASTLE, Odeon
Sat. 14, ‡ ● BRADFORD, Gaumont
Sun. 15, MANCHESTER, Palace
Mon. 16, RUGBY, Granada

Tues. 17, WOLVERHAMPTON, Gaumont
Wed. 18, LIVERPOOL, Odeon
Thur. 19, ‡ * DONCASTER, Gaumont
Fri. 20, SHEFFIELD, Gaumont
Sat. 21, ‡ ● HANLEY, Gaumont
Sun. 22, MORECAMBE, Winter Gardens
Mon. 23, BRIXTON, Granada
Tues. 24, BOURNEMOUTH, Gaumont
Wed. 25, KILBURN, State
Thur. 26, WATFORD, Gaumont
Fri, 27, ROMFORD, Odeon
Sat. 28, ‡ * LEWISHAM, Odeon
Sun. 29, BRIGHTON, Hippodrome

* Barron-Knights not appearing these dates   ‡ Mike Sarne appearing these dates only
● Pretty Things not appearing these dates   ‡ Simon Scott appearing this date only

WITH **THE PRETTY THINGS**

KIM WESTON and the
EARL VAN DYKE
QUARTET

THE TEA TIME
FOUR

THE LE ROYS
DON SPENCER

THE BARRON-KNIGHTS

ON SPECIFIED DATES

MIKE SARNE   SIMON SCOTT

Numerous beat groups turned to Chuck Berry's Chess LPs as regularly as monks to the Bible, and felt privileged to support whenever he toured Britain.

Brand leaders of the 'Andover Sound', the Troggs – (left to right) Reg Presley (vocals), Chris Britton (guitar), Pete Staples (bass) and Ronnie Bond (drums) – pose with another icon of the mid-1960s.

Opposite page, top Screaming Lord Sutch (dark jacket) congratulates Eastleigh's Big T Show, runners-up in 1965's *Melody Maker* band competition, with (left to right) Jenny, Penny and Fran, once a Basingstoke folk club trio, as 'white Supremes'. *(Penny Hicks)*

Opposite page, left Tich (obscured) and Dave Dee soundchecking for their first *Ready Steady Go* appearance. *(Alan Clayson Archives)*

Opposite page, right Viv Prince, Pretty Thing and Soho club host of Knuckles, recorded a solo single in 1966, 'Minuet For Ringo'. *(Jackie Ryan)*

The Move, January 1966: (left to right) Trevor Burton (guitar), Roy Wood (guitar), Bev Bevan (drums), Carl Wayne (vocals) and Chris 'Ace' Kefford (bass). *(Jim Simpson/Big Bear Music Group)*

Brian Poole (centre, back) and the Tremeloes – (left to right) Ricky West (guitar), new boy Len Hawkes (bass), Alan Blakely (guitar, keyboards) and Dave Munden (drums) – were recording separately by mid-1966, but it wasn't until a university booking the following year that Brian finally parted from his backing group. *(Brian Poole)*

Ready Steady Go compere Cathy McGowan and, in trendy military attire, Manfred Mann, August 1966. *(Alan Clayson Archives)*

Manfred's Menn: Klaus Voorman (flute), Tom McGuinness (guitar), Mike Hugg (drums) and (obscured) Michael D'Abo, ex-Band of Angels, who took over as vocalist from Paul Jones in July 1966. *(Alan Clayson Archives)*

Wayne Fontana's first national TV broadcast without the Mindbenders. *(Alan Clayson Archives)*

Inset 'Here's a young man who could make a profound impression in the future,' reckoned the *NME* after Jimi Hendrix's teeth-gnashing British TV debut in December 1966 with his Experience, which included bass player Noel Redding (background). *(Alan Clayson Archives)*

Below Steve Winwood and Eric Clapton at Blind Faith's Hyde Park concert, 7 June 1969. *(Roger Barnes)*

1969: A veteran of Glasgow's Chris McClure Section, Candy Floss and the John Wayne Band, Sandy Newman (guitar, vocals) was to assume leadership of Marmalade in the 1970s.

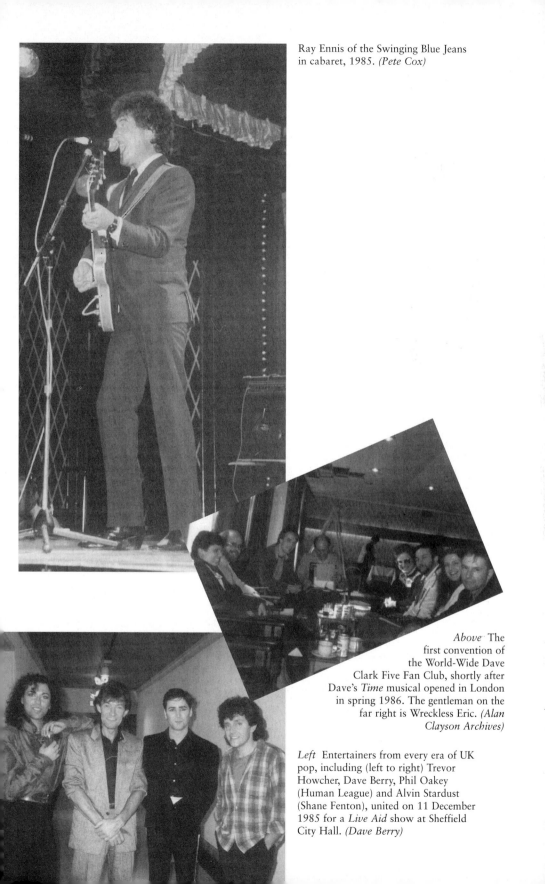

Ray Ennis of the Swinging Blue Jeans in cabaret, 1985. *(Pete Cox)*

Above The first convention of the World-Wide Dave Clark Five Fan Club, shortly after Dave's *Time* musical opened in London in spring 1986. The gentleman on the far right is Wreckless Eric. *(Alan Clayson Archives)*

Left Entertainers from every era of UK pop, including (left to right) Trevor Howcher, Dave Berry, Phil Oakey (Human League) and Alvin Stardust (Shane Fenton), united on 11 December 1985 for a *Live Aid* show at Sheffield City Hall. *(Dave Berry)*

Above Dave Berry rocks and the author rolls at Southsea pier, March 1986. *(Peter Rowe)*

Below In the early 1980s, Ringo Starr (centre, foreground) wandered artistically from pillar to post. He seems to be doing exactly this in the 1982 video shoot for Paul McCartney's 'Take It Away' with (left to right) former Mindbender (and 10cc) Eric Stewart, George Butler, Linda McCartney and Paul. *(Ian Drummond)*

Below Dozy, Beaky, *a* Mick and Tich.

Adam Faith at the 1986 launch of a new series of BBC TV's *Rock 'n' Roll Years*, produced by Ann Freer. *(Alan Clayson Archives)*

Accompanied by Cornwall's Face Value, political leader Screaming Lord Sutch on campaign at the Burstow Inn, Bow, on 15 August 1987. *(Kevin Delaney)*

A six-piece Fourmost perform before a mock-up of the Cavern wall and the ghostly image of Rory Storm at a charity function at Liverpool's Grafton Rooms, May 1989. *(Dave Humphreys)*

The British Invasion All-Stars, 1992, with North American fan Mike Ober (far right) who financed an array of products by (left to right back) Dick Taylor (Pretty Things, guitarist), Keith Grant (Downliners Sect, bass) and Matthew Fisher (Procol Harum, ex-Sect, keyboards) plus (left to right front) Eddie Phillips (Creation, guitarist), Don Craine (Sect, guitarist), Ray Phillips (Nashville Teens, singer) and Jim McCarty (Yardbirds, drummer). *(Don Craine)*

Above The Merseybeats in 1989 with ex-Beatle Pete Best replacing the late John Banks. *(Dave Humphreys)*

Left Traveller of a mighty rough road since forming an instrumental outfit with his uncle in 1961, a rejuvenated Ace Kefford was recording with Fairport Convention in 1994. *(Murat Ozkasim)*

Below (Left to right) Guitarist Peter Pye, drummer Ann 'Honey' Langtree and singer Denis D'Ell from the 1964 edition of the Honeycombs joined with Simon Wyatt (bass) and Paul Price-Smith (keyboards) for an anniversary bash at London's Mildmay Tavern thirty years after their 'Have I The Right' chart-topper. *(Denis D'Ell)*

Above Cliff Bennett, 1992.

In November 1990, Mike Smith (ex-Dave Clark Five) broke cover with *It's only Rock 'n' Roll,* his first solo album. *(Bruce Fleming)*

Dave Dee, Sandy Newman and Alan Blakely (left to right foreground) onstage with other ravers during the finale of a German 1960s extravaganza in 1993. *(Peter Oelker)*

An exhibit from *The Beatles Story*, now one of Liverpool's most popular tourist attractions. *(Mike Byrne)*

Yet the only Apple act other than the Beatles to attain any measure of chart longevity were Badfinger, once the Iveys, who had stemmed from the Masterminds and the Calderstones, two minor Merseybeat acts formed by lads who'd coughed up the one-shilling membership to catch the Hollies time after time at the Cavern. After backing David Garrick, they were spotted by a Beatles lackey and, with their pedigree an asset, groomed for greener pastures.

That Apple didn't throw down a line to the likes of Freddie Garrity – who was interviewed by Yoko Ono, now John Lennon's paramour and artistic collaborator – and the Remo Four may have been because their very names were too directly associated with dear, dead Merseybeat. Yet they were probably best off out of it because nothing he did on Apple would make Jackie Lomax rich, despite costly publicity photographs and a full orchestra or one of these new-fangled Moog synthesizers if he needed one. Helping out on one of his sessions, Eric Clapton gave him as a relic to guard for life, the Gibson SG heard on Cream's double-album, *Wheels of Fire*.

Trios were 'it' then. Cream, the Jimi Hendrix Experience, Rory Gallagher's Taste and, after Christine Perfect left for Fleetwood Mac, Stan Webb's Chicken Shack. Most harked back to the Big Three's guitar-bass-drums test case. Yet John Mayall dispensed with drums for a while, and Traffic – now down to three lanes too – surged to keyboards-drums-woodwinds climaxes all the more rewarding for a low-volume restraint.

Less intense than gut-wrenching, Cream had gone from a Willesden scout hut to grander platforms in the USA where, in the late 1960s, collegiate youth seemed fair game to purchase anything British labelled 'heavy' or – surely taking coals to Newcastle – 'blues'. On stage, Cream's musical sensitivity was lost to 'endless, meaningless solos,' reflected a perplexed Clapton. 'We were not indulging ourselves so much as our audiences – because that's what they wanted.'[167] They especially liked it when he went *diddle-iddle-iddle-iddle-iddle-iddle* way up the neck of his guitar. As long as customers went as ape over clusters of bum notes as they did over the band's most startling moments, Cream in stagnation broke box office records in Uncle Sam's baseball parks before a calculated disbandment in November 1968.

Clapton and Ginger Baker then amalgamated with Steve Winwood and Rick Grech, bass player from Family, as Blind Faith who, so a letter in *Melody Maker* wrongly predicted, would achieve 'almost Beatle status'.[167] The situation in the States didn't change as Winwood made the exasperated discovery that, as it had been with Cream, 'We could play really terrible and get the same reaction as if we played good.'[166]

The rest of Traffic checked in at the inevitable rural hideaway with ex-member Dave Mason and Wynder K. Frog, a former Fairy. Wooden Frog didn't last long. Poignantly, the last hop was at Kidderminster Town Hall where the Hellions used to play. As well as an instrumental version of 'Born Under a Bad Sign' from *Wheels of Fire*, the set also embraced the murder ballad 'Long Black Veil' that Bob Dylan's backing Band had lately resurrected.

Blind Faith and the Rolling Stones too displayed evidence of having fallen under the spell of the Band's True West blend of electric folklore, nurtured over many a rough night in hick Canadian dance halls before the musicians landed the Dylan job. Bob's own *John Wesley Harding* had, in its unvarnished arrangements and lyrical directness, also helped steer pop away from backward-running tapes, sitars and self-conscious symbolism that disguised many essentially vapid perceptions.

With ex-Bluesbreaker Mick Taylor where Brian Jones had once been, the Stones were back on the road again. Rather than thirty closing minutes a night on the scream circuit, they were now delivering three-hour concerts in the USA where matches would be lit and held up *en masse* in trendy approval. On the minus side, discomforted snarls had replaced 1967's love-and-peace as everyone with the same-priced tickets pushed towards the protective cordon of hired police. Onstage silences and *pianissimos* were undermined by a barrage of stamping, whistling, and, worst of all, bellowed demands for the good old good ones.

What if you hadn't got any good old good ones for anyone to bellow for? A troubled US tour by Family was epitomized by an in-concert punch-up in the wings of New York's Fillmore East between Roger Chapman and promoter Bill Graham, who reckoned that they were the worst group he'd ever heard. Not the least of their distinctions was Chapman's fully-developed, nanny-goat vibrato and and the soon-departing Rick Grech's quirky violin fiddlings. What had that to do with heads-down no-nonsense rock?

A sign of the times back home was John Peel – not as 'beautiful' as he'd been in 1967 – no longer inserting twenty-minute ragas between 'progressive' fare on *Top Gear*. An electric sitar, however, was a selling point on both US group the Box Tops' 'Cry Like a Baby' and an inspired adaptation of George Formby's 'Hindu Meditating Man' by Birmingham's Alan Randall. 'Nobody's trying to fool anyone about it being an Indian instrument,' said Chris Spedding. 'It's a sound effect. Every time I use it, I charge ten pounds apart from my session fee.'[168]

Yet Radio One disc jockeys were 'into' Zen macrobiotic cookery and yoga – and old colleagues Eric Clapton and Tom McGuinness would gather thoughts on religious matters in the respective self-penned hymns 'Presence of the Lord' on Blind Faith's only LP, and 'I Will Bring To You' – which found its way into British primary school hymnals. More specifically committed, former Graham Bond Organization guitarist 'Mahavishnu' John McLaughlin had converted to the doctrines of Bengal holy man Sri Chinmoy while Bond himself was so fascinated by the occult that he'd start professing that his father was the much-misunderstood black magician Aleister Crowley.

If less pin-ups now than slightly dotty uncle figures too, the Beatles were not so far above the adoration of schoolgirls that they didn't have recent group photographs – albeit unsmiling and disunited – available on request for *Jackie* or *Rave*! To the general public, Beatle John seemed the most changed – funny peculiar rather than funny ha-ha – though some wondered if Beatle George wasn't as just as screwy on the quiet. Courtesy of George was the piloting into the Top 20 of 1969's 'Hare Krishna Mantra' by the Radha Krishna Temple, the strangest act ever since the Joystrings were invited to be on *Top of the Pops*.

David Bowie's first hit, 'Space Oddity', was a more pertinent artefact of the year of the Moon landing. There hadn't been much else to get worked up about. Incidents like a fatal stabbing at a free Rolling Stones concert near San Francisco and the Sharon Tate bloodbath horrified TV news viewers as much a shoot-out in a spaghetti western nowadays. Was it only the previous October that *International Times* had proclaimed 'Charlie Manson is just a harmless freak'?[169] He and his 'Family' had had *The Beatles*, the double-LP that followed *Sgt. Pepper*, on instant replay as they prepared for the Tate murders having heard revolutionary 'messages' to do so in certain tracks.

'Revolution is this year's flower power'[170] – so Frank Zappa had summed up the previous year when, with Vietnam the common denominator, kaftans had been mothballed as their former wearers followed the crowd to genuinely violent anti-war demonstrations. Few pop stars joined in – as Mick Jagger did – or came up with even another anthem as irresolute as the Beatles' 'Revolution', but they were active after a arm-wavingly detached, pop-starrish fashion in verbal support of pacifism.

Philanthropy was also popular. Marc Bolan – now a cult figure with the Tyrannosaurus Rex duo – berated his manager for being too 'hung up' about 'bread', and, on leaving Fleetwood Mac, Peter Green would command his accountant, on pain of a sock on the nose, to redirect incoming monies to the poor. Of a 1968 field visit to Bangladesh, Cliff Richard made the uneasy admission that his patronage of the Evangelical Alliance Relief (TEAR) Fund 'was to give me a sense of satisfaction and fulfilment, and I won't pretend I felt any heartache for the people in the Third World or anyone else for that matter'.[171]

Other entertainers were fixtures at the free concerts that marked the counter-culture's social calendar in post-flower-power Britain. So common were these altruistic if publicity-worthy affairs that response when scanning billings in *Time Out* or *International Times* had shifted from a cynical, 'Yes, but how much is it to get in?' to a jaded, 'Hmmm, is that all that's on this time?' Most such extravaganzas were triumphs because everyone wanted them to be, though occasional disruptions by 'skinheads' – youths with Prussian haircuts out for 'bovver' – caused some to suggest the formation of vigilante squads.

Shirt-sleeved bouncer-types were in evidence when Blind Faith made its concert debut free of charge in Hyde Park's natural arena. A few weeks later at the same spot, the Stones hosted the largest assembly for any cultural event London had ever known. With sets by Alexis Korner, Family and new sensation King Crimson, this buckshee bash was seen as a memorial for Brian Jones who had drowned two days before.

Tiring of psychedelia as they had, the Stones dug down to a three-chord bedrock in 1968 for 'Jumping Jack Flash', perhaps their most enduring single. It was included in ten sensational minutes at the *NME* Pollwinners show which the group set alight like gin-sops at a temperance meeting. Nevertheless, the three years after 1968 would see a petrification of UK pop's turbulent adolescence. *Top of the Pops* had already brushed its 1960s nadir one schmaltzy week in 1968 when the only group featured was the Tremeloes – who, before they started casting aspersions in the press about the IQs of fans of their 'rubbish', were, with Love Affair and Marmalade, a prong of a grinning triumvirate that ruled this silver age of British beat.

In March 1969, a Benny Hill TV sketch concerned a disc jockey on an early morning radio show after a night on the tiles. Aggravating his hungover queasiness was a listener's request for 'any platter by Grapefruit, Cream – or Marmalade!' This gag acknowledged unconsciously the commercial apogee of Glaswegian pop which, prior to Marmalade's four-year chart run, had been restricted to sporadic Top 30 forays by Lulu and the Luvvers and the Poets. Marmalade's tenacity had been rewarded in June 1968 when they penetrated the Top 10 at last with 'Lovin' Things', orchestrated in a style reminiscent of Love Affair. Their third hit, 'Ob-la-di Ob-la-da' from *The Beatles*, reached Number One – which Marmalade celebrated by miming it on *Top of the Pops* in sporrans, gorgets, clan tartans *et al.*

Beneath them, the charts were constipated with further harmless purveyors of popular song like the Casuals, Cupid's Inspiration, Plastic Penny, Butterscotch, Pickettywitch, Arrival and all the rest who endured for maybe two Top 40 showings. With a nod towards North America's cartoon Archies and the Don Kirschner 'bubblegum' factory, some of these acts (e.g. Springwater) had no physical form beyond television and recording studios.

Chargeable for a fair amount of these were Rogers Cook and Greenaway, united for composition and production work, but functioning separately as occasional recording artists – as instanced by Cook's fronting of chartbusting Blue Mink, and Greenaway's smash with 1970's 'Gimme Dat Ding' as one of the Pipkins, a clownish duo with another ex-Kestrel, Tony Burrows. This was but one landmark in a golden year for Tony who, in his capacity as a session vocalist, also attended to hits by Edison Lighthouse, White Plains and Brotherhood of Man.

Between the limits of these disposable cash-ins and the most way-out progressive band, pop artists in the latter half of the 1960s were inclined to become polarized in particular styles as jazz had been for years. There was a traditional school wide enough to contain both Cilla Black and *mucho macho* Tom Jones. Mainstream could be represented by Marmalade and Amen Corner, while the likes of Ten Years After and, despite 'Love Is Blue', the Jeff Beck Group, had enough class to muscle in amongst modernists like Jethro Tull and a reformed Traffic. No more teenage fun than Engelbert was, Soft Machine and the Third Ear Band roamed the distant reaches of the avant-garde. Some acts belonged in more than one section – as the Beatles did by selecting both mock-vaudeville ('Honey Pie') and freak-out tape collage ('Revolution Nine') on the same double-album – and what of 'Throw Down a Line', Hank Marvin's 1969 single with Cliff Richard, featuring him in Hendrix mode?

The Bystanders were to cross categories in another more successful form. Though they'd had a minor 'mainstream' hit with '98.6' in 1967, 'Cave of Clear Light' from 1968 gave more overt clues of what they were to become after they were joined by guitarist Deke Leonard from the Dream to become Man, perhaps the Land of Song's foremost progressive outfit. Years of struggle under another name – the Spectres – had a similar effect on Status Quo who had finally struck gold in 1968 with the psychedelic 'Pictures of Matchstick Men'. Another change of policy was to bring them more lasting success as blues-boogie merchants of the 1970s.

Four years later 'Let The Sun Shine In', the Peddlers came up trumps again when an invigorating CBS contract launched *Freewheelers* into the LP chart. This heralded a Top 10 strike with the self-composed 'Birth', a smaller hit in its follow-up, 'Girlie', and the Peddlars' highest climb up the album list with *Birthday*. The long-term benefits for the trio included providing musical interludes for TV chat-shows – and higher fees for their stock-in-trade cabaret bookings.

The Peddlers' return coincided with but was not related to a rock 'n' roll revival as Bill Haley and Buddy Holly re-issues crept into the charts, and medleys of classic rock closed the shows of 'nice little bands' whose names – Tea-and-Symphony, Warm Dust, Audience, Puce-Exploding Butterfly – implied musical insights less immediately graspable. Entertaining a truer underground than these denizens of Students Union stages were provincial combos led by extant Teddy Boys like Crazy Cavan and Shakin' Stevens and others who carried a torch for the 1950s.

Not quite so obviously 'regressive' were contemporary singles like the Move's 'Fire Brigade' with its antique Duane Eddy twang, and 'Lady Madonna', its rhythm track reminiscent of Humphrey Lyttelton's 'Bad Penny Blues'. The Beatles were now adhering to a production criterion that attempted to marry Merseybeat to advanced technology. This, however, only hastened their sour freedom from each other as, killing two birds with one stone, a film crew documented the sessions for a new album, *Let It Be*, with a high retail price (£3!) that would be the basis of the movie they owed to United Artists. Most viewers would watch it to the bitter end – as they had *Magical Mystery Tour* – though they might not have done if it'd been, say, Unit 4 + 2 getting on each others' nerves, going on irresolute musical ambles down memory lane, and coming to grief as soon as they tried anything new.

There'd be a shortfall of quality too on *Jamming With Edward*, a budget-priced jam with three Stones, Nicky Hopkins and Ry Cooder. This sort of thing and albums galore by soloing individuals and splinter units like John Entwistle's Rigor Mortis would make collecting every disc associated with a favourite group economically unsound.

Various personnel from the Beatles, Stones, Blind Faith and Joe Cocker's Grease Band were heard on numerous records by a cabal of expatriate Americans who, after an age of anonymous studio drudgery, were now breathing the air round British pop musicians, whether pot-boiling with comparative unknowns like Audience and Third World War or proudly augmenting the Rolling Stones.

When Blind Faith's six weeks on the road in the States was perverting the 'gentle surprise'[172] of Hyde Park in to ham-fisted resignation, Eric Clapton loafed around with the package's small fry, seeking the particular comradeship of a workmanlike group, Delaney and Bonnie and Friends, made up of Los Angeles session players nicknamed the 'Blue-Eyed Soul School'. That faintly sickening word 'funky' was used to describe the relentless snappy jitter and economic 'tightness' of the rhythm section, and a shrill, simple and neatly dovetailed repertoire.

From Clapton's own pocket came the outlay for the aggressively friendly Friends' European tour on the understanding that he was to be their lead guitarist. When George Harrison was roped in too, Beatlemania seemed like a previous life as a slight figure in nondescript denims was obscured by those drawling exuberantly at the front microphones. No 'in crowd' was ever so insufferably smug as these interchangeable 'supersidemen' – Bobby Whitlock, Bobby Keyes, Leon Russell *ad nauseum* – plus a smaller handful of British 'heavy friends' who, exchanging smirks over London consoles, introduced a dogmatic conformity, as if rock couldn't be played in any other way or by any other folk than that *crème de la crème* whose only contact with Dullsville was through managers, runarounds and narcotics dealers.

Conversation was bloated with hip restricted code and male chauvinist piggery. Warming up for the next track, someone might kick off a boring, boring instrumental jam. With big names dropping by to indulge as well, it was thought prudent to keep the tape rolling. George Harrison's flabby *All Things Must Pass* solo triple-album was to contain two whole sides of such interminable meanderings.

On the boards, some 'supersidemen' joined the oversubscribed ranks of Joe Cocker's Mad Dogs and Englishmen, a mobile debacle that toured endless US cities to capitalize on Joe's success there. After an *Ed Sullivan Show*, he and the Grease Band had slain the half-million drenched Americans who'd braved Woodstock, which when viewed from a distance of years was seen as the climax of hippy culture and, via its spin-off movie and albums, the measure by which future Cocker performances would always be judged.

Whilst briefly an attraction separate from Joe Cocker, the Grease Band came to be recognized as a competent session team, sometimes serving the selfsame artists as Chris Spedding who fell back on such employment (as well as northern cabaret for entertainers such as Dusty Springfield) to finance his own projects – notably the co-founding of the jazzy Battered Ornaments with Cream lyricist Pete Brown. When Brown left in 1969, Chris took over as lead singer weeks before the group had the unenviable task of preceding the Stones onstage at Hyde Park.

The Inland Revenue would drive the Stones into tax exile within a year. The Beatles would be more conclusively absent in 1969 after *Abbey Road* which was – as Debussy said of Wagner's *Rheingold* – 'a glorious sunset mistaken for a dawn'. The four who had soundtracked the Swinging Sixties would prove unable as ex-Beatles to so minister to the 1970s.

More old heroes went down – the Small Faces, Unit 4 + 2, the Dave Clark Five – and the Hermits would be out on a limb after Herman had his only solo hit, 'Oh You Pretty Thing' (written by David Bowie), in 1971. Colin Blunstone almost surrendered to Rod Argent the task of singing 'Time of the Season', the opus that ensured that the Zombies went out with a bang in 1969. Spurred by snowballing North American airplay, this elegy was near the top of the Hot 100 when it was discovered that the group had already told the whole fairweather industry to get stuffed by quietly disbanding. Not even a five-figure sum for just one little concert could put them back together again – though a rash of other outfits began accepting illicit bookings under the Zombies' name.

Most of the real Zombies were to reform on a casual basis years later, but such a possibility was denied to the Jimi Hendrix Experience after the death of its figurehead in 1970 – though Noel Redding had been emerging as quite a star in his own right. Coerced into a Mothers of Invention comedy sketch at a London concert in 1968, he was greeted with delighted cheers. That summer, he'd formed Fat Mattress with ex-members of the Loving Kind, initially as a vehicle for his songs and a preferred role as lead guitarist. After a *Top of the Pops* appearance, Noel went so far as to suggest that the new group might be a suitable support act to Hendrix. Though Fat Mattress did, indeed, open during a 1969 tour of the USA, Redding's tenure with the Experience was coming to an end – but then so was the Experience itself.

After pioneering spirit Graham Nash slipped his cable, many imagined that the Hollies were finished too, yet they milked the Top 50 for a further six years, despite the death of 'L. Ransford', the man who never was. As well as the catalogues of Tin Pan Alley tunesmiths like Chip Taylor and Mike Batt, they also rifled those of lesser-known performers such as the Greatest Show on Earth, whose music was like that of both the Hollies and Crosby, Stills and Nash.

When Allan Clarke briefly flew the nest in 1971, the Hollies thought enough of Bamboo, a Swedish band that would connect genealogically with Abba, to shanghai its vocalist, Mikael Rickfors. However, Allan's lone ventures elicited as lukewarm a response as *Romany*, the new Hollies LP. After 'Long Cool Woman in a Black Dress', an old track sung and co-written by Clarke, slinked up the US Hot 100, the prodigal returned.

Another lead singer, Carl Wayne, on quitting the Move in 1969, pursued the path of the all-round entertainer, going the whole hog by playing a milkman in *Crossroads*, and marrying in real life the actress who played its Miss Diane. On leaving the Rockin' Berries, Geoff Turton had a solo windfall in the US charts under the pseudonym 'Jefferson', and, after The Quiet Five faded away, Richard Barnes placed two solo 45s in 1970's Top 40 – but, as Cliff Bennett and Colin Blunstone could have told both Geoff and Richard, a mere Great Voice wasn't enough.

Dying on their feet were the Poets and the Downliners Sect. In slower decline, the Troggs lost both Chris Britton and bass player Pete Staples, and Reg Presley and Ronnie Bond made solo records. Yet there'd be enough life left in the old dogs for an unexpected South African Number One with 'Feels Like a Woman' in 1972.

It wasn't until the summer of 1969 that the Troggs' exhausted blood-brothers, Dave Dee, Dozy, Beaky, Mick and Tich, had their last hit, 'Snake in the Grass'. Had they not split in two at this point, it's possible that they might have revived as they had after the comparative failure of 'Touch Me Touch

Me' in 1967. As it was, Dee followed a middle-of-the-road path – with Peter Lee Stirling as his musical director – and the rest as 'DBMT' courted the 'progressive' audience.

The Kinks' sojourn in the Top 20 was nearly spent, but, augmented by the Mike Cotton Sound – now reduced to just its horn section – they gave free rein in both stage and studio to Ray Davies' increasingly theatrical leanings. Beneath pop's capricious quicksand was a sufficient substratum of encouragement assuring them that it was worth carrying on. To a smaller degree, the same applied to the Pretty Things whose *Parachute* was 1969's Album of the Year in *Rolling Stone* magazine.

Manfred Mann was still doing TV commercials after his group fragmented in 1969. All former members were to achieve further success in the music industry – most conspicuously Tom McGuinness whose McGuinness-Flint outfit with ex-John Mayall drummer Hughie Flint had two hit singles in the early 1970s, and Manfred himself who had a longer chart stay later in the decade with Manfred Mann's Earth Band.

If Mann, Georgie Fame and Alexis Korner could do ITV advertisements, then there was nothing shameful in old pop stars becoming regulars on the channel's children's hour. Freddie Garrity and Dreamer Pete Birrell were general factotums on *Little Big Time*; Billy J. Kramer compered *Lift Off*, and Gerry Marsden turned up on *Junior Showtime*. On a further horizon was Ringo Starr's narration of the adventures of movable models known to infant viewers as *Thomas the Tank Engine and Friends*. Merseysiders all, each relied on forthright but amiable impudence and, like every northern comic from Askey to Tarbuck, the conveyance of a feeling that everyone knows him and he them.

On collecting their cards from Jeff Beck, Rod Stewart and Ron Wood had amalgamated with three former Small Faces. As ordinary-sized 'Faces' with Rod as Jack-the-Lad front man, the quintet were to be the Woodstock Generation's Brian Poole and the Tremeloes, though their infectious, boozy flair didn't always translate too well onto vinyl.

Humble Pie's main men were the other ex-Small Face and the Herd's Peter Frampton. While Frampton had been *Rave!*'s 'Face of '68', Steve Marriott's hairline was already receding – but not as much as Van Morrison's. Marriott, Morrison and Eric Burdon too had Gone West; Steve to build on the Small Faces' slight gains in the States after Humble Pie had acquired both a solitary UK Top 20 entry and a reputation for boorish behaviour on *Top of the Pops*. Choosing not to bury themselves in groups, Van and Eric each had a crack US session team whose blithe dedication to their craft was refreshing after those with whom they'd once been on equal terms in Them and the Animals.

However, a clutch of familiars – his 'Heavy Friends' (including Nicky

Hopkins, Jimmy Page and Noel Redding) did their duty by their old boss, Screaming Lord Sutch, after his part in a show at Los Angeles' Thee Experience club lead to a profitable two-album deal with Atlantic Records. Both sold well in the USA, even making the Hot 100.

Sutch, sly old rascal, finished the 1960s on an upswing while brethren like the Swinging Blue Jeans and the Nashville Teens were being displayed as curios from the recent past in an outer darkness of the dancehall orbit of northern Europe – but, briefly sporting shoulder-length hair and a trendy beard, Dave Berry remained hot property in The Netherlands where 'This Strange Effect' yet rippled.

Outlasting nearly all the beat groups, high street musical equipment emporiums waited to buy back saleable instruments taking up cupboard space, and monolithic speaker cabinets serving as room dividers. The last edition of *Rave!* was in the shops in March 1969, and, finally, both Cliff Richard and John Lennon turned thirty.

THE WORST THING IN THE WORLD

Nineteen-seventy began and ended with the respectively undiggable sounds of Edison Lighthouse and 'Grandad' Clive Dunn. The anthem of a wet summer was 'In the Summertime' by Mungo Jerry, virtually a skiffle group. The same raggedly carefree *joie de vivre* was heard too in later hits by McGuinness-Flint, Medicine Head – produced by Keith Relf – and Lindisfarne, once a Tyneside trio named Coloured Rain after a number by Traffic, who had themselves recently recorded 'John Barleycorn', that most exquisite English folk air, and further from Ray Charles than any Spencer Davis Group fan could have imagined in 1965. As iconoclastic too were the Nashville Teens' 'Widecombe Fair' (despite a heavy metal touch-up) and Alan Price's 'Trimdon Grange Explosion'.

The hit song of 1970, however, was Free's 'All Right Now' which, owing much to the Rolling Stones' 'Honky Tonk Women' of 1969, was an album-enhancing 45 that would pulsate from college jukeboxes along with fare from Humble Pie, Black Sabbath and their ilk, appealing to male consumers recently grown to man's estate. Heavy-rock fanaticism was such that 'headbangers' would insert their bruised bonces into yawning speaker bins to receive the full mega-decibel blast of bass guitar. With Deep Purple as link, this category stretched towards jazz-rock – which in Britain spawned respectable names like East of Eden, Colosseum (who were enlivened in 1970 by the presence of Chris Farlowe) and John McLaughlin's Mahavishnu Orchestra, and the 'technoflash' pomp-rock of Yes and Emerson, Lake and Palmer – ELP – of whom the 'P' was Carl Palmer, drumming *wunderkind* from Farlowe's Thunderbirds, and the 'E', Keith Emerson, ex-keyboard player in Gary Farr's T-Bones and the Nice.

Reaching out to self-doubting adolescent diarists rather than headbangers was a mostly North American school of singing composers so bound up in themselves that their most trivial emotions were translated into song. It was called 'self-rock' if you liked it and 'drip-rock' if, like *Melody Maker*'s Allan Jones in a scathing article, you didn't. Over here we had the likes of Elton John (ex-pianist with Long John Baldry's backing-group), Gary Farr, Bridget St John, and Cat Stevens, former teen idol and writer of the Tremeloes 'Here Comes My Baby'. No Mick Jaggerings were necessary. All you did was sit on a stool, whinge 'beautiful' cheesecloth-and-denim ballads and, like Freddie

Garrity with his 'just a minute!', emit a small, sad smile now and then.

More than gruff heavy metal or pomp-rock, drip-rock had caught the tenor of the hungover morning after the Swinging Sixties. The house band was the suitably anodyne Crosby, Stills, and Nash who at Woodstock, their second booking, had been joined by Neil Young, a drip-rock colossus whose 'Southern Man' got what it deserved in a version by Dave Clark and Friends – Clark, Mike Smith and personnel from Blue Mink.

Groups like DBMT, Marmalade, the Searchers, the Tremeloes and the Shadows (as 'Marvin, Welch and Farrar') developed a new introspection. DBMT's 'For the Use of Your Son', also sniffed the same wind as the Kinks' 'Every Mother's Son', the track from *Arthur* that protestors sang outside the White House during the Vietnam moritorium. Just as solemn, Marmalade's 'Reflections of My Life' was their only major US chartbuster. Yet their last British hit for a while was the up-tempo 'Radancer' – from Hibernian slang – which alluded to unlooked-for publicity after their ex-drummer had sold relevations of his old comrades' sexual encounters on the road to a Sunday newspaper.

'Radancer' was a blip on the test-card of a pop era without colour, daring or humour. Headbanging and streaking were among wretched pastimes that caught on in the years leading to British beat's 1974 nadir. At roughly the same mental level was the 'high energy' of units like the Climax Blues Band (formerly Hipster Image), Supertramp (formerly the Joint) and Led Zeppelin. While he had come to despise it, Jeff Beck was tarred with the same brush even after he demonstrated his skills on BBC2's *Guitar Workshop* on which other guest tutors were Julian Bream and John Renbourne. Captivated by jazz-rock, Beck declined a post with the Rolling Stones in order to record *Wired* with former Mahavishnu Orchestra keyboard player, Jan Hammer. On a subsequent tour, Beck emerged as one of few rock guitarists capable of playing 'fusion' music convincingly.

Top 40 pop was far behind Jeff now. Let someone else have their turn as the teenagers' fave rave. Yet, if 'Rollermania' was rampant among schoolgirls for several months in the mid-1970s, neither The Bay City Rollers – bowties and half-mast tartan trousers – Hello, Kenny or any other UK newcomers shaped up remotely as new Beatles, Rolling Stones, Kinks, Yardbirds or Animals. Though the Beatles had been superceded by Creedence Clearwater Revival at the top of the *NME*'s popularity poll in 1971, coming second was pretty good for a group that didn't exist any more, and, despite Lennon and McCartney sniping at each other in the press and even in record grooves, the Fab Four's regrouping was seen then as inevitable by even the most marginally hopeful outsider.

A second bite of the showbusiness cherry had already been granted to certain beat musicians, even if none were to leave as insidious a legacy to pop as they had in the 1960s. Ex-Creation singer Kenny Pickett struck gold with his co-writing of 'Grandad'. Six years later, Euro-disco behemoths Boney M would dig up the Creation's 'Painter Man' as they had the Yardbirds' 'Still I'm Sad'.

Colin Blunstone's biggest solo success came in 1972 with an exact copy of 'Say You Don't Mind', Denny Laine's first single on leaving the Moody Blues in 1967. Not up to the original's fighting weight either was 'I Love You' when unearthed in 1974 by People, an obscure Californian combo – though not so obscure after their version of this 1965 B-side by Blunstone's own Zombies climbed up the Hot 100.

'I Love You' composer Chris White wrote for Rod Argent's eponymous new group whose first two US 45s had been attributed falsely to the Zombies. The unit's initial personnel also included Zombies' drummer Hugh Grundy as well as veterans of the Hunters, the Mike Cotton Sound, the Roulettes and Unit 4 + 2. Elements of pomp-rock pervaded much of the output of Argent (the group) but they weren't above tossing the odd Chuck Berry opus into their stage set. In the singles chart, they peaked in 1972 with the million-selling 'Hold Up Your Head'. That same year, guitarist Russ Ballard's confidence as a writer was boosted when his 'God Gave Rock and Roll To You' was also a hit. As a composer too, he swept into the US Top 10 with 'Liar' as covered by Three Dog Night, and would likewise service America (a group), Hot Chocolate and the Deep Purple offshoot, Rainbow.

The Fortunes had broken into the US Hot 100 with 'Rainy Day Feeling' and regained a hold on the British Top 10 after a six-year absence with 'Freedom Come Freedom Go'. They proved that this hadn't been a fluke either by doing it again in 1972 with 'Storm in a Teacup'. Ex-Merseybeat Billy Kinsley was also to get lucky twice in the UK Top 20 with his Liverpool Express, while Karen Young, once 'featured singer' in Johnny Tempest and the Cadillacs, had had a Top 10 hit in late 1969 with 'Nobody's Child', and the Sorrows' Don Maughn – as 'Don Fardon' – whooped it up to Number Three in 1970 with 'Indian Reservation'.

While Peter Lee Stirling, grizzled and renamed Daniel Boone, realized a middle-of-the-road chart bonanza in the early 1970s, Joe Brown latched onto country-rock in Brown's Home Brew, a sextet with wife and former Vernons Girl Vikki, and ex-Bruvver Peter Oakham. When this ultimatum to the contemporary pop mainstream was rejected, he returned to his previous well-paid living in pantomine, cabaret *et al*, a decision that did not mar the respect that has always been accorded him as a musician – and a Joe Brown 45, 'Hey Mama', made the Top 40 as late as 1973.

The Bee Gees and, as the Real Thing, ex-members of the Chants were back

too – as paladins of disco fever, then sashaying towards its John Travolta
zenith. In Britain, disco's epicentre was Wigan Casino Soul Club where discs
like the Chants' 'Baby I Don't Need Your Love', Herbie Goins' 'Number One
In Your Heart' and – both B-sides – Wayne Fontana's 'Something Keeps
Calling Me Back' and 'Better Use Your Head' from ex-Honeycomb Denis
d'Ell found their way onto the turnable to become much-requested 'Northern
Soul' classics.

A more likely cool cat than Denis, Georgie Fame, was issuing curate's egg
albums like *Seventh Son* and 1973's *Georgie Does His Thing With Strings*.
The former was supervised by Alan Price whose more visible alliance, Fame
and Price Together, almost reached the Top 10 in 1971 with 'Rosetta'. Other
of Price's diverse activities were acting and writing film soundtracks – both at
the same time in *O Lucky Man* and *Between Yesterday and Today*, an
exploration of Alan's northern roots, and the source of his final Top 10 entry,
1974's 'Jarrow Song'. Meanwhile, Georgie had hit the road with a new Blue
Flames, a shambling exercise that fizzled out with nobody rediscovering any
roots.

Syd Barrett went back to his roots in Cambridge after retiring as a
professional musician following two solo LPs. Nourished by half-truths and
media fiction, the 1960s myth would outlast the frailer mortal. During Jim
McCarty's more finite 'wilderness years', he penned selections on the new
Renaissance's *Prologue* and 'If You've Got a Little Love to Give' on the only
LP by Dave Clark and Friends. Resuming his own recording career in a then-
unfamiliar role on lead vocals and keyboards, he released *On the Frontier*
with Shoot, a combo that fired commercial blanks. He may have been better
off commercially had he beaten Cozy Powell, fresh from the Jeff Beck Group,
to Top 20 success with what had been perceived as a market void for a Sandy
Nelson of the 1970s.

The Cliff Richard of the 1970s was Cliff himself who, aided by younger
minds than Norrie Paramor's, finally made the US Top 20 after a twenty-year
wait. Accompanied by *I-never-thought-he-had-it-in-him* reactions, a surge of
higher chart placings at home might have been simply because he was still
there like a tree, blooming again after the decay of autumn and the snows of
winter.

Paul Raven was another 1970s star that had cut his first disc in the 1950s.
Back from Germany, he'd jumped a few more bandwagons (including a 1969
cover of the Beatles' 'Here Comes the Sun' as 'Paul Munday') until – as
'Gary Glitter' – he was washed up near the top of both the British and US
charts in 1972 with 'Rock 'n' Roll Part 2', a number built round a call-and-
response chant and a martial beat. Of much the same football terrace stamp,
further massive sellers – including a hat-trick of UK Number Ones –

established Paul-Gary in his trademark silvery suit as overlord of glam-rock.

Up there with him was T Rex, fronted by Marc Bolan – whose talkative conceit on attaining renown infuriated contemporaries. When he implied in the press that the squealing 'T Rexstasy' that attended his concerts was one in the eye for the Stones, Jagger sneered that he was 'not interested in going back to small English towns and turning on ten-year-olds'.[173] Yet *Born To Boogie* – a T Rex documentary – was Ringo Starr's first essay as a film director, and, behind the cameras at Wembley's Empire Pool, scene of much Beatles mayhem in the old days, it must have been strange for Starr to be completely ignored as hysterical girls clambered to get at Marc.

This mini-beat boom of sequins and mascara was that once-in-a-lifetime opportunity for other 1960s group veterans – most significantly, David Bowie, Roy Wood, Mud, the Sweet (formerly Wainwright's Gentlemen), Slade and Suzi Quatro's backing unit. The brains behind the Rubettes was the former 'Lennon-McCartney' of the Pete Best Four – Wayne Bickerton and Tony Waddington – and Fine Art student Bryan Ferry had fronted a 1960s Tyneside soul outfit, the Banshees, when Roxy Music wasn't even a glint in his eye.

Slade were Wolverhampton's as the Beatles were Liverpool's, notching up more chart enties than the Fab Four did when still together – even if the number of weeks spent there were less impressive. In 1973, the Gerry and the Pacemakers to Slade's Beatles were Wizzard, formed when Roy Wood had quit the Electric Light Orchestra – ELO – who, rising from the ashes of the Move, were exploring the more grandiloquent aspects of the Beatles' psychedelic period. However, on *Top of the Pops*, a commercially-expedient toy windmill twirled on new leader Jeff Lynne's hat when he lip-synched ELO's debut 45, '10538 Overture'. Emphasizing the glam elements they'd always had were Alex Harvey – bombastic leader of the Sensational Alex Harvey Band – the Faces and the Kinks, now little more than Ray Davies' backing group.

Glam's grip on singles charts was – with North America a glaring exception – world-wide, but sixth formers and undergraduates were more inclined to find *Tea for the Tillerman* by Cat Stevens or Deep Purple's *Machine Head* in their Christmas stockings. Heard but not really listened to as they revised for their exams was *Streetwalkers*, a collaboration mostly by Roger Chapman and ex-Family guitarist Charles Whitney. Far less pretentious than Family, they drew much inspiration from R & B and soul stylings. They were a popular attraction on the college circuit – especially in Germany – and their next LP, *Red Card*, breached the UK Top 20, a feat dampened by internal difficulties.

From his Manchester audio business, ex-Mindbenders bass player Bob

Land was persuaded to join Racing Cars whose sights were set on more than local bookings. Reaching Number Thirty-nine in the UK album list, the band's debut, *Downtown Tonight*, also produced an unexpected Top 20 entry in 'They Shoot Horses Don't They'. Before a lengthier chart future with 10cc, another former Mindbender, Eric Stewart, had been in one-hit wonders Hotlegs with ex-Mockingbirds, Kevin Godley and Lol Creme. Eric and business partner Graham Gouldman were amassing capital to expand their Strawberry Studio project, then humbly situated above a Stockport hi-fi shop. Signed to Jonathan King's UK label, 10cc – Eric, Graham, Kevin and Lol – had their first chart-topper with 1973's 'Rubber Bullets' which, like its Top 10 predecessor, 'Donna', was ostensibly a border-line comedy disc with neo-'baby' lead singing and deep bass second vocal.

As 10cc took off, the Faces touched down; this was caused mainly by the greater success of Rod Stewart's solo records, and his untimely public criticisms of Faces output. Another crack appeared with Ron Wood's solo LP, *I've Got My Own Album To Do* – featuring 'If You Gotta Make a Fool of Somebody' which Rod high-stepped Freddie-style when guesting on Ron's promotional showcase in London. The album was notable for its star-studded sleeve credits which included Keith Richards – through whom Ron became a full-time Stone and Ian McLagan a temporary one. After Keith Moon's body's final rebellion after a lifetime of violation, Kenney Jones would take his place in the Who.

Less fortunate jobbing musicians would switch off when required to pound fashionable Leon Russell-type descending piano inversions or *Shaft* chukka-wukka guitar for the millionth time – though quite a few eventually landed on their feet too. Never short of work, ex-Merseybeat Johnny Gustafson was among Roxy Music's pool of bass players, and drummer 'Dinky' Diamond from Aldershot's Sound of Time became a mainstay of Sparks, an Anglo-American glam outfit produced by Muff Winwood, freelance until 1978 when CBS made him an offer he couldn't refuse. At continental jazz and blues festivals, the sharp-eyed might spot another ex-Spencer Davis man, Pete York, sweating it out with some band or other until 1977 when he joined Chris Barber's Jazz and Blues Band.

As a healthy diet contributed to the stamina necessary to his musical calling, Pete and his wife opened a restaurant in Berkshire, catering largely for the horsey fraternity. Bill Wyman saw to the needs of more urban stomachs with his Kensington eaterie, *Sticky Fingers*. Speculating in non-musical diversions too were George Harrison as grey eminence of HandMade Films; Reg Presley with his patenting of a fog dispersal system, and Roger Daltrey as Hungarian composer Franz Liszt in Ken Russell's *Listzomania*. Daltrey and Peter 'Herman' Noone would also try light opera as, respectively, Macheath in *The Beggar's Opera* and Frederick in the *The Pirates of Penzance*.

Some were now above the tour-album-tour sandwiches incumbent upon poorer stars, and could wait until they felt like going out on the road again or making a new record. Yet, after picking and choosing from both friends and the most voguish, highly-waged LA studio cats, none of them would accomplish what the old beat groups, for all the casually-strewn errors, had committed to tape instinctively.

That the Fab Four had been together – albeit not at the same time – on the *Ringo* album in 1973 was enough to feed dreams that soon everything would be OK; the Beatles would regroup officially to tour and make the chart-toppers that John and Paul, all friends again, would be turning out once more. In reality too, sales of records by the four as individuals did not yet depend upon commercial viability. An ex-Beatle was assured at least a minor hit, even with drivel.

The world was, nevertheless, becoming wiser. After his guitar divinity peaked with Cream, only a miracle could have rescued Eric Clapton, now dependent on heroin, even if media build-up had warded off an immediate Blind Faith backlash. He either couldn't or wouldn't play like he had with Cream or John Mayall; neither was he an outstanding singer or composer. Yet he and George Harrison breaking sweat on duelling guitars during 'While My Guitar Gently Weeps' was one of the most thrilling moments of *The Concerts for Bangla Desh*, George's finest hour, in which he held at bay misgivings about treading the boards again to raise funds that would eventually mitigate homelessness, lack of sanitation, cholera and starvation in East Bengal. Instructing Allen Klein to book no less a venue than Madison Square Garden on 1 April 1971, he'd mustered up whatever musicians he could to support him. Newly domiciled in France, Mick Jagger was prevented from taking part because his visa couldn't be cleared in time. The coup of the decade would have been the regrouping of the Beatles, but he only managed to procure Ringo.

Pop's upper echelon was now inhabiting a world more exclusive than even that of the Bangladesh 'superstars', and more cultivated than that of a Scotch of St James rave *circa* 1965. The new rock squirearchy began taking up recreations recommended by those born into privilege. Steve Winwood, owner since 1970 of a manor not far from the ancestral Cotswolds home of the Mitfords, had an open invitation from one of his monied neighbours to take part in the disgusting aristocratic passion for blood sports. Huntin', fishin' and shootin' might not have lured others, but Clapton, Jagger, Bill Wyman, Jim Capaldi and a now short-haired Phil May were all rubbing shoulders with professional cricketers like Ian Botham and Mike Gatting.

Other companions in revelry might have included Elizabeth Taylor,

Formula One racer Jackie Stewart and Princess Grace of Monaco as a zest for the social whirl became so voracious that you'd hide rings under the eyes with the mirror sunglasses that became a standard party accoutrement from that period. Some still adored being in the limelight, seldom missing opportunities to be the focal point of eyes grateful to them for just existing. How would Ringo Starr have felt if polite clapping rather than a foot-stomping ovation had greeted him when he mounted his drum podium for just the finale of *The Last Waltz*, the Band's all-star concert farewell to 'the road' after sixteen years. At dazzling showbiz *soirées* where guests sipped poised cocktails like melted crayons, a murmur would reach a crescendo that Mick Jagger had arrived. This wasn't television or a picture in *Fabulous*. He was actually within, asserting his old power in abundance as the younger pop stars and their acolytes droned round him like a halo of flies.

Yet Mick would be derided by hippies as another bourgeois liberal with inert reactionary tendencies. Indeed, the bit about 'help me cope with this heavy load' from George Harrison's 'Give Me Love', and lines concerning the problems of running a country estate in Traffic's 'Memories of a Rock 'n' Rolla' might have prodded a raw nerve or two in Britain's dole queues. Yet surely it was no sin to make a fortune out of harmless entertainment, was it? Who could begrudge a lad from a back-street terrace or middle-class semi-detached a cosseted retirement in his mid-thirties? During the 1960s, he'd been treated like a pigeonhole in a self-service cafeteria. No more could it be taken for granted that he existed only to vend entertainment with a side-serving of cheap insight. The world wouldn't let him stroll unmolested in a public park so he'd had to buy one of his own. Unobserved, he'd stride forth on a clear, dew-sodden morning into the woods and pastures of his acres. At one with nature, all the intolerable adulation his life had contained, the Number Ones, the money down the drain, could be transformed to matters of small importance.

Once you'd seen too much of him but now John Lennon was sighted less often than the Loch Ness monster since he'd left England forever in 1971. McCartney had settled for a 'simple life' on a Sussex farm, but London's Little Venice was a haven for rich pop stars who preferred the city. You could enjoy the best of both by buying a spread in 'Hollywood-on-Thames', the areas round Windsor, Ascot and Henley, which threw together the most disparate of neighbours. Thespians such as Susan George would fill petrol tanks at the same garage as comedian Ernie Wise, and fete-opening 'personalities' like Rolf Harris, Freddie Starr or Vince Hill might be vaguely impressed when told that the guffawing drinkers in the next bar of the local pub were members of Deep Purple.

A regular at South Stoke's Perch and Pike, former Bonzo Dog drummer

'Legs' Larry Smith was a lesser light in what became known as the 'Henley Music Mafia' who played together either in the privacy of their own homes or on stages like those in Watlington's Carriers Arms or the Crown in Pishill, running through selections drawn largely from classic rock and 1960s beat. From these casual ramblings came more palpable liaisons. While house-hunting in the area, the Hollies' Tony Hicks stayed at Kenny Lynch's place where owner and lodger wrote songs that would be unveiled on *Romany*. There'd be a similar collusion between ex-Herman's Hermit Karl Green and Ten Years After organist Ric Lee.

Freeing themselves from the constraints of a hired studio, well-off musicians would order the construction of electronic dens, enabling them to potter about with sound and tape the wackiest demos. For some, every note of their public output could be hand-tooled in sophisticated private recording complexes, often technological steps ahead of London. Quadrophonic speakers and the latest transitorized toys would come and go, and instructions to engineers would be dotted with new jargon like 'pan-pots' (stereo channel potentiometers), 'EQ' and 'carbon faders'.

Most of the rock *nouveau riche* ensconced themselves in the oak-beamed gentility of hamlets buried in the woods surrounding a reach of the river where sheep nibbled on grassy old Saxon battlegrounds. Only the whoosh of an occasional Concorde from Heathrow miles away need remind you of the twentieth century. While Deep Purple's drummer might attend village bazaars in undisguised anonymity, an ex-Beatle dipping into the bran tub might be as profoundly disturbing as finding the Prince of Wales bowling for a pig. George Harrison seldom descended into Henley from Friar Park, the pile that would be as synonymous with his name as the Queen's with Windsor Castle (virtually next door to Jimmy Page). Ringo Starr dwelt in a mansion off Ascot's main thoroughfare to London; Jon Lord was squire of Hambledon; Rod Stewart lived over in Bray; Joe Brown in Skirmett; Alvin Lee in Goring, and Mick Ralphs (ex-Mott the Hoople) in Nettlebed.

Before they were able to lay any such foundations, tax laws might have liberated the gypsy in many a soul. While the Stones fled to France, Bee Gee Maurice Gibb chose the nearer Isle of Man, and Tony Sheridan applied for Irish nationality. A bothersome Inland Revenue demand led Roger Cook to migrate to Nashville to pen C & W Number Ones for artists like Crystal Gale and Don Williams. The land of opportunity also beckoned Dave Clark to spend a year in California – and Graham Nash much longer in Hawaii on discovering that mere pop stars in Britain were lionized as Artists in enthusiastic North America. Greeted by familiar faces in recording studios, many UK British beat musicians were now contemplating permanent moves to New York or Los Angeles. Dave Mason and Marmalade's Dean Ford and

Pat Fairlie were three that took the plunge; Pat eventually becoming landlord of the Scotland Yard, a pub frequented by other expatriate Britons of the Hollywood Raj.

If of sufficient means, others preferred to roam from hotel to hotel where switchboard or room service would relay flattery without friendship to one whose every action was worth a half-page in *The Sun* or *Los Angeles Times*. A mollycoddled but empty life led you to sometimes shun the sun and the 'beautiful people' to excitedly develop some flash of musical inspiration for the next album but, after strumming, twiddling or pounding a bit, the phone might ring. If not, dinner was getting cold or *M*A*S*H* just starting on TV. Maybe you'd have another go tomorrow. All the fragments of song would sound the same, infantile vibrations hanging in the air. Languor would set in and your mind would drift off again to the TV, the drinks cabinet, the refrigerator.

Knuckling down to another album would be further impeded by accepting more record dates that were earning legion – if frequently pseudonymous – credits on albums by old pals and contemporary celebrities. You'd use the famous-cast-of-thousands approach yourself but, beneath the back-slapping, a sense of simply going through the motions once more was evidenced by dispiriting slickness keeping pace with close-miked lethargy.

Your moderately successful moderate records would hover round the same worn-out formula melodies and buzz-words, but writer's blocks and ante-start agonies would not prevent more than a little off-hand breast-beating to intrude on vinyl output which, like the drip-rockers and John Lennon, tended to be more autobiographical now; one man's vision of his immediate world. Most blatant was George Harrison's liberty-taking with the Everly Brothers' 'Bye Bye Love' with revised lyrical digs at his wife and her lover, Eric Clapton.

Whether you had or hadn't lost the knack of writing hits, why shouldn't you indulge yourself with old favourites penned by other people? David Bowie, Bryan Ferry, Jonathan King, John Lennon and the Hollies all cut entire LPs of oldies, and there were singles of the same by the likes of Jim Capaldi, Zoot Money, the Troggs (an incredible 'Good Vibrations'), Colin Blunstone and Keith Richards – whose Rolling Stones were one of many 1970s acts to record songs with 'rock 'n' roll' in the title. Renewed interest in 1960s instrumentals put Bert Weedon abruptly at the top of the album lists in 1976 with *22 Golden Guitar Greats*.

'Works' – which also meant not having to come up with hit singles – were very much the order of the day as well. With *Tubular Bells* setting the standard in 1973, Allan Clarke and Colin Blunstone were among helpers on Alan Parsons Project's *I Robot*, and Dave Dee, several worlds from 'Xanadu', sang on *Few and Far Between* by Jean Musy, an intensely bearded Frenchman. Steve Winwood had a bigger say in the overblown *Go* by Japanese percussion virtuoso Stomu Yamash'ta.

Another alternative was to stop trying to prove yourself. Instead you could go on more holidays than the Duchess of York. What was escapism for most of the world could be where you lived. When in Paris, no waiter's eyebrows would rise if you ordered egg-and-chips to go with a minor Beaujolais in Montparnasse restaurants where only the likes of Dali, Fellini, Warhol, Hemingway and Bardot could afford to clatter cutlery on plate. Borabora in the Tahitian archipelago was so remote that it could only be reached by boat. Yet, on its beach, your lilo would be adjacent to that of, say, Charlton Heston or Raquel Welch. In common with dolphins you might have sighted there, you devoted your life to the pursuit of pleasure.

Who cared if Paul McCartney, still an international chart assailant, was accorded forty-two lines in *Who's Who* while you languished with the likes of Bill Haley and the McCoys in *Whatever Happened to . . .* 'the great rock and pop nostalgia book'?[174] As Paul was on nationally-televised chat-shows, so a 1960s has-been retold the old, old story on local radio, answering perfunctory enquiries about his latest record that the interviewer may or may not have heard. It'd be played but faded out to fit in the on-the-hour news.

Already the halcyon world-conquering 1960s seemed so far away. As your photo hadn't been in the music press for years, how strange – and sometimes amusing – it often was to be a nobody again. Billeting himself on his parents one summer, Joe Cocker had spent an evening in a Sheffield inn where he'd been stimulated sufficiently to sing with the incumbent pianist and drummer. Afterwards, he was offered a booking by a landlord unaware of the guest vocalist's global renown. In the same city, Frank White was wowing packed houses at a Friday night residency at the Pheasant with *de rigeur* strangled vocals and note-bending on a single-neck guitar rather than his fantastic Gibson.

Even more of the old haunts were no more; gone to warehouses, sports pavilions and multi-storey car parks. While a supermarket thrived on the site of Sheffield's Azena, the Esquire – now rechristened the Leadmill – still presented pop, and the Wilson Peck music equipment shop yet prospered, even if no longer the biggest ape in that particular jungle. The 2i's was now a trattoria, and Aldershot's Queen's Palais a radio rental. The sinking of an underground railway shaft had meant the final demolition of the Cavern in 1976, and alarm bells and sirens would execute a discordant threnody as the Rialto Ballroom crumbled in a haze of smoke and powdered plaster when the festering unrest in Liverpool's most depressed districts exploded during the humid July of 1981.

The Moody Blues had been lining up a tour – a sentimental journey – of Black Country R & B pubs in 1980. Albeit with modernized interiors, other familiar places still bore their original names such as the Elbow Room – though Wolverhampton's Blue Flame, an old Mod hangout, was now the Lafayette – and would be included on the Sex Pistols' 'secret tour' date sheet in 1977. For its earlier glory, the Golden Eagle was picked by Robert Plant for an unpublicized piece of market research for his new material. Its doors would be closed forever in 1984; the biker regulars bidding farewell by trashing the place.

Over in Hamburg, an erotic cinema was on the old site of the Star-Club which, now owned by the Rattles, had been relocated – as a discotheque with occasional 'live' shows – in the Grossneumarkt, further from the disreputable heart of Die Grosse Freiheit which, now under government licence, was not as open-minded about temptations of the flesh as it had been. Visiting 1960s veterans couldn't help but visualize certain people in some fixed attitude, doing what they did way back when – and, sure enough, there was Tony Sheridan at the new Star-Club in 1974, brushing aside the centuries since 1960 like matchsticks. For sale in the foyer was his new LP, *World's End*, produced by Klaus Voorman who had also returned to Germany. Both had continued to look up old mates from the past as Tony did Pete Best when both chanced to be in Los Angeles; Pete to speak about his Beatle days on TV.

With a happy marriage and two lovely daughters, he regarded himself as more fortunate than alcoholic Ringo who on another US talk programme had been the worse for booze. Since accidentally running over his chauffeur in 1970, Keith Moon had been afflicted with worsening black-outs through consuming up to four decanters of spirits within two hours of rising. Eric Clapton's heroin odyssey had caused a retreat from pop until his so-called 'comeback' concert in 1974, with famous cronies at London's Rainbow, formerly the Finsbury Park Astoria.

Addled by narcotics and music industry thuggery, Joe Cocker had gone home to mother again, spending a year under self-imposed house arrest, apart from excursions to the boozer. Parallels might be drawn between Joe's breakdown and other wandered souls like Chris Curtis, P.J. Proby, Peter Green, Syd Barrett and, after severing all direct links with pop to become a furniture salesman back in Leicester, Rick Grech, who was die at the age of forty-four of debilities not unrelated to the hard drugs that had been common currency when he was a 'superstar'.

Also prone to bouts of drug addiction, Graham Bond had been at a personal and professional low in 1974. Whether he fell or was overcome by a sudden urge to end it all, he finished under the wheels of a London tube train. As pitiful in its way had been the passing of Rory Storm in 1972 after an injudicious quantity of whisky washed down tablets prescribed for a chest complaint. A couple of the national tabloids that picked up the story carried a quote from Shane Fenton – now exhumed and back in the Top 10 as 'Alvin Stardust' – who compared his brother-in-law favourably with Rod Stewart.

Chewed upon and spat out by the Swinging Sixties too, the likes of Tommy Quickly, Wayne Fontana, Billy J. Kramer and Keith Richards were bobbing like corks on shoreless seas. Keeping the company only of those with the same destructive tastes, their consumption of tranquillizers, Scotch, cocaine – whatever the drug of choice – became so immoderate that tabloid journals would hint of sojourns in clinics to sweat out the blue devils. In the throes of paranoia, mounting business difficulties, vocational frustrations and personal desolations, they made no long-term plans. How could they?

When in Dave Berry's Cruisers, I once shared a hotel room with Wayne Fontana who, for all his bygone fame, was reaping the church mouse harvest of executive incompetence. He was also dejected by former colleagues distancing themselves such as Graham Gouldman with his curt telephone manner. Though the slightly rakish good looks of his 'Game Of Love' prime were still apparent, that great leveller alopaecia had attacked Wayne's scalp as it had his brothers before him. Despite an outward cheerfulness, there was definitely something sad about the boy. Anxiously looking homeward to his wife and cockatoos, he seemed to kill a lot of time in the company of Messrs Pimms and Johnny Walker.

Wayne and Billy J. had joined many old mates on 'British Invasion' revival tours of North America in the mid-1970s that also reunited Herman with his Hermits and made the Searchers give 'em a fifteen-minute work-out of 'Southern Man' to show that, if they'd never worn headbands or played Woodstock, they were still with-it. Most of the participants then fell back on the civic halls and social clubs that had become their lot since the bubble burst.

Though Holland was still his, Dave Berry had made his cabaret debut in Newcastle. Yet he was resilient. Clothed in black as always, he was still making his suspensory Grand Entrance, and all the essential elements remained intact – the hand ballets, the microphone *glissandos*, the kismet supercool. Time would unwind, and he'd appear as lean, saturnine and outrageous as he'd been in 1964. He'd be rebooked before he'd even left the building. Afterwards there might be an occurrence like the one reported in the *NME* in 1978 when a starstruck girl asked Dave in all seriousness why he'd left Roxy Music. That he was still thought worthy of the odd mention in the music press put him above other 1960s stars in the same boat, and there was a sense of marking time on the understanding that, sooner or later, another song as good as 'The Crying Game' would come his way.

Ten years after the frenzy of your first hit, there were no more screams but an unsettling hush after the kind of facetious build-up that an uninterested old group would hear over and over again these days: 'Without further ado, ladies and gentlemen, I'd like to bring on a bunch of grrrrrreat entertainers I know you're all going to enjoy – well, my great aunt was very fond of them . . .' In a vocation founded on short-lived novelty, running through your best-loved songs for the people who loved them – and you – best of all in some back-of-beyond palais might not have been such a bad place to end up. If you had a big enough backlog, you'd do some of your hits as a medley so none could complain that you hadn't played their favourite.

You were submerged in a netherworld where current chart status had no meaning. It was the same endless-highway dilemma as that faced by rock 'n' roller or black bluesman of a pre-Beatle epoch for whom singing or playing an instrument was their only saleable trade. The road was obscure and quiet; a humdrum, dusty road that did not look as if it led anywhere. Yet you could be bought for more than you'd ever earned in the 1960s – for smartly-dressed audiences rotten with money, who'd downed a skinful of pricey liquor and guzzled their supper by showtime.

On the same bill as vile comedians and corny variety acts, you'd become the epitome of the financially-secure Adam Faith's assertion that 'the worst thing in the world is to be an ex-pop singer doing the clubs'. You'd cut corners with a second-rate *one* guitar-bass-drums unit who couldn't reproduce the original arrangement and sometimes insisted on its own spot in the act – but you couldn't afford better any more.

Every year you seemed a little shabbier, others a little less respectful. Stray newspaper paragraphs might mention litigation against venues for breach of contract or 'loss of reputation' after the cancellation of a widely advertised show at short notice. After a four-day hearing, Dave Dee won £27,181 damages from Blazer's in Windsor. 'Few of the Sixties bands made any money because they never took care of business,' he told the *Sun*, 'Most of them who are still working today are not wealthy people. It was time I stood up to be counted.'[175] The Troggs' new guitarist, Richard Moore, was stabbed at Farnborough Technical College, and a package containing Screaming Lord Sutch and Cliff Bennett, stranded in Spain through a promoter's inefficiency, was rescued by Ronnie Knight, a businessman sought by Scotland Yard to help with their enquiries.

Gone were the days of open-handed conviviality round a manager's desk. When challenged with, say, a tax bill that had amassed since 1965, you began to take an intense and unwelcome interest in his handling of affairs. Storm clouds of legal mumbo-jumbo gathered in tandem with your new willingness to credit alarmist tales about his transgressions in the 1960s when contracts could be mapped out on a serviette over lunch, as Billy J. Kramer's had been with Brian Epstein. It might transpire that your manager is not a gentleman – but perhaps he never had been in the first place. You wriggle from his clutches, and the mazy balance sheets and blizzards of writs subside into complicated but fixed channels whereby assorted incoming monies are divided as agreed and sent to the frequently disgruntled parties.

After all that you either try to take care of yourself or start looking for a new minder, an enterprise as tricky as looking for a new girlfriend. Gradually you get more embodied in cash-flow problems, talking more and more about the lack of work. It's nothing very tangible, just a steady gnawing away with little peaks and troughs. You get a week supporting Freddie 'Parrot Face' Davies in a new club just opened on the Isle of Wight, but a venue where you'd always gone down well changes its policy and you don't belong any more. Things would get so bad that it seems fanciful to look to future victories – and, for some, the worst is yet to come – but from this, British beat's darkest hour, the slow pageant of sunrise would soon begin.

25 THE CHANGELESS AND
THE CHANGED

On any Tuesday throughout 1984, you could have seen the Pretty Things for 50p in the functions room of a Little Venice hostelry. Even more of a bargain was Wednesday nights in the Station Tavern along Latimer Road with the Jim McCarty-Top Topham Blues Band. Fifty miles away, the Nashville Teens rocked out every few weeks for the bikers at High Wycombe's Nag's Head, and Trevor Burton who quit the Move in 1968 after 'Blackberry Way', their only Number One, had returned ultimately to his Brumbeat womb to front a band once a week in a Harborne tavern.

Finding yourself at the same venues time and time again, you had at least the opportunity to form genuine friendships with managers, staff and patrons, who now understood how ordinary – even boring – you were. Nevertheless, both you and the doting members of your fan club – if you still had one – would be proud, even boastful, about how well you still went down after all this time.

Two Merseybeats' devotees drove almost two hundred miles from east Kent to Reading's Top Rank suite where, between games of bingo, the group laid on a non-stop intermission hour that included a medley of hits by the Searchers, Billy J. *et al*, Beatles numbers and, of course, their own cache of lovelorn smashes – 'I Think of You', 'Wishin' and Hopin' and so forth. As a handful of aging ravers bopped round their handbags, the set caught fire during 'Sorrow' and the encore – of 'Hi Ho Silver Lining' – though while its last chord yet resounded, the legs-eleven patter recommenced.

In a Dutch conference centre, I'd glowed with patriotic pride when the Fortunes' 'Let It Be Me' filled the dance area with smoochers. What was happening? This was the Fortunes, damn it, who'd made Cliff Richard sound like Zappa jamming with Hendrix during a mid-1960s Top 20 sortie that had excited no positive response from me. Yet here I was, tapping my feet to 'Here It Comes Again', 'This Golden Ring' and everything else I'd despised – probably because it made more rock 'n' roll sense without the session orchestra that had soaked through the records.

Still, at least the Fortunes had had hits. In 1988, Mike Sheridan celebrated thirty years without any, though he'd become a Birmingham institution to the degree that the Applejacks, after reforming two years earlier, had been quite amenable to backing him. Pondering his fate as a big fish in a small pond, he had 'seen a lot of changes over the years; the most noticeable being the decline in venues'.[176]

Like Mike and the Applejacks, the Rockin' Berries had found more time for impersonations and knockabout clowning within the staple diet of the stuff they'd always played. Stuck forever on the nostalgia circuit now, they 'undoubtedly stole the show'[177] at an under-forties weekend at a Hopton-on-Sea holiday camp in 1987.

Further from his roots, Carl Wayne had entertained at a Brighton Dome summer season in 1976. He'd preceded Essex pianist Mrs Mills whose beefy mitts had pounded out 'Bill Bailey', 'When You're Smiling' and like singalongs. To a backwash of the house band and Pisces, a winsome boy-girl harmony quartet that I disliked intensely, Carl burbled mush of the 'Help Me Make It Through the Night' calling. As the grannies clapped along to his 'Y Viva Espana', I fought a temptation to barrack for 'Night of Fear' and 'I Can Hear the Grass Grow'.

Of the same vintage as Carl and his Vikings were the Dominettes who'd become the Ugly's. The only constant Ugly, singer Steve Gibbons, drew his first Steve Gibbons Band from ex-members of the Move – including Trevor Burton – Tea-and-Symphony and the Idle Race. Interpreting hard rock with a feel gentler than that of Black Sabbath, they ticked off a British hit in 1977 with Chuck Berry's 'Tulane' – and, if that sort of thing matters to them, then the Steve Gibbons Band, a 1960s beat group beneath it all, can die easy.

Six years after being booed at the Rolling Stones' Hyde Park relaunch, Chris Spedding's time had come, too, when he was dragged into the Top 20 with 'Motorbikin'' – all guitar tremelo, snarling carburettors and a sullen lout 'too fast to live/too young to die'. Helping Chris look the part was his resentment at foregoing a rumunerative studio date for a *Top of the Pops* spot to plug what was to be his only hit.

This paradise had nearly been the Citizens' – who had been little more than a name even in their native Sheffield. As resplendently whiskered Bitter Suite, however, they try-tried again, and always there was a stint on *Radio One Club*, or some other small incentive to carry on. Their steadfastness seemed rewarded when 'Goodbye America', via publicity stunts in stars-and-stripes costumes, charted in Portugal and Holland – though it was hampered in Britain by a BBC technicians' strike.

After singing in another Yorkshire outfit of the 1960s, Mickey's Monkeys, John Parr had come up through the ranks of Bitter Suite to go solo. As such, he was an icon of young America for a while. Yet he could walk without hindrance through a Rotherham department store both before and after 'St Elmo's Fire' leapt into the UK Top 10 in 1985.

A further latecomer, Joe Fagin – once Joe Feegan of the Strangers, active during the Liverpool era – Made It in 1984 when 'That's Livin' Alright' from ITV's *Auf Weidersehen Pet* series reached Number Three – though a 1989 Merseybeat revival show in the Grafton Rooms, scene of many a rough night in the early days, wasn't the time or place for Joe to parade his marvellous achievement. Instead, he gave 'em a gripping 'Stand By Me' with Faron's Flamingos while Faron himself got his breath back.

A much-changed Marmalade had come in from the cold as a quartet. Most conspicuous onstage under this regime was the gifted Sandy Newman, guitarist and lead vocalist, who'd cut his teeth at the Picasso with the Chris McClure Section while second guitarist, Charlie Smith, had been one of the Dream Police, another Glasgow combo, that also contained future Average White and Sensational Alex Harvey Bandsmen. The new Marmalade scored straightaway with 1976's 'Falling Apart at the Seams' at Number Nine, but impressions of a continuing chart renaissance were not corroborated as subsequent 45s each bit the dust.

After accumulating considerable goodwill in cabaret where proficient comedy always commands high fees, the Barron-Knights bounced back into the charts too with 1977's 'Live In Trouble' followed by 'A Taste of Aggro'. Further evidence of the power of persistence came with a best-selling LP, *Night Gallery*, and a TV series.

A Kinks Komeback would be pulled off when the abrupt rise of *Low Budget* into the US album list in 1979 ended years in the middle league of the 'adult-orientated rock' hierarchy. That year, the Searchers also proved to be more than the has-beens once imagined. Not as novel as it seemed was a *Melody Maker* review of an engagement at Rhydyfelen Non-Political Club – because the Searchers had just been signed to the hip Sire label. This venture was well-received critically, and a 45 from one of the two albums had a close shave with the Top 50. Yet backstage at London's Nashville Rooms, some dingbat asked Mike Pender how the new boy was settling in, meaning not Billy Adamson, drummer since 1967, but Frank Allen, a Searcher since 1964.

The Tremblers was the means whereby Peter Noone also attempted to re-enter pop on a contemporary footing. The content of an LP, *Twice Nightly*, was reflected in interviews during which Noone – looking more like Brian Jones than Herman – professed a liking for New Wave acts such as the Pretenders and Elvis Costello, and inserted a few un-Herman-like swear words. However, Noone-Herman encountered the same difficulties as DBMT, LA, the Tremeloes, the Searchers and everyone else who'd tried – few were able to disconnect him from his previous incarnation.

Other 1960s artists past their sell-by date still made new records, but it made more sense to plug the timeless chartbusters while leaving what might be an annual new single – recorded almost for form's sake – to fend for itself.

Some almost talked rather than sang the greatest hits now, like venerable luvvie actors, over arrangements that had grown coarser over the years. Where there had once been baroque wistfulness, a wah-wah guitar now squittered and a synthesizer rolled like treacle, but never enough to mar the good old good ones played in the good old way with all the mistakes – deliberate or otherwise – that only old pros could make. What would not be pardoned, however, was any fracturing, perhaps with a solitary word – like Tony Crane singing 'stink' instead of 'think' on the last line of 'I Think of You' – of the emotive intent of the most nostalgic songs ever recorded.

Many 1960s classics had long been available on budget labels. The strongest fiscal opportunity of all had been in leasing the rights to a firm like K-Tel with its saturation TV commercials that might perk up sales from tens of thousands to a quarter of a million a year. As well as triumphs of album repackaging by the likes of the Who, the Moody Blues, the Dave Clark Five and the Hollies, a 1976 re-release of Vince Taylor's 'Brand New Cadillac' nearly made the Top 50, but all these were nothing to the chart-swamping aftermath following EMI's repromotion of all twenty Beatles singles on the same spring day in 1976. In Britain alone, seven breached the Top 40, causing a *Time* correspondent to enquire rhetorically, 'Has a successor to the Beatles finally been found? Not at all – it is the Beatles themselves.'[178]

At the Parisian grave of the Doors' Jim Morrison, a mourner reasoned that these and later seasons of revivals were because 'the sixties music was much better than stuff now'.[179] The decade had already been lamented in nice-little-band Barclay James Harvest's 'Titles' 45 which span in specific sad-eyed homage to the Beatles, seated at the table head of the 1960s Valhalla. Not a week would go by without some twerp in the media asking when they were going to reform. It had been only George and Ringo in *The Concerts for Bangladesh* but still headlines had shrieked 'Beatlemania Sweeps a City!'[180] and even 'The Beatles Are Back!'[181] However, that all four were losing their grip one way or another wasn't the soundest foundation for a second coming.

Yet attempts at 1970s rebirths on vinyl and stage had been made by the Animals, *a* Big Three, the Easybeats, the Spencer Davis Group, Dave Dee, Dozy, Beaky, *a* Mick and Tich, the Temperence Seven, the Tornadoes and the Walker Brothers. Formed by Paul Jones and Tom McGuinness in 1979, the Blues Band would be as near as you'd get to Manfred Mann, leaning as heavily as they did on the Mann repertoire just as the Jim McCarty-Top Topham Blues Band did on that of the Yardbirds.

The Downliners Sect were back as well after seeing for themselves the 'street level' acclaim granted to pub-rockers like Kilburn and the High Roads, Dr Feelgood and Ace (with Paul Carrack, long after hanging up his drumsticks with the Saville Row Rhythm Unit). What with Johnny Kidd's

Pirates and even the lowly Rockin' Vickers trying again, surely there was a place in the nicotine-clouded pub-rock sun for the Sect too? Indeed there was, and the Sect came belligerently alive when the lights hit them. The crowd responded by sending reissues of the old LPs high up independent charts throughout Europe.

A regrouping of the Small Faces seemed a natural regression too as both the Faces and Humble Pie were no more. The only fly-in-the-ointment was Ronnie Lane, content with his new outfit, Slim Chance. A replacement was enlisted, however, in time for a Small Faces UK tour which, to symbolize the desired revitalization, began in Sheffield, scene of their first booking in 1964.

Nevertheless, despite fullish houses whenever they appeared, precious few 1960s acts became challengers again as poor sales of 'comeback' records against healthy returns for reissues demonstrated that fans, old and new, wanted the sounds of yesteryear. While 'House of the Rising Sun' and 'Itchycoo Park' span on Radio One's *All Our Yesterplays*, Mr and Mrs Average became Swinging Sixties teenagers again, lovestruck and irresponsible.

Not forestalling tumbles into the bargain bin either were *in extremis* re-recordings of old hits by the Nashville Teens, Downliners Sect, Mike Smith, Denny Laine, Brian Poole, the Tornadoes, Colin Blunstone, Dave Berry, the Troggs, Alan Price, the Hollies and Ringo Starr. Some resulted from legal problems over straight re-releases and, as such, copied the first versions with cheese-paring precision as Blunstone would on a *third* 'She's Not There' – for a British Telecom ITV commercial. If some indefinable something was missing – the margin of error – it wasn't obvious, and dare I say that I prefer the Downliners Sect's revival of 'Glendora' to the 1966 original?

The Hollies revamp of 'Just One Look', however, didn't appeal at all. It was all a bit too lush – especially when the snotty synthesizer came in. Revamps like this tended to be rather too premeditated modern reconstructions. 'Art' intruded upon guts and left a peculiar afterglow – especially if the dusty old 45 had emotional significance. Too often, prevailing fads were imposed – say, a disco jitter or punk thrash – or, lending no drive or transcendental edge, the latest studio gimmick: drum machine time-keeping of Japanese water-torture exactitude and the squeaky-clean 'funky' neatness of flatulent clavinet and the 'twanging plank' bass that plagued pop throughout the 1980s.

Pop movies harked much more convincingly back to the past than the remakes. Set in 1959–60, *That'll Be the Day* had starred David Essex and Ringo Starr. Bit-parts had been given to Keith Moon, Graham Bond and Vivian Stanshall – and Billy Fury, about to undergo a second heart operation, was a touching instance of type-casting as, in silver jacket and hair stiff with lacquer, he sang with Bickerstaffe Happy Holiday Camp rock 'n' roll combo,

Stormy Tempest and the Typhoons, in a bowdlerization in more than name of Rory Storm and the Hurricanes.

In the sequel, *Stardust*, the David Essex character became a mid-1960s pop star with Adam Faith taking over from Ringo as his confidant because Starr had felt that his circumstances in the role would condone a story-line too close for comfort to that of the Beatles.

The Who were an almost unseen presence in *Quadrophenia*, the Mod retrospective movie, and right in yer face for *The Kids Are Alright*, 1979's celluloid portrait of them with commentary from many of their 1960s peers.

One of Pete Townshend's broken guitars had been among the dearest lots at perhaps the very first pop memorabilia auction, held in New York in 1970. Soon olde-tyme pop would be so beyond a joke that, rather than throw such an artefact onto a bonfire, it'd be guarded like a splinter from the True Cross. Under the hammer at Sotheby's in 1983 would be a toilet removed from a house where a Beatle had once lived. This was displayed and sold as solemnly as if it had been a Duchamp 'ready-made'.

Well before this and the publication in 1979 of the first edition of *Record Collector*, the growth of specialist 'fanzines' like *Zabadak!* – 'the magazine about Dave Dee, Dozy, Beaky, Mick and Tich' – *Yardbirds World*, *Trogg Times*, and *Carousel*, about the Hollies, encouraged hearts to pound in anticipation as collectors squeezed between hags blocking access to a pile of scratched 45s on a white elephant stall.

I went through that phase myself in the early 1970s when at college. In the bar, I'd yell 'N4!' whenever anyone approached the jukebox. N4, see, was the selection number of 'Three Rooms and Running Water', Cliff Bennett and the Rebel Rousers' unwarranted flop from 1965. Somehow escaping purging by the rep for seven years, it was the sole oasis in the vinyl desert of that particular nickelodeon. My unorthodox vision was shared and, with other disenchanted renegades, my nature dictated the scouring of the bazaars and second-hand emporiums of Reading and neighbouring towns for artefacts from earlier musical eras.

Once I voyaged to the end of the world to Let It Rock, a vintage record shop – one of London's first – in Chelsea. From less manifest sources came the Fabulous Fleerekkers EP, 'Chaquita' by the Dave Clarke Five, *The Zombies Begin Here*, *sans* cover, and the sheet music to 'Still I'm Sad' with the Yardbirds' teeth blacked-in. The Pretty Things' 'Rosalyn' turned up for 2p at a Methodist fete, and I nearly had kittens when the rarest Kinks track, the B-side, 'You Do Something To Me', was uncovered a week later in a Pangbourne Oxfam shop.

Glorious days! What could recapture the illicit bliss of cutting lectures, and hightailing in Tim Fagan's VW Beetle to Basingstoke, Camberley, Maidenhead, Crowthorne or Aldershot. Mecca, however, was Swindon where every other shop, it seemed, bore the sign 'junk', or 'bric-à-brac'. The ghastly present with its Elton Johns, ELPs and *Eric Clapton at the Rainbow* was kept at arm's length as a handful of young people from all walks of life joined together with a sense of purpose that time would never erase! My first social invitation to my future wife was to a jumble sale to look for records.

In Tim's VW, tall stories were told about lost icons of adolescence. You can hear Phil May drop his maraccas at the end of 'Rosalyn'. My aunt's friend's daughter knows somebody whose sister slept with Wayne Fontana. On the French picture sleeve of 'Tell Me When', you can see one of Megan Davies' nipples. Honestly. When challenged for proof of a rare disc allegedly owned, an adequate response was to snarl that nobody gets to *look* at it, let alone *hear it*.

If an expedition wasn't that rewarding, there might follow an enthralling evening of B-sides of the calibre of 'I Want You' by the Troggs, 'He's a Raver' from Dave Dee and Co., Dave Berry's 'Don't Gimme No Lip, Child' and the Merseybeats' 'Really Mystified' to hum on the way home. On other occasions, there'd be experimental deceleration of singles to 33 rpm whereby the Small Faces would sound just like Howlin' Wolf. Further education certainly broadens your outlook.

During this idyll, record sessions would evolve into attempts at reproducing the outmoded sounds on guitar, voice and piano. At some point during the fun and games, we mulled over suitable names for a group that could perform these numbers, and someone jokingly suggested 'Billy and the Conquerors'. The story of this astonishing group must wait until my autobiography, but there were other better-known outfits of like motivation. The exhilaration of the impromptu was also prized infinitely more than supersideman-esque technical accuracy by such outfits like Duke Duke and the Dukes, fronted by a balding, bespectacled Bristol bus conductor, and the Count Bishops who were like a 1964 R & B combo that had been in suspended animation for ten years. Luton's Stargazers had been in it for twenty. Managed by 'Let It Rock' proprietor Malcolm McLaren, the Sex Pistols' exploratory stumblings in late 1975 included a majority of 1960s beat classics and obscurities that included 'Whatcha Gonna Do About It', 'He's a Raver', 'Substitute' and 'Don't Gimme No Lip, Child', while roly-poly Frenchman Little Bob Story's best-remembered release was a revival in 1977 of the Animals' 'I'm Crying'.

There were also the first stirrings of a Medway towns group scene as self-contained in its quieter way as Merseybeat. Over it presided the Milkshakes, Thee (*sic*) Mighty Caesars, Thee Headcoats (with guest singer Don Craine) and others of the same retrogressive bent. Indeed, the Milkshakes' twenty-track mono LP would contain nothing but 'The Hippy Hippy Shake', 'Sweet Little Sixteen', 'Money', 'Carol', 'Boys', 'Some Other Guy' and all the rest of them. The sleeve notes would spin a likely tale of how 'our fathers recorded this for a large record company in the sixties, but it was regarded as too primitive at that time. We wanted the record released as a kind of tribute to their memory.'

You wouldn't be sure either how you were meant to take Neasden's Mari Wilson and the Imaginations. Fun while they lasted, they'd come on like a sort of back-dated white soul revue with strong 1960s Mod overtones, and a set of genre originals such as 'Beat the Beat' (the debut 45), '(Beware) Boyfriend' and the show-stopping 'Rave!'

Surprisingly, the *NME* was tacitly supportive of such radical grassroots backsliding in its journalists' lampooning of 'dinosaur bands' as either over-the-hill like Crosby, Stills and Nash, or wholesomely Americanized like Fleetwood Mac who were as far from the rough-and-ready blues band they once were as Steve Winwood would be from even Traffic with his 1982 solo album on which more electronic gadgets and US sound laboratories would receive 'special thanks' on its inner sleeve than people.

Billy and the Conquerors, the Count Bishops, Duke Duke, the Sex Pistols, the Milkshakes, Mari Wilson — all were a reaction against this distancing of the humble beat group from its teenage audience. Why pay through the nose to see some remote supergroup forever in America but deigning to top the bill at the Reading Festival when in the jovial surroundings of licensed premises, there was no unending *diddle-iddle-iddling* or lyrics that made you embarrassed to be alive, but an outfit playing with more thought for the customers than any old millionaire having a fit of pique amid the backstage disarray at Washington Stadium, and keeping everyone waiting? With ex-Beatle albums joining ex-Beatle singles on British deletion racks, who cared if they never reformed?

26 HERE IT COMES AGAIN

A moth-eaten old Mod had a daughter at art college who kept talking about the Sex Pistols. Punk was a fierce time and no mistake. Every week threw up another hot act ringing some changes. Most of them were just like the Sex Pistols: guitars thrashed at speed to machine-gun drumming behind a ranting johnny-one-note who'd given himself a self-reviling name like Kenny Dreadful: onetwothreefour dah dah dah dah dah-dah DAH! We mean it, maaaaaan! Superficially rousing but lacking the musical strength of both the 1960s beat boom and psychedelia, punk was always doomed to be ineffectual.

Yet, as the Beatles had divided the previous decade, 1970s pop tends to be dated either pre- or post-Sex Pistols. Though the Pistols dismissed the Beatles as 'scouse gits' and would fire their Glen Matlock for liking them, there was plenty of kowtowing to 1960s groups within the new regime, most blatantly in respective revivals of 'Help!', 'Glad All Over', 'This Strange Effect', 'We Love You', 'Shakin' All Over', Lord Sutch's 'She's Fallen In Love With the Monster Man', 'You're a Better Man Than I' and 'Pretty Face' by the Damned – who'd felt honoured one evening to bear Sutch's coffin on stage – The Rezillos, The Spectres, Cock Sparrer, Generation X, the Revillos, Sham 69 and Jean-Jacques Burnel of the Stranglers, whose splinter group, the Purple Helmets, would play only 1960s stuff.

The old school were not in agreement about punk. Cliff Richard 'didn't like it at all. None of them could play, and hardly any of them could sing'[182] while Reg Presley 'loved it. I saw it as energy, but I didn't see any melody. Just afterwards, you got the melody back with the energy. That was a good time, was that.'[183] When punk came in, there was Andy Somers from Zoot Money's Big Roll Band on guitar with the Police, and Chris Spedding supervising the Pistols' first demos, and dusting off 'Motorbikin'' when backed by the Damned at 1976's Punk Rock Festival in the 100 Club when he was the only oldie allowed on the bill. Dave Berry had rated too. As special guest of Adam and the Ants at the Strand Lyceum, the Berry experience was as new and disquieting for most punks as it had been for their Swinging Sixties forerunners.

As punk sold music papers in the late 1970s, interviews with less esteemed old timers would be slotted well towards the back just before the box adverts for disco equipment. Polished, pleasant and infrequent, their albums were never expected to be astounding. As they had aged, so had the topics tackled by them or their wordsmiths. In a realistic, conversational flow, marital strife, mortality and the passing time were filtered through clever arrangements and technological innovations that often camouflaged nondescript songs in need of editing.

It's rather a sweeping generalization, but as playing and production got better, standards of composition fell in favour of the blinded-by-science sound at any given interval. Somehow, most of it was a bit too pat, too dovetailed, too American – and it was no longer so easy for new records by old icons to be approved without comment by record labels' quality controllers, voracious as always for new faces to exploit and discard for a fickle public. In 1977, Warner Brothers signed the Sex Pistols and, shockingly, erasured Van Morrison from its books for not being sufficiently 'current'.

Now that more had to be done than just mailing review copies of your latest LP to the music press, it helped if you shaved off your scrappy Woodstock beard and undertook a media itinerary that would include appearances on, say, BBC 2's 'progressive' showcase, *The Old Grey Whistle Test*, or NBC's *Saturday Night Live* in New York. If you weren't an actor, the video now needed to go with the single wouldn't project you in a dramatic situation but adhere to a straightforward synchronization of a musical performance.

You'd never be off tabloid pop pages with quotable jocularities, and – if you weren't in it – withering attacks on the latest Top 20 in a manner reminiscent of a middle-aged square in the 1960s going on about the Stones – or me today in full philistine flood about rap, or Joe Brown on modern pop in general. 'It bores me,' he told a periodical called *Mature Times*, 'It doesn't seem to sustain itself.'[184]

No longer ploughing energy into keeping out of the public gaze, there Steve Winwood was in autumn 1987, flogging 'Valerie' which, when first issued as a UK single five year earlier, had stopped short of the Top 50. Miming on *Top of the Pops*, *Wogan* and the new pop series, *The Roxy*, he seemed at an endearing loss when the record stopped but, with his schoolboy grin and freckles, he held his own amid Me-generation acts such as the Christians and Level 42. 'Virtually forgotten by the rock world for a decade'[185] began the maximum-impact announcement on BBC breakfast TV. In the subsequent chat from one of his homes, Steve – whose discs shot to triple-platinum Number One in the States – played up to the prologue with a quip about 'the autumn of my career', sipping tea nonchalantly from fine porcelain on a George III silver tray.

Artists of his means cropped up more often in high society gossip columns than *Melody Maker* now. Winwood and a 'young Nashville socialite' were spotted at a £100-a-head charity party, keeping a wide berth of the first Mrs Winwood who posed for a piquant *Daily Express* photograph with Patti Boyd, former spouse of both George Harrison and Eric Clapton, and – looking rather down-in-the-mouth – philandering Bill Wyman's ex-girlfriend. Viscount Linley and two ex-Beatles were among the vetted guests at Elton John's lavish birthday party in a London night club, but the Queen's nephew was not to hear George Harrison's after-dinner laudation to Eric Clapton when Elton, Bill, Ringo, Phil Collins – all the usual shower – gathered at the Savoy Hotel to celebrate Slowhand-God's first quarter-century as a professional guitarist.

Eric's reassuringly more ordinary albums still shift millions, bought out of habit by the kind of consumer for whom information that a preferred performer's latest disc is just like the one before is praise indeed. Eric also forged an unofficial second career with psychiatrist-couch discourses to his eulogists about his life, his soul, his torment. Always, he bitched about the Yardbirds.

A group called the Yardbirds took the Marquee stage on 22 July 1983 as part of the club's anniversary celebrations. As Keith Relf had been killed by electrocution in 1976, and neither Clapton, Jeff Beck or Jimmy Page could be persuaded to pitch in too, Jim McCarty, Paul Samwell-Smith and rhythm guitarist Chris Dreja went the distance with substitutes. After a second show in Surbiton, this Yardbirds recorded an LP which reached Number Forty-Five in the US list under the guise of a Box of Frogs with contributions from the late Rory Gallagher and Beck, who was among spectators during the ongoing residency of McCarty's blues band – minus Anthony 'Top' Topham by 1992 – at the Latimer Road pub.

Jeff would be thinking aloud about either a finger-style acoustic album, one with a big band or finally, a Gene Vincent and the Blue Caps tribute that would recall his apprenticeship under Cal Danger and Kerry Rapid. Meanwhile, Led Zeppelin had packed it in after John Bonham's over-imbibing of vodka finished him off in 1980. Like the Searchers with 'Southern Man', Led Zeppelin had showed how hip they were by visiting a London punk club to check out the Damned before it was too late. It wouldn't be that long before the Damned were smooth enough to score their biggest hit with 'Eloise', lovingly copied from Barry Ryan's violin-drenched 1968 original.

Punk was succeeded by a hyped fad for 'power-pop' like the 'Thamesbeat' of the Pleasers, who shook their moptops, went 'ooo' and spoilt it by reviving the Who's 'The Kids Are Alright' rather than 'Love Me Do' for their first single. Nevertheless, at the *Beatlefests* that were now becoming annual fixtures in cities throughout the world, other groups cloned the Beatles more precisely, right down to big-nosed sticksmen, moon-faced bass players and handles like Cavern, Abbey Road and, mild sensations of *Merseybeatle '90* at Liverpool's Adelphi Hotel, the Soviet Union's own Beatles Club. From the *Beatlemania* musical in London's West End, the Bootleg Beatles, the most accurate imitators of all, were formed from members of the cast.

Similar events that paid homage to other 1960s groups drew far smaller crowds. Richard MacKay lost his shirt when only around fifty devotees turned up in the cavernous Oxford hall he'd booked for the first ever Yardbirds convention. Richard may be comforted to know that in 1986 only a dozen or so showed up when Herman Hamerpagt, a Dutch accountant, organized a fan get-together in London on behalf of the Dave Clark Five, even though Dave's musical, *Time* – starring Cliff Richard and Sir Laurence Olivier, and commended mostly for its spectacular visual effects – had just opened in the West End.

Though he recorded a medley of his Dave Clark Five smashes in 1985 – 'as an exercise to learn new recording technology' – it took until 1990 for Mike Smith to truly break cover with *It's Only Rock 'n' Roll*, a proficient if unambitious first solo LP. Other beat group musicians had also indulged individual post-punk recording whims, beginning with Paul Jones' extraordinary version of the Sex Pistols' 'Pretty Vacant' and Gary Brooker's near-hit with 'Say It Ain't So, Joe' – produced by George Martin. In 1982, Hank Marvin managed a Top 50 entry with 'Don't Talk', meant initially for Cliff. Carl Wayne had some airplay but no chart action with 'Deeper Than Love', its B-side penned by producer Jeff Lynne. Billy J. Kramer was still functioning as a recording artiste too with the finger-snapping 'Rock It', the first of two singles in 1982.

Paradoxically, Bill Wyman's long-promised resignation from the Rolling Stones appeared less inevitable when that year's witty 'Si Si Je Suis Un Rock Star' was the highest hit parade strike for any solo Stone. Using the group's mobile studio, Wyman also searched Britain for deserving unknown bands via Ambition Ideas Motivation and Success (AIMS), a project that fizzled out when Pernod withdrew its financial support. Yet this and other of Bill's Good Works were less intriguing to a nosy world than his courtship of and troubled marriage to a teenager, and his 1990 no-stone unturned autobiography.

Meanwhile, the Stones *in toto* carried on with much the same sort of music they'd always played. On the boards, though the girls gasped rather than screamed when he took off his shirt, Mick was as poutingly athletic as ever and the group still rode 'em on down with sets in which ambles down memory lane were laced with more recent smashes like 'Start Me Up', a 1986 revival of 'Harlem Shuffle' and 1994's 'Love Is Strong'.

Some other outfits from the 1960s were plugging away undismayed with new(ish) discs as well. The Tremeloes' 'Words' was deemed worthy of a video during a chart match lost against a version by an F.R. David, but the Hollies could only be the sole competitors with 1981's 'Holliedaze' retrospective medley at Number Twenty-Eight, thirty places higher than the previous year's 'Soldier's Song', in the then-popular 'historical' style absorbed by Adam and the Ants.

Billy Fury's 'Devil or Angel' of 1982 would stick at Number Fifty-eight too. Within a year, as he might have wished it, he passed away with a single in the UK charts – 'Forget Him' – though he was denied a scheduled returned hero's tour of Britain or the completion of an album, *The Only One*. His fans' sorrow was either exorcized or exacerbated by a special edition of *Unforgettable*, Channel Four's nostalgia series.

On a world scale, Billy's heart attack was overshadowed by the slaying of another of British beat's Grand Old Men two years earlier in a travesty of legitimate admiration by a 'fan' who was nuts about him. 'Are you John Lennon?' asked a cop in the squad car in which the victim was rushed to a New York hospital. 'Yeah,' choked John. Then he died.

'John who?' Pete Best, shaving in the bathroom, had spluttered when his wife had shouted the news up the stairs on that creepy December morning. On the stop-starting drive to work, Pete saw images of his former colleague on TV sets in electrical goods shops. As Elvis had demonstrated in 1977, a death in pop could still revive a flagging chart career, and, before they'd even wiped away the tears, record company moguls wondered what Beatles/ Lennon tracks they'd be entitled to rush-release if John didn't recover from being dead. Ghoulish Beatlemania would give him a hat-trick of UK chart-toppers within a month of his cremation, and, for the first time since *Two Virgins*, his first album with Yoko Ono, Lennon's bum made the cover of *Rolling Stone*. Michael d'Abo played him in the Royal Court Production, *No One Was Saved*, and the Downliners Sect's 'A Light Went Out in New York' in 1992 was one of the more poignant tributes, certainly knocking the hastier likes of George Harrison's 'All Those Years Ago' into a cocked hat.

Inactivity might have been John's worst enemy during the five years of cheerful artistic lassitude that had preceded 1980's *Double Fantasy*, a his-and-hers album that could almost be filed under 'easy-listening'. With such innovations as graphic equalizers, programmable desks and even synthesized drums to do battle against adverse acoustics, the notion of touring again had become sufficiently attractive to him and contemporaries of the same standing to blank out how ghastly it has been in the distorted 1960s. On the back of a Mod revival *circa* 1979, the Who had been on stage again – and so soon would be others for whom the only reminders of the squalid holocaust over the hills in London, New York and Hollywood were gold discs lining balustraded stairwells.

On the road, security was stepped up after the awful release of John Lennon's spirit, but even the more famous faces in pop became less fearful of being stalked by an autograph-hunter with a gun. George Harrison took his son to Sydney's Sea World; back in Henley, Tony Hicks presented fun-run prizes; Paul McCartney travelled second-class on a train to London, and Steve Winwood perused a record stall's wares at Fairport Convention's annual reunion bash at Cropredy. Years away from the public eye may have assisted re-entries into a wider world – and, in any case, Harrison, Hicks, McCartney and Winwood could be reassured by the fact that they'd never be in the same vulnerable league as Lennon, Dylan and other possessors of more provocative originality than orthodox talent.

Death still lurked in the skies and on the highway, but testing the water with one-off bookings often led to full-scale tours with corporation sponsorships. On phone lines in frantic offices were stadium managers from each continent, all of them yelling 'Klondike!' at the prospect of a carnival of the magnitude of a British Invasion *blitzkrieg*. In 1982, the original Animals reformed for a world tour, despite tabloid headlines like 'Why I Despise Alan Price by Eric Burdon'. The other three were out of practice but the employment of auxiliaries – including Zoot Money – steered them out of danger. Price was prime mover at rehearsals and in the arranging of the inevitable new album and single (*Ark* and 'The Night'), while his restive assistant, Eric, looked forward to meeting his estranged daughter in the USA.

While they might have filled, say, Caerfilly's Double-Diamond club for an entire week, it might have been unwise for other 1960s acts to have shouldered the same commitments. While one of the Animals' performances was screened mid-evening on BBC1, the Nashville Teens – with only Ray Phillips left from the 1960s – were on *Unforgettable* at the lonely mid-week hour of 3.45 p.m., promoting drastic rearrangements of 'Tobacco Road' and 1965's 'Find My Way Back Home' as they hadn't had enough hits to compile bite-sized chunks of them into one of the 'Holliedaze'-type medleys that were popular in the early 1980s – 'Beatles Movie Medley', 'Hooked on Number Ones' (by The Fortunes, who never had any, Marmalade and Mungo Jerry) and Tight Fit's 'Back to the Sixties'.

Another common (but generally unviable) practice was to rehash an item from the hit repertoire of a contemporary. In 1988, for instance, Dave Berry fired a pot-shot with Chris Farlowe's 'Out of Time' while Farlowe himself tried with 'Let the Heartaches Begin'. There was also Dave Dee, Dozy, Beaky, Mick and Tich's 'Do Wah Diddy Diddy' and Sandie Shaw with Cilla's 'Anyone Who Had a Heart'.

A more successful strategy was teaming-up with other – often unlikely – artists. We Britons were stunned to notice Joe Cocker at Number One in the States in 1982 with 'Up Where We Belong', a duet with C & W star Jennifer Warnes and, seven years later, by Van Morrison and Cliff Richard on *Top of the Pops* with 'Whenever God Shines His Light'. Suzi Quatro and Reg Presley revamped 'Wild Thing' for the disco floor, and Dave Dee's second 'Zabadak!' was with German comedy duo, Klaus and Klaus. A more reconcilable alliance had Brian Poole, Reg Presley, Tony Crane, Mike Pender and the Foundations' Clem Curtis in what was known collectively as the Corporation for a sprightly 'Ain't Nothing But a House Party'. Brian's brainchild, it tiptoed into the lowest reaches of the charts – the first such entry for those taking part in many a year.

Marmalade were (and still are) often fronted by Dave Dee for half of their show. With him, too, they made 'Scirocco', a 1989 single written and produced by Sandy Newman. Whilst engaged in a household chore, I found myself humming this fusion of the salient points of 'Zabadak!' and 'The Lion Sleeps Tonight', and wondering whether Marmalade with Dee's chances of a hit were entirely improbable.

As enterprising in its way was Pete York's 'Blues Reunion' tours with variable personnel drawn from those whom the blues had made more famous than it had many of the black originators who'd captured their adolescent imaginations. Some customers were susceptible enough to think that a 'Blues Reunion' quartet of 1985 was a reconstituted Spencer Davis Group. Mounting the stage at Putney's Half-Moon was, yes, Spencer Davis . . . and there's Pete York. For most, credulity wouldn't stretch to the Winwood brothers. Instead you got Rocket 88's bass player and, on synthesized organ, Brian Auger, who'd beaten Steve in the keyboard section of 1969's *Beat Instrumental* poll.

Among other old pals called upon to partake were Chris Farlowe and Zoot Money. There was a friendly downhome ambience about the proceedings – especially in Pete and Zoot's bantering continuity about the old days and older. Yet it is frequently revealing to discover the actual depth to which those who happen to be in the same profession know each other, although in showbusiness it's easy to get a different impression. Entering a Southsea hotel bar one evening in 1988, a puzzled Dave Berry was embraced by Gerry Marsden who'd become buoyant with sentiment for the Swinging Sixties. Dave hardly knew Gerry then.

Gerry would be to the fore in a more transient 'supergroup' than the Corporation on Channel Four's *Brookside* soap-opera with Pete Best, bass-playing Don Andrew from the Remo Four and Swinging Blue Jeans guitarist Ray Ennis. A more durable combine surfaced via the home counties' old boy network. Yet the British Invasion All-Stars were less remarkable for their music than how they were turned into a cottage industry by a certain Michael Bernard Ober who, as a New York schoolboy in 1964, had conceived a lifelong passion for British beat: 'sounds that made love to my mind'. In 1975, he mentioned some in a letter to a UK pop weekly about his own group, That Hideous Strength, whose EP included 'Vintage English Rock 'n' Roll' – 'our tribute to the English groups of the 60s – Downliners Sect, Pretty Things, Who, Creation, Move etc.'

Don Craine had kept a cutting of that letter, and would meet its writer when Mike Ober arrived in London in 1989. So began a liaison that was to bring Craine and other of Mike's now middle-aged idols to a wider public than they might have warranted in the normal course of events. Via Ober's Brisk Productions company and Promised Land record label, there followed a vast array of goods intended to capture 'the sound of the future, the beat of the past'.

The venture kicked off with a spoken-word cassette by Craine – a sort of premeditated Troggs Tape – and amateurish videos like a *Guide to Yardbirds Drumming* by Jim McCarty and *the Downliners Sect Story*, i.e. the present-day Sect holding forth in a local pub with mimed musical interludes in a rehearsal studio. Next up was a 'historic jam' shot during one sweaty summer's night at Latimer Road. There, the Sect and McCarty's resident combo ran through items known to both.

From this chaotic evening, Brisk/Promised Land's flagship act smouldered into form. The British Invasion All-Stars began as an amalgam of Don, Keith Grant, Jim, Ray Phillips and the Creation's Eddie Phillips (no relation). *Regression*, the debut album of 'the ultimate supergroup of the new decade' was a rushed job – Brisk, in fact – and the clouds parting on the gods at play revealed not magic but mere music in competent tries at 'House of the Rising Sun', 'Tobacco Road', 'Summertime Blues', 'My Generation' and other mutually familiar items. Likewise, the attendant video went in one eye and out the other, but the All-Stars seemed to have fun. Afterwards, they looked at each other, shrugged their shoulders and returned to everyday activities.

Regression, however, was only the tip of Ober's iceberg. After supplementary albums of *Regression* out-takes, false starts and dubious 'extra tracks', another beer-sodden 'historic jam' was frozen on film: Eddie Phillips' weekend combo with ex-personnel from the Creation, the Kinks and, from the 1970s, Guys and Dolls. Though I must add the raw information that the initial batch of Promised Land merchandise proved a worthwhile commercial undertaking, particularly in Japan and the USA, it was pretty much of a muchness. Outlines dissolved and contents merged. For example, with the exception of Jim's drum tutorial and Don's cassette, each audio or visual item included a go at 'Route 66', a song that I now hear no more than a pop star in the 1960s heard screams.

Matters improved though. Pieced together by multiple overdubbing on a console in his garage, Eddie Phillips' solo release, *Riffmaster of the Western World* – with lyrics by Ober – was a melodious adventure, and the follow-up to *Regression* demonstrated that these British Invasion boys might have potential after all. A partiality for Berry, Waters, Diddley *et al* remained apparent on *United*, but the lads were now mining less constricting seams with originals like McCarty's 'Heavy Weather' – which went down as well as the Yardbirds' smashes with his R & B unit.

When Chris Dreja sat in during a set at the 100 Club, Ober felt entitled to call the resulting *au naturel* cassette *The Yardbirds' Reunion Concert*. On the boards, the Downliners Sect too balanced the old and the new – much of the latter off *Savage Return*, from 1991. Formerly the laggards of the pack, the Sect's lean drive and strong songwriting on this outing might have given their Crawdaddy colleagues, the Rolling Stones, pause for thought had they ever listened to it.

Through the auspices of Mike too, the Inmates and two Pretty Things – who'd had Glen Matlock in their ranks briefly – powered through *A Whiter Shade of Dirty Water*, their readings of the best-known songs of the Standells, Seeds, Strangeloves and other US 'garage bands' the Things had inspired. With the masters at work, it was almost a matter of course that '96 Tears', 'I Want Candy', 'Kicks' and so forth would be played with more guts and abandon than by the callow apprentices – as the Sect's versions of Lennon-McCartney obscurities on *A Light Went Out in New York* turned out better than those heard on Beatle bootlegs.

If rumours about the Fab Three reforming had substance, a *Beatles Sing the Downliners Sect* LP would have been unlikely. However, Mike Ober had been pushing for the living Yardbirds to record an interpretation of the first Led Zeppelin LP. The closest he got was in 1994 on *The Yardbirds Experience* – the All-Stars plus Noel Redding – which included a couple of Zeppelin items amid previously-released tracks from *United* and barrel-scraping items from the repertoires of each All-Star's usual group.

Soon after *The Yardbirds Experience* was mastered, Ober's day job took him back to New York from whence he tried to negotiate a Yardbirds Experience tour of the continent whilst overseeing Brisk Productions in the same manner as George III fought the American War of Independence from Whitehall. Nevertheless, over his ledgers and computer run-offs, Mike continues to daydream about a wondrous parallel universe of pop in which the likes of Madonna, Take That and Snoop Doggy Dog mean nothing, and the Sect, Pretty Things *et al* reign supreme.

The only difference, in my *humble* opinion, between the British Invasion All-Stars and the Traveling Wilburys was the backing of an organization of much more import than Brisk. This gathering of George Harrison, Jeff Lynne, Bob Dylan, Roy Orbison and Tom Petty was not intended as any ongoing 'supergroup', that most fascist of pop cliques, just five blokes messing about in Dylan's garage over a long afternoon. After completing *Volume One* in 1988, the Wilburys had gone back to separate projects but, bound by their 'brotherhood', each implemented services for the others. Dylan, for instance, penned a track for an Orbison LP – though this was never taped owing to the ill-starred Texan's sudden death – and it was alleged that the four surviving Wilburys played unannounced floor spots in and around Los Angeles.

Back in England, both Eric Clapton and Steve Winwood had rolled up with acoustic guitars to the disbelief of respective folk club audiences in Surrey and Birmingham, reinforcing Winwood's statement that 'you can't really say that you have to play one thousand times better in front of twenty thousand than you do in front of twenty'.[186] In a burst of exuberance, he'd also sat at a piano in a London pub and banged out 'Gimme Some Lovin'' and a Traffic instrumental.

Steve's 'Valerie' had been one of ten post-Traffic selections on *Chronicles*, a compilation that would see action in the Christmas charts against other 'best of' offerings by Paul McCartney, George Harrison and Bryan Ferry. Teenagers, you see, were no longer pop's most vital consumers, having been outmanoeuvred by their Swingin' Sixties parents and young marrieds who had sated their appetites for novelty. As in the pre-Bill Haley era, the young had to put up with much the same music as their elders liked.

Edited 'highlights' of *Ready Steady Go* and *Beat Club* on Channel 4, and Radio Two's *Sounds of the Sixties* helped nurture nostalgia for 1960s pop. Out of step with the strident march of hip-hop, acid house *et al*, the Len Bright Combo – 'Wreckless' Eric Goulden and two ex-Milkshakes – propagated a comically seedy image and the artistic style of an olde tyme beat group. Like a Viking longship docking in a hovercraft terminal, the Combo's do-it-yourself air and endearing imperfections were a V-sign at all that they – and I – detested about 1980s mainstream pop.

An unsolicited letter in 1986 inquiring whether I'd be interested in running a course entitled *Sound of the Sixties* at a Watford adult education centre spurred me to seek similar work, and I accrued an itinerary stretching into the 1990s. Among *bona fide* icons of the era invited as guest speakers was Reg Presley whose thought-provoking stint at Swindon College had a bizarre repercussion when a female student wanted to retrieve the cigarette ends that had graced his lips during the lecture. Unhappily, these had been cast out by one ignorant of their value. However, the girl was satisfied with the butts from my car ashtray which her hero had filled as I drove him from Andover.

If you were unemployed, as British school leavers often were in the austere 1980s, your UB40 would have guaranteed you free admission to some of my courses, as it would for ones about Etruscan vases or French humanism. You could even con grants out of the government to form a group – even if, in the same defeated climate, record companies were no longer chucking blank cheques about. At every turn, you'd missed the boat. Resurgences of Mod, psychedelia and other 1960s movements were all less than how they had been portrayed in *Quadrophenia* and in your mother's fond memories of the UFO. The sap of young adulthood was rising, yet AIDS and further sexual ailments of the 1980s cramped your style. Soon it wouldn't be safe to masturbate.

There was always beer. Yet even up the pub were mementos of all you'd missed. As well as old classics on the jukebox, disco turntable and bar band set, the original performers would sometimes still be setting up their equipment at opening time, as was John Mayall, coming up for his sixtieth birthday, at London's Town and Country where, though his name had been mis-spelt on the ticket, he was as ecstatic as his cramped fans that he was so rabidly remembered.

Contradicting Billy J. Kramer's single of 1983, 'You Can't Live On Memories', a swarthy youth removed his jeans to the accompaniment of 'Stand By Me' in an ITV advertisement, and suddenly the whole country was awash with yearning for the 1960s. Snippet coverage in a lager commercial sent the Hollies' nineteen-year-old 'He Ain't Heavy (He's My Brother)' to Number One in 1988. After Colin Blunstone's second re-make of 'She's Not There', British Telecom moved on – or back – to a Merseybeat medley while 'Catch Us If You Can' was worked into an advert for shoes. 'Tired of Waiting For You' plugged shower gel as 'Gimme Some Lovin'' did tea. 'Gimmie Shelter', 'Baby Please Don't Go', 'Wild Thing', 'All Day and All of the Night' likewise broke up evenings in the late 1980s sabotaged by snooker. Time almost stopped when one week's Top 10 contained only one entry that wasn't either a re-issue or a revival. No time was better for the publication of Pete Best's autobiography[187] or Cathy McGowan's arrival from Twickenham motherhood to present an afternoon chat-show on television.

Roger Chapman's agonized singing was heard in a specially-written vignette for Brutus jeans, and the most unexpected acts released new records that verified the value of sweating over promising new material rather than merely overhauling oldies. With a new single, 'Sensitive Kind', John Mayall indicated that a return to a qualified prominence was not laughable. Out of the blue in 1986, Dave Berry became a critical *cause celebre* via a new album, *Hostage to the Beat*, in which I was inescapably involved as composer and producer of several tracks. Five years later, 'The Moonlight Skater' was what those who hadn't heard much of Dave since 'This Strange Effect' may have imagined he sounded like nowadays.

Onstage, he looked pretty much the same as he did in 1965, and the very fact that one such as Dave Berry was making records again indicated that the nostalgia circuit was no longer such a netherworld. No 1960s relic grew old there any more. Each was still a legendary hero who, like an updated Caesar deified by the Gallic peasants, would offend none by refusing to autograph a dog-eared EP cover depicting him with most of his hair still on his head. Some, like the Searchers, attracted a surprisingly young crowd that, not wanting its 1960s medicine neat, mouthed the words to the yet unrecorded 'I Can't Cry Hard Enough' as accurately as those of 'Sweets for my Sweet'.

Neither they nor incorrigible old Mods, Rockers and hippies minded squeezing into the smart casuals that were expected at the Sixties Club in Marbella, Frimley's Lakeside, Caesar's Palace in Luton, Maidenhead's Silver Skillet and other citadels of 'quality' cabaret where there were near-capacity crowds on 'Sounds of the Sixties' nights – or for events like the Solid Silver Sixties Christmas tour of 1988 with the Searchers, Dave Berry, Gerry, Freddie, The Fortunes, Dave Dee and Marmalade, and the Merseybeats.

After a packed Hollies concert in June 1984 at Reading's Hexagon auditorium, a housewife remarked: 'I always thought that the Status Quo show was the best thing I'd seen, but this was better.' In the same hall, three original (or near enough) Hollies and four younger musicians had been bemused by standing ovations. As well as the hits, even tracks from the latest LP earned wild applause. Most striking of all was a version of the Supremes' 'Stop in the Name of Love' which they'd taken into the US Top 20 the previous spring.

Most of the Hollies' 1960s music had been transferred onto compact disc on which you could almost make out the dandruff falling from Graham Nash's hair. The selling of CD reissues was but one aspect of the persisting demand for 1960s music and musicians. There were also *Top of the Pops* visitations – either on video or in the flesh – by such young hopefuls as the Rolling Stones, the Kinks, Paul McCartney, Tom Jones and George Harrison, all outside the nostalgia orbit through a combination of pulling unexpected strokes, stubbornly following unfashionable routes and yet maintaining a lingering hip sensibility.

The Kinks reappeared after an eleven-year absence with 'Come Dancing'. Though their mark on pop would have been indelible even if they'd retired after 'Waterloo Sunset', their 1960s accomplishments and the slump that followed blinded many critics to the quality of their later output. 'Quiet Life', Ray Davies' solo donation to the movie soundtrack of 1986's *Absolute Beginners*, for example, was the equal of many of his best-known songs. Each new Kinks release is still, as far as I'm concerned, a special event. If flawed in places, 1993's *Phobia* justified the words of John McNally of the Searchers: 'You don't have to be young to make good records.'[188]

In a similar way to the Searchers, the Troggs counterpoise sporadic new records – notably *Athens to Andover* in 1991, assisted by trendy REM – and raising the roof with 'Wild Thing' at Harvest Home dances in the West Country where they are still based. The 1980s had ended with Chris Britton back in the fold, and the sacking of Ronnie Bond (who died in 1992), and if *Athens to Andover* and its 'Don't You Know' 45 failed to sustain a comeback, the Troggs mightn't have needed one in the first place.

For all the 'good' foreheads, chicken necks and belts loosened to the last hole, such campaigners still intrigued the young, envious of an unquiet journey to middle life. Partly, it was a symptom of artistic bankruptcy among newer artists, content to imitate or exalt old heroes. Saddest of all, perhaps, was *Sgt Pepper Knew My Father*, a charity LP on which several new acts depped for the Lonely Hearts Club Band for a remake of the Beatles' most famous record; Wet Wet Wet having a Number One with 'With a Little Help from My Friends' – as they would too in 1994 with a remake of the Troggs' 'Love Is All Around', complete with state-of-the-art over-embroidered lead vocals. Also as a film tie-in, Boy George was in the top 30 in 1993 with 'The Crying Game', and Pato Banton at Number One in 1994 with 'Baby Come Back'. For years, the Kinks' 1960s catalogue had been the source of hits for many artists including the Jam, Pretenders, Fall, Stranglers and Kirsty MacColl. 'Roadie For the Kinks' by the Nonce from San Francisco and Psychic TV's 'Godstar' – about Brian Jones – were among salutes to a more vibrant past, while link-ups with the Art of Noise would deliver both Duane Eddy and Tom Jones back into the Top 20.

Gerry Marsden had been at the very top of it in 1985 as leader of the Crowd, an all-star aggregation, with a money-raising remake of 'You'll Never Walk Alone' for victims of the *Herald of Free Enterprise* shipwreck. Three years later, he was up there again singing 'Ferry Across the Mersey' – with Paul McCartney, Elvis Costello and members of Frankie Goes To Hollywood, the Christians and other Scouse bands – when it was used likewise in aid of a Liverpool FC relief fund for the families of the ninety-five crushed to death during an away-match in Hillsborough.

With *The Concerts For Bangla Desh* as the starting point, other milestones along pop's road to respectability included a 1986 performance at Birmingham's National Exhibition Centre involving Brum Beat exponents such as Denny Laine, Jeff Lynne and Robert Plant, you name 'em, all doing their bit for 'Heartbeat '86', a committee headed by ELO's Bev Bevan to procure cash for Birmingham Children's Hospital. A finale of 'Johnny B.

Goode' had all the guitarists barring the over-familiar chord changes, and it was appropriate that, as one of Brum Beat's leading lights from the onset, Ace Kefford's joyous 'Goodnight, Birmingham!' was the last frame in the resulting video.

Ace's lad Gary had drummed in a punk unit. He was one of many chips off various old blocks. The son of Rick Huxley, from the Dave Clark Five, as well as playing keyboards in a group, also engineered the laser show during the party that followed the premier of *Time*, and one of Brian Jones' progeny was employed behind-the-scenes by the Stones. Ginger Baker's boy, Kofi, toured the USA with a unit that also contained Jack Bruce's son Malcolm. Similarly, Elizabeth Price, as well as singing with father Alan's band, was in Burn, a Bristol ensemble with Georgie Fame's two sons. As solo vocalists, the daughters of Marty Wilde and Joe Brown – and the son of Len Hawkes of the Tremeloes – had UK chart success, as did Paul McCartney's young step-sister, Ruth, in Russia. Making headway as recording artists of the 1990s too were Brian Poole's girls as 'Keren and Chelle' who started as pre-emptors of Shampoo before attempting material of a less light-hearted nature. Michael Rogers, son of Twinkle, has became the Weatherman, an up-and-coming studio creator of 'rave' music.

The sons of Keith Relf passed through several Bracknell groups that worked much the same local venues as the Next, who'd rehearsed in a disused lodge on the estate of drummer Zak Starkey's moneybags of a father. Pete Townshend considered this eldest child of Ringo Starr 'the most accurate emulation of Keith [Moon]'s style. Luckily Zak has a style of his own but many have been moved to say "My God! It's him!".'[189]

There'd been hearsay that, as well as a reformed Who, Julian Lennon and his sire's former Beatle *confreres* could perform together at Live Aid. The ease with which Lennon *fils* had secured a record deal with a label with preconceived ideas about his ability might be the most renowned example of a 1960s surname opening doors, and furnishing a pop career with both the best and worst start.

27 HIGHWAYS 61– 67 REVISITED

Whether the Barron-Knights on the chicken-in-a-basket trail or the Rolling Stones amid a sky-clawing stage set at Wembley, all an act still intact from the 1960s needs to do to please the crowd is to be an archetypical unit of its own, spanning every familiar trackway of its professional career – all the timeless hits, each change of image, every bandwagon jumped. Yet who could have pretended that this is what it must have been like down the Cavern when the *Mersey Reunion* tour hit Guildford Civic Hall in 1992? The show, nevertheless, belonged to the Merseybeats, perhaps the most vibrant paradigm of the Liverpool beat explosion that Joe Average is ever likely to encounter these days.

No one whose life was soundtracked by pop during the 1960s should've missed Roy Wood's UK tour either, despite an unpromising support act in the Jim Onslow Experience, trundling if competent rock 'n' roll revivalists. Like Wood, Onslow had been in Gerry Levene and the Avengers back in Birmingham when the world was young.

As he all but retired in the late 1970s, Roy may have predicted less than half-capacity crowds. Unperturbed, he drew instant rapport by starting at the end of the beginning with 'California Man', the Move's Top 10 swansong, and closing on an emotional high with a jubilant audience blasting up chorus after unaccompanied chorus of 'Blackberry Way'. As impressive were four new numbers, disadvantaged only by the hits' head start of up to a quarter of a century.

You don't need me to tell you that the Kinks are still wild onstage too. Now containing the Davies siblings plus ex-members of the Hunters, Unit 4 + 2, Argent and others of the Hertfordshire school, their press handout calls them 'a unique 90s band', but there's no shortage of the 1960s classics, although many are presented as mere flashes of past glory by Ray Davies on lone acoustic guitar – though there were full-scale versions of as many others. Obscurer items ranged from 'Oklahoma USA' (off *Muswell Hillbillies*, 1971) to 'Aggravation', a 1980s epic, complete with a shadow-play-cum-mini-ballet by two females who reappeared in apposite garb for 'Sleazytown' during the 'unprepared' encore section. The latest single, 'Only a Dream', was laid on with a trowel with Ray trying to work it up as a rowdy singalong – but will it be a hit? The present chart climate begs the question: who wants proper songs any more – least of all ones with the class of 'Only a Dream', 'Scattered' and everything else they did from *Phobia*? I took my sons then aged eleven and nine to this, their first pop concert – our family's equivalent of a *bar mitzvah* – and it was entirely fitting that it starred the Kinks, who were everything I hoped they'd be.

Searching for other extant units from the golden age of British beat can be both intriguing and depressing. With a front man like Freddie Garrity, who cared about the identity of the Dreamers behind him? The same applies to the too-youthful accompanists of John Mayall, Dave Berry, Wayne Fontana, Screaming Lord Sutch or Billy J. Kramer – whose wan croon has dropped an octave over thirty years.

Though performance can transcend deceit, where there is less of a demarcation line between group and singer, it's often not quite the full shilling. Whither Dozy, Beaky, Mick and Tich with a new Mick and Beaky and no Dave Dee or a Love Affair consisting almost entirely of slim-hipped young herberts for whom the big beat was a playpen memory at most? A Manfred Mann with no Manfred had been the concluding turn at 1986's *Heroes and Villains* London charity spectacular of 1960s acts. The present Tornadoes features a female singer, and only one original, Clem Cattini. 1994 brought Animals II built round original guitarist and drummer, Hilton Valentine and John Steel. The same northern promoter has also scratched-up a Yardbirds and an entity connected with the Move.

It seemed that you required just the rights to an old name, no matter how obscure, to find work. Roaming Britain in 1992 was a Hedgehoppers Anonymous with only the most tenuous association with either the 1965 one-hit-wonders or Wittering, the town they came from. As dubious was a Unit 4 + 2 out there while members of the 1960s edition were up to their necks in the writing and production of a London musical play about Leonardo da Vinci.

On the other hand, Gary Kane and the Tornadoes are still functioning with only one personnel change in thirty-five years, and the original Moontrekkers were reconstituted in 1991 initially for some Joe Meek memorial concerts. The Creation also returned intact to pick up where they'd left off in 1968. Flying in the face of documentary evidence, Barry Noble and his Sapphires were made out to have 'achieved a couple of minor hits'[45] – but what was true was that they contained all the 'chartbusting' team of 1962 – as did the Javelins who, at the instigation of their ex-lead singer Ian Gillan, now of Deep Purple, reunited in 1993 for an album of selections from their St Dunstan's Youth Club repertoire. The following year saw the release of the 'debut' album by the Quarry Men featuring Rod Davis and John Lowe (also a Four Penny in 1994) from the John-Paul-George days.

Back too were a number of backing groups who, either by choice or circumstance, operated without their 1960s focal point. A reformed Hurricanes is active on Merseyside, mostly on the strength of renewed interest stoked up by no less than two locally-presented plays, *The Need For Heroes* and *The King of Liverpool*, centred on the character of Rory Storm. The Dakotas were also performing with no Billy J.

In 1994, a Shadows in all but name got by with Hank Marvin and Brian Bennett with their respective sons on rhythm guitar and bass. Likewise, Darren Bullis, son of Ronnie Bond, has served as a temporary Troggs drummer just as Led Zeppelin enlisted the similarly placed Jason Bonham.

With Herman's Hermits' lead guitarist Derek Leckenby playing his final dates in a wheelchair, and naming a successor on his death bed, there's no reason why a 1960s group shouldn't go on forever. However, a social secretary might have to check which Searchers he'd be booking. Distressing particulars of why Mike Pender left to form 'Mike Pender's Searchers' in 1986 are not relevant here. His departure was considered regrettable but by no means disastrous by the 'official' Searchers who continued with a replacement – though the situation was complicated further four years later by the debut of a combo fronted by Tony Jackson, earning ovations with versions of Searchers hits on which he may or may not have been heard.

There are also two Honeycombs on the circuit; one with three of the original five for special occasions, and, with their assent, a more dedicated Honeycombs led too by Denis D'Ell, who moonlights with the most un-Have I The Right-like Southside Blues Band. Not obliged to maintain a defined image, ex-Sorrow guitarist Phil Witcher and Dave Berry's former drummer, Ray Pinfold, are mainstays of Torquay's Brummies In Exile.

Still with no participation by the Mann himself, the 1965 line-up of Manfred Mann undertook tours in the 1990s as the Manfreds with Michael d'Abo on keyboards. With his own Mighty Quintet, d'Abo specializes in hunt balls, private parties and corporate functions, and, as a West Country radio presenter, 1960s music programmes with guests that have included Lonnie Donegan, Reg Presley, Georgie Fame, Gerry Marsden, Alan Price, Joe Brown, Manfred Mann and fellow disc-jockeys like Noddy Holder (from Manchester's Piccadilly Radio), Brian Poole (in training for BBC Essex) and Paul Jones. Of the latter two, Brian is also negotiating with publishers over a book he's written about colloquial English, while, as well as his blues series on Radio Two, Paul is omnipresent on children's TV and West End musicals like *Cats* and *Guys and Dolls*, and remains much in evidence whenever the Blues Band decides to work again as they did at a Hamburg show – with Mitch Mitchell depping for the usual drummer, Rob Townsend (ex-Family) – which also starred Chicken Shack, Man and Ten Years After.

On prime time *Live at the London Palladium* in 1987, another old bluesman, Joe Cocker, was introduced by MC Jimmy Tarbuck as 'a man who's been to hell and back'. Now blessed with a happy marriage, oceanside contentment in Santa Barbara, and an angling river running through his vast acreage in Colorado, the man who was Vance Arnold is now a fully-integrated constant of the 'contemporary rock' mainstream. His sell-out UK tour of 1992 included an eagerly anticipated engagement in Sheffield. It was noticed that he was bulkier; his spastic stage motions had been moderated, and that this unlikely Judy Garland of British beat still swilled back a routine three pints of ale before going on.

As well as 'men from hell', the pop world is fascinated by recluses. To certain of his devotees, it was Syd Barrett's misfortune not to die after shedding his commercial load. In recent photographs, he appears overweight, scruffy and balding, yet Syd looks no worse essentially than other former colleagues, also well into middle age. In the teeth of dull truth, Barrett still preoccupies countless fans as well as record business moguls who continue to scrape the barrel for anything on which he even breathed.

Whispers from Merseyside suggest that Chris Curtis is singing to his own guitar in local pubs, but Chris, Syd, Peter Green – 'the werewolf of Richmond' – Tommy Quickly and everyone else in the legion of the lost tend to be spoken of as if they were old nags put out to grass. Like an inverse of a 'happy ending' in a Victorian novel, they live outwardly unproductive lives in which nothing much is calculated to happen, year in, year out. Yet some of the faithful still expect them to reappear from Rip Van Winkle-esque suburban slumber, rejuvenated and contemporary, debunking the myth of an artistic death.

How different it might have been. Let's transfer to a parallel dimension, and a front page of *Melody Maker* in 1970: 'Ending three years of rumour by ratifying composer, guitarist and lead singer Syd Barrett's break with The Pink Floyd, a spokesman added, "Syd's new band is already in rehearsal with Scott Walker sharing vocals, Ace Kefford on bass, Chris Curtis on drums, and, on the rebound from Fleetwood Mac, Peter Green on second guitar. Syd calls them 'The Madcaps'. Like Blind Faith last year, they'll kick off with a free concert in Hyde Park." Barrett is also keen for this latest 'supergroup' to tour the States soon to capitalize on the Floyd's recent breakthrough in *Billboard*'s Top 20 with 1969's UK smash, "The Old Woman and a Casket".'

No matter how legitimate or lucrative the set-up, nothing would coax builder Johnny Hutchinson, driving instructor Mick Wilson, butcher Kingsize Taylor, or Kerry Rapid, now Alan Hope, Deputy Mayor of Ashburton, back into the fray. Not wishing to play Pop Stars any more either, London resident Scott Engel agreed with Bob Dylan that 'the moment I speak, I become my enemy' – though prior to 1995's *Tilt* LP the ex-Walker Brother had been glimpsed momentarily in the Sixties black-and-white of a 1988 commercial for orange juice in a cast that also included Dave Dee, Georgie Fame, the Tremeloes, Dusty Springfield and Eric Burdon.

Out of the blue, another pop hermit, Ace Kefford, telephoned in April 1994 to invite me to his Bradford flat for an interview – his first since leaving the Move in 1968. He'd resisted efforts by Jeff Beck and Ozzy Osbourne (ex-Black Sabbath) to enlist him into their respective ensembles during a tragic aeon of drug abuse, suicide attempts, incarceration in asylums, divorce and the estrangement of his children. A recurring sentence during our long and frank discussion was 'my head had gone'. The tide of Ace's life, however, has finally turned, albeit with majestic slowness, and he is composing songs again; many of them reflective of hard-won religious convictions but with the rock 'n' roller of old still peeping out. In terms of experience, image and ability, if anyone qualifies as Bill Wyman's permanent replacement in the Stones, it is surely Christopher John Kefford, voyager of a mighty rough sea since forming an instrumental group with his uncle in 1961.

Treasure from the ship that came in for Reg Presley with Wet Wet Wet's 'Love Is All Around' may be ploughed back into research on crop circles, a subject he discusses sometimes on *Is Anyone Out There?* his regular UFO show on Andover's cable TV station where a latter-day Troggs bass player is employed. Now a Basingstoke electrician, the 1960s bass man, Pete Staples, had lost touch with the other Troggs, but had carried on writing and recording. On a holiday cruise in 1992, he was recognized and coaxed into taking the stage with the liner's band to thunderous applause from onlookers that included a booking agent from Moscow. 'He explained that the Russian authorities were anxious to broaden their knowledge of western art, culture and music. He asked me if I'd be prepared to go there to perform, talk to groups about how the English pop scene has evolved and discuss ideas for developing pop music in Russia. I told him that it sounded a fascinating project, and he said he'd be contacting me later this year.'[190]

Another bass guitarist called Pete was a self-employed artist in Canada. An exhibition in 1994 by ex-Kink Pete Quaife – now Peter Kinnes – includes some autobiographical illustrations such as 'Baked Beans', showing a hand removing a housefly from a plate of baked beans. ('People think that we always ate in fancy restaurants. We didn't. All we had time for was baked beans and toast'.) Another depicts a highway and trees. ('All we saw was highway after highway as we toured from city to city'.) Then there's one of a stern-looking hotel receptionist registering the group members.

Ron Wood began exhibiting his oil paintings in the late 1980s during one of progressively longer breaks in the Rolling Stones' schedule – and while the

Stones embarked on their twelfth US tour in thirty years in 1994, Dave Clark turned down another multi-million dollar offer to reform the Five.

Another ex-drummer in a 1960s outfit, Pete Best, had worked his way up to deputy manager at a Liverpool job centre. On leave, he'd bank extra brass by speaking at Beatle-associated events, and by naming his new group after a now very collectable US album from 1965, *Best of the Beatles*. Best of luck to him.

One of the Pete Best All-Stars, Wayne Bickerton, had superceded Roger Greenaway as chairman of the Performing Rights Society, and it was whispered that Pete's successor in the Beatles was to drum for the Who in the London group's twenty-fifth anniversary tour. With no new LP in the shop and no recent hits to slip in, they were fixing solely and unashamedly on their back catalogue. Now their afficionados could not refute the claim that the Who were in the same bag as other huge but stagnant headliners like the Beach Boys and the reconstituted Monkees.

There was also the borderline case of Jack Bruce and Ginger Baker on a trek round the US with a band that broke the ice each night with an hour's worth of old Cream numbers. Shortly before he perished in a fire in his Essex home in 1991, Steve Marriott had been trying to reassemble Humble Pie with Peter Frampton who was among those attending the funeral where 'All or Nothing' – very atmospheric in context – was spun as Steve's requiem.

Adjectives like 'atmospheric', 'shimmering' and 'caressing' cropped up in critiques of what was called either New Age, New Instrumental or Adult Contemporary Music – the only wave of principally instrumental music to reach a mass public since jazz-rock. Its undynamic nature is akin to Indian music, Gregorian chant and other reference points once associated with the Yardbirds and their more subdued offshoots. Indeed, Stairway – probably the best-loved British New Age outfit – is actually Jim McCarty and former Renaissance colleague, Louis Cennamo, reactivating aspects of their pioneering pasts in the new idiom.

Portfolios of other ex-beat group musicians have embraced New Age too; among them Rod Argent, Van Morrison, Andy Somers, Rory Gallagher, ex-Hipster Image guitarist Pete Haycock, former Georgie Fame sideman Ray Russell and Steve Winwood's replacement in the Spencer Davis Group, Eddie Hardin. Argent and McCarty in particular allow their old beat groups to peer out with one or two tartly-arranged songs – amid the pervading instrumental swirl on each album; a few such items are as innovative in their way as any in the Yardbirds' or Zombies' canon. Moreover, a 1992 Stairway offering, *Medicine Dance*, features Jim pounding a full drum kit, almost *Five Live Yardbirds*-style on some tracks, and judging by the quality of the first McCarty solo album, *Out of the Dark*, the best might be yet to come – but whether a mass public will ever hear it is another matter. In any event, to the man-in-the-street, neither McCarty, Argent or anyone else will ever be as great as they were in the 1960s.

Ace Kefford, Joe Cocker, Eric Clapton and quite a few more were lucky to be even *compos mentis* again with hands no more a-tremble or nose enpurpled. When obliged to by the law, Keith Richards had kicked heroin with acupuncture. Via a spell in a nursing home and the love of a good woman, Wayne Fontana overcame his dependence on Valium and was no longer a booker's risk. By 1991, he was very much back in business, backed by a new Mindbenders (alias Manchester's Mike Sweeney and the Thunderbyrds).

After the indignity of being jeered at Reading's Hexagon in 1985 and the breakdown of his marriage, Billy J. Kramer moved to New York where, after joining Alcoholics Anonymous, he persevered with teetotalism. Ringo Starr's rise from the same pit became most perceptible in 1989 when he set the wheels in motion for an autumn tour of North America and Japan with a hand-picked (and all-American) 'All Starr Band' in 'towns that weren't built the last time I did this'.[191] His part in the proceedings boiled down to about ten 'songs you know and love' for those who'd nearly but not quite engulf his singing after a Max Miller cry of, 'All together now!'

Whether looking forward to the past is a healthy situation for an artist is open to conjecture. Perhaps I imagined this, but there was a frozen moment at Blazer's in 1986 when Dozy's mask slipped as, hunchbacked behind the drum kit during 'Mick's' lead vocal spot, he snarled, 'Here's another hit from the *fabulous* Sixties,' with the underlying venom born of weary repetition.

If they still made records, the output of the nostalgia groups was in keeping with the stage act: perhaps a third LP remake of the old hits and the likes of Freddie Garrity's 'I'm a Singer in a Sixties Band' and Ray Ennis' 'I'm an Old Rock 'n' Roller' — statements that both tacitly reiterate whenever Freddie does 'I'm Telling You Now' or the Swinging Blue Jeans close the show as always with 'The Hippy Hippy Shake'.

George Harrison seemed to come to terms with both the 1960s and his present situation with 'When We Was Fab', a happy invocation of the Beatles with 'fab! gear!' vocal responses and a coda of wiry sitar, backwards tapes and further psychedelia. Peaking at Number Twenty-five in the UK chart, 'When We Was Fab' did better than the retrospective efforts of Freddie, Ray and other less bankable contemporaries, partly because George could afford the expensive services of Godley and Creme from 10cc — now an in-demand audio-visual production team — to direct a video in which he and Ringo donned the Sgt. Pepper costumes that their respective offspring had been borrowing for fancy dress parties.

Gaps between releases might lengthen, but there's no reason why 1960s groups and individuals with the resources to do so shouldn't still be making records in old age – even placing them high in the charts as George, the Kinks and others did in the 1980s, and the Rolling Stones still do, with Keith Richards even predicting a second golden age for them to anyone still listening.

EPILOGUE: *NOT FADE AWAY?*

A Mrs J. Drabble and John, her three-year-old son, were walking through a department store in Sheffield when the toddler fell over Dave Berry's famously big feet. Both parties were the souls of smiling apology, and the incident was chronicled by his mum in John's Baby Record Book. While crow's feet round the eyes are the most obvious external sign that Dave has passed his half-century, Mother Nature has been less kind to his old local rival, Jimmy Crawford, who, after a sojourn as a pub landlord in Cornwall, was espied singing in one of the working men's clubs where he'd started – and those who remembered wouldn't let him quit the stage without giving 'em his 'I Love How You Love Me' any more than Dave could without 'The Crying Game', Animals II without 'The House of the Rising Sun', the Kinks without 'You Really Got Me' or any edition of the Searchers without 'Needles and Pins'.

In the longer term, if ever a ballroom is built on Mars, there might still be a Herman's Hermits, a Bootleg Beatles or an Animals DCLXVI playing 'Sounds of the Sixties' nights, and a sound-checking drummer still being hailed, 'Oi, Ringo!' by a janitor wishing him to shift his bloody junk away from the safety curtain.

There may also be evenings given to 'tributes' to Gary Glitter, Slade, David Bowie or even the Sex Pistols, one of the best-known challengers for the title of 'The Last British Beat Group'. Later contenders have included the Len Bright Combo, the Rapiers, Mike Sweeney and the Thunderbyrds and few others. Perhaps I'm mistaken, but, as the millenium approaches, there doesn't seem to be much going on in Britain – no equivalent of skiffle, beat, psychedelia or punk, no Donegan, Beatles, Stones, Slade or Pistols at the height of their respective powers, no focus comparable with any of them.

In 1965, fifteen of the thirty best-selling US singles were British, in 1993, two. Yet it's feasible that a musical movement from these islands might once again bare its teeth to the world – because the eternal verities that detonated the earlier explosions live on in bored teenagers – and outside a village hall in Midshire, a singer screaming 'Waaaaaah!' into a microphone stabs the night air.

NOTES

All unattributed quotes are from my own correspondence and interviews. In addition I have used the following sources which I would like to credit:-

1. *Step Inside* by C. Black (Dent 1985)
2. *Everybody's Weekly*, 3 July 1957
3. *Melody Maker*, 8 January 1966
4. World-wide Dave Clark Fan club newsletter, No. 58, December 1984
5. *The History of Rock*, Vol. 1, No. 5 (Orbis, 1982)
6. *Picturegoer*, 1 September 1956
7. *Record Mirror*, 21 January 1956
8. *New Musical Express*, 24 February 1956
9. *Melody Maker*, 29 March 1958
10. *Skiffle* by B. Bird (Robert Hale, 1958)
11. *Midland Beat*, No. 1, October 1963
12. Sleeve notes to Drake's *Hello My Darlings* EP (Parlophone GEP 8720)
13. *New Musical Express*, 1 November 1957
14. *Daily Mirror*, 8 April 1957
15. *Sounds of the Sixties*, Radio Two, 15 June 1987
16. *Sunday Times*, 7 March 1958
17. *Zabadak!* No. 8, July 1989
18. *Everybody's Weekly*, 23 June 1956
19. 'A musicologist' on *Six-Five Special*, 18 January 1957
20. *Pops with a Purpose* (Tower LLM-SP-101)
21. *Liverpool Institute Magazine*, Vol. LXVIII, No. 1, February 1960
22. To Louise Jury
23. *The Times*, 24 January 1981
24. *New Gandy Dancer*, undated 1984
25. The kit used by the first British rock 'n' roll drummers was a standard dance band set-up which, by the late 1950s, was bass drum and pedal (right foot), small tom-tom (mounted on bass drum), floor tom (right hand), snare drum for the off-beat (right hand), two cymbals ('crash' for accentuation, and 'ride' for continuous playing) mounted on stands. To the left, hi-hats (two cymbals facing each other) were brought together with a snap by a foot pedal to provide a 'matching' but more obtrusive off-beat to the snare. Later, the hi-hat was heightened to be within easy reach of a stick. The drum shells were usually of wood. Throughout the 1950s and early 1960s, US drums could not be imported because of government trade embargos to protect Premier, Carlton and other British makes.
26. *Acker Bilk* by G. Williams (Mayfair, 1962)
27. Sleeve notes to *Neil Christian and The Crusaders* (See For Miles SEECD 342, 1992)
28. *Melody Maker*, 16 December 1962
29. *The Eamonn Andrews Crackerjack Book* (DM, 1962)
30. To Ray Coleman
31. *South West Scene*, Vol. 3, No. 1 (undated, 1963)
32. *Call Up the Groups!* by A. Clayson (Blandford, 1985)
33. *New Musical Express*, 3 August 1962

34. World-wide Dave Clark Fan Club newsletter, No. 57, July 1984
35. *Tutti Frutti* (John Byrne), BBC 1, 1987
36. *Reading Evening Post*, 28 December 1989
37. *Herald of Wales*, June 1964
38. To Pete Frame
39. *Midland Beat*, No. 8, May 1964
40. *Daily Mirror*, September 1960 (precise date obscured)
41. On commencing a solo career, bass player Chris Morris (from Birkenhead) would be renamed 'Lance Fortune' by Larry Parnes.
42. Quoted in *Swinging Sheffield* by A. Clayson (Sheffield Museum, 1993)
43. Polydor press release, 1962
44. *Herald of Wales*, June 1965
45. To Mike Neal and Christine Bones (*The Beat Goes On*)
46. *Crawdaddy*, February 1977
47. *Fiesta*, May 1975
48. BBC Radio Bedfordshire, 29 December 1985
49. *Greatest Hits*, February 1981
50. *Midland Beat*, No. 31, August 1966
51. *Melody Maker*, 1 August 1964
52. *Rolling Stone*, June 1972
53. To Billy Shepherd (*The True Story of the Beatles* by B. Shepherd, Beat, 1964)
54. *Melody Maker*, 23 April 1966
55. Press conference transcript, 2 June 1962
56. *Disc*, 24 November 1962
57. *Hit Parade*, June 1963
58. *Fabulous*, 19 February 1964
59. *Beatles Monthly*, October 1982
60. *The Beat Goes On*, April 1991
61. *Sunday Times*, 27 February 1982
62. *Merseybeat*, 15 February 1962
63. *Merseybeat*, 19 April 1962
64. John Lennon's sleeve notes to *Off the Beatle Track* by the George Martin Orchestra (Parlophone PCS 3057, 1964)
65. *New Musical Express*, 26 October 1962
66. *Peterborough Standard*, 7 December 1962
67. *Merseybeat*, 3 July 1963
68. *New Musical Express*, 1 February 1963
69. *Melody Maker*, 14 November 1964
70. *Melody Maker*, 7 May 1963
71. *Top Star Special*, May 1963
72. *New Musical Express*, 16 March 1963
73. To Spencer Leigh
74. *Liverpool Institute Magazine*, Vol. LXXXI, No. 2, July 1963
75. *Merseybeat*, 29 November 1962
76. *Merseybeat*, 1 January 1964
77. *The Independent*, 8 February 1989
78. *Melody Maker*, 3 August 1963
79. *Midland Beat*, No. 3, November 1963
80. *Midland Beat*, No. 14, November 1964
81. *Melody Maker*, 14 June 1963
82. For *Radio Luxembourg Record Stars Book*, No. 5 (Souvenir Press, undated)
83. *Worcester Whisperings*, April 1964
84. *New Musical Express*, 5 April 1963
85. *Sunday Times*, 13 November 1966
86. *Melody Maker*, 20 February 1965
87. *Merseybeat*, 9 April 1964
88. Radio Merseyside, 26 March 1994
89. *Melody Maker*, 5 January 1966
90. *The Fab Four* (French), March 1975
91. *Melody Maker,* 27 November 1963
92. *Melody Maker*, 2 December 1967
93. Sleeve notes to *The Very Best of Kenny Lynch* (See For Miles, SEE 207), 1987
94. *Melody Maker*, 15 October 1966
95. *Our Own Story by the Rolling Stones* by P. Goodman (Corgi, 1964)
96. *British Beat* by C. May and T. Phillips (Socion 1974)
97. *New York Times*, 30 December 1964
98. Quoted in *Jimi Hendrix* by B. Mann (Orion, 1993)
99. Who was to take up residency in Halifax.

100. *Midland Beat,* No. 11, August 1964
101. To Fred Dellar
102. *Midland Beat,* No. 15, October 1965
103. *Herald of Wales,* July 1964
104. *Midland Beat,* No. 7, April 1964
105. Quoted in *Slade* by G. Tremlett (Futura, 1975)
106. *Ptolemaic Terrascope,* May 1990
107. The song's co-writer – and father of Elvis Costello
108. *New Musical Express,* 12 February 1966
109. On posters for his appearance at Redhill Market Hall on 30 January 1964
110. *Record Collector,* No. 176, April 1994
111. *Midland Beat,* No. 27, October 1966
112. *New Musical Express,* 26 June 1966
113. *Melody Maker,* 26 June 1966
114. *Melody Maker,* 23 November 1968
115. *Watlington Gazette,* 11 March 1964
116. *The Guardian,* 31 March 1964
117. *Beat Instrumental,* February 1966
118. *Here Are the Beatles* by C. Hamblett (Four Square, 1964)
119. *Havant News,* 2 December 1963
120. *Fleet Times,* 15 January 1964
121. *All Night Stand* by T. Keyes (WH Allen, 1966)
122. *Melody Maker,* 12 December 1971
123. *Melody Maker,* 5 June 1964
124. Quoted in *Ginsberg* by B. Miles (Viking, 1990)
125. Italian Broadcasting Company, *circa* autumn 1963
126. *New York Times,* 3 August 1963
127. Veronica TV (Dutch) archives (undated)
128. *New Musical Express,* 24 May 1963
129. *Goldmine,* February 1982
130. *'Twixt Twelve and Twenty* by P. Boone (Prentice-Hall, 1959)
131. Milwaukee press conference, 4 September 1964
132. *Playboy,* 19 October 1964
133. *Billboard,* February 1964
134. *Melody Maker,* 13 August 1966
135. *Rolling Stone Interviews* (Straight Arrow, 1971)
136. *Beat Instrumental,* April 1968
137. *Record Song Book,* December 1964
138. Quoted in *The Kinks* by J. Savage (Faber & Faber, 1984)
139. Not Paul Rodgers, the Middlesbrough vocalist who was a founder member of Free in 1968.
140. *Sunday Times,* 13 November 1966
141. *You Don't Have to Say You Love Me* by S. Napier-Bell (New English Library, 1982)
142. Quoted in *Experimental Pop* by B. Bergman and R. Horn (Blandford, 1985)
143. *Sunday Times,* 10 July 1994
144. *New York Times,* 20 December 1964
145. *Daily Express,* 3 December 1964
146. *Beatles Down Under* by G.A. Baker (Wild and Woolley, 1982)
147. *Melody Maker,* 26 June 1966
148. *Melody Maker,* 11 February 1967
149. *Melody Maker,* 4 March 1967
150. *Merseybeat,* 23 April 1964
151. *Sunday Times,* 29 December 1963
152. *Herald of Wales,* June 1966
153. *Leader* by G. Glitter (Ebury, 1991)
154. *The Stage,* 19 November 1987
155. *Melody Maker,* 16 March 1968
156. *Sunday Express,* 4 March 1968
157. *Ptolemaic Terrascope,* July 1992
158. *Sounds of the Sixties,* Radio Two, 8 November 1986
159. *International Times,* 17 May 1967
160. Extract from Y. Ono's Speech at Everson Art Museum, 9 October 1971
161. *Record Mirror,* 30 July 1970
162. *Rare Records* by T. Hibbert (Proteus, 1982)
163. *New Musical Express,* 15 June 1967
164. *New Musical Express,* 16 December 1967

165. *Time Out*, 4 September 1988
166. Quoted in *Back in the High Life* by
    A. Clayson (Sidgwick and Jackson,
    1988)
167. *Melody Maker*, 22 April 1969
168. Quoted in *Vox Pop* by M. Wale
    (Harrap, 1972)
169. *International Times*, October 1968
170. *Village Voice*, September 1968
171. *Which One's Cliff* by C. Richard
    (Coronet, 1977)
172. *Melody Maker*, 13 June 1969
173. Quoted in *The Wit and Wisdom of
    Rock and Roll* ed. M. Jabubowski
    (Unwin, 1983)
174. *Whatever Happened To . . .* by
    J. Brunton and H. Elson (Proteus,
    1981)
175. *The Sun*, 2 December 1988
176. *The Stage*, 19 November 1987

177. *The Stage*, 3 December 1987
178. *Time*, 21 May 1976
179. *The Guardian*, 5 July 1989
180. *The Sun*, 2 August 1971
181. *Evening Standard*, 1 August 1971
182. *Ptolemaic Terrascope*, January 1991
183. *Ptolemaic Terrascope*, January 1992
184. *Mature Times*, May 1994
185. Breakfast TV, BBC 1, 29 November
    1987
186. *Goldmine*, September 1981
187. *Beatle*! by P. Best and P. Donaldson
    (Plexus, 1985)
188. *Sunday Times*, 5 May 1990
189. *The Sun*, 23 September 1982
190. *Basingstoke and North Hampshire
    Gazette*, 4 September 1992
191. New York press conference, 20 June
    1989

INDEX